CHINA'S

RESPONSE

TO THE WEST

Prepared in coöperation with the
International Secretariat of the
Institute of Pacific Relations

CHINA'S

RESPONSE

TO THE WEST

a documentary survey
1839–1923

Ssu-yü Teng

with
E-tu Zen Sun
Chaoying Fang
and others

John K. Fairbank

Harvard University Press

Cambridge · 1961

CONTENTS

ACKNOWLEDGMENTS

William L. Holland, Secretary General of the Institute of Pacific Relations, originally inspired this volume. Its completion has been aided by grants from the Institute and from the Humanities Division, Rockefeller Foundation. From its inception this has been a joint enterprise among a number of specialists in Chinese studies, whose contributions in varying degree have been so numerous and pervasive that detailed acknowledgment would require a statement more complex than a holding company's income tax return. We have been aided most tangibly in the process of production by Chaoying Fang and E-tu Zen Sun, whose contributions have principally concerned the nineteenth and twentieth centuries, respectively. They are co-authors, though not to be held responsible for the final product. Knight Biggerstaff, E. R. Hughes, K. C. Liu, Earl Swisher, C. Martin Wilbur, and Mary C. Wright have contributed either manuscript materials or copious comments on the first draft, which was circulated in September 1950. For less extensive though similarly appreciated criticism and suggestions we are indebted among others to Banno Masataka, Theodore de Bary, Frank L. Benns, Eugene P. Boardman, Derk Bodde, Conrad Brandt, Ch'en Shou-yi, Kaiming Chiu, Martha Davidson, Immanuel C. Y. Hsu, William Hung, Marius Jansen, Joseph R. Levenson, Ralph Powell, Benjamin Schwartz, Kuan-wai So, Stanley Spector, T. H. Tsien, Hellmut Wilhelm, Karl A. Wittfogel, Arthur F. Wright, Lien-sheng Yang, and Zunvair Yue. In particular we wish to thank Dr. Hu Shih for helpful criticism of Chapter XXVI. We are immensely indebted to Ai-li Chin for expert help on the Bibliography and Glossary, to Rosamond Chapman for editorial assistance, and to Margaret Teng for preparing the index. For the mechanics of this work, see the companion volume.

Note: The companion volume, entitled *A Research Guide for "China's Response to the West,"* has been published separately so that this main volume may be more easily available to interested readers. The *Research Guide* contains the brief reference notes corresponding to the numbers in the text, together with extensive discussions of Sources, a full Bibliography of Western, Chinese, and Japanese works, and a Glossary of Chinese terms. All of this data, however, is prepared only for sinological specialists. Though such specialists are in our view an important national asset, they are unfortunately rather few in number, and the materials which we have compiled especially to assist their research are therefore published separately.

S. Y. T.
J. K. F.

September 1953

Reigns of the
Ch'ing (Manchu) Dynasty

Shun-chih	1644–1661
K'ang-hsi	1662–1722
Yung-cheng	1723–1735
Ch'ien-lung	1736–1795
Chia–ch'ing	1796–1820
Tao-kuang	1821–1850
Hsien-feng	1851–1861
T'ung-chih	1862–1874
Kuang-hsü	1875–1908
Hsuan-t'ung	1909–1911
Republic of China	1912–

A Note on Style of Translation. Our first draft of September 1950 reproduced Chinese names literally, as given in the original sources — thus Ku Yen-wu was at times referred to by his other name, Ku T'ing-lin; Prince Kung by his personal name, I-hsin; or Tseng Kuo-fan by his posthumous name, Tseng Wen-cheng-kung. Similarly, Shanhaikuan, where the Great Wall meets the sea, when referred to by the single character *kuan* was translated as "the Pass (i.e., Shanhaikuan)"; and we generally inserted parentheses around phrases implied by but not literally expressed in the Chinese original. This scholarly exactitude, while reassuring to other scholars for whom it was unnecessary, could only distract and bewilder the uninitiated general reader. To avoid perpetuating that sterile esotericism which has bedevilled the Chinese people and their Western students throughout history, we have now simplified the text. One man is cited by one name, not several. An emperor is known by his reign title, e.g., K'ang-hsi. Our translations try to give the full meaning of the original, even if part of it was only implied by the context. *Square brackets* enclose material added by way of editorial explanation, including page numbers from the original text. Capitalization in translations is used to indicate the Chinese elevation (to the top of the next line) of characters referring to the emperor, the dynasty, and the like. *Dates* given for memorials are normally those on which they were seen by the emperor, i.e., later than the actual date of composition.

1

THE PROBLEM AND ITS

BACKGROUND

CHAPTER I. INTRODUCTION

This is a survey of one of the most interesting, but neglected, aspects of modern history — the way in which the scholar-official class of China, faced with the aggressive expansion of the modern West, tried to understand an alien civilization and take action to preserve their own culture and their political and social institutions.

Since China is the largest unitary mass of humanity, with the oldest continuous history, its overrunning by the West in the past century was bound to create a continuing and violent intellectual revolution, the end of which we have not yet seen. The traditional system of tribute relations between the ancient Chinese empire and the "outside barbarians," who had formed the rest of China's known world, came to an end with the Anglo-Chinese treaty of Nanking in 1842. For a full century after 1842, China remained subject to a system of international relations characterized by the "unequal treaties" established by the Western powers, beginning with the treaty of Nanking, and not formally abolished until 1943.

Throughout this century of the "unequal treaties," the ancient society of China was brought into closer and closer contact with the then dominant and expanding society of Western Europe and America. This Western contact, lent impetus by the industrial revolution, had the most disastrous effect upon the old Chinese society. In every sphere of social activity the old order was challenged, attacked, undermined, or overwhelmed by a complex series of processes — political, economic, social, ideological, cultural — which were set in motion within China as a result of this penetration of an alien and more powerful society.

The massive structure of traditional China was torn apart much as the earth's crust would be disrupted by a comet passing too near. In the end, the remnants of the old China — its dress and manners, its classical written language and intricate system of imperial government, its reliance upon the extended family, the Confucian ethic, and all the other institutional achievements and cultural ornaments of a glorious past — had to be thrown into the melting pot and refashioned. The old order was changed within the space of three generations.

The ancient Chinese society, which had grown and developed through four millennia as the world's most populous and in many ways most highly cultured state, has been remade within a few score years. Rapid change is nothing new to

Westerners, but the rate of social change in modern China has exceeded anything we can imagine for it has included the collapse of old ways and the growth of new ways on a scale and at a tempo unprecedented in history.

Modern China, a Problem in Understanding

The West may well be disconcerted to note that this strenuous century of modern Chinese contact has now finally resulted in the rise to power of Chinese Communism. Since this event is certainly the most portentous in the whole history of American foreign policy in Asia, every intelligent American must strive to understand its significance. Does the Chinese communist victory constitute, as it seems to some, a rejection of the West? Or is it, in a sense, a final step in accepting certain aspects of the West? Or again, is it merely the latest phase of a continuing process within the body of Chinese society? Final answers to such oversimplified questions cannot be expected. Evidence may be cited to support all three of these suggested interpretations and several more besides: the new order at Peking is nationalistically committed to rejecting all forms of inferiority to the West, such as the "unequal treaties"; it is a genuine and thus far (1953) quite orthodox branch of the international communist movement, although few may wish to call that movement a proper form of "Western" influence; and it is at the same time obviously the climax of a revolutionary process long endemic in the Chinese body politic.

Underlying this book is the belief that modern China, including the communist rise to power there, can be understood only against the background of its contact with the West. A knowledge of China's growth as a traditional society is, of course, prerequisite. But the contemporary scene within the Middle Kingdom cannot be understood merely by reference to classical worthies like the Duke of Chou (*ca.* eleventh century B.C.) or the philosophical maxims of Confucius (551–479? B.C.) and Mencius (390–305 B.C.) or the thought of a medieval scholar like Chu Hsi (A.D. 1130–1200). New forces are at work, induced by the modern experience of the Chinese people. The origin and growth of these forces can be studied only within the context of the century of Western influence. Nationalism, party dictatorship, the cult of the masses, the worship of technology, the leadership of youth, and the emancipation of women — all these are new elements inspired mainly by Western contact. On the other hand, the Christian West will disclaim credit for that indoctrination of the mind and police control of the person which are integral parts of Chinese Communism and yet reminiscent also of China's past.

In spite of all the furor of change in recent decades, the hold of the past is still curiously strong in present-day China. Not far below the surface lies the ancient civilization of the Middle Kingdom, a subsoil which limits and conditions the new growth. Our efforts at analysis inevitably differentiate between the ancient Chinese heritage and modern Western influences. We assume that they each contributed, in varying degree, to the modern society which we knew up to 1949 (Communist China, so little known and difficult to appraise, is beyond the scope of this volume). Exactly how the heritage from the past and the influences from abroad have interacted within Chinese society during the last century is, of course, the nub of our problem. In many instances the conflict between traditional China and the West no doubt produced a stalemate. In the realm of law, for example, it might be argued (until such time as legal scholars apply themselves more fully to Chinese studies) that the impact of Western law served to undermine the Confucian ethic as a basis for administration and the achievement of social justice, without being able to take its place. It may be that the weakening of the ethical basis of the Confucian state was not compensated by a firm establishment of

Western legal institutions, and that China has been left somewhere in between.

In this volume we study the period from 1839 to 1923 because it spans the century from the first arrival of the Western powers in force to the first acceptance of Marxism-Leninism. In 1839 Commissioner Lin Tse-hsü (1785–1850) strove to settle the opium problem by destroying the opium stocks of foreign merchants, thereby precipitating the showdown between China's ancient tributary system and the expanding power of Britain. In 1923 Sun Yat-sen (1866–1925), having already led a republican revolution which ended the ancient imperial system in 1912, finally adopted some of the methods (although not the creed) of the Russian Communists. Between these two leaders of their generations who appear at the opening and close of our period lies an enormous gulf, so vast that they would have had great difficulty in understanding each other's conversation. Commissioner Lin had been trained in the Confucian classics, Dr. Sun in Western medicine. Lin represented an imperial potentate whose dynasty was the twenty-ninth in succession to have its history recorded as ruling all or part of the Chinese empire since its first unification in 221 B.C. Sun had worked most of his life to destroy that empire. In the end, he accepted communist help only in order to create a regime adequate to take the empire's place.

Paradoxically, however, these two men exemplify the unity which underlies the amazing diversity of modern China's history. Both Lin, the old-style mandarin, and Sun, the modern revolutionist, were concerned with the government of the Chinese state. Both felt the Western stimulus and reacted strongly to it. Both were patriots. Like all other Chinese officials, scholars, and revolutionists who will be quoted in this book, they were vitally concerned with the fate of China, its civilization, and way of life. Behind all the variety of viewpoints, assumptions, analyses, and proposals put forward for China's salvation during this century of change and collapse there has been a cultural bond, a strong consciousness of China as an entity and of the Chinese people as a unit in history. "All-under-Heaven" (T'ien-hsia, the empire) and the "Middle Kingdom" (Chung-kuo, China) have remained primary concepts, starting points of the reformer's thinking. Thus the leadership of modern China in the period 1839–1923 remained ethnocentric and China-centered. Many students of Chinese history doubt that the Chinese Communists can remain otherwise, in the long run, even though students of international communism agree that nationalistic independence of Moscow, or "Titoism," is a very rare phenomenon among communist movements.

Any study of the acculturation of one society by another involves a number of independent variables. One must appraise and characterize the value systems or ideals of both societies, and this requires one to generalize upon a scale so broad as to be sometimes almost meaningless. The "American way of life" must be compared with the "Chinese way of life." Not only must the student of cultural miscegenation turn from one culture to the other, ambivalently, but he must also live in the past as well as the present, and appreciate the Confucianism of old China as well as the utilitarianism of Victorian England. This is a well-nigh impossible task at a time when we know so little of the actual content of life and thought in premodern China. But the attempt must be made, sooner or later, as best we can. The documents and commentaries in this volume are presented as a first step in this direction.

Some Preliminary Definitions

Let us begin by clarifying certain concepts. First of all, it would be quite unrealistic to think of premodern or "traditional" China (or the "Confucian state") as archaic and static, backward and unchanging. Chinese society has always been in a process of change, older values and institutions giving way gradually to newer ideals and forms. Through this evolutionary development, China's ancient ways have undergone continuous modification as century followed century. The China of 1839 was vastly different from that of Confucius or Mencius, and also very different from the medieval China of Neo-Confucian philosophers like Chu Hsi. When we call the Chinese society of the early nineteenth century "traditional," we are only stressing its close continuity with its own China-centered heritage from the past.

Secondly, we face the problem, what was the general nature of this traditional Chinese society? It was most unlike that of Western Europe and America; but how? Among several answers that could be given, one of the most illuminating (for those who seek to put societies in categories) is the concept of old China as an example of "Oriental Society." Even before Karl Marx used the term "Asiatic mode of production," Western scholars like J. S. Mill had noted certain general characteristics which seemed to make the ancient empires of the Near East and Asia quite different in kind from the society of Europe. Social historians today are developing this concept; while we can hardly try to summarize it here, we can note certain features. Traditional China, like other ancient empires, came to be organized under a centralized monolithic government in which the official bureaucracy dominated most aspects of large-scale activity — administrative, military, religious, economic, political. This agrarian bureaucratic state got its revenue largely from the agricultural production of the illiterate peasantry, who also provided the manpower for the conscript armies and for the corvée labor which was used to control the water supply through diking and ditching. Large-scale public works, like the Great Wall or the Grand Canal, comparable to roads and airfields today, have been built by this mass-labor force, mobilized and superintended by the officials. The latter were of course drawn from the small literate element of the Chinese population, the literati who could transact public business using the intricate Chinese writing system. Since only the well-to-do could normally afford the years of study required for literacy in the classics, officials came more from the landlord-gentry class than from the peasant masses. Thus the landlords produced scholars, and the scholars became officials, forming a complex upper stratum so closely interrelated and interdependent that the ideal men of distinction were landlord-scholar-officials, rather than generals or merchants.

In this society, the individual was generally subordinated to his family group. The scholars and administrators, like the emperor above them, were expected to follow an ethical rather than a purely legal code of conduct. A Western-type individualism and the supremacy of law never became established, nor the personal freedom under law represented by our civil liberties and institution of private property. (The legal safeguards of personal liberty are, to be sure, a rather recent and not yet perfect achievement in the West.) At any rate, the old China was based on the farming family and ruled by the bureaucrat. It was politically centralized while economically decentralized, and strong in the customary ethical sanctions which preserved the patriarch and the ruler at the top of the social hierarchy, while weak in the institutions of property and enterprise. All this has affected the capacity of the Chinese state to follow the Western pattern of capital investment and industrialization. As we shall note below, China's modern industrial enterprises had to be under official patronage if not control, yet the tradition was to invest one's personal savings in land rather than in productive industry. This undoubtedly impeded China's industrialization.

Perhaps enough has been said to indicate how the institutional patterns of old China influenced her response to the West in every sphere — economic and political as well as military, social, and intellectual. We forego at this point any further effort to define the general nature of the old Chinese society. Although we are about to look at bits of the record, we cannot expect to see the whole picture in detail ahead of time; for the detailed picture has still to be put together.

Our explanation of terms may conclude with two further points. First, to say as some do that nineteenth-century China was "feudal" or "semi-feudal" seems to us not very meaningful, if we judge these terms by their use in European or Japanese history. China does not fit into the proper institutional pattern. Second, the terms "stimulus" (or "impact") and "response" are not very precise. We are in danger of assuming that there was a previous "Western impact" merely because there was later activity which we call a "Chinese response." This "Chinese response" or activity is the thing we want to study, but it obviously was part of Chinese conduct as a whole. In other words, the Western impact was only one of many factors in the Chinese scene. The response to it can only be unscrambled with difficulty from Chinese history in general. Until we can work out a more precise analytic framework, the title of this study will remain more metaphorical than scientific.

The Scope of this Volume

These considerations give us a limited objective — to mark some of the broad outlines and trace some of the main patterns in the intellectual history of modern China's attempt to comprehend the West and adjust to it. We proceed on the assumption that Western influence did indeed precipitate the remaking of Chinese life and values. Every patriot and statesman since the time of Lin Tse-hsü has had to consider China's relationship to the West as one of the primary problems confronting the Chinese state and its people. Beginning with the movement for coastal defense, there has been a succession of formulations and reformulations of the ancient "barbarian problem." The imitation of Western arms, the program of "Self-strengthening" through Western studies, later through industrialization and eventually through institutional reform, the movement for revolution and republicanism, the cult of "Science and Democracy," the literary "Renaissance," the adoption of party tutelage and "democratic centralism" — all these and many other programs have had their day and contributed to the long struggle for the remaking of Chinese life. All of them have been related, in greater or less degree, to the Western influence on China, even down to the alleged "American imperialism" which helps today to sanction the power of the Chinese Communists.

Within this single volume we make no formal effort to describe or define the Western impact. The inequalities of the treaties are well enough known: the foreign consuls' legal jurisdiction over their nationals known as extraterritoriality; the conventional treaty tariff and the commercial exploitation that went hand in hand with it; the treaty ports which, as Chiang Kai-shek so fervently declared in China's Destiny, became centers of infection whence the old social order was contaminated and broken down. Less has been written to evaluate the social influence of the great Protestant, and also the revived Catholic, missionary movements of the nineteenth century. Similarly the influence of Western studies in China and of Chinese students who had studied in the West has been only imperfectly evaluated. The monographic work essential to scholarship has not yet been done. Scholarly conclusions can hardly yet be formed.

Our main effort, therefore, is to stimulate and assist the kind of monographic study necessary to any intellectual progress in this field. It will not be enough for Western social scientists to apply new interpretations to the meager record of modern Chinese history thus far available. Not enough facts are known. We cannot rely on propagandist "scholarship," with its dogmatic disregard for the truth —

or rather, its Procrustean regard for the truth as a relative matter — to give us the real story. It is necessary for trained and competent Asian and Western scholars alone and in collaboration to spend long periods of time in translation and research, else we shall never know what has really happened in China since its opening to the West.

The memorials, essays, and diaries of Chinese statesmen and reformers form perhaps the most convenient and practicable avenue of approach to this immensely difficult subject. Texts are artifacts. Their original meaning can be wrung out with patience. In the process, reflections and interpretations will occur to the translator. The corpus of Chinese literature is well organized, within its own universe of discourse. Statements of fact and idea can often be cross-checked and verified. Every author whose writings are quoted below could profitably become the subject of monographic research. To this end, we have given bibliographical suggestions, in our *Research Guide* (see *Notes and Sources*), which are intended to supplement the aid to be found in Dr. A. W. Hummel's invaluable *Eminent Chinese of the Ch'ing Period 1644–1912*, 2 vols., (Washington, D. C., 1943–1944). We have tried in our own commentaries to avoid duplicating the material presented by Fang Chao-ying, Tu Lien-che and the various other contributors to that biographical dictionary. It is assumed that the user of this volume will have it at hand.

Since so many of these items are memorials addressed to the emperor, it should be explained to non-specialists that official business in the Chinese empire was formally transacted and decisions made by the process of proposal from the high officials and decision by the ruler and his advisers. It was almost literally a case of "Man proposes, God (or the Son of Heaven) disposes." Consequently, for a policy to get any official result, it had to be embodied in a proper document or report ("memorial") from one of the emperor's officials, whereupon an imperial edict or decree could be issued to summarize, comment upon, or confirm it. Whether or not an edict was to follow, the emperor was expected to append at the end of a memorial, after he had read it, a brief comment, even so brief as "Noted" or "I am informed" (equivalent to "OK"), just to show that he was on the job. This comment is usually called a "vermilion endorsement," since the emperor used red ink. The recorded date of a memorial was normally the day when the emperor saw it, not the actual date of writing.

The bold new program of translation and comment which this volume represents will in the course of time seem to have been overbold, if not foolhardy, and no longer new. But it is our thesis that the field of modern Chinese intellectual history has lain fallow far too long. Our selections of material have had to be arbitrary and without benefit of prolonged research on all the persons and movements dealt with, but this is a pump-priming operation, conducted on the assumption that Western students of China will increase in number and productivity, and that they will not fail to meet the intellectual challenge of modern China's metamorphosis.

CHAPTER II. SOME ELEMENTS IN THE CHINESE INTELLECTUAL TRADITION

In nineteenth-century China, more than in most times and places, the problems of the day were met in terms of the past. During China's long history, orthodoxy of thought had been stressed by one ruler after another, ever since the first emperor of the Ch'in in 213 B.C. burned the books hostile to his regime. A great continuity of intellectual tradition had thus been established, constantly preserved by the official historians and by the literati who mastered the ancient classics. The orthodoxy of ideas inculcated in this way was used by the imperial government to ensure the loyalty and obedience of its subjects. Consequently, both unorthodox ideas and foreign ideas were potentially dangerous to the regime in power.

Here we see one channel of Western influence — Western ideas could become weapons in the struggle for power within China. Both the institutional reformers of 1898 and the republican revolutionists of 1911 eventually demonstrated this. Even the Taiping rebels of 1850–1864 invoked the Christian Bible to support their cause. More recent and successful rebels have used Marx and Lenin. Yet the process of ideological change in modern China had to begin with the reinterpretation of the Chinese heritage, rather than with its denial and rejection.

In this chapter, therefore, we must take note of three major elements in the intellectual background of nineteenth-century Chinese thinkers: one was the ethnocentric, even "nationalistic," ideology of certain scholars who had opposed the alien rule of the Manchus; the second was the influence left by the early Catholic missionaries; the third was the traditional attitude of the Ch'ing court toward the West.

a. Some Early Ch'ing "Nationalist" Thinkers

These independent-minded Chinese scholars of the early Ch'ing period (1644–1911) courageously challenged the orthodoxy which the new Manchu rulers were fostering. While remaining within the bounds of the Chinese classical tradition, they boldly questioned some of the doctrines of the day, especially the philosophy of Wang Yang-ming (1472–1528). Beginning in the last years of the Ming Dynasty (1368–1644), they argued against certain traditional interpretations of Confucianism and demanded drastic re-examination of the classics, thus setting a precedent and providing a stimulus for the scholars of the late nineteenth century. The precedent that they set, however, should not be exaggerated — the methods and interpretations of these seventeenth-century scholars did not come down in an unbroken tradition out of which the late Ch'ing reformers emerged. On the contrary, some of them were all but forgotten and were rediscovered only after Western contact had obliged Chinese reformers to look in their own past for precedents which would justify their new interpretations of Chinese tradition. It was in this way, as convenient predecessors in the exposition of ideas they now found necessary, that the reformers of 1898 used seventeenth-century scholars like Ku Yen-wu and Huang Tsung-hsi. Among other things, these men had opposed alien rule, by the Manchus or any other non-Chinese. Two centuries later their writings naturally became of value to patriotic scholars who sought an ideological basis for modern Chinese nationalism.

One major form of China's response to Western contact has thus been the reappraisal of Chinese tradition, in the effort to use it for modern purposes. The next few pages illustrate the type of writings available for this endeavor.

Huang Tsung-hsi (1610–1695) was a famous scholar of the late Ming, whose political treatise, written in 1663, was called *Ming-i tai-fang lu.* (For data on this and other works, see our separate *Research Guide.*) The tenets of this work were derived from two sources: a) Mencius' thesis, that the people are the most important members of any state, while the ruler is less significant; b) a chapter of the *Book of Rites* (*Li-chi*) which presents the idea that "the empire is for the public," *T'ien-hsia wei-kung,* i.e., it is not for one person. (This was a slogan later used by Sun Yat-sen. For these Chinese characters, see list in the *Research Guide.*)

The main points of Huang's political philosophy were that the institution of ruler is for the benefit of the people and the ruler and his ministers are public servants of the people. A good ruler should be loved by the people as their parent, but a bad ruler should be killed. Huang approved tyrannicide. After the legendary golden age, he argued, political disorder in China had resulted from the neglect of duty by rulers who considered the empire their private property. Huang still believed in enlightened monarchy, although he disapproved the practice of "patterning after the ancestors" or ancestral law (fa-tsu), according to which all emperors of a dynasty should obey the regulations laid down by the dynastic founder. He also argued that a good legal system is of primary importance, while able administrators are secondary. One of the reformers of 1898, T'an Ssu-t'ung (see Ch. XVI below), is said to have printed several hundred thousand copies of excerpts from Huang's Ming-i tai-fang lu for secret distribution, to promote his own ideas of reform. These excerpts strongly influenced the thinking of the late Ch'ing period.

Writing "On the ruler," Huang says: [1] *

At the beginning of creation, every man was selfish and every man was self-seeking. There was public good in the empire but probably no one cared to promote it; there was public evil in the empire, but probably no one cared to get rid of it. Then there appeared a man who did not consider his personal interest as the object of benefit but made it possible for the people of the empire to share the benefit. . . The assiduous toil of this man must have been a thousand or a myriad times more than that of the people of the empire. Well, after spending himself a thousand or a myriadfold in assiduous toil, he still did not enjoy the benefit. . . Rulers of later ages were different. They considered that the authority to bestow benefit and harm was entirely concentrated in their own hands; the benefit of the empire was entirely received by them, while the harm of the empire was entirely given to others [p. 2]. . . They considered the empire as their chief item of personal property. . . In ancient times the people of the empire were the primary interest, the ruler was secondary, and what the ruler planned and did was for the empire. Now the ruler has the primary interest, the people of the empire are secondary . . . and the one who does great harm to the empire is the ruler. . . In ancient times the people of the empire loved their ruler, comparing him to their parents, respecting him as Heaven; that was indeed not too much. Now the people of the empire hate their ruler, looking on him as an enemy, calling him a dictator (tu-fu); this is certainly the position he occupies.

On the subject of the minister, Huang says [p. 3], "When I enter government service, I work for the empire, not for the ruler; for the myriads of the populace, not for one family." In his chapter "On the law," he writes [p. 5]:

What is called law is for the protection of the one imperial personage and is not the law for the sake of society as a whole. . . Some critics say that each dynasty should have its own laws, and that to obey ancestral law is filial piety. . . These are plagiarized statements of vulgar scholars [p. 6]. . . Some commentators even say, there is government by man, no government by law; I should say, government by law should come before government by man.

* The reader's attention is called to the Note on page vii.

Ku Yen-wu (1613–1682), also known as Ku T'ing-lin, was a very learned scholar who with Huang Tsung-hsi and others tried to restore the Ming dynasty. He traveled extensively in North China, carrying on a kind of geographic, topographic, and economic survey. Stressing agriculture, irrigation, and rural economics, he encouraged the use of labor-saving machinery and the opening of mines. As a reaction against the philosophy of Wang Yang-ming, Ku advocated the pursuit of knowledge "of practical use to society," *ching-shih chih-yung*. Among his famous works are the *Jih-chih lu* (Notes of daily accumulation of knowledge), dealing with a large variety of subjects; and the *T'ien-hsia chün-kuo li-ping shu* (A book on the strategic and economic advantages and disadvantages of the counties and states of the empire), author's preface dated 1662. He was also a pioneer scholar in Chinese philology and he emphasized the inductive method of research in classics and history.

Living in the same environment, Huang and Ku both reacted against the political oppression of the early Ch'ing period. Their thinking was largely similar, but in attacking despotism Huang took the people as the fundamental element of the state, while Ku did not consider them of such cardinal importance. Ku attacked the overconcentration of authority in the hands of the emperor. Although he eulogized ancient feudalism as a means of sharing the empire among the public, he still did not think that it should be restored. Instead, he favored the division of state authority among local magistrates who should have full power in developing education, agriculture, and military affairs. The power of each magistrate should be again divided among the heads of small political divisions, where the people should have considerable right of self-government. He hated the way in which the scholar-literati acted as a law unto themselves in rural communities and objected to the legal restriction of the people's freedom.

Ku Yen-wu was in favor of reform: "If the laws or institutions are not reformed, it will be impossible to meet the present crisis. We are already in a situation where we must reform, yet we still try to avoid actually doing it. . . This will certainly cause great corruption." [2]

Ku favored thorough reform, not a patchwork; reform based on present conditions and not restricted by ancestral law:

When our predecessors initiated legislation, they could not thoroughly study the facts and circumstances and prepare in advance for future revision. Their successors followed what was already a corrupt practice, and were restricted by the established statutes which they could not change, or had to make by-laws, to amend them. Thereupon, the more numerous the laws, the more they were abused. All the affairs of the empire became more vexatious. The result was that the laws were not understood and not enforced. The upper and the lower classes tried to fool each other, the only consideration being that they should not neglect the system laid down by their ancestors. This state of affairs was most prevalent in the Ming dynasty.[3]

But Ku Yen-wu searched for a golden age in the past. His political purpose was "to make use of Chinese institutions and to transform the barbarians" (*yunghsia pien-i*). He tried to restore the self-confidence of the Chinese people, to develop the Chinese traditional ethics and wisdom. In a letter to a friend he says that his purpose in writing the *Jih-chih lu* was "to disperse rebellion and to cleanse away the dirt of politics, to model after our antiquity and to use the political and social systems of the Hsia [ancient China], to supply more information to future students and to wait for a good time of administration by future emperors." [4]

Fortunately Ku Yen-wu was not bigoted nor bound by Chinese traditionalism. He recognized the good points of the barbarians also: "There are some Chinese customs which are inferior to those of foreign countries." He admired the frugal, assiduous, and military spirit of the Khitans. He praised the honest customs of the Uigurs, who made only slight differences of rank between the ruler and his ministers. He thought the system of encouraging the cultivation of arable land and its equal distribution under the Toba Wei dynasty (A.D. 386–535) in Northwest China might serve as a model for later ages.[5]

Wang Fu-chih (1619–1692), also called Wang Ch'uan-shan, was a renowned historical critic and a voluminous writer. After the Ming dynasty was overthrown he retired to a small boat-shaped island in Hengyang, Hunan, where he lived the life of a hermit, writing books for some forty years. Because he had little association with other scholars, he became an independent thinker.[6] From his historical and inductive approach to political problems, he built up his theory of evolution — that the legal system should be changed from time to time and in each dynasty be a single unit. Accordingly Wang objected to all conservative attempts at restoration of the past; it is futile, he thought, to imitate antiquity. The society of ancient times was rightly governed by ancient law; the political system of today cannot rightly be enforced in the society of the future. The administration of each dynasty should fit the needs of its time and be adjusted to contemporary conditions. For instance, in the old days, it was a good system for soldiers to become farmers and vice versa, but in modern times when warfare has become far more complicated, it is necessary to have well-trained, specialized soldiers; untrained farmers cannot at the same time serve as soldiers.[7]

Wang Fu-chih discovered another theory — that every species and race, all the way from insects to human beings, aims at its own preservation and organization. Self-preservation is a natural law. Even the ants know how to protect themselves; human beings are certainly not to be excepted. Since the forming of groups is inherent in human nature and the establishment of a ruler is for the purpose of protecting the group, it is logical and necessary for the group to govern itself. Each race should be controlled by its own ruler, and should never allow any encroachment by an alien race. In other words, all states should be national states and self-governing. He would rather have even a usurper on the throne than a foreign race dominating China.[8]

Still another of Wang's new ideas was that differences of culture are produced among various races which live in different geographical zones. Since the barbarians and the Chinese were bred in different places, their spirit, actions, and customs also differed. China should not allow barbarians to invade her territory and her culture. Wang considered that culture fluctuates and civilization does not stay in one place. He observed that in many cases culture has progressed from barbarism to civilization, while in other cases it has remained stagnant. He thought there was a possibility of China being reduced to a barbarous or savage condition. Wang's method for forestalling a barbarian invasion was to make good use of the time element. "He who would succeed in controlling barbarians should have a good knowledge of the times and seasons. When the combination of circumstances favors attack, he attacks; when it favors defense, he defends."[9]

Chu Chih-yü (1600–1682), also called Chu Shun-shui, was another ethnocentric thinker who had great influence in both China and Japan. Born in the same district as Huang Tsung-hsi, he fled to Annam and Japan to request aid against the invading Manchus. Having failed in repeated attempts to overthrow the Manchu rule, he remained in Japan after 1659. His scholarship attracted the attention of Japanese savants who not only studied under him but recommended him to be a teacher of Prince Tokugawa Mitsukuni, grandson of the great Ieyasu. Under

Mitsukuni's auspices he prepared a detailed description of the Chinese state worship of Confucius and gave advice on the compilation of the colossal *Dai Nihon shi* or "History of Great Japan," a work which later influenced the leaders of the Meiji Restoration of 1868.

Chu was a man of great integrity and an advocate of pragmatism. His anti-Manchu writings, entitled *Yang-chiu shu-lueh*, were to be a great stimulus to rebellious Chinese youth near the end of the Ch'ing dynasty. Before his death Chu requested that his body should "not be returned to China so long as the Manchus rule." [10]

The Literary Inquisition

The growth of Chinese "national" feeling against the Manchu regime, stimulated by writers like Huang Tsung-hsi, Ku Yen-wu, Wang Fu-chih, and Chu Chih-yü, was suppressed by the literary inquisition. This reached its height under Emperor Ch'ien-lung (1736–1795), when more than two thousand selected Chinese works were wholly or partly destroyed. The partisans of the Ming had given the Emperor K'ang-hsi (1662–1722) much trouble and, even after their political suppression, had left many writings which expressed dissatisfaction or resentment against the Manchus. A purge of such works had actually begun with the first Manchu emperor after 1644.[11]

As an example of the inquisition, we may note the case of Lü Liu-liang (1629–1683) and Tseng Ching (1679–1736). Lü was a classicist as well as a pamphleteer. He refused to take the civil service examinations but instead wrote commentaries on Sung philosophy in which he openly deplored the plight into which China had fallen and the inability of the Chinese people to check the disaster of the Manchu invasion. His expression of anti-Manchu sentiment was quite influential and during the Yung-cheng period (1723–1735) led a certain Tseng Ching, a *chü-jen* (provincial graduate) of Hunan, and his disciples to attempt to overthrow the Manchu government. Tseng was so much interested in Lü Liu-liang's writings that he sent one of his loyal students to read them all at the latter's home in Chekiang, and to get acquainted with Lü's disciples. In 1728 Tseng Ching sent the same student to persuade the governor-general of Szechwan and Shensi to rebel against the Manchus. This was reported to the court and ruthless punishment was dealt to the partisans, descendants, relatives and disciples of all the persons involved. Most of the writings of Lü and Tseng were destroyed. But from the *Ta-i chueh-mi lu*, a work which consists of all the arguments of Emperor Yung-cheng in defense of himself and his throne, as well as from the testimony of Tseng Ching, one can still trace a little of the nationalist spirit behind this abortive rebellion.[12]

Ideas and events of this sort were known to the Chinese scholars of the nineteenth century as part of their native tradition. In their response to the West they were necessarily more under the influence of this tradition than of any other. Just as the China of today can be more thoroughly understood by reference to the nineteenth century, so the record of Chinese thought must be pursued farther back, in order to gain that over-all perspective which the historian seeks. Is it not possible, for example, that the effectiveness with which the Ch'ing government suppressed the growth of creative and ethnocentric anti-Manchu thought in the eighteenth century contributed directly to China's inability to respond more vigorously to the Western stimulus a century later?

After the literary inquisition had reached its height in the late eighteenth century, the "nationalist" movement was represented chiefly by secret societies of various names and forms which sought to overthrow the Manchus. Some of these societies contributed, in some degree, to the Taiping Rebellion and subsequently to Dr. Sun Yat-sen's revolutionary movement. The study of the secret societies deserves separate monographic treatment, beyond the scope of this volume.[13]

b. *The Early Jesuit Influence in China*

The first extensive cultural contact between China and Europe began near the end of the sixteenth century, when the Jesuit missionaries, in the wake of the Portuguese, reached China by sea. Their dual function is well known: they not only diffused Western ideas in China, including elements of mathematics, astronomy, geography, hydraulics, the calendar, and the manufacture of cannon, but they also introduced Chinese (particularly Confucian) ideas into Europe.[14] The Jesuits found it easier to influence China's science than her religion. Perceiving this, they used their scientific knowledge as a means of approach to Chinese scholars. Although a small number of their Chinese converts took part in the translation and compilation of religious and scientific books, the majority of the native scholars, entrenched in their ethnocentric cultural tradition, were not seriously affected by the new elements of Western thought.

The great Jesuit pioneer, Matteo Ricci (1552–1610), tried to fit Catholicism into Chinese thought. In general he accepted Confucianism in its most ancient phase but rejected the Confucian development after Han and T'ang, especially the Neo-Confucianism of the Sung. He accepted the term *Shang-ti*, the highest deity in the Confucian classics, but not the *T'ai-chi* or "Supreme Ultimate" of the Neo-Confucians. Ricci and his followers likewise accepted the *hsien-ju*, the early Confucianists, but not the *hou-ju*, the Confucianists of later ages.[15]

The cosmological ideas of the Roman Catholic Church and of Neo-Confucianism differed in several important respects: a) the Neo-Confucians did not recognize a creator or almighty God in the universe; instead, they believed that the growth of creatures is by *li* or "natural law"; b) they recognized the existence of *hsin* (mind or conscience), which is somewhat comparable to the soul of Christianity, but they did not believe that this mind or conscience is bestowed by God; c) they acknowledged that every human being has the power and free will to reach his best state of development, to be free from sin or crime, and without God's help to go to Heaven. While both the Catholics and the Neo-Confucianists sought to understand the universe, to distinguish truth, to cultivate virtue and to teach people how to be good, their purposes appear to have been just sufficiently similar to bring them into rivalry and conflict.[16]

The Various Forms of Chinese Interest

Those Chinese scholars who accepted both Christianity and Western science, like Hsü Kuang-ch'i (1562–1633) believed that Western learning overcame the shortcomings of Confucianism and replaced Buddhism; and that Confucianism and Christianity could be developed in China in parallel fashion. Their acceptance of what Ricci had to offer was based first of all on a rational appreciation of the Jesuits as philosopher-gentlemen. One late Ming writer says: [17]

The *T'ien-chu kuo* [the Lord-of-Heaven country, i.e., the Catholic state, presumably Italy], lies further to the west from the Buddhist state [India]. Their people understand literature and are as scholarly and elegant as the Chinese. There is a certain Li-ma-tou [Matteo Ricci] who came from the said state, and after four years reached the boundary of Kwangtung by way of India. Their religion worships *T'ien-chu* ["the Lord of Heaven," the Catholic term for God], just as the Confucianists worship Confucius and the Buddhists, Buddha. Among his books there is one entitled *T'ien-chu shih-i* (The true meaning of Christianity) which frequently explains the truth by comparison with Confucianism but sharply criticizes the theories of nothingness (*hsü-wu*) and emptiness of Buddhism and Taoism. . . I am very much delighted with his ideas, which are close to Confucianism but more earnest in exhorting society not to resemble the Buddhists, who always like to use obscure, incoherent words to fool and frighten the populace. . . He is very polite when he talks to people and his arguments, if challenged, can be inexhaustible. Thus in foreign countries there are also real gentlemen.

Firearms and applied science further commended the Jesuits to the court of Peking, as they already had to the daimyo of Japan. Long before Ricci finally received a court stipend in Peking in 1601, European weapons had been introduced into South China. But apparently they were not widely welcomed until Japan invaded Korea in 1592. The Japanese, benefiting by the early Portuguese importation of firearms after 1542, won victories in Korea, and the Chinese recognized the necessity of improving their weapons. In 1622 the Ming emperor, already threatened by the new Manchu power beyond the Wall, sent an envoy to Macao seeking Jesuit help in casting cannon. In the following year Westerners were summoned to the capital for this purpose. Ch'ü Shih-ssu (Thomas Ch'ü, 1590–1651) memorialized the throne in 1628 requesting the study of Western cannon and other weapons; he declared that in 1619 an imperial decree had ordered Hsü Kuang-ch'i to search for Western weapons and that he had obtained four cannon. Li Chih-tsao (d. 1630) had secured twenty-three more from Canton in 1621. Thus the Ming sought Western cannon for defense against the Manchus much as the Manchu government two centuries later was to seek Western cannon and the help of the "Ever Victorious Army" at Shanghai to suppress the Taiping Rebellion. The Ming dynasty attempted to acquire Portuguese artillery and three or four hundred men from Macao to repel a Manchu invasion; but apprehension over having Western soldiers in China led to the cancellation of the mission at Nanchang. Only the commander, Gonzales Tedeira, and a few others continued to Peking.[18]

Thereafter in the waning years of the Ming not only Jesuits but also other foreigners from Macao went to Peking, both to make weapons and to serve in the Chinese forces. In 1639 Franciscus Sambiaso presented to the emperor many gifts, including a clock, binoculars, maps, an organ, a mirror, and a parrot. He submitted a memorial to the throne calling attention to the need for a good calendar, the selection of ores, the promotion of international trade and the purchase of Western guns. This actually constituted a modernization program for China; but the Ming dynasty was busily engaged in warfare against the Manchus and among these recommendations the Chinese emperor took an interest only in the calendar and the guns.[19]

While the conversion to the Roman Catholic faith of such Chinese scholar-officials as Hsü Kuang-ch'i and Li Chih-tsao is well known, it nevertheless poses several questions. First, what element in Christianity was responsible for its friendly reception by certain scholars and members of the imperial family, several score of whom are said to have been converted by 1640? [20] Did their baptism mean acceptance of basic Christian tenets, or were these converts won over by rationalism (as opposed to faith), because they believed Christianity to be less unworldly than

Buddhism and Taoism? Both Hsü and Li were also interested in Western guns and cannon, and on his part Matteo Ricci accepted some Chinese phraseology (e.g., *Shang-ti*), and admitted the validity of ancient Confucian teachings. Do these signs indicate that, rather than a fundamental conversion to a new faith, the Chinese acceptance of the Christian religion was only a manifestation of tolerance?

Secondly, it is noteworthy that the immediate Jesuit influence in China was through items of practical significance, such as cannon, the calendar, or Ricci's map of the world. Why is so little trace of Christian doctrine to be found in the writings of Chinese scholars in the subsequent century? If this is to be explained by the fact that government suppression cut off contact and the relatively few professed converts had few successors, we still face the question why the minds of the non-Christian scholars were not more permanently influenced by Western knowledge or ideas.

Such questions raise the knotty problem of the Chinese religious consciousness. The long and complex religious experience of the Chinese people had included, among many other faiths, the great flowering of Buddhism in the seventh and eighth centuries, a religion characterized by belief in an incarnate yet divine savior. We know that Chinese Buddhism had a profound influence upon the subsequent Neo-Confucian philosophy, although the extent of this influence is still being appraised. It is plain that China's early experience of Buddhism lay behind her later reaction to Christianity, in ways that remain to be studied.[21]

If we turn the other way and look at the centuries after the Jesuit contact, we may assume that the use of Western cannon in the seventeenth century served as a useful precedent in the minds of officials in the nineteenth century. The authentic record of the use of Western cannon two-centuries before must also have helped the nineteenth-century officials to admit the superiority of Western arms.

The Conservative Antagonists of Western Christianity and Science

Opposition to the Jesuits and other Western missionaries was motivated partly by the xenophobic suspicion that foreigners were spies; partly by ethical scruples against Christian religious ceremonies which seemed contrary to Chinese customs such as the veneration of Heaven, ancestors and Confucius; and partly by professional jealousy, on the assumption that if Catholicism were to become prevalent in China, the decline of the doctrines of Confucius, Buddha, and Lao-tzu would damage the position of their protagonists. Soon after Ricci's death in 1610, troubles had begun.

The Chinese Buddhist leadership appears to have been vehemently anti-Catholic. Meanwhile most Chinese scholars remained dogmatically opposed to the Westerners' religion. Lacking enthusiasm for their religion, they also disliked their science. From 1659 on, the scholar Yang Kuang-hsien (1597–1669) wrote a number of treatises denouncing the Christian religion and criticizing the calendar made by Adam Schall von Bell. In 1664 he charged Schall with errors in astronomical calculation, and accused the missionaries, with their "million followers" scattered throughout the land, of plotting against the state and indoctrinating the people with false ideas.[22]

The calendar controversy in particular was caused by the opposition of traditionalists. In a sense, it represented a first symptom of unrest in the Chinese academic world caused by Westerners, just as the Opium War of 1840–1842 was to be the first such disturbance in China's modern political history. The conservatives objected to Western scientific instruments, arguing that clocks were expensive but useless, that cannon could not annihilate enemies but usually burned the gunners first, and that on Ricci's map of the globe China was not in the very center and was not large enough. They also objected to Western painting because it lacked forceful strokes.[23]

Since such objections were not conclusive, the conservative scholars adopted another tactic, quoting irrelevant Confucian classics to refute the newly introduced Western knowledge. Yang Kuang-hsien says that the calendar of the legendary Emperors Yao and Shun should be used, even though its predictions may be inaccurate. Juan Yuan (1764–1849), a nineteenth-century representative of the anti-Western-science school, says that it is unbelievable that the earth is rotating and he who believes it rebels against the Confucian classics.[24] A more powerful line of attack was to make a forced interpretation of Western discoveries, cite some vague references from the Chinese classics, and claim a Chinese origin of Western science. In this way it was claimed that the Western calendars were derived from the chapter "Yao-tien" in the Book of History; the essential ideas of Western discussions of the earth were derived from the commentary on the tenth chapter of Tseng-tzu; [25] and the formula for computing the circumference of a circle had been figured out and handed down by Tzu Ch'ung-chih (429–500).[26] As for algebra, it was said to have been the method of Li Yeh of the Yuan dynasty, while other elements of Western mathematics were derived from the ancient mathematical classic, Chou-pi suan-ching.[27]

Behind all this condemnation of Western learning lay the basic political fact that the Manchu rulers of China could not tolerate the propagation of a foreign religion which asserted the spiritual supremacy of Rome over Peking. By 1640 Japan, under the Tokugawa, had proscribed Christianity and foreign contact (except for the Dutch in Nagasaki) as politically dangerous. In China by the end of the seventeenth century there were Catholic congregations in all but two of the provinces; the Roman Catholic faith was banned in the Yung-cheng period (1723–1735), though less drastically than in Japan (Chinese Christians were compelled to follow the example of those in Japan and trample on the cross).[28] Even before 1773, when the Jesuit order was dissolved by the Pope, the missionaries at the Chinese court had been limited to serving as technical personnel — painters, musicians and architects — rather than as persons of intellectual importance. They had lost influence as a link between Western and Chinese culture.

The Jesuits and Chinese Science and Technology

It remains an interesting question what influence the Catholic missionaries had on the native Chinese tradition in mathematics, medicine, and similar fields. We know that Western military superiority, which forced China into closer contact with Europe and America, was a product of technology. Like the tank-and-airplane team today, British gunboats in the 1840's proved decisive in battle. The inadequacy of China's military techniques — her musketeers, mounted archers, and banner-decked war junks — was a symptom of scientific backwardness. Yet it would be quite wrong to conclude that Chinese society had always lagged behind the West in her material culture. On the contrary, medieval China's earlier use of printing, the compass, and gunpowder had indicated her comparative advancement over medieval Europe. The native roots of science and technology in China have not yet been thoroughly examined, although the modern world has already gained useful drugs (like ephedrine) from the old Chinese pharmacopoeia, and the products of many Chinese craftsmen and artists have long been recognized as without peer abroad. How far Chinese technology was influenced by the West before the nineteenth century is still uncertain.

The superiority of the Jesuit knowledge of mathematics was soon recognized by Chinese scholars. Since the thirteenth century, when the abacus had begun to replace the old Chinese calculating rods,[29] the Chinese mathematics based on the latter method of calculation had fallen gradually into neglect. By the late sixteenth century even the foremost scholars knew practically nothing about higher mathematics. Hence the publication of the Chinese translation of Euclid's *Elements of Geometry* in 1607, and certain Jesuit works on mathematics and calendric calculation in subsequent years, created a new interest among the scholars in mathematical studies.[30] The Western method of calculation, writing down the progress and results of reasoning step by step, probably had more appeal for Chinese scholars than the use of the abacus. Under the first four Manchu emperors, the Imperial Board of Astronomy was almost continuously entrusted to one or more Catholic missionaries in Peking. Emperor K'ang-hsi himself studied mathematics under several Jesuits and so did certain selected officials in a special school.[31] Thus, for more than a century, Chinese mathematicians learned only from Western teachers or translated texts. It was not until the 1770's that rare ancient Chinese textbooks on mathematics began to be reprinted and studied.[32] As more and more masterpieces of Chinese mathematics reappeared, the history of its development before the fourteenth century became better known. Yet the Western methods of calculation remained prevalent and, because they were sufficient as a means for understanding and solving the problems posed in ancient Chinese texts, few scholars bothered to learn again how to manipulate the cumbersome calculating rods. Thus an interest in ancient Chinese mathematics was revived in the late eighteenth century, while Western mathematics as introduced in the preceding century continued to be fully accepted and studied. More modern Western texts were translated after 1850.[33]

The Chinese level of mechanical technology, as summarized in the work, *T'ien-kung k'ai-wu* (Natural resources utilized for manufacturing) of 1637, was probably as high as the material resources and sciences of the day permitted. The early Jesuits introduced some ideas about labor-saving machines but they failed to rouse any general interest. Among the Western manufactured articles that were admired most in China were clocks, organs, telescopes, and eyeglasses, but only the last of these was imitated by Chinese artisans.[34]

Similarly, in medicine, a Jesuit work on anatomy printed in 1635 did not arouse much interest among Chinese physicians. Certain new drugs such as quinine were imported but in quantities too small to have any lasting influence. The real beginning of Western medicine in China was Dr. Alexander Pearson's introduction of vaccination against smallpox in 1805. Although limited at first to Canton, this technique soon spread to other parts of China and was also adopted by Chinese physicians. In the 1830's the Protestant missionaries began to establish free clinics and hospitals as the best means to promote Christianity, having found that the Chinese officials and gentry usually would permit and occasionally even sponsor such philanthropic institutions. Thereafter modern medicine and medical education had a steady growth in China. Yet at the same time the old Chinese medicine, except in the field of surgery, has widely persisted.[35]

Surveying and map-making were other kinds of Western technology that the Jesuits brought to China. A general cartographic survey of the empire in the period 1707–1717 was conducted by teams of Jesuit fathers with trained Chinese students, one of whom later took an active part in the surveying of the newly conquered area in Turkestan and Ili (1755–1759). All this produced a number of the most accurate maps of Eastern Asia which had yet been made; but in China some of them were not even printed and those that were published did not have much circulation. Only in Europe were these maps put to good use. After the middle of the eighteenth century the technique of surveying and map-making was lost among the Chinese. It had to be learned as a new subject more than one hundred years later.[36]

All in all, the residual influence of the Western technology made available to China through the early missionaries seems to have been rather slight. Even when present, it was seldom acknowledged. Meanwhile an anti-Western political tradition had become well established.

c. The Attitude of the Ch'ing Court toward the Westerners

The Chinese monarchy under the Manchus continued to be a powerful and centralized institution. The emperor was expected to carry a heavy administrative burden day by day, to rule as well as reign. All official business of any importance was supposed to pass before him. The Son of Heaven at the top of the Chinese social pyramid was indeed expected to perform a superhuman function, supervising the major personnel, the use of funds and military forces, public works and ceremonies, on a vast and intricate scale.

Two results flowed from this emphasis on the monarchy: one was that a ramified and conservative administrative mechanism had to be maintained at Peking to carry on the various imperial functions under the emperor's aegis. The other was that the emperor himself, as a single man, had all he could do to keep up with his daily duties and meet the dynasty's problems, without seeking further fields of activity outside the court. He was not easily susceptible to new influences coming from abroad, yet his response to them was an essential act of leadership if the Chinese state was to make any response at all. The attitude of the emperor, or the court which surrounded and assisted him, was therefore of prime importance in China's relations with the West — a circumstance which the Jesuits had clearly perceived.

Since the court's attitude was to play a great part in the nineteenth-century acceptance of the West, let us note briefly the precedents which the early Ch'ing emperors bequeathed to their less fortunate successors of a later day.

When the Manchu conquerors first came to Peking in 1644, they found the Jesuit Adam Schall there, in charge of a bureau compiling a set of monographs on Western methods of calculation for making the calendar. Schall was permitted to continue his work, and when he had the new calendar for 1645 prepared in time for publication, his position as head of the Imperial Bureau of Astronomy was confirmed. During the following two hundred years, except for a short interruption, some Catholic missionary was always in charge of that Bureau. The first Manchu emperor in China, Shun-chih (1644–1661), was very friendly towards Schall and sometimes sought the aged missionary's advice. His successor, K'ang-hsi (reigned 1661–1722) was even more conciliatory towards the Jesuits and made use of their services to a considerable extent. During a controversy in 1669, when their predictions concerning astronomical phenomena were proved correct, he became interested in Western mathematics. Thereafter, the emperor studied Western mathematics and scientific subjects and kept several of the Jesuits near at hand to provide information or translations. In 1689 he sent two of them with the embassy from China which went to negotiate a treaty with the Russians at Nerchinsk — a treaty demarcating the Sino-Russian boundary in the northeast which remained in force down to the 1840's. For more than a century after 1689, Western missionaries at Peking served as interpreters whenever Russian or other European diplomatic missions came there. K'ang-hsi also employed them to teach selected young students mathematics and art, and to supervise the repairing of clocks and music boxes. In the last decade of his reign, as we have noted, he sent them out in teams to conduct a cartographic survey of the whole empire.

He also tried his best to arbitrate rationally in the so-called rites controversy between the Jesuit and other Catholic orders. The tolerance of this illustrious ruler, however, did not always stretch to the point of permitting missionary work in the entire empire. Evidently fearing that political repercussions would follow provincial proselytizing, K'ang-hsi introduced a system of passports in order to allow only certain missionaries in Peking and Macao. This policy was followed by his successors.[37]

Yung-cheng (1723–1735) developed a dislike for Western missionaries because some of them had taken the side of his opponents on the issue of his succession to the throne. Those who had official posts in Peking he tolerated, but he deported many others who were working in the provinces.[38] Under Ch'ien-lung (1736–1795), European mechanics were still employed to assemble and repair the clockworks and other devices brought from Europe, and several Jesuit missionaries served as architects of the buildings and landscape garden in Italian style which formed a part of the Old Summer Palace. About 1747 a fountain in the Western style was constructed by Michel Benoist, and this became the nucleus of a group of buildings in the Italian style designed by Castiglione.[39] By the last years of Ch'ien-lung, however, when the Macartney embassy of 1793 visited Peking from England, the Europeans had ceased to play much part at the Ch'ing court. Their long-continued activities there, perhaps because more technical than ideological, had evidently not given the Manchu rulers any real understanding of the West. The center of contact shifted to Canton.

Until this time, the missionaries at Peking had usually been referred to as "men of the Western Ocean" (*Hsi-yang jen*), meaning Europeans. But as Sino-Western contact and conflict increased in the early nineteenth century, the generic term "barbarians" (*i*), long applied to the Europeans at Canton, came into more general use. In the traditional Chinese society, every person had his place and designation; and since the early Portuguese adventurers who reached China by sea after 1514 were non-Chinese in culture, and also inclined to piracy and rapine, this appellation had been fitting both in the old Greek sense of "barbarian" as "outlandish" and in the later sense of the term as "barbarous." The non-Chinese of Inner Asia had provided an inexhaustible reservoir of "barbarians" since the beginning of Chinese history. There was nothing novel in the idea of bellicose foreigners turning up on the Chinese frontier. The Portuguese and their successors had been assimilated into the Confucian scheme of things by being allowed to dwell on the southeast coast at Macao or Canton under a careful, if polite, quarantine. The success of the Jesuits at Peking had been an inside job, quite distinct from the trade of Western merchants on the South China coast. By the end of the eighteenth century, the Western world was represented there chiefly by the British East India Company trading at Canton, where a complex of Sino-Western problems was gradually accumulating over such questions as diplomatic equality, taxation of trade, and legal procedures. It was most unfortunate for the Manchu dynasty at Peking and the Chinese and Manchu officials who represented it at Canton that the Chinese concept of the West had been so little developed.

Knowing little of the West in fact, China's ruling class applied to it the ancient theory of tributary relations — the grand and ancient concept that the Middle Kingdom was indeed the center of civilization, that the Son of Heaven actually represented all mankind in his functions as a moral and ceremonial intermediary between human society and the unseen forces of Nature, and that all the surrounding tribes and peoples should naturally recognize this central fact. The Chinese theory of state, in short, was that of a universal empire. Foreign rulers who wished contact or trade with the empire should first enroll as tributaries, accept investiture, send envoys to perform the kotow (three kneelings and nine prostrations) before the Son of Heaven, and otherwise obey the regulations for tributary intercourse. As European contact increased, the Ch'ing court persisted in the effort to fit Western nations into this traditional and outmoded tributary framework.[40] Perhaps the most famous example of this attitude is the lofty and condescending edict of Ch'ien-lung to King George III in 1793, which read in part: [41]

AN IMPERIAL EDICT TO THE KING OF ENGLAND: You, O King, are so inclined toward our civilization that you have sent a special envoy across the seas to bring to our Court your memorial of congratulations on the occasion of my birthday and to present your native products as an expression of your thoughtfulness. On perusing your memorial, so simply worded and sincerely conceived, I am impressed by your genuine respectfulness and friendliness and greatly pleased.

As to the request made in your memorial, O King, to send one of your nationals to stay at the Celestial Court to take care of your country's trade with China, this is not in harmony with the state system of our dynasty and will definitely not be permitted. Traditionally people of the European nations who wished to render some service under the Celestial Court have been permitted to come to the capital. But after their arrival they are obliged to wear Chinese court costumes, are placed in a certain residence, and are never allowed to return to their own countries. This is the established rule of the Celestial Dynasty with which presumably you, O King, are familiar. Now you, O King, wish to send one of your nationals to live in the capital, but he is not like the Europeans, who come to Peking as Chinese employees, live there and never return home again, nor can he be allowed to go and come and maintain any correspondence. This is indeed a useless undertaking.

Moreover the territory under the control of the Celestial Court is very large and wide. There are well-established regulations governing tributary envoys from the outer states to Peking, giving them provisions (of food and traveling expenses) by our post-houses and limiting their going and coming. There has never been a precedent for letting them do whatever they like. Now if you, O King, wish to have a representative in Peking, his language will be unintelligible and his dress different from the regulations; there is no place to accommodate him. . .

[P. 14] The Celestial Court has pacified and possessed the territory within the four seas. Its sole aim is to do its utmost to achieve good government and to manage political affairs, attaching no value to strange jewels and precious objects. The various articles presented by you, O King, this time are accepted by my special order to the office in charge of such functions in consideration of the offerings having come from a long distance with sincere good wishes. As a matter of fact, the virtue and prestige of the Celestial Dynasty having spread far and wide, the kings of the myriad nations come by land and sea with all sorts of precious things. Consequently there is nothing we lack, as your principal envoy and others have themselves observed. We have never set much store on strange or ingenious objects, nor do we need any more of your country's manufactures. . .

In such terms the Englishmen and Scotsmen who were about to batter down the gates and destroy the Middle Kingdom's ancient superiority over all other peoples were still categorized as uncultured barbarians outside the pale of civilization. Chinese and Manchu officials, making systematic reports in their memorials to the emperor, regularly applied to the British and Americans at Canton the same terms that were traditionally used with reference to the Burut and other tribes of Central Asia or to the Lo-lo and Miao-tzu aborigines of southwest China. Curiosity about Europe and America appears to have been very slight among the ruling class of China. The confusion based on ignorance was confounded by the difficulties of translation between the Chinese and European languages. The Portuguese had been called *Fo-lang-chi* ("Franks") because they came from the same region as the Franks who had fought the Saracens at the time of the Crusades. When the French arrived, France (*Fo-lang-hsi*) was confused with Portugal. The union of Spain and Portugal in the late sixteenth century confused those two countries in the Chinese mind. The presence at Portuguese Macao of Italian Jesuits identified Portugal with *I-ta-li*. Meanwhile the Dutch from Holland (*Ho-lan*) were confused with the French, and when a Dutch king took the British throne, Holland became confused with England.[42]

If the names of the European barbarians were topsy-turvy, their habitat was even more so. Since they all arrived by ship from the "Southern Ocean" (*Nan-yang*), through which Chinese merchants plied their trade by junk with Southeast Asia, it was often assumed that these European barbarians dwelt somewhere to the southwest, beyond the minuscule sultanates and ports-of-call like Sungora, Patani, and Johore which were strung along the Malay peninsula. When Europe was assigned to its proper place in the "Western Ocean" (*Hsi-yang*), confusion still resulted from the fact that this had been the very logical name anciently assigned to the Indian Ocean west of Malaya. Europe had to be called "Great Western Ocean" (*Ta-hsi-yang*) to distinguish it.

The personal characteristics of the strange people who came to China from Europe were well known to the Chinese linguists, hong merchants, and compradores who specialized in the foreign trade. But to most of the empire, Europeans were known only through rumor and folklore. Some of the latter has been enshrined in books of the period, which comment on the barbarians' "dazzling white" flesh, high noses, and "red hair" (*Hung-mao*, the name of the Dutch in particular). "Their custom is to esteem women and think lightly of men. Marriages are left to mutual arrangement," says one imperial compilation of the 1750's,[43] thereby indicating the curious and chaotic state of Western mores. But this Chinese observation of the West hardly went beyond the superficialities of manners — "they wear short coats and tip their black felt hats as a sign of politeness. The Swedes take snuff, which they carry in little containers made of golden thread." This appears to have been about the level of understanding of the West which prevailed in China in the period when the industrial revolution was beginning to remake the world. The diplomatic effort of Lord Amherst at Peking in 1816, like that of Macartney in 1793, was labeled a "tribute mission from the King of England" and did little to educate the Chinese upper class. After all, between 1655 and 1795, there had been some seventeen missions from Western countries, including Russia, which got as far as audience with the emperor, and all but the British had performed the kotow. The record contained nothing to show that Europeans were not tributary to China like other countries, whenever they wanted relations with China at all. Indeed, the Chinese records available to Commissioner Lin Tse-hsü in 1839 also state *pro forma* that Macartney performed the kotow, although we know he did not.[44]

As the export trade in teas and silks at Canton grew in volume and value, a few accounts of it and of the foreign trading nations were drawn up by Chinese chroniclers. One of these accounts, the "Maritime record" (*Hai-lu*), was taken down by a scholar from the lips of an old blind interpreter who in his youth had sailed the seas.[45] He describes the many-storied houses of England, the three bridges of London and its plethora of prostitutes, how the soldiers wear red and the women wear narrow-waisted dresses, tight above and full below — all exotic enough, but hardly enlightening. This and other works of its kind do state, however, that England lives by overseas trade and by seizing profitable posts like Bombay, Bengal, and Singapore. At the beginning of our story in 1839, the British position in India was well-known and the strength of England's naval guns had already been exhibited on the coast of China. Yet the Chinese officials of the 1840's seem to have been profoundly ignorant of what they faced. One of their first efforts, aside from self-defense, had to be the study of Western geography, to learn the name, location, products, and size of each country — almost like children in school.

2

RECOGNITION OF CHINA'S NEED

TO KNOW THE WEST, 1839–1860

CHAPTER III. COMMISSIONER LIN'S PROGRAM

FOR MEETING BRITISH AGGRESSION

Unlike the Japanese, the Chinese of a century ago did not look back on a tradition of borrowing from abroad. The empire was vast and its institutions were slow to change. It took the rulers of China two decades, after the first defeat by British arms in 1840, to acknowledge the necessity of studying the West — a necessity which many Japanese students of the "Dutch learning" had recognized even before the arrival of Commodore Perry in 1853. Japanese scholars, though secluded from foreign contact, were evidently more curious about the Western world than their contemporaries in China, who knew of the Western merchants at Canton but made little effort to seek them out.[1]

Since the Chinese officials were supremely ignorant of the West but well-versed in human nature and in Chinese tradition, they at once applied to the British those concepts and practices which had become traditional in China's dealings with barbarians — particularly the joint methods of coercion and persuasion which have so often been combined in Chinese statecraft. This was the approach of the famous Commissioner Lin Tse-hsü when he precipitated the Opium War in 1839 by blockading the British merchants at Canton and destroying their opium. His letter to Queen Victoria which forms our first document below was an appeal to conscience, just as his drastic action at Canton was a resort to force. Unfortunately for Lin, this combined approach failed in both its aspects; for British gunboats soon retaliated with superior power, while the British refused to acknowledge that the opium trade was the main and only point in dispute. To the Western mind, important questions of diplomatic equality, freedom of trade, and legal safeguards for foreigners in China were also at issue. Chinese opinion saw only the evil of the opium trade, which poisoned an increasing number of Chinese smokers and drained China's vital silver supply out of the country. But this was too simple a view of the problem which China faced.

We present below two brief items by Lin Tse-hsü. One was written when he tried to chastise the British, and one afterward. There follows a longer selection from the first famous geography of the 1840's, a book which tried to describe the West, almost for the first time in Chinese history. Finally, we note the early growth of nationalistic anti-foreignism at Canton, a sentiment which was eventually to motivate great changes.

In the first document, the righteous moral tone of Commissioner Lin's appeal to Queen Victoria in 1839 is certainly striking. It indicates that the opium question in the minds of Chinese officials was not entirely, as some have alleged, a matter of economics; the responsibility of the Confucian monarch for the welfare of the common people was also involved. Lin Tse-hsü had reached Canton as imperial commissioner on March 10, 1839, and soon coerced the British merchants into surrendering their opium stocks, which were publicly destroyed. But by August it had become apparent to him that the opium trade could be finally checked only at its source. This famous letter to "the ruler of England" (Ying-kuo wang, i.e., without distinction of sex) was therefore a further and unprecedented effort to solve an insoluble problem.

Lin's phraseology toward the British ruler is courteous within the limits of traditional tributary language. His theory that the barbarians must perish without the rhubarb,[2] tea, and other exports from China is a manifestation of Chinese egocentricity which has not been entirely absent in recent times. Lin's use of rewards and punishments to make merchants calculate their advantage and disadvantage is in the Chinese tradition of administrative law. It is plain that the imperial commissioner expected human nature to be the same in Britain as in China. More important, he expected it to respond equally to the dictates of moral conscience.

DOC. 1. LIN TSE-HSÜ'S MORAL ADVICE TO QUEEN VICTORIA, 1839 [3]

A communication: magnificently our great Emperor soothes and pacifies China and the foreign countries, regarding all with the same kindness. If there is profit, then he shares it with the peoples of the world; if there is harm, then he removes it on behalf of the world. This is because he takes the mind of heaven and earth as his mind.

The kings of your honorable country by a tradition handed down from generation to generation have always been noted for their politeness and submissiveness. We have read your successive tributary memorials saying, "In general our countrymen who go to trade in China have always received His Majesty the Emperor's gracious treatment and equal justice," and so on. Privately we are delighted with the way in which the honorable rulers of your country deeply understand the grand principles and are grateful for the Celestial grace. For this reason the Celestial Court in soothing those from afar has redoubled its polite and kind treatment. The profit from trade has been enjoyed by them continuously for two hundred years. This is the source from which your country has become known for its wealth.

But after a long period of commercial intercourse, there appear among the crowd of barbarians both good persons and bad, unevenly. Consequently there are those who smuggle opium to seduce the Chinese people and so cause the spread of the poison to all provinces. Such persons who only care to profit themselves, and disregard their harm to others, are not tolerated by the laws of heaven and are unanimously hated by human beings. His Majesty the Emperor, upon hearing of this, is in a towering rage [p. 34]. He has especially sent me, his commissioner, to come to Kwangtung, and together with the governor-general and governor jointly to investigate and settle this matter.

All those people in China who sell opium or smoke opium should receive the death penalty. If we trace the crime of those barbarians who through the years have been selling opium, then the deep harm they have wrought and the great profit they have usurped should fundamentally justify their execution according to law. We take into consideration, however, the fact that the various barbarians have still known how to repent their crimes and return to their allegiance to us by taking the 20,183 chests [4] of opium from their storeships and petitioning us, through their consular officer [superintendent of trade], Elliot, to receive it. It has been entirely destroyed and this has been faithfully reported to the Throne in several memorials by this commissioner and his colleagues.

Fortunately we have received a specially extended favor from His Majesty the Emperor, who considers that for those who voluntarily surrender there are still some circumstances to palliate their crime, and so for the time being he has magnanimously excused them from punishment. But as for those who again violate the opium prohibition, it is difficult for the law to pardon them repeatedly. Having established new regulations, we presume that the ruler of your honorable country, who takes delight in our culture and whose disposition is inclined towards us, must be able to instruct the various barbarians to observe the law with care. It is only necessary to explain to them the advantages and disadvantages and then they will know that the legal code of the Celestial Court must be absolutely obeyed with awe.

We find that your country is sixty or seventy thousand *li* [three *li* make one mile, ordinarily] from China. Yet there are barbarian ships that strive to come here for trade for the purpose of making a great profit. The wealth of China is used to profit the barbarians. That is to say, the great profit made by barbarians is all taken from the rightful share of China. By what right do they then in return use the poisonous drug to injure the Chinese people? Even though the barbarians may not necessarily intend to do us harm, yet in coveting profit to an extreme, they have no regard for injuring others. Let us ask, where is your conscience? I have heard that the smoking of opium is very strictly forbidden by your country; that is because the harm caused by opium is clearly understood. Since it is not permitted to do harm to your own country, then even less should you let it be passed on to the harm of other countries — how much less to China! Of all that China exports to foreign countries, there is not a single thing which is not beneficial to people: they are of benefit when eaten, or of benefit when used, or of benefit when resold: all are beneficial. Is there a single article from China which has done any harm to foreign countries? Take tea and rhubarb, for example; the foreign countries cannot get along for a single day without them. If China cuts off these benefits with no sympathy for those who are to suffer, then what can the barbarians rely upon to keep themselves alive? Moreover the woolens, camlets, and longells [i.e., textiles] of foreign countries cannot be woven unless they obtain Chinese silk. If China, again, cuts off this beneficial export, what profit can the barbarians expect to make? As for other foodstuffs, beginning with candy, ginger, cinnamon, and so forth, and articles for use, beginning with silk, satin, chinaware, and so on, all the things that must be had by foreign countries are innumerable. On the other hand, articles coming from the outside to China can only be used as toys. We can take them or get along without them. Since they are not needed by China, what difficulty would there be if we closed the frontier and stopped the trade? Nevertheless our Celestial Court lets tea, silk, and other goods be shipped without limit and circulated everywhere without begrudging it in the slightest. This is for no other reason but to share the benefit with the people of the whole world.

The goods from China carried away by your country not only supply your own consumption and use, but also can be divided up and sold to other countries, producing a triple profit. Even if you do not sell opium, you still have this threefold profit. How can you bear to go further, selling products injurious to others in order to fulfill your insatiable desire?

Suppose there were people from another country who carried opium for sale to England and seduced your people into buying and smoking it; certainly your honorable ruler would deeply hate it and be bitterly aroused. We have heard heretofore that your honorable ruler is kind and benevolent. Naturally you would not wish to give unto others what you yourself do not want. We have also heard that the ships coming to Canton have all had regulations promulgated and given to them in which it is stated that it is not permitted to carry contraband goods. This indicates that the administrative orders of your honorable rule have been originally strict and clear. Only because the trading ships are numerous, heretofore perhaps they have not been examined with care. Now after this communication has been dispatched and you have clearly understood the strictness of the prohibitory laws of the Celestial Court, certainly you will not let your subjects dare again to violate the law.

We have further learned that in London, the capital of your honorable rule, and in Scotland (Su-ko-lan), Ireland (Ai-lun), and other places, originally no opium has been produced. Only in several places of India under your control such as Bengal, Madras, Bombay, Patna, Benares, and Malwa has opium been planted from hill to hill, and ponds [5] have been opened for its manufacture. For months and years work is continued in order to accumulate the poison. The obnoxious odor ascends, irritating heaven and frightening the spirits. Indeed you, O King, can eradicate the opium plant in these places, hoe over the fields entirely, and sow in its stead the five grains [i.e., millet, barley, wheat, etc.]. Anyone who dares again attempt to plant and manufacture opium should be severely punished. This will really be a great, benevolent goverment policy that will increase the common weal and get rid of evil. For this, Heaven must support you and the spirits must bring you good fortune, prolonging your old age and extending your descendants. All will depend on this act.

As for the barbarian merchants who come to China, their food and drink and habitation are all received by the gracious favor of our Celestial Court. Their accumulated wealth is all benefit given with pleasure by our Celestial Court. They spend rather few days in their own country but more time in Canton. [p. 35] To digest clearly the legal penalties as an aid to instruction has been a valid principle in all ages. Suppose a man of another country comes to England to trade, he still has to obey the English laws; how much more should he obey in China the laws of the Celestial Dynasty?

Now we have set up regulations governing the Chinese people. He who sells opium shall receive the death penalty and he who smokes it also the death penalty. Now consider this: if the barbarians do not bring opium, then how can the Chinese people resell it, and how can they smoke it? The fact is that the wicked barbarians beguile the Chinese people into a death trap. How then can we grant life only to these barbarians? He who takes the life of even one person still has to atone for it with his own life; yet is the harm done by opium limited to the taking of one life only? Therefore in the new regulations, in regard to those barbarians who bring opium to China, the penalty is fixed at decapitation or strangulation. This is what is called getting rid of a harmful thing on behalf of mankind.

Moreover we have found that in the middle of the second month of this year [April 9] Consul [Superintendent] Elliot of your nation, because the opium prohibition law was very stern and severe, petitioned for an extension of the time limit. He requested a limit of five months for India and its adjacent harbors and related territories, and ten months for England proper, after which they would act in conformity with the new regulations. Now we, the commissioner and others, have memorialized and have received the extraordinary Celestial grace of His Majesty the Emperor, who has redoubled his consideration and compassion. All those who within the period of the coming one year (from England) or six months (from India) bring opium to China by mistake, but who voluntarily confess and completely surrender their opium, shall be exempt from their punishment. After this limit of time, if there are still those who bring opium to China then they will plainly have committed a wilful violation and shall at once be executed according to law, with absolutely no clemency or pardon. This may be called the height of kindness and the perfection of justice.

Our Celestial Dynasty rules over and supervises the myriad states, and surely possesses unfathomable spiritual dignity. Yet the Emperor cannot bear to execute people without having first tried to reform them by instruction. Therefore he especially promulgates these fixed regulations. The barbarian merchants of your country, if they wish to do business for a prolonged period, are required to obey our statutes respectfully and to cut off permanently the source of opium. They must by no means try to test the effectiveness of the law with their lives. May you, O King, check your wicked and sift your vicious people before they come to China, in order to guarantee the peace of your nation, to show further the sincerity of your politeness and submissiveness, and to let the two countries enjoy together the blessings of peace. How fortunate, how fortunate indeed! After receiving this dispatch will you immediately give us a prompt reply regarding the details and circumstances of your cutting off the opium traffic. Be sure not to put this off. The above is what has to be communicated. [Vermilion endorsement:] This is appropriately worded and quite comprehensive (*Te-t'i chou-tao*).

In retrospect it is plain that the Manchu-Chinese defiance of Britain never had the slightest chance of military success. Confident of their power, the British

soon opened hostilities, and in 1840 Commissioner Lin was recalled from Canton
in disgrace for having produced a war instead of a settlement. As punishment
he was ordered to start on his way into exile in Ili.[6] On the basis of his recent
experience with the British at Canton, he wrote letters in 1842 to various friends
frankly admitting China's military inferiority to the West and favoring her purchase and manufacture of ships and guns patterned after the Western model.
This confession is in sharp contrast with his former intransigent action in
Canton. Had his plans for making modern weapons been carried out, China's
modernization movement might have been advanced twenty years. Unfortunately,
with the Court opposed to it, he dared not make an overt advocacy of Westernization but told only his friends and asked them to keep it confidential. One of
these letters, translated below, was addressed to Wu Tzu-hsü,[7] a compiler of
the Hanlin Academy and a good friend of Wo-jen and Tseng Kuo-fan (on these
men, see Chapter VI and Doc. 18).

DOC. 2. A LETTER OF LIN TSE-HSÜ RECOGNIZING WESTERN MILITARY SUPERIORITY, 1842 [8]

[Lin describes to his friend how impossible it proved to control the
barbarians, p. 19.] The rebels' ships on the open sea came and went as they
pleased, now in the south and now suddenly in the north, changing successively between morning and evening. If we tried to put up a defense everywhere, not only would we toil and expend ourselves without limit, but also
how could we recruit and transport so many troops, militia, artillery, and
ammunition, and come to their support quickly? . . .

When I was in office in Kwangtung and Kwangsi, I had made plans regarding the problems of ships and cannon and a water force. Afraid that
there was not enough time to build ships, I at first rented them. Afraid that
there was not enough time to cast cannon and that it would not be done
according to the regulations, I at first bought foreign ones. The most painful
thing was that when the Hu-men [the Bogue or "Tiger's mouth," the entrance
to the Canton River] was broken into, a large number of good cannon fell
into the hands of the rebellious barbarians. I recall that after I had been
punished two years ago, I still took the risk of calling the Emperor's attention to two things: ships and guns. At that time, if these things could have
been made and prepared, they still could have been used with effect to fight
against the enemy in Chekiang last fall [1841]. Now it is even more difficult
to check the wildfire. After all, ships, guns, and a water force are absolutely
indispensable. Even if the rebellious barbarians had fled and returned beyond the seas, these things would still have to be urgently planned for, in
order to work out the permanent defense of our sea frontiers. Moreover,
unless we have weapons, what other help can we get now to drive away
the crocodile and to get rid of the whales? . . .

But at this time I must strictly observe the advice to seal my lips as one
corks the mouth of a bottle. However, toward those with identical aims and
interests, I suddenly spit out the truth and am unable to control myself.
I extremely regret my foolishness and carelessness. Nevertheless, when I
turn my thoughts to the depth of your attention to me, then I cannot conceal
these things from myself. I only beg you to keep them confidential. By all
means, please do not tell other persons.

Lin Tse-hsü's concern over the British problem had led him while at Canton to compile information on the West and to suggest strategic principles for holding Britain at bay. As the British Governor of Hongkong wrote later, "When Lin . . . got involved with Europeans, he availed himself of the aid of interpreters, and of every work he could procure, either native or foreign, to obtain a knowledge of . . . every country of the world beyond China . . . the Missionary Tracts, the Chinese Monthly Magazine, a Treatise on Commerce, a Description of the United States and of England, a work on Geography, etc., which were all, more or less, abridged or abstracted. Translations were also made of all such articles in the newspapers as contained anything concerning China, and especially opium." [9] The result was a famous geography book on the "maritime countries" (Hai-kuo t'u-chih) which was compiled by the well-known scholar Wei Yuan (1794–1856), making use of Lin's materials. Some sections of the work name Lin as the compiler. Wei Yuan's first acknowledgment at the beginning of his preface is to the "Gazetteer of the four continents" (Ssu-chou chih), which was probably a compilation of translations from Murray's Cyclopaedia of Geography and was published by Lin in 1841.[10] After Lin was dismissed in disgrace, Wei Yuan completed the compilation and revised it several times. The first edition, 50 chüan, was published in 1844, the second in 60 chüan in 1849, and the third in 100 chüan in 1852.[11]

Wei Yuan had published in 1842 his famous "Record of imperial military exploits" (Sheng-wu chi) in which he surveyed the campaigns of the Ch'ing dynasty since its founding. He was a good scholar of military history and economic geography and a critical student of the classics. Indeed, his academic position in the mid-nineteenth century was almost comparable to that of Ku Yen-wu in the seventeenth and Tai Chen (1724–1777) in the eighteenth. During the Opium War, however, Wei Yuan was a minor civilian official at Yangchow and he did not receive the chin-shih degree until 1844. While he was familiar with the British military campaigns, his views on strategy and high policy undoubtedly derive from those of Lin Tse-hsü.

In the following section on military strategy against the British, there crops up the doctrinaire fallacy into which so much Chinese scholarly thinking was inclined to fall — a tendency to settle strategic questions on the basis of theories, closely reasoned but inadequately based on fact. Even so, his advocacy of land defense rather than sea battles is sensible and he at least explodes the theories so widely expounded in memorials of the period that British vessels could be sunk by divers boring holes in their bottoms, or burned by fireships floating against them.

In the field of diplomacy, Lin and Wei Yuan enunciate principles which were time-tested in their day and have been used effectively since. "Using barbarians to control barbarians," the Chinese counterpart of the balance-of-power concept in Western Europe, is not a foolproof stratagem (any more than is the balance of power). But like that similar device of empires, "divide and rule," it is often inexpensive and requires only a modest investment of force. "Learning the superior skills of the barbarians" strikes a more novel note, although it was soon to become the spirit of an entire epoch in nearby Japan and the slogan of many Chinese reformers.

In applying the principle of using barbarians, Lin at once hit upon the possibility of getting the Russians to invade India, which would indeed have put a stop to the British foray in China. The idea of using France and the United States against England was a similar shot in the dark, but wider of the mark. Exactly how far the Americans and French actually sought to mediate in the Opium War is not yet known.[12]

Lin's practical proposals to translate Western books, to build shipyards and arsenals, ships and guns, to hire foreign technical instructors and train selected Chinese personnel, and to alter the military examinations, all forecast the main line of China's development. The great question is, why was all this delayed for almost exactly twenty years?

DOC. 3. WEI YUAN'S STATEMENT OF A POLICY FOR MARITIME DEFENSE, 1842 [13]

Plans for Maritime Defense. Section a, discussion of defensive strategy, first part

Ever since the barbarian incident, the strategy which has been contrived in the generals' tents and which has been carried out in the field has been, if not war, then peace; if not peace, then war. No one has yet devoted himself to the discussion of defensive measures. . .

There are two policies for self-defense. First, to defend the open ocean is not as good as to defend the seaports, and to defend the seaports is not as good as to defend the inland rivers. Second, the transferring of distant troops from other provinces is inferior to the training of local troops, and the transferring of water forces is inferior to the training of local marines. There are two methods of attacking the barbarians, namely, to stimulate countries unfriendly to the barbarians to make an attack on them, and to learn the superior skills of the barbarians in order to control them. There are two methods of making peace with the barbarians, namely, to let the _ various trading nations conduct their trade so as to maintain peace with the barbarians, and to support the first treaty of the Opium War so as to maintain international trade. Now let us first speak of defense. . .

He who intends to control the enemy must cause the enemy to lose his basis of superiority. Does the superiority of barbarian ships lie in warfare in the open sea or in the inland rivers? There are only two measures we can use to resist the enemy: one is to attack them with cannon and the other is to attack them with fire. . . If our cannon merely hit the side of a ship, a ship in the open ocean, easily maneuvered on deep water, it simply shudders and withdraws; it will neither be broken [p. 2] nor sunk. We must hit the mast and the bridge before it is rendered unnavigable, yet immediately a steamboat will tow it to another harbor to repair it overnight. Only when we hit the ammunition hold will there be an explosion causing it to turn over or sink. There is no such thing as to have someone swim to the bottom of the ship to bore a hole and make it sink. This is the first difficulty. If we have fire ships put out to sea to burn the barbarian warship, the hull material is so solid and thick that even if it is burned it will not catch fire. It is necessary to use fire arrows or rockets to burn the sails, ropes, oil, fuel and munitions, and attack the rudder and bridge of the ship. Yet, on the top of the mast of a barbarian ship there is always a barbarian soldier with a telescope looking into the distance. Before our fire ships reach them, they will long since have cut their anchors and escaped. This is the second difficulty.

[The author goes on to say that it is better to attack foreign ships in inland rivers where Chinese guns can hit them and where they will be unable to maneuver in the more shallow and narrow waters; where iron chains and sunken boats can hinder their movement and fire ships can be sent from all directions to burn them. In this situation, it is argued, the guns of the foreign ships cannot hit the Chinese soldiers, who will lie behind thick walls.]

[P. 3b] The phrase "enticing the enemy to enter the inland rivers" means that soldiers, guns and mines are sown on land and in the water as if making a pit to wait for tigers, or setting a net to wait for fish. We must make sure that we have control over their fate before we let them enter our strategic area. It does not mean that we should open the door and invite the bandits in as guests. . .

[P. 13] The Japanese barbarians [who raided China in the sixteenth century] were strong in land fighting and weak in water warfare, because the pirates who came were all desperadoes from poor islands, who had no means to build large ships and big guns, but relied upon sheer courage to cross the ocean, and depended upon their swords and spears to invade China. Therefore, whenever they went ashore it was impossible to resist them. But when the Japanese ships met the junks of Fukien and Kwangtung, then they were like rice on a grindstone. If the Japanese ships met big cannons and firearms, they would be like goats chased by wolves. . . In general, the strength of the Japanese was on the land. To attack them on the open ocean was to assail their weak point. The strength of the British barbarians is on the ocean. Wait for them in the inland rivers. Wait for them on the shore and they will lose their strength. Unfortunately, the Ming people, in warding off the Japanese, did not know how to oppose them on the ocean, and nowadays those who are guarding against the British do not lay ambushes in the interior. Thus, the really effective ideas in the world must necessarily be contrary to the opinion of the multitude of mediocre minds. . .

Plans for maritime defense. Section c, discussion of offensive strategy

[P. 36] The inland defense having been consolidated, let us now discuss the external offensive. Yo Fei [1103–1141] says that to use a government force to attack pirates is difficult; to use pirates to attack pirates is easy. . . What is the method for using sea barbarians to fight against sea barbarians?

To plan barbarian affairs it is necessary to know first the barbarians' conditions. To understand the barbarians' conditions it is necessary first to know the barbarians' geographical situations. Now let us first explain their circumstances.

The enemy countries of which the British barbarians are afraid are three: Russia, France, and America. The vassal states of our country of which the British are afraid are four: the Gurkhas [i.e., Nepal], Burma, Siam, and Annam. The methods for attacking England are, first, from the land; and second, from the ocean. The method of attacking her from the land lies in India. The countries which are close to India are Russia and the Gurkhas. The Russian capital and the English capital are separated by a few countries and not connected by land routes. But by water, one route is by the Mediterranean sea and the other one by the Baltic sea, where a force that sails from Russia in the morning could reach England in the evening. In 1691 the King of England [sic] used warships to attack Russia by the Mediterranean sea but failed and returned home. Thereafter, the two countries had no intercourse and their military struggle was concentrated in India.

India is on the southwest of the Onion Range, and adjacent to our further Tibet, the Gurkhas, and Burma. From the homeland of the British barbarians, India is several myriad *li*. The British barbarians used warships and occupied the three parts of India, in the east, the south, and center. The Russian troops then, from the space between the Yellow Sea and the Caspian Sea, attacked and subdued the various nomadic tribes and made connection with the two western and central parts of India. They were only separated by the Himalayas. Each side was guarded by heavy garrisons of troops. From Bengal to Malwa in East India and from Bombay to Madras in South India opium is prevalent. The British barbarians annually collect from opium taxes more than ten million (taels) silver, and the Russians are jealous. When the British barbarians mobilized Indian [p. 37] troops and warships to invade China, they were greatly afraid that Russia might take advantage of their weakness to invade Hindustan (Author's note: in central India). There was also a rumor that Russian messengers had started a trip from Petersburg to China (Author's note: Petersburg is her eastern capital), and the British were scared of the two ox horns [i.e., pincers]. . . Therefore, the British barbarians' fear of Russia lies not in her national capital but in India. This is one opportunity which might be used.

The Gurkhas are in the western part of further Tibet and are close to eastern India. When in the middle of the Ch'ien-lung period our troops invaded the Gurkha barbarians, the British barbarians' warships in India also took that opportunity to attack their eastern boundary. So after the stoppage of commerce with the British barbarians last year, the Gurkha barbarians immediately informed our Imperial Resident in Tibet that they were willing to send troops to attack India. At that time, if the Gurkhas had been permitted to cause trouble on their east and Russia to invade on the west, then India might have been collapsed and the enemy vessels would have had anxiety over their internal garrisons. This is a second opportunity which might have been used. Thus, when there were opportunities which might have been taken, they were not utilized; this is not because the outer barbarians cannot be used, but because we need personnel who are capable of making arrangements with them.

There is no better method of attacking England by sea than to use France and America. France is very close to the English barbarians, being separated only by an arm of the sea. America and the English barbarians, on the other hand, are separated by a great ocean. Beginning from the period at the end of the Ming and the beginning of this dynasty, France colonized the northeast territory of America. Cities and towns were built, markets and ports were opened. The British barbarians suddenly attacked and seized them. Thereupon the French barbarians and the English barbarians became bitter enemies. Later on the British barbarians levied numerous and heavy taxes which caused the thirteen parts of America to start a righteous revolt to drive them out. At the same time the Americans asked France to help them. Several hundred warships of the three countries, and several hundreds of thousands of soldiers and seamen were kept on duty for several years.

The Americans cut the British supply lines. The British soldiers were in hunger and distress, and the British ceded territory and asked for peace. The Americans then entirely recovered the twenty-seven parts of their original land [p. 38], and the British barbarians only retained the four parts in the northeast corner [i.e., Canada]. They did not dare invade the United States any more.

Even the land of India was also opened by Holland and France, but was taken over by the British barbarians. . . This is the condition of the various countries.

As for commerce at Canton, the British barbarians are the most fierce and arrogant while France and America are the most amicable and obedient. After the stopping of trade, the British barbarians even used warships to prevent other countries trading with us. The various countries were all resentful and said that if the British barbarians did not withdraw their troops for a lengthy period, they would each be obliged to go home and send ships of war to dispute the issue with them. Last year [1840] after the General for Rebellion Pacification [14] had mobilized his troops, the barbarian headman among the Americans at Canton at once came to mediate. Thereupon, Elliot submitted a document saying that he was only asking that he might carry on trade as usual. He dared not make demands even regarding the cost of the burned opium and the status of Hongkong. This is the third opportunity which might have been used.

Unfortunately, when the peace negotiations had not yet been settled, our troops suddenly attacked the barbarian factories and unexpectedly injured several Americans by mistake. Thereupon, the American headman no longer made any effort to mediate. But France, after the British barbarians for the second time had broken the truce, in the winter sent a military officer with a ship of war to Canton. . . [The author then describes how, through suspicion and bureaucratic delay, China failed to take advantage of an alleged French offer to mediate with the British.]

The situation today is this: if there is a discussion about getting and using Western warships, then someone is sure to say that he fears borrowing aid from the outer barbarians would show our weakness. Yet when suddenly our weakness has been several times more fully exposed than this would have involved, they have been glad to do it without shrinking. If there is a discussion about building ships, making weapons, and learning the superior techniques of the barbarians, they say it is too expensive. But when suddenly the cost is ten times more than this, they again say it is a matter of exigency to meet an emergency and is not regrettable. If there is a discussion about the translation of barbarian books and prying into barbarian affairs, they are sure to say it would cause trouble. (Note: during the reign of Chia-ch'ing there was someone in Kwangtung who intended to publish a book giving transliterations of Chinese and barbarian characters, which would be very convenient for Chinese translating their characters. Yet it was forbidden by the Kwangtung authorities.) When suddenly something has happened, then they ask, "What is the distance between the English capital and the Russian capital?" Or, "Via what route can the English barbarians communicate with the Mohammedan tribes? . . ."

Regarding these countries, with which we have had trade relations for two hundred years, we indeed know neither their locations nor their inter-relations of friendship or enmity. Can it even yet be said that we are paying attention to frontier affairs? In the Han Dynasty, the Western Regions were utilized to attack the Hsiung-hu [Huns]. In the T'ang Dynasty, Turfan was utilized to attack India and the Uighurs were utilized to attack Turfan. Emperor K'ang-hsi used the sailing ships of Holland to attack Formosa and he also allied with the Russians to exert pressure on Djungaria. From ancient times those who tried to control the outer barbarians only prevented their alliance with our enemies to plan against us, but did not prevent their alliance with us to attack our enemies; they only prevented the leaking of Chinese intelligence to the outside, but we have not heard that they prohibited the conditions of foreign countries being revealed to China. Thus, he who wishes to control the outer barbarians must [p. 40] begin by understanding their circumstances, and he who wishes to understand their circumstances must begin by establishing a bureau for the translation of barbarian books. He who wishes to train men of ability in frontier affairs must begin by using the governors general and governors who pay attention to frontier affairs. . .

Before the peace settlement, it behooves us to use barbarians against barbarians. After the peace, it is proper for us to learn their superior techniques in order to control them. The superior techniques of the barbarians are three: (1) warships, (2) firearms, and (3) methods of maintaining and training soldiers. Let us give an account of the past events of this dynasty.

At the beginning of the K'ang-hsi period, the sailing ships of Holland were sent to suppress Formosa. The European Nan-huai-jen [Ferdinand Verbiest] was ordered to make cannon to suppress the rebellion of the three feudatories; [15] and Europeans were selected and appointed to the Imperial Board of Astronomy to be officers in charge of the calendar. Today the British barbarians not only have occupied Hongkong and accumulated a great deal of wealth as well as a proud face among the other barbarians, but also have opened the ports and cut down the various charges so as to grant favor to other barbarians. Rather than let the British barbarians be good to them, in order to enlarge their following, would it not be better for us ourselves to be good to them, in order to get them under our control like fingers on the arm? . . . [This was the reasoning behind China's acceptance of the most-favored-nation clause and her extension to the other Western nations of the treaty privileges given the British in 1842–43.]

[Wei Yuan then describes Western shipbuilding.] The materials in their shipyards are piled up like hills and craftsmen congregate there like a cloud. [P. 41] Within twenty or thirty days a large warship can be completed. They can instantly spread the sails and adjust the tiller with a few shouted orders. Their craftsmen compete with each other in their talents and abilities. In construction they compete for speed and in navigation also. Construction goes on all year long, the fire illuminates the sky, and the noise shakes the earth. Thus, while the British ships and guns are regarded in China as due to extraordinary skill, in the various countries of Europe they are considered as quite ordinary. In Canton international trade has been carried on for two hundred years. At first the products of their strange skills and clever craftsmanship were received, and then their heterodox religions and poisonous opium. But in regard to their conduct of war and the effectiveness of their weapons, we are learning not a single one of their superior skills. That is, we are only willing to receive the harm and not . . . the benefit of foreign intercourse.

Let us establish a shipyard and an arsenal at two spots, Chuenpi and Taikoktow [16] outside of the Bogue in Kwangtung, and select one or two persons from among the foreign headmen who have come from France and America, respectively, to bring Western craftsmen to Canton to take charge of building ships and making arms. In addition, we should invite Western helmsmen to take charge of teaching the methods of navigating ships and of using cannon, following the precedent of the barbarian officials in the Imperial Board of Astronomy. We should select clever artisans and good soldiers from Fukien and Kwangtung to learn from them, the craftsmen to learn the casting of cannon and building of ships, and the good soldiers to learn their methods of navigation and attack. . . In Kwangtung there should be ten thousand soldiers; in Fukien, ten thousand; in Chekiang, six thousand; and in Kiangsu, four thousand. In assigning soldiers to the ships we must rely on selection and training. [P. 42] Eight out of ten should be taken from among the fishermen and smugglers along the sea coast. Two out of ten should be taken from the old encampments of the water forces. All the padded rations and extra rations of the water force should be . . . used for the recruiting and maintenance of good soldiers. We must make the water forces of China able to navigate large (lit., "storied") ships overseas, and able to fight against foreign barbarians on the high seas. . .

While Chinese officials like Lin and Wei Yuan were reacting to the British invasion by formulating theories of statecraft, another type of reaction became manifest among the Cantonese populace. In 1841, after British forces had fought their way up the river to the great walled metropolis, exacted a "ransom," [17] and then withdrawn, there began an anti-foreign movement which seems to have been one of the first stirrings of modern Chinese nationalism. From this time on, in a succession of "incidents" recorded in British blue-books, hostile placards were posted denouncing the presence and activities of foreigners, and those who ventured too far into the countryside were occasionally stoned or beaten and in some cases even killed. The background of this anti-Western feeling around Canton has not yet been thoroughly studied. It is plain, however, that members of the scholar-gentry class, with official backing from the imperial government, gave the popular movement leadership and encouragement if not actual inspiration, much as was later to be the case in North China in 1900. The resulting "Canton city question" (focused on the issue of admitting Westerners within the city walls, as distinct from the Thirteen Factories outside the walls) remained a diplomatic storm center until the Anglo-French occupation of Canton in the second war of 1858–1860. To indicate the violent spirit of this Cantonese proto-nationalism, we quote part of the famous denunciation posted by the villagers of San-yuan-li after the British had withdrawn their forces in 1841. The villagers, who had suffered economically from the war, maintained an armed resistance and claimed to have repulsed the British. This "Placard of the patriotic people of Kwangtung denouncing the English barbarians" was in vigorous and often vulgar terms, though obviously not the composition of a mere peasant.

DOC. 4. CANTONESE DENUNCIATION OF THE BRITISH, 1841 [18]

The thoroughly loyal and patriotic people of the whole province of Kwangtung instruct the rebellious barbarian dogs and sheep for their information. We note that you English barbarians have formed the habits and developed the nature of wolves, plundering and seizing things by force [p. 16]. . . In trade relations, you come to our country merely to covet profit. What knowledge do you have? Your seeking profit resembles the animal's greed for food. You are ignorant of our laws and institutions, ignorant of right principles. . . You have no gratitude for the great favor of our Celestial Court; on the contrary you treat us like enemies and do us harm. You use opium to injure our common people, cheating us of our silver and cash [p. 17]. . . Although you have penetrated our inland rivers and enticed fellows who renounce their fathers and their ruler to become Chinese traitors and stir up trouble among us, you are only using money to buy up their services — what good points have you? . . . Except for your ships being solid, your gunfire fierce, and your rockets powerful, what other abilities have you? . . .

[P. 19] We patriots have received the favor of the Celestial Dynasty in nourishing us for two centuries. Today, if we do not exterminate you English barbarians, we will not be human beings. You have killed and injured our common people in many villages, and seriously hurt the universal harmony. You also completely destroyed the coffins in several places, and you disastrously damaged the Buddhist statues in several monasteries. This is properly a time when Heaven is angered and mankind is resentful; even the ghosts and spirits will not tolerate you beasts. . .

[P. 20b] Our hatred is already at white heat. If we do not completely exterminate you pigs and dogs, we will not be manly Chinese able to support the sky on our heads and stand firmly on the earth. Once we have said this, we will never go back on it, even if frustrated ten thousand times. We are definitely going to kill you, cut your heads off and burn you to death! Even though you ask people to admonish us, we will not obey. We must strip off your skins and eat your flesh, and then you will know how tough (li-hai) we are. . . We ought really to use refined expressions. But since you beasts do not understand written characters, therefore we use rough, vulgar words to instruct you in simple terms. . .

This type of inflammatory anti-foreignism remained endemic at Canton until after 1858 and embarrassed the officials on both sides who sought to develop peaceful Sino-Western relations.

CHAPTER IV. THE POLICY OF CONCILIATION

The alternative to Commissioner Lin's policy of coercing the barbarians was to conciliate them. This required the use of negotiation instead of force, but it was still within the Chinese traditional pattern of relations with the barbarians. It did not involve any borrowing from the West or reform of Chinese ways. The militant defiance of the Opium War period gave way to the conciliatory policy under which the first treaties were signed: with Britain at Nanking in 1842, and with the Americans and French in 1844. On the basis of the treaties the first treaty ports were opened for foreign residence and trade under the protection of foreign consuls and gunboats — at Shanghai as well as Canton, Amoy, Foochow, and Ningpo. Yet this new order of Sino-Western relations, having been obtained by force, was grudgingly conceded. The treaties represented a defeat of the Ch'ing regime, even though they were euphemistically referred to as means of "pacifying" the barbarians or "bringing them under control" through the imperial "compassion for strangers coming from afar."

As has long been noted, the policy of conciliation or appeasement was carried out mainly by Manchus — notably by Ch'i-shan in 1840–41 and by the imperial clansman Ch'i-ying from to 1842 to 1848 — whereas the policy of non-appeasement was represented mainly by Chinese such as Lin Tse-hsü in 1839–40 and Yeh Ming-ch'en at Canton from 1848 to 1858. The Manchu element in the Ch'ing government of China appears at this time to have been concerned for the welfare of the dynasty more than for that of China as a whole. At least they were more willing than the Chinese officials to buy off the barbarians by concessions which would preserve the dynasty even though sacrificing a certain amount of Chinese cultural pride and economic interest. Whether or not this generalization can stand, it seems evident that the negotiators of the first treaties, under the pressure of *force majeure*, were relatively heedless of the long-term economic repercussions of the treaty settlement. They confined their attention mainly to the immediate problem of mollifying the invaders and keeping them from further warlike acts. For this purpose, Ch'i-ying in particular exerted himself over a period of several years to establish and maintain an intimate personal relationship with the foreign envoys: Sir Henry Pottinger (1789–1856) who negotiated for the British, the American Caleb Cushing (1800–1879), and the Frenchman Th. de Lagrené.[1] Ch'i-ying's obvious intent was to achieve a sort of personal ascendancy by which to influence the course of the barbarians' policies and actions in China. He also tried to use the United States and France against England.

Since this personal contact with the invaders put any Ch'ing official in mortal danger of denunciation as a traitor or dupe of the foreigners (on a theory of "guilt by association") Ch'i-ying was obliged constantly to excuse and defend himself on this score in his memorials to the throne. His two-faced position between the emperor and the barbarians is well illustrated in the following document — the famous memorial which he wrote after he had negotiated the early British, American, and French treaties. It was later found by the British among the archives of the Canton governor-general, Yeh Ming-ch'en, at the time when that obstinate xenophobe was captured in 1858 during the Anglo-French war with China. Thomas Wade translated it and took it to Tientsin, where the aged Ch'i-ying, then in his seventy-second year, had suddenly appeared as a treaty negotiator. His appointment, however, incurred the jealousy of the imperial negotiators already on the spot and was rejected by the British and French envoys. Confronted in 1858 with this memorial of fourteen years before, Ch'i-ying lost countenance, withdrew from the negotiations, and was graciously permitted by the emperor to strangle himself with a silken bowstring.[2]

DOC. 5. Ch'i-ying's Method for Handling the Barbarians, 1844 [3]

Ch'i-ying presents a supplementary memorial: with further reference to the management of the barbarian affairs of the various countries, his receptions of or interviews with the barbarian envoys and his controlling them as the circumstances allowed — your slave has already from time to time presented memorials and reports. . . He is mindful that the English barbarians were finally brought to the point of reconciliation in August 1842, and the American and French barbarians have also followed in their footsteps in the summer and autumn of the present year. Throughout this period of three years the barbarian situation has undergone deceptive changes in many respects and has not produced a unified development. The methods by which to conciliate the barbarians and get them under control similarly could not but shift about and change their form. Certainly we have to curb them by sincerity, but it has been even more necessary to control them by skillful methods. There are times when it is possible to have them follow our directions but not let them understand the reasons. Sometimes we expose everything so that they will not be suspicious, whereupon we can dissipate their rebellious restlessness. Sometimes we have given them receptions and entertainment, after which they have had a feeling of appreciation. And at still other times we have shown trust in them in a broad-minded way and deemed it unnecessary to go deeply into minute discussions with them, whereupon we have been able to get their help in the business at hand.

This is because the barbarians are born and grow up outside the frontiers of China, so that there are many things in the institutional system of the Celestial Dynasty with which they are not fully acquainted. Moreover, they are constantly making arbitrary interpretations of things, and it is difficult to enlighten them by means of reason. Thus for example when Imperial Utterances [i.e., edicts and decrees] are handed down, they are all received and acted on by the Grand Councillors, but the barbarians respect them as being written by the Imperial hand; if they were definitely informed that these are not from [p. 19] the Imperial brush, then there would be no means of maintaining their confidence. This, then, is something that ought not to be made known to them.

When the barbarians meet together and eat, it is called "a banquet." [4] Generally they assemble a large number of people at a great banquet and eat and drink together for the fun of it. When your slave has been at the Bogue, Macao, and such places, and has entertained the various barbarians with a feast, their chieftains, leaders, and headmen have come, to the varied number of ten or more, or up to twenty or thirty persons. When on one occasion your slave has gone to the barbarians' storied residences or to the barbarian ships, the leaders and others have sat around in a circle in attendance upon him, competing to bring him food and drink — he could not but share their cup and spoon so as to hold their hearts.

Moreover, the barbarians commonly lay great stress on their women. Whenever they have a distinguished guest, the wife is certain to come out to meet him. For example, the American chief Parker and the French chief Lagrené both brought their foreign wives along with them, and on occasions when your slave has gone to the barbarians' storied residences to discuss business, these foreign wives have rushed out and saluted him. Your slave was confounded and ill at ease, while they on the other hand were deeply honored and delighted. Thus in actual fact the customs of the various Western countries cannot be regulated according to the ceremonies of the Middle

Kingdom. If we should abruptly rebuke them, it would be no way of shattering their stupidity and might give rise to their suspicion and dislike.

Furthermore, the various barbarians have come to live at peace and in harmony with us. We must give them some sort of entertainment and cordial reception; [5] but we are on guard against an intimate relationship in intercourse with them. For this reason at those times when the treaties with the various countries were to be discussed and settled in succession, your slave has always ordered the provincial treasurer Huang En-t'ung [d. 1881] to tell the various barbarian envoys clearly that Chinese high officials when managing public affairs with other countries on no account can overstep the bounds and have personal relations; if there should be gifts which they desire to present as a courtesy, we can only firmly decline to accept them. If they were accepted in an underhanded manner, the ordinances of the Celestial Dynasty are extremely strict; not only would such an official injure the fundamental institutions of government, he would also have difficulty in escaping punishment according to the statutes of the realm. The barbarian envoys in question have heretofore had the sense to obey this instruction. But at times when they have been received in interviews, they have occasionally had small gifts to present, such as foreign wine or perfume, or the like. The value of these things has been very slight, and the barbarians' intention has been quite sincere. It has been inconvenient, right before their faces, to throw such gifts back at them. But he (Ch'i-ying) has conferred on them such things as snuff boxes and ornamental purses which are carried on the person simply in order to uphold the principle that though little is received, much should be given. . .[6]

As to these various countries, although they have rulers, they may be either male or female, and they may rule variously for a long or a short time, all of which is far beyond the bounds of any system of laws. For example, the English barbarians are ruled by a female, the Americans and the French are ruled by males, the English and French rulers both rule for life, while the ruler of the American barbarians is [p. 20] established by the campaigning of his countrymen, and is changed once in four years — after he leaves the position, he is of equal rank with the common people.

The official designations by which they call themselves also differ. (In China) most of them assume Chinese characters [i.e., titles of office] to make a false display and boast about themselves, as self-important as the Yeh-lang [the barbarian tribe who asked the Han envoy which state was larger, Yeh-lang or Han]. Those actions of course pay respect to their rulers, and have nothing to do with us. If we restrained them by the ceremonial forms used for dependent tribes, they would certainly not consent to retire and remain in the status of Annam and Liu-ch'iu, since they do not accept our calendar nor receive an Imperial patent of investiture.

With this type of people from outside the bounds of civilization, who are blind and unawakened in styles of address and forms of ceremony, if we adhered to the proper forms in official documents and let them be weighed according to the status of superior and inferior, even though our tongues were dry and our throats parched (from urging them to follow our way), still they could not avoid closing their ears and acting as if deaf.

Not only would there be no way to bring them to their senses, but also it would immediately cause friction. Truly it would be of no advantage in the essential business of subduing and conciliating them. To fight with them over empty names and get no substantial result would not be so good as to pass over these small matters and achieve our larger scheme.

The several measures stated above are all methods based on close investigation of the barbarian situation, an estimation of the exigencies of the times, and a thorough judgment as to the importance or unimportance, urgency or lack of urgency involved, and have had to be adopted as expedients and modifications to fit the circumstances. Either because the affairs were fundamentally of little importance or because the needs of the time were too urgently pressing, your slave has not ventured to memorialize especially and intrude them one by one upon the Sacred Intelligence. Now, since the barbarian affairs have been roughly brought to a conclusion, as is proper he states them, one and all, in a supplementary memorial.

[Vermilion endorsement:] They could only be managed in this way. We thoroughly understand it.

The problems of diplomatic intercourse which were faced by the Manchu grandee Ch'i-ying were met with every day on a more intimate plane in the treaty ports. There the mandarins whose careers depended upon their getting along with the foreigners studied at first hand how to deal with them. The Western trade and population rapidly increased at Shanghai and friction occurred at all the ports. But the rise of the great Taiping Rebellion which engulfed the interior of South China after 1851 (see Ch. Vc) weakened the position of the Ch'ing government. The new emperor, Hsien-feng, who reigned from 1851 to 1861, was narrowly anti-foreign and abetted the short-sighted Cantonese contempt for the West, but his regime was powerless to expel the barbarian and had to continue a half-hearted policy of conciliation. This left it up to the Ch'ing officials at the ports to get on with the foreigners as best they could. We quote below a description of the methods of conciliation used by an able military commander at Shanghai in 1854–55, Chi-er-hang-a (d. 1856). This Manchu official had been rapidly promoted to the governorship of Kiangsu because of his success in obtaining foreign assistance and coöperation when rebels occupied the old walled city of Shanghai (Sept. 1853–Feb. 1855) and so endangered the foreign settlement nearby.

When in 1853 the British barbarians saw the many difficulties in our domestic situation, and straightway became warlike, Chi-er-hang-a brought them under control [p. 5] by the use of right principles and subdued them by his spirit, while also showing his confidence in them by getting together with them, as a result of which he was able to turn them to our use. His method of showing confidence in them was first of all, necessarily, to break down their suspicions. Those of whom these barbarians are most suspicious are the high officers of China who do not memorialize their complaints truthfully to the Emperor. . . Chi-er-hang-a scrupulously took their reasons for complaint and if they happened to be things that could be done, he would at once tell them that he was memorializing on their behalf according to the facts. If they were things that could not be done, then he would say to them, "You want me to memorialize on your behalf; I cannot but memorialize, but as soon as I have done so, His Majesty the Emperor will certainly remove me from office and have me tried. We have been mutually friendly — let me take this gauze cap [symbol of office] and hand it over to foster our friendship, it is of no importance; but I do not know whether you gentlemen will feel at ease or not." If they put forth statements which were perverse or erroneous, he would reply directly, "My head can be cut off, but this cannot be done." The barbarians considered that he was not deceiving them and respectfully called him "Lord Chi" and so in their inner hearts were sincerely submissive.

The danger of any association with foreigners and the difficulty of dealing with them led to the emergence in the new treaty ports of a special class of Chinese officials who were specialists on the barbarian problem, comparable to the so-called "Far Eastern experts" of latter day America. One of the most competent of these men was the scholar-official Hsü Chi-yü (1795–1873), who helped to carry out Ch'i-ying's policy at the treaty ports of Amoy and Foochow in Fukien. His grandfather had been a provincial graduate (chü-jen) and his father a metropolitan graduate (chin-shih), which Hsü Chi-yü also became in 1826, so that his unorthodox interest in the West was that of a reputable scion of the established order. After service in the Hanlin academy at Peking and as a censor, he became the chief "barbarian controller" in Fukien, holding the posts successively of financial commissioner and governor between 1843 and 1851. His first foreign contact appears to have occurred at Amoy early in 1844, where an unfortunate British acting-consul was having a hard time doing business with the local Chinese authorities: lacking a competent interpreter, the Englishman in an interview would address his remarks in English to a Singapore Chinese, who would repeat them in Fukienese to a local Chinese, who would then state them in mandarin (Pekinese) to the officials.[8] The local American missionary, Rev. David Abeel, who could understand "a good deal" of mandarin though not speak it, was called in to help stave off the resulting chaos. Thus it happened that Hsü Chi-yü met a Westerner of literary interests, who showed him an atlas of the world. After borrowing Abeel's atlas, Hsü took up world geography as a hobby. Abeel said of him, "He is the most inquisitive Chinese of a high rank I have yet met." Abeel gave him instruction in geography and history and other foreigners like Capt. Smith of H. M. S. Druid also helped him.[9]

Hsü's eventual product, "A brief description of the ocean circuit" (Ying-huan chih-lueh), was completed in 1848 and printed in 1850. It was shorter and less broadly discursive than Wei Yuan's Hai-kuo t'u-chih; but as a straight summary of world geography based on Western sources it was more handy and succinct — one might say "scientific." Hsü's maps, for example, were careful copies of Western maps, vastly more accurate than the old-style sketch-maps used by Wei Yuan.

Hsü Chi-yü fitted into the post-treaty phase of conciliation, for he was concerned less with military strategy against the British invasion than with the study of Western society as a proper subject of scholarly interest. While his official memorials inveighed against the twin evils of foreign opium and missionaries in the fashion of the period, he is known to have gone rather far in friendly contact with foreigners. After Hsü began service in the Tsungli Yamen (1865–69, see Ch. Va) the Ying-huan chih-lueh was reprinted by it in 1866.

The extracts translated below on Britain and the United States are in the form of digested statements, evidently based rather directly on Western sources, which are then followed by Hsü's own comments of a more interpretive nature. Thus the British institutions of parliament and jury trial are succinctly described, but without much comment, whereas the expansion of British power in America and India receives comment of what might now be called a "geopolitical" nature. The exploits of the American father of his country, "Ton" (i.e., Washington, see Doc. 6), are played up, though perhaps no more than in American textbooks of the day. Governor Hsü's researches laid before his countrymen enough data on the economy and political institutions of the West to make it plain that the Western barbarians represented an entirely different and very powerful society. The difficulty lay in absorbing the lesson of this difference and applying it to statecraft.

DOC. 6. HSÜ CHI-YÜ'S ACCEPTANCE OF WESTERN GEOGRAPHY, 1848 [10]

[On Britain and her empire] The population of England is dense and the food insufficient. It is necessary for them to import from other countries. More than [p. 44] 490,000 people are engaged in weaving. The weaving machine is made of iron, and is operated by a steam engine, so it can move automatically. Thus labor is saved and the cost of production is low. Each year more than 400,000 piculs [1 picul equals 133 lbs.] of cotton are used, all of which are shipped in from the five parts of India and America. . . Silk is purchased and shipped from China and Italy. The work of manufacturing guns, cannon, knives, swords, clocks, watches, and various kinds of utensils and tools for daily use is done by about 300,000 people. Each year the income from the various products is worth approximately ten million taels or more. Their commercial ships are in the four seas; there is no spot which they do not reach. The great profits go to the merchants and dealers, while the workers are poor.

[Hsü then describes the British Parliament and its activities, and the system of trial by jury]

The English procedure of legal inquiry is that, when there is evidence of crime, the offender is arrested or sent to the court. When he is about to be examined, six persons of good reputation are first selected from among the common people and the offender is also ordered to select six persons for himself. Together the twelve persons make the inquiry, and decide the merits of the case before they report it to the judge. The judge then examines it and the law is executed. . .

[Commentary, p. 45b] England consists merely of three islands, simply a handful of stones in the western ocean. Her area is estimated to be about the same as Taiwan and Ch'iung-chou [Hainan]. . . Even if the soil is all fertile, how much can be produced locally? The reason for her becoming suddenly rich and strong, exerting political influence here and there beyond tens of thousands of li is that in the west she obtained America and in the east she obtained the various parts of India. The land of America hangs isolated on the globe, and since ancient times it has been little known. In the Wan-li period (1573–1620) of the Ming, it was discovered, and then a rich soil of ten thousand li was added to Great Britain, soon making her immensely rich. Even though the land of America is separated from England by ten thousand li, the British are skilled in ocean navigation, and make the voyage as easily as crossing a marshy ground with weeds. When the southern part was ceded to the United States of America, the northern part [i.e., Canada] which, though vast, is as barren and cold as Chinese Mongolia (was retained by the British). After England lost this part [U. S. A.], she almost lost her prosperity [lit., color].

The five Indias lie on the southwest of China. . . In 1755 Bengal was annexed, and taking advantage of their victories the English stealthily encroached on the various states like silkworms eating mulberry leaves. The various parts, scattered and weak, could not resist, and consequently more than half became British colonies. The land produces cotton and also opium. After opium became popular in China, ten-fold profits were made. The revenue collected by the English in large measure comes from the five Indias. To have lost in the west [America] and yet to have made it up in the east [India] — how fortunate she is!

After the English obtained the five Indias, they gradually expanded toward the southeast. Along the eastern coast of the Indian Ocean, ports were opened everywhere. . . Malacca and Hsi-li (author's note: that is, Singapore) were exchanged with Holland. Eighty or ninety per cent of the wealth of the Small Western Ocean (Note: the Indian Ocean), came under British control. In the farther east, of the states on the various islands in the southern ocean of China, except Luzon which belongs to Spain, the rest are all trading ports of Holland. The luxurious places like Ko-lo-pa (Note: that is, Java), the strategic areas like Manila (Note: that is, small Luzon) also were coveted by the English. Unfortunately other people already possessed them; she had no reason to take them by force. And yet, she goes to and fro on the eastern sailing route, using the two places as her hostelries, and Spain and Holland dare not offend her in the least. . . At the present time, what Britain relies upon to be her outside treasury and to extend the power of her nation lies in the five Indias. The territory is on the southwest of further Tibet, whence it only takes twenty or thirty days to go to Canton by sea. This colony of the British has been for a long time close to our southern frontier, and yet our critics merely know that England proper is over 70,000 *li* away.

England herself is geographically small in area, but very numerous in population. The arable land is not sufficient to supply food for one-tenth of the population. Before the ceding of North America, the unemployed British subjects usually sailed westward to seek sustenance. After the ceding of America, the remaining land of England in the northern region [i.e., Canada] was too cold for farming. Even though the large territory of the five Indias was obtained, there were originally inhabitants in that area, and there was no unoccupied territory. Although many English people went to live there, after all they could not reverse their guest position to become the hosts [p. 47], and therefore they were anxious to find new places. In recent years, the great island of New Holland [New Zealand] has been obtained. The grass and weeds have been cut down in order that criminals may be banished to that place. The poor people, who have no means of making a living, were also taken there for settlement. In moving these people over a distance of 80,000 *li*, it was a hard and painstaking job (for the government) to plan to feed and accommodate the people. [End of commentary]

The annual revenue of England, apart from paying the interest to merchants, is approximately Tls. 200,000,000 [11] and more. The expenditure is also more than Tls. 200,000,000. The size of the regular army of England proper is 90,000 men. In India, the British soldiers are 30,000, and the local troops 230,000, who are called "sepoy" soldiers. She has more than 600 warships, large and small, and more than 100 steamships. Their sailors wear blue uniforms and their army wear red. The navy is stressed but the army is slighted. They depend entirely upon rifles and guns, and are not skillful in boxing. Excepting knives and swords, they have no other weapons.

[In the succeeding section of commentary, the author describes the types and sizes of British warships and their structure, and notes that the foreign ships are not afraid of storms but are vulnerable to rocks in the sea. He also describes Western cannon and the structure of steamships and their operation. His details indicate an understanding of the theory of steam propulsion. He also states that the steam engine was first used in Europe for weaving, later on extended to steamships, and in recent years in America extended to locomotives.]

[On the American revolution and the U. S. A.] [12]

In the middle of the Ch'ien-lung period (1736–1795), England and France were engaged in a war which lasted for years without being settled. Hundreds of methods had been used to raise provisions, and the rate of taxation was doubled. According to the old regulation, the seller of tea had to pay a tax; the British then ordered the purchasers also to pay a tax. The Americans could not bear this. In 1775, the local gentry gathered together in a public building, wanting to discuss the problem with their resident chieftain. The chieftain [i.e., British official] drove away the petitioners and urged the levy of the tax even more harshly. The multitude of the people were so irritated that they threw the tea from the ships into the sea, and they planned to raise an army to fight against the British.

There was a certain Washington (Hua-sheng-tun; note: also written Wang-hsing-t'eng and Wa-sheng-tun), a native of another part of America [i.e., not of Massachusetts], born in 1731 [1732]. When he was ten he lost his father, and his mother educated him and brought him up. He had cherished great ambitions in youth and was gifted in both literary and military matters. He was unusually gallant and robust. Once [p. 15] he served as a British military officer. . . When the time came for the multitude of the people to revolt against the British, they urged Washington [lit., Tun, i.e., taking the last syllable as surname] to be their commander. . . The army of Washington was defeated, and his followers were so discouraged that they wished to be disbanded and to go away. Washington maintained his spirit as usual. He gathered his forces and grouped them into an army to fight again, and he was victorious. Thus in eight years of bloody war, he was repeatedly defeated, but he also repeatedly refused to be discouraged. . .

After Washington settled his country's affairs, he gave up arms and intended to return to his farm. The multitude could not bear to leave him, but insisted on electing him the head of the state. Then Washington held a discussion with the multitude, saying that to establish a state and to hand it down to his descendants would be selfish; the duty of looking after the people should be carried on by selecting those who have virtue. The traditional divisions [pu, parts] were set up as individual states, and each state has a commander [i.e., governor]. . . The leaders of the villages and towns write down the names of those whom they are going to elect and put them in a box. After this is finished, the box is opened, and the one who has obtained the most votes is established as governor. Whether he is an officer or of the common people, there is no restriction according to his previous status, and after retirement, the governor is still considered an equal of the common people. . .

[P. 16b] The whole continent of America reaches the great western [i.e., Atlantic] ocean in the east, and the great ocean sea [i.e., Pacific Ocean] in the west. The United States are all in the eastern part. . . The unculti-vated region in the west is all occupied by the aborigines. Whenever new territory is to be opened, at first hunters are employed to kill the bears, deer, and wild oxen, and then the unemployed people are allowed to cultivate the land. When forty thousand inhabitants have been gathered together or born in the region, then a city is built which is given a name as a territory [*pu*] attached to the whole group of states. At present, apart from the states, three territories have been added.

[P. 33] The various states of America have an equable and normal climate. In the north it is like Chihli and Shansi and in the south it is like Kiangsu and Chekiang. The river currents are gentle and the soil is good. There is no desert and little plague. (Note: in the south there is a pestilential vapor, but it is not very poisonous.) The land is level and fertile and suitable for the five grains. Cotton is the best and the most produced, whence the various countries like England and France all get their supplies. There are all kinds of vegetables and fruits. Tobacco leaves are extremely good and are circulated far and wide. In the mountains coal, salt, iron, and white lead are produced. Within the country there are many small rivers, and the Americans have dredged them from place to place in order to facilitate water transportation. Steam locomotives [lit., fire-wheel carts] are also made. Stones are used to pave the road bed and they melt iron and pour it like a liquid in order to smooth the running of the train. Within one day it can run more than 300 *li*. Steamships are even more numerous, running back and forth on the rivers and seas like shuttles, because the land produces much coal. . .

Once every two years, one person is elected for his outstanding ability and point of view out of every 47,700 people to stay at the capital city to participate in and discuss the national affairs. In the capital, where the president lives, there is a congress (*kung-hui*) representing all the states, each of which elects two wise men to participate in this congress and decide great political issues such as making an alliance, declaring war or adopting defensive measures, determining the rate of customs and taxes on trading transactions and the like. The full term is six years. In each state there are six judges to take charge of making verdicts or imprisonments. They are also elected to fill these positions. If there is anyone who is prejudiced or unfair, he may be removed by public opinion. . .

The standing army of the United States of America is not more than 10,000, who are distributed among various forts and strategic points. Except for scholars, physicians, and astronomers, the rest of the people — farmers, workers, and merchants — from twenty to forty years old are subject to selection by the officials to serve as militia [*min-ping*] and are issued registration cards. . . The militia system of about 1,700,000 men is fundamentally identical with the method of our ancient people who quartered troops on the farmers.

[P. 34b] In the United States of America, all the white men have immigrated to live there; there are people from all countries of Europe but those coming from England, Holland, and France are the most numerous. Among these three countries, England again provided more than one-half. Therefore, the spoken and written language is the same as that of England. . . The business and transportation work is all done by the white people. The people are docile, good-natured, mild, and honest. They do not have the fierce and cruel bearing of birds of prey. They work very hard in making a living and their merchant ships sail the four seas. All the states of America accept the religion of Jesus [i.e., Protestant Christianity], and are fond of academic discussions and activities. Everywhere there are schools. Their scholars in general are divided into three kinds: namely, academic, studying astronomy, geography, and the tenets of Christianity; medical, for curing diseases; and legal, for training lawyers and judges.

CHAPTER V. THE EMERGENCE OF THE THEORY OF SELF-STRENGTHENING

By 1860 the rulers of China had wasted twenty years in refusing to face the problems created by Western contact. These lost decades, to be sure, had seen the outbreak of a great rebellion against the Manchu dynasty which for some time threatened it with extinction and absorbed its waning energies. Simultaneously there continued to develop those points of friction — at Canton, in the opium trade, and elsewhere along the coast and in the treaty ports — which led eventually to the second war between Britain and the Ch'ing empire, in which France also joined. Negotiations for treaty revision having been frustrated by Chinese intransigence, the British and French finally seized convenient pretexts, sent a joint expeditionary force, occupied Canton, and negotiated treaties at Tientsin (as the Americans and Russians did also) in 1858. At first glance this would seem to be a plain case of the imperialist powers taking advantage of China's domestic difficulties to force their will upon her, and we may indeed judge this to be the general pattern of China's modern experience among the nations. Yet a view of China's nineteenth-century foreign relations which saw only the aggression of the West would certainly be one-sided. Chinese-Manchu attitudes and reactions were an essential factor in the historical process, as can be illustrated by a comparison of the periods just before and after 1860.

In the year preceding, when the ratifications of the treaties of Tientsin were to be exchanged, the Ch'ing court conceived and executed a bold stratagem to ambush the barbarian envoys and forestall their approach to the capital. In hostilities at Taku, outside Tientsin, they were for the moment victorious, and the British force retired in defeat. This only set the stage, however, for a second campaign in 1860, in which Anglo-French troops fought their way to Peking,

forcing the emperor to flee, and secured by force a confirmation of all their demands. From that time foreign ministers were to reside at the capital, foreign
ships to ply the Yangtze, and foreign goods and missionaries to penetrate into the
interior. This utter failure of Ch'ing power to hold off the West, by either force
or conciliation, finally brought a change in the court's attitude and policy.

The years after 1860 saw a hopeful effort to develop new Chinese institutions,
particularly for the conduct of foreign relations and the collection of customs
duties, and to secure foreign advice and assistance, particularly against the rebels
in South and Central China. Who knows what might have been accomplished if
such policies had been adopted earlier? To suggest that they could have been
instituted in the 1840's or 1850's is, of course, to overlook the facts of the historical
situation. Our point is that the historical forces of the time had to become manifest through a specific change in attitude, in the Chinese response to the Western
problem. For this reason the reversal of policy at Peking in 1860 merits our close
attention.

a. *Prince Kung and the Tsungli Yamen*

In May of 1860 the defeat of the regular Ch'ing forces by the Taiping rebels at
Nanking forced the central government to relinquish its time-honored policy of
centralization of power and yield great freedom of action to the provincial governors general, most of whom were Chinese. Four months later, in September,
came the events noted above — the British and French allied army routed the
Manchu troops assembled to defend Peking, the emperor had to flee, and the
demands of the foreign powers, which the emperor had stubbornly resisted at
enormous cost since 1851, had to be completely accepted. The shocking realization by the court that the two main supports of the Manchu throne — the Manchu
army at Peking and the Chinese troops in each province — had both been shattered brought about a reversal of policy towards the Westerners that was to prevail for over twenty years. This new attitude was particularly in evidence during
the first decade after the debacle of 1860, the decade of the "T'ung-chih Restoration," when the decline of the dynasty was temporarily checked by a reassertion
of the Confucian principles of civil government.

As the Emperor Hsien-feng fled from Peking he had designated his younger
half-brother, I-hsin (1833–1898), commonly called Prince Kung, as his representative to deal with the victorious British and French envoys. There was nothing
the prince could do at that time but sign a convention confirming the treaties
drawn up two years previously and meeting all further demands. Being entrusted
with the fulfillment of the obligations specified in the new treaties, he found it
essential to create a new office for foreign affairs, free from the traditions and
precedents that dominated the old administration at Peking. In late 1860 the
foreign troops had begun to withdraw to Tientsin, so as to set sail before the
river was frozen over. When the prince and his two major assistants began to
evolve a definite plan to deal with the Western powers, the result was the following memorial submitted by Prince Kung, Kuei-liang, and Wen-hsiang, received
at Jehol on January 13, 1861, and at once read and approved by the emperor and
the grand councillors.

DOC. 7. THE NEW FOREIGN POLICY OF JANUARY 1861 [1]

After the exchange of treaties, the barbarians have returned to
Tientsin and sailed hurriedly back to the south in groups. Moreover, they
still base their demands on the treaties. This shows that they do not covet

our territory and people. Hence we can still through faithfulness and justice tame and control them while we ourselves strive towards recovery. The present case is somewhat different from the (barbarian invasions) of former dynasties. . . Now the Nien rebellion [1851–1868] is ablaze in the north and the Taiping in the south, our military supplies are exhausted and our troops are worn out. The barbarians take advantage of our weak position and try to control us. If we do not restrain our rage but continue the hostilities, we are liable to sudden catastrophe. On the other hand, if we overlook the way they have harmed us and do not make any preparations against them, then we shall be bequeathing a source of grief to our sons and grandsons. The ancients had a saying, "Resort to peace and friendship when temporarily obliged to do so; use war and defense as your actual policy." This is truly a well-founded statement.

The situation today may be compared (to the diseases of a human body). Both the Taiping and Nien bandits are gaining victories and constitute an organic disease. Russia, with her territory adjoining ours, aiming to nibble away our territory like a silkworm, may be considered a threat at our bosom. As to England, her purpose is to trade, but she acts violently, without any regard for human decency. If she is not kept within limits, we shall not be able to stand on our feet. Hence she may be compared to an affliction of our limbs. Therefore we should suppress the Taipings and Nien bandits first, get the Russians under control next, and attend to the British last. . .

If we follow our plan at the present time, we should act according to the treaties and not allow the foreigners to go even slightly beyond them. In our external expression we should be sincere and amicable but quietly try to keep them in line. Then within the next few years [p. 19], even though occasionally they may make demands, still they will not suddenly cause us a great calamity. After careful deliberation on the whole situation we have drafted six regulations:

(1) To establish at the capital the Tsung-li ko-kuo shih-wu ya-men ["office in general charge of foreign affairs"; i.e., the "Tsungli Yamen"] . . . under the direction of princes and ministers. . . As soon as the military campaigns are concluded and the affairs of the various countries are simplified, the new office will be abolished and its functions will again revert to the Grand Council for management so as to accord with the old system.

(2) To establish the offices of high commissioners to facilitate the handling of affairs respectively at the northern and southern ports. [Here follow details on the office of superintendent of trade for the five southern ports: Canton, Foochow, Amoy, Ningpo and Shanghai, and the superintendent of trade for the three northern ports: Newchuang, Chefoo and Tientsin. (3) To arrange for maritime customs collections at the treaty ports and on the Russian frontier; (4) to ensure mutual information among officials handling foreign relations, so as to prevent errors.]

(5) To select two persons from Canton and two from Shanghai who understand written and spoken foreign languages and send them to Peking for consultation. [This is the initiation of the interpreters' college, T'ung-wen Kuan, discussed further in Ch. VIII below. (6) In each seaport, the internal and external commercial conditions, as well as foreign newspapers,

should be reported in communications to the Tsungli Yamen once a month to supply material for official perusal.]

Thus was created the Tsungli Yamen, a special board or subcommittee under the Grand Council which was to concern itself with all aspects of relations with the Western powers. While not a genuine ministry, it served as the prototype of a foreign office until the creation of the Wai-wu-pu, Ministry of Foreign Affairs, in 1901. In fact, its temporary and special status made it possible to select for service in the Tsungli Yamen some of the ablest personnel and most powerful officials.

As head of the new office, Prince Kung succeeded in establishing a working relationship with the British, French, American, and Russian envoys, in starting a Western-trained Manchu army using Russian guns, and in reinvigorating the central government at Peking. When the emperor died a year later, the prince emerged as regent for the new T'ung-chih Emperor of the period 1862–1874. From 1861 to 1884, the year of his dismissal from the Tsungli Yamen, Prince Kung seems to have concentrated mainly on keeping the peace with the Western powers, almost at any price, in order to give China time to become strong. His internal policy from 1861 to 1865 was also one of relative meekness towards the able Chinese administrators in the provinces, who were allowed a great deal of freedom in their conduct of the civil war against the Taipings and other groups of rebels. The final victory over the Taipings in 1864 was partly due to this policy.

Prince Kung was not a man of great abilities or personal ambitions. However, he was wise enough to listen to his advisers in the central government. He never issued arbitrary orders, but, in matters of importance, consulted the leading provincial officials before making a decision — a procedure that remained standard practice down to the end of the dynasty. At Peking he worked closely with two principal assistants, Kuei-liang and Wen-hsiang. Kuei-liang (1785–1862) was the prince's father-in-law and had had a good deal of experience in dealing with Westerners at Canton, Shanghai, and Tientsin, but he was by 1860 old and ill. Hence much of the routine was handled by Wen-hsiang (1818–1876), a Manchu official known for his integrity and intelligence and a member of the Tsungli Yamen from 1861 until his death in 1876. The fact that he was brought up in poverty at Mukden probably enabled him to see things more realistically than his fellow-nationals accustomed to the luxuries of Peking.[2]

The new dispensation in China's foreign relations symbolized by the Tsungli Yamen was only an aspect of the general process of dynastic revival which occurred during the "Restoration" of the T'ung-chih period. Essentially this was a process of temporary resuscitation rather than of innovation, an Indian summer of a declining regime rather than the creation of a new one. The Restoration period saw the pacification of the Taiping and other rebellions, resumption of the examinations and reinstitution of civil administration over wide areas, reduction of the land tax and other measures of relief for the agrarian economy, and a vigorous effort to select and train men of talent and imbue them with the principles of Confucian morality. This reaffirmation of the Confucian ideology of scholar government, the core of the Restoration movement, called for the application of traditional principles to the new situation of the 1860's. Reform of old institutions and establishment of new policies were therefore the order of the day, but both were sought within the framework of the orthodox Confucian system. Intellectual leadership was taken by scholar-officials who were steeped in the classical teachings of loyalty and ethical government. One of the most influential, though least known, of these men is discussed in the next section, with special reference to his attitudes and suggestions concerning relations with the West.

b. *Feng Kuei-fen and his Essays*

Feng Kuei-fen (1809–1874), a scholar of Soochow, was probably the first man to apply to China's modern problems the term *tzu-ch'iang* (lit., "self-strengthening," or "to make ourselves strong"). His ideas also anticipated the famous phrase *Chung-hsueh wei-t'i, Hsi-hsueh wei-yung* ("Chinese studies [learning, culture, values] for the base [fundamental structure, framework], Western studies for use [practical application]"), a slogan to be made famous a generation later by Chang Chih-tung in the 1890's (see Ch. XVII).

Feng obtained a *chin-shih* degree with high honors in 1840, and thereafter was a compiler of the Hanlin Academy for seven years — a position which enabled him to know government problems from the inside. He was well read and widely interested not only in the classics but also in mathematics, philology, astronomy, geography, agriculture, irrigation, and other subjects. He served as an assistant to Lin Tse-hsü and as secretary to Li Hung-chang (see Ch. VII) and other high dignitaries at various intervals over a period of many years. During the Taiping Rebellion he had organized a volunteer corps to defend Soochow; his letter to Tseng Kuo-fan in 1861 helped the latter to dispatch Li Hung-chang to Kiangsu province. This period of service made it possible for Feng to have direct contact with foreigners. In the meantime, he became concurrently director of two academies, one in Shanghai and one in Soochow. After the suppression of the rebellion he acted as Li Hung-chang's adviser for more than a year, and at his suggestion a school of Western languages and sciences was established in Shanghai in 1863, and the taxation in the region of Soochow was reduced in 1865.

The *Chiao-pin-lu k'ang-i* or, roughly translated, "Personal protests from the study of Chiao-pin," consists of forty essays which deal with governmental, financial, educational, and other aspects of China's modernization. The essays were first written in Shanghai around 1860, compiled under the above title with an author's preface in 1861, and were then presented to Tseng Kuo-fan, who intended to have them published. The author, however, very modestly declined, although he allowed his friends to read them or make copies.[3] In 1898 *Chiao-pin-lu k'ang-i* was finally brought to the attention of Emperor Kuang-hsü, who ordered the Grand Secretariat to make a thousand copies to be distributed to, and discussed by, all government offices. Most of the essays were also reproduced in the various collections of *Huang-ch'ao ching-shih wen-pien*, or "Essays on administration of government during the Ch'ing Dynasty," [4] an indication that they had far-reaching influence.

The following translations indicate Feng's recognition of the fact that the changing modern world had become much larger than anything ever imagined in ancient China. He recognized, too, the importance of Western sciences as necessary auxiliaries of Chinese knowledge. It was Feng who suggested the study of Western languages and sciences, which resulted in the establishment of the Kuang fang-yen kuan at Shanghai, which was an extension of the T'ung-wen Kuan (see Ch. VIII). In foreign affairs, he advocated a fair deal for the foreigner, and sought to get rid of Chinese jealousy and suspicion by turning from the general concept held before 1860, that all barbarians were of bad faith, to a new view that the barbarians were of good faith and should be treated with sincerity and respect.

Judged by these trenchant essays, written in a trim and condensed classical style, Feng Kuei-fen was most remarkable for his realistic appreciation of the importance of genuine learning. His contempt for the Canton-style "linguists," through whom Western lore had been murkily filtered into China, springs from this attitude, as well as his demand for language training, translations, and the study of mathematics and sciences, as the only possible basis for a mastery of the fundamental principles from which the barbarians got their power. His independence of mind is evident in the short shrift he gives to Wei Yuan's ideas, and in his readiness to tamper with the sacrosanct examination system.

DOC. 8. ON THE ADOPTION OF WESTERN KNOWLEDGE [5]

The world today is not to be compared with that of the Three Dynasties (of ancient China). . . Now the globe is ninety-thousand *li* around, and every spot may be reached by ships or wheeled vehicles. . . According to what is listed on the maps by the Westerners, there are not less than one hundred countries. From these one hundred countries, only the books of Italy, at the end of the Ming dynasty, and now those of England have been translated into Chinese, altogether several tens of books. Those which expound the doctrine of Jesus are generally vulgar, not worth mentioning. Apart from these, Western books on mathematics, mechanics, optics, light, chemistry, and other subjects contain the best principles of the natural sciences. In the books on geography, the mountains, rivers, strategic points, customs, and native products of the hundred countries are fully listed. Most of this information is beyond the reach of our people.

Nowadays those familiar with barbarian affairs are called "linguists." These men are generally frivolous rascals and loafers in the cities and are despised in their villages and communities. They serve as interpreters only because they have no other means of making a livelihood. Their nature is boorish, their knowledge shallow, and furthermore, their moral principles are mean. They know nothing except sensual pleasures and material profit. Moreover, their ability consists of nothing more than [p. 38] a slight knowledge of the barbarian language and occasional recognition of barbarian characters, which is limited to names of commodities, numerical figures, some slang expressions and a little simple grammar. How can we expect them to pay attention to scholarly studies? . . .

If today we wish to select and use Western knowledge, we should establish official translation offices at Canton and Shanghai. Brilliant students up to fifteen years of age should be selected from those areas to live and study in these schools on double rations. Westerners should be invited to teach them the spoken and written languages of the various nations, and famous Chinese teachers should also be engaged to teach them classics, history, and other subjects. At the same time they should learn mathematics. (Note: All Western knowledge is derived from mathematics. Every Westerner of ten years of age or more studies mathematics. If we now wish to adopt Western knowledge, naturally we cannot but learn mathematics. . .)

I have heard that there are large collections of books in the Mei-hua shu-kuan [American Presbyterian Press] and in the Mo-hai shu-kuan [London Missionary Society's Printing Office]. Moreover, in 1847 the Russian barbarians presented us with more than one thousand books which are preserved in the Fang-lueh-kuan [Military Archives Office, in Peking]. These books should be sent to the new schools so that the valuable ones may be selected and translated. . .

After three years all students who can recite with ease the books of the various nations [p. 39] should be permitted to become licentiates; and if there are some precocious ones who are able to make changes or improvements which can be put into practice, they should be recommended by the superintendent of trade to be imperially granted a *chü-jen* degree as a reward. As we have said before, there are many brilliant people in China; there must be some who can learn from the barbarians and surpass them. . .

If we let Chinese ethics and famous [Confucian] teachings serve as an original foundation, and let them be supplemented by the methods used by the various nations for the attainment of prosperity and strength, would it not be the best of all procedures?

Moreover, during the last twenty years since the opening of trade, a great many of the foreign chiefs have learned our written and spoken language, and the best of them can even read our classics and histories. They are generally able to speak on our dynastic regulations and government administration, on our geography and the state of the populace. On the other hand, our officers from generals down, in regard to foreign countries are completely uninformed. In comparison, should we not feel ashamed? The Chinese officials have to rely upon the stupid and silly "linguists" as their eyes and ears. The mildness or severity, leisureliness or urgency of their way of stating things may obscure the officials' original intent after repeated interpretations. Thus frequently a small grudge may develop into a grave hostility. At the present time the most important administrative problem of the empire is to control the barbarians, yet the pivotal function is entrusted to these people. No wonder that we understand neither the foreigners nor ourselves, and cannot distinguish fact from unreality. Whether in peace negotiations or in deliberating for war, we can never achieve the essential guiding principles. . .

If my proposal is carried out, there will necessarily be many Chinese who learn their written and spoken languages; and when there are many such people, there will certainly emerge from among them some upright and honest gentlemen who thoroughly understand the fundamentals of administration, and who would then get hold of the essential guiding principles for the control of foreigners. . .

DOC. 9. ON THE MANUFACTURE OF FOREIGN WEAPONS [6]

The most unparalleled anger which has ever existed since the creation of heaven and earth is exciting all who are conscious in their minds and have spirit in their blood; their hats are raised by their hair standing on end. This is because the largest country on the globe today, with a vast area of 10,000 *li*, is yet controlled by small barbarians. . . According to a general geography by an Englishman, the territory of our China is eight times larger than that of Russia, ten times that of America, one hundred times that of France, and two hundred times that of England. . . Yet now we are shamefully humiliated by those four nations in the recent treaties — not because our climate, soil, or resources are inferior to theirs, but because our people are really inferior [p. 41]. . . Why are they small and yet strong? Why are we large and yet weak? We must try to discover some means to become their equal, and that also depends upon human effort. Regarding the present situation there are several major points: in making use of the ability of our manpower, with no one neglected, we are inferior to the barbarians; in securing the benefit of the soil, with nothing wasted, we are inferior to the barbarians; in maintaining a close relationship between the ruler and the people, with no barrier between them, we are inferior to the barbarians; and in the necessary accord of word with deed, we are also inferior to the barbarians. The way to correct these four points lies with ourselves, for they can be changed at once if only our Emperor would set the general policy right. There is no need for outside help in these matters. [Here Feng goes on to point out that the only help China needs from the West is in modern arms, and claims that in recent contests with Western troops the Chinese army has not been inferior in physical qualities, nor even sometimes in morale, but always in arms.]

What we then have to learn from the barbarians is only the one thing, solid ships and effective guns. When Wei Yuan [in his *Hai-kuo t'u-chih*, see Doc. 3 above] discussed the control of the barbarians, he said that we should use barbarians to attack barbarians, and use barbarians to negotiate with barbarians. Even regardless of the difficulties of languages and our ignorance of diplomatic usages it is utterly impossible for us outsiders to sow dissension among the closely related barbarians. Moreover, he considered the various barbarian nations as comparable to the Warring States [403–221 B.C.], but he did not realize that the circumstances are different. Wei saw quite a number of barbarian books and newspapers and should not have made any such statement [p. 42]. It is probably because in his life and academic ideas he was fond of regarding himself as a political strategist.[7] In my opinion, if we cannot make ourselves strong [*tzu-ch'iang*] but merely presume on cunning and deceit, it will be just enough to incur failure. Only one sentence of Wei Yuan is correct: "Learn the strong techniques of the barbarians in order to control them. . ."

Funds should be assigned to establish a shipyard and arsenal in each trading port. Several barbarians should be invited and Chinese who are good in using their minds should be summoned to receive their instructions so that they may in turn teach many artisans. When a piece of work is finished and is indistinguishable from that made by the barbarians, the makers should be given a *chü-jen* degree as a reward, and be permitted to participate in the metropolitan examination on an equal footing with other scholars. Those whose products are superior to the barbarian manufacture should be granted a *chin-shih* degree as a reward, and be permitted to participate in the palace examinations on the same basis as others. The workers should be double-paid so as to prevent them from quitting.

Our nation has emphasized the civil service examinations, which have preoccupied people's minds for a long time. Wise and intelligent scholars have exhausted their time and energy in such useless things as the eight-legged essays [highly stylized essays for the civil service examination, divided into eight paragraphs], examination papers, and formal calligraphy. . . Now let us order one-half of them to apply themselves to the pursuit of manufacturing weapons and instruments and imitating foreign crafts. . . The intelligence and wisdom of the Chinese are necessarily superior to those of the various barbarians, only formerly we have not made use of them. When the Emperor above likes something, those below him will pursue it even further, like the moving of grass in the wind or the response of an echo. There ought to be some people of extraordinary intelligence who can have new ideas and improve on Western methods. At first they may learn and pattern after the foreigners; then they may compare and try to be their equal; and finally they may go ahead and surpass them — the way to make ourselves strong actually lies in this. . .

[P. 43] Two years ago the Western barbarians suddenly entered the Japanese capital to seek trade relations, which were permitted. Before long the Japanese were able to send some ten steamships of their own over the western ocean to pay return visits to the various countries.[8] They made many requests for treaties which were also granted by these countries, who understood Japan's intentions. Japan is a tiny country and still knows how to exert her energy to become strong. Should we, as a large country, alone accept defilement and insult throughout all time?. . . We are just now in an interval of peaceful and harmonious relations. This is probably an opportunity given by heaven for us to strengthen ourselves. If we do not at this point quickly rise to this opportunity but passively receive the destiny of heaven, our subsequent regret will come too late. . . If we live in the present day and speak of rejecting the barbarians, we should raise the question as to what instruments we can reject them with. . .

Some suggest purchasing ships and hiring foreign people, but the answer is that this is quite impossible. If we can manufacture, can repair, and can use them, then they are our weapons. If we cannot manufacture, nor repair, nor use them, then they are still the weapons of others. When these weapons are in the hands of others and are used for grain transportation, then one day they can make us starve; and if they are used for salt transportation, one day they can deprive us of salt [p. 44]. . . Eventually we must consider manufacturing, repairing, and using weapons by ourselves. . . Only thus will we be able to pacify the empire; only thus can we play a leading role on the globe; and only thus shall we restore our original strength, and redeem ourselves from former humiliations.

DOC. 10. On the Better Control of the Barbarians [9]

Today our country considers barbarian affairs to be the first important matter of government, and the suppression of the bandits to be the second. Why? Because the bandits can be exterminated but it is impossible to do so with the barbarians. . . If a plan of controlling the barbarians is not devised, then when it behooves us to fight, we, on the contrary, may negotiate peace; or when it behooves us to negotiate peace, we, on the contrary, may fight on; and so the barbarian problem will become worse. Or if we vacillate between peace and war, the barbarian problem will also become worse. . .

Today peace has been negotiated; we should devote ourselves to peace.

We should treat the barbarians with entire candor. Traces of jealousy and suspicion will not avail us anything. . .

Should we then force ourselves to comply with every demand? The answer is, no. My opinion is simply that to submit outwardly, but to be jealous and suspicious inwardly, is not a good policy. The barbarians always appeal to reason. We should forthwith take their methods and apply them in return. According to reason, if a demand is acceptable, then we should accept it; according to reason if it is not acceptable, we should try to convince them on rational grounds. The various barbarians, though ignorant of our "three bonds" [the relation between prince and minister, father and son, husband and wife] still know one thing, namely, good faith. Not because they are naturally trustworthy, but because, if one nation breaks faith, then a hundred nations will rise in a group to attack and oppress her so that she is obliged to keep faith. . . Can peace be maintained for a long time? We know that the various barbarians cannot be without improper aims. But for the next several years to come, there will be no war. China is the largest country on earth with ample, fertile plains and marshes, numerous people and abundant resources. Naturally the mouths of all nations are watering with desire. For years past they have extensively compiled maps including tracks of roads and footprints all the way to Yunnan, Kweichow, Szechwan, and Shensi. What is their intention? Nevertheless, at present there will be no incident, because the four countries, Russia, England, France, and America, have too much uncultivated land, equal power, outward harmony, and covert jealousy to act together and force a submission, and no one dares to make the first move [p. 46b]. . . The Tientsin incident of 1858 was started by England, but the other three countries were necessarily involved. They all came together for no other reason than that England dared not monopolize the gain; she feared the other three countries would plot behind her back. In 1860, when the barbarians stopped as soon as they had obtained a proper excuse, it was also because they feared that Russia and America would plot behind their backs. . . In the future, if the relations among the four nations should become consolidated, they might coöperate to plot against us; or if the four countries fought among themselves, one country might be victorious and the three others might fall under her control, and then the victor might encroach upon us. Thus, the mutual hatred among the four countries will take precedence over their hatred of us. Their relations can never be consolidated and the date for the struggle between them must not be far away. This warrants our anxiety. . .

Recently we have heard that the footsteps of the Russian barbarians have reached the region of the Sui-fen River [p. 47] which is not far away from the Ch'ang-pai mountains and Kirin, and this merits even greater anxiety.

c. The Taiping Rebels' Interest in Modernization

Like most writers on nineteenth-century China, we have referred to the Taiping Rebellion (1851–1864) several times in preceding pages without trying to sum it up. The many records concerning it are still being studied and generalizations such as are made about the French Revolution or the American Civil

War are not yet possible. But a contemporary observer estimated that the rebellion took, all told, some twenty million lives, and it would not be wrong to class it among the great social upheavals of modern times. The ground for the rebellion was prepared by a variety of social conditions and circumstances, such as the incidence of population growth, economic depression (possibly connected with changes in foreign trade), the growing corruption of the Ch'ing officialdom, and the lowered prestige of the dynasty as a result of the Opium War. Protestant evangelism also played its part, and the leader of the movement, Hung Hsiu-ch'üan (1814–1864), used certain aspects of Christian doctrine in setting up his personal theocracy. As the movement got under way, a multitude of poverty-stricken peasants were joined by secret society members who had cherished anti-Manchu sentiments since the beginning of the dynasty and by jobless coolie porters, opium smugglers, and pirates from the Canton area. Starting in the mountains of Kwangsi, west of Canton, the rebels advanced rapidly northward through Hunan to the Yangtze and down it to Nanking, which they chose in 1853 to be the capital of the Heavenly Kingdom of Great Peace (*T'ai-p'ing t'ien-kuo*). They aimed not only at driving out the Manchus, as the founders of the Ming Dynasty had driven out the Mongols, but also at setting up a kind of communistic and theocratic state. They failed to reach this goal for many reasons, among them the united opposition of the privileged classes, led by the Confucian scholar-official Tseng Kuo-fan (1811–1872), the help given the imperial forces by the Western powers after 1860, and perhaps most important, the Taipings' own lack of competent leaders and adequate methods. While the rebel movement in many ways harked back to China's past, it is interesting for our purposes in this volume to note its reforming zeal, which in favorable circumstances might conceivably have developed a program of modernization for China. Even in the midst of constant warfare, the rebels tried or intended to secure an equal distribution of the land, to simplify the Chinese language, to enforce monogamy (among the common people), and to prohibit prostitution, footbinding, the sale of slaves, opium smoking, adultery, witchcraft, and gambling.[10]

It is interesting, of course, to speculate on the relations with the West which might have developed had the Taiping rebels been victorious. On the subject of modernization and reform of Chinese customs and institutions, the thinking of some Taiping leaders seems to have been more advanced, or at least more imaginative, than that of the opposing Ch'ing officialdom, as may be seen in the next document we quote.

Hung Jen-kan (1822–1864), a relative of Hung Hsiu-ch'üan, the founder of the Taiping kingdom, did not join in the military campaigns of 1851–1859, but took shelter in Hong Kong, where he received more training from Western missionaries than any other Taiping leader. He studied Christian doctrine with the Reverend Theodore Hamberg (1819–1854), to whom he supplied the basic information about Hung Hsiu-ch'üan that resulted in Hamberg's book, *The Vision of Hung-Siu-Tshuen and the Origin of the Kwangsi Insurrection* (Hong Kong, 1854), one of the basic English sources on the Taiping Rebellion. For three years he was employed by James Legge (1815–1897) in the London Mission at Hong Kong. Through long association with Westerners, he learned something of astronomy and other sciences.

In 1854 Hung Jen-kan tried to go to Nanking via Shanghai but was unable to get beyond the latter city and had to return to Hong Kong. When he finally reached Nanking in 1859, he was warmly welcomed by Hung Hsiu-ch'üan, who was said to trust no one but his brothers and other relatives with the handling of important affairs after the internal dissensions of 1856. Hung Jen-kan was soon made minister of foreign affairs and prime minister but, not having fought for the

Taiping empire in its early years, he was afraid that the old comrades might be jealous of him. He therefore presented to the Heavenly King his book, *A New Work for Aid in Administration* (*Tzu-cheng hsin-p'ien*), printed in 1859, which became one of the two chief Taiping writings on political ideology.[11]

Hung's reform program reflects his Western contact. Impressed by what he heard of the rapid progress in Westernization of Siam and Japan, he planned to abolish such customs as the wearing of long fingernails, footbinding, the raising of birds, and the wearing of ornaments. He suggests that calligraphy and painting, gold and jewels should be esteemed less than steamships, trains, thermometers, barometers, binoculars, and other scientific instruments. For institutional reforms, he recommends the inauguration of railroads, steamships, banks, post offices, newspapers, hospitals, institutions for the blind and the deaf, the prohibition of infanticide and of the sale of slaves, a ban on the performance of plays for religious or superstitious purposes, and the transformation of monasteries into hospitals. This indicates that he had in mind a sort of industrial and economic program for China. Many of his suggestions were carefully noted by Hung Hsiu-ch'üan, the Heavenly King himself, who wrote in the top margin, comments such as "I concur" or "This policy is perfectly correct." Nevertheless, in reading the following document one cannot help wondering exactly to what degree Hung Jen-kan knew what he was talking about. At any rate, he had linguistic difficulties in explaining new ideas by classical Chinese expressions.

DOC. 11. HUNG JEN-KAN'S PROPOSALS, 1859 [12]

(1) [Authority should be centralized and applied to all the people. On the other hand, the people's opinion should have ready access to the government.]

(2) The promotion of the facilities of communication [lit., carriages and horses] is aimed at convenience and speed. If someone can make a locomotive such as those made in foreign countries, which are capable of seven or eight thousand *li* in a day and a night, let him be permitted to monopolize the profit [i.e., patent], and after a certain limit of time let other people be permitted to imitate his invention. If he does not wish to monopolize the profit but to let society have the benefit, he should petition the government for permission to give up his monopoly in order to prevent bad practices [patent claims by people who would be less public-spirited]. At first, we should construct twenty-one main railroads in the twenty-one provinces, to serve as the veins of the whole country, and when the traffic is in good circulation, the nation will be healthy. . .

(3) The promotion of ships, which should be solid, nimble, and fast. Whether fire, steam, (human) energy or wind is to be used for power should be decided by the inventor. . . At present there is a steamship [p. 15] which can run more than two thousand *li* within a day and a night and which a great merchant can use to transport passengers and . . . commodities, while the government could use it for war or for defense and patrolling. . . If the Heavenly Kingdom could promote this craft, then the Yellow River could be dredged and made to flow into the sea. Shipping on the Yangtze and the Huai rivers could be used for the exchange of products between the places where they are produced and to take them to others where they are

lacking. In strategic spots steamships could be used to ward off trouble, and in drought or flood they could serve in famine relief. . .

(4) The promotion of banks. If a rich man wants to open a bank, he shall first report and deposit his deeds and other securities in the national treasury, whereupon he will be allowed to issue one million and a half (taels of) bank notes, which will be inscribed with very elaborate designs, stamped with the state seals, and be exchangeable for silver or commodities or for other bank notes and silver. On all these bank notes it will be allowed to charge three per cent interest. . .

(5) The promotion of patents for inventing utensils and for various arts. If there are those who can make very fine, unusual and convenient articles, they alone shall be permitted a manufacture and sales monopoly. Imitators shall be considered to have committed a crime and shall be punished. . . As a reward for a small article, there shall be a five-year (period of monopoly rights) and for a large one, ten years. . . After the time limit, other persons shall be allowed to make them.

(6) The promotion [i.e., exploitation] of hidden treasures. If there are people who discover gold, silver, copper, iron, tin, coal, salt, amber, oyster shells, jade, precious stones, and other materials, they shall be required to report this to the government. They shall be appointed as the chief superintendents and be permitted to employ people to mine. Twenty per cent shall be given to the chief superintendents, twenty per cent to the national treasury, and sixty per cent to the miners. . .

(7) [P. 16] The promotion of a postal service to transmit state documents, post offices to circulate all kinds of private letters, and newspaper offices to report frequent changes of current affairs.

(8) The promotion of Court investigators [to establish the facts officially, etc.]. . .

(9) The promotion of official reporting officers [lit., newspaper officers] in all provinces. These officials shall have duties but no authority. They must be honest and impartial, so that they will be independent and not controlled by other government officers nor should they try to control other officers. They will devote their time to collecting news from the eighteen provinces and a myriad of other places. . .

(10) [P. 17] The promotion of money and grain storehouses in the provinces, counties, and districts to take care of the salaries and public funds for civil and military officers. Officers should be established to take charge of monthly reports. If there are those who, apart from their salaries, illegally take one cent of bribery from the people, a punishment should be meted out to them.

(11) The promotion of public organizations for the populace [shih-min kung-hui]. Those who are rich and philanthropic, and who respect the sacred humanitarian hearts of the Heavenly Father and the Heavenly Elder Brother [i.e., Jesus Christ], should be allowed to make contributions at their pleasure in order to help the distressed and the endangered and the ignorant.

(12) The promotion of hospitals to relieve those who are ill and in

suffering. . . Physicians shall be installed but they must have passed several examinations before they can be employed. . .

(13) The promotion of rural officers [to be supported by public contributions and to maintain local order, etc.].

(14) The promotion of rural soldiers. . . In the daytime they shall supervise all the families in cleaning the streets or roads in order to get rid of the dirt and poisonous things that cause injury to the people. They are also to arrest those who fight and steal, and to summon the bystanders to the office of the county officers to be witnesses and help render a verdict. Those who give false evidence shall be punished. . .[13]

The rest of the book deals with the abolition of group punishment, arguing that only the culprit himself should be punished, while his family members and others should be spared; with the prohibition of infanticide, of the sale of slaves, etc., as summarized above; with the prohibition of personal visits to official residences in order to avoid the solicitation of favors; with the conversion of temples into churches; and with the criteria for a good soldier and general. Needless to say, Hung Jen-kan had no chance to carry much of his program into effect.

3

THE DESIRE FOR WESTERN

TECHNOLOGY, 1861–1870

CHAPTER VI. TSENG KUO-FAN'S ATTITUDE

TOWARD WESTERNERS AND THEIR MACHINERY

By 1861 the main ideas of the Restoration period, as illustrated in the memorials of Prince Kung and his colleagues or the essays of Feng Kuei-fen, had been enunciated, while the Ch'ing victories over the Taipings in that year marked the turning of the tide in favor of the established dynasty. For the next decade, until his death in 1872, a significant share of the moral leadership of the Chinese state rested with the chief architect of victory over the rebellion, Tseng Kuo-fan (1811–1872). So outstanding was this one individual, as a leader of men and an embodiment of the Confucian principles of administration, that it will be quite impossible to do him justice here. In what follows we confine ourselves to excerpts from Tseng's day to day writings, to indicate some of his comments on and attitudes toward the Westerners. Absorbed as he was in the problems of domestic government, it is uncertain how far Tseng Kuo-fan ever faced up to the implications of the technological superiority of the Western world.

Born into a Hunan farmer's family, Tseng first learned to write eight-legged essays and classical poems in order to pass the civil service examinations. He developed a great interest in the moral principles of Sung Neo-Confucianism and made a study of ancient philology. By the time he was twenty-eight, he had become a very assiduous student, although he was a man of only moderate scholastic aptitude. The years from twenty-eight to forty-two he spent in Peking, where he obtained his *chin-shih* degree, became a member of the Hanlin Academy, and made friends of many leading scholars and officials. Between the ages of forty-two and sixty-two, he had a strenuous military career, spent mainly in suppressing the Taiping rebels and some of the Nien bandits. By 1864, when the Taiping Rebellion was put down, Tseng Kuo-fan had acquired enormous prestige and influence. It was typical of his disciplined Confucian character, however, that his loyalty to the Manchu Son of Heaven never wavered. Rather than seek personal power, he led the Restoration movement to meet China's problems along traditional lines. As a representative of the landlord-scholar-official class, he identified his interests with those of the Confucian monarchy.

Tseng Kuo-fan's policy for dealing with the West, revealed mainly in his letters to Li Hung-chang and other officials, stressed the old Confucian virtues of sincerity and good faith. His progress from writing eight-legged essays to taking an interest in Western ships and guns was gradual and can be traced in his voluminous diary. His first turning in this direction was in order to improve China's defenses. As early as 1853 he recognized the need of a naval force and memorialized accordingly.[1] He became interested also in Western methods of training soldiers; and not only in purchasing foreign guns, but also in their imitation and manufacture by his own people. In 1855 he established small arsenals in Kiangsi. When he moved his headquarters to Anking in 1861, he established both an arsenal and a shipyard there.[2] In his diary entry of June 3, 1862, Tseng recorded a conversation with his staff members as follows: [3]

If we wish to find a method of self-strengthening, we should begin by considering the reform of government service and the securing of men of ability as urgent tasks, and then regard learning to make explosive shells and steamships and other instruments as the work of first importance. If only we could possess all their superior techniques, then we would have the means to return their favors when they are obedient, and we would also have the means to avenge our grievances when they are disloyal. If on our side we have no instruments to depend upon, then when we are wrong, we naturally take the blame; when we are right, we also take the blame. If we hate them, we shall be blamed; if we favor them, we shall also be blamed. Though all the people in the interior flatter the barbarians, we certainly have no power to forbid them to do so. Even if everybody hated the barbarians, we could not take advantage of it.

On a visit to Shanghai in June 1868, Tseng wrote in his diary: [4]

I saw landscape pictures through a foreign glass [stereoscope] which was brought here by Governor Ting [Ting Jih-ch'ang]; they are very beautiful. [On the following day, he writes:] I went to Yang-king-pang [the part of Shanghai along the later Avenue Edward VII] to return a visit of the French Consul-general Pai-lai-ni [M. Brenier], who entertained us very cordially. Even the bedrooms of his mother and his wife were prepared in advance to be shown to us. He conducted me, the governor, and the provincial commander-in-chief up through every floor of his four-storied residence. The splendid rooms and magnificent terraces, with bronze sculptures and colorful decorations, are probably superior even to the palaces of Chinese emperors.[5]

Three days after this visit, the *North China Herald* published a rather sarcastic account, guessing quite wrongly that a bad impression "must have been made on the mind of the august visitor who passed through our midst." [6] Actually Tseng steadily developed his interest in Western science. At Nanking he had a big model of the earth and frequently consulted the *Ying-huan chih-lueh* of Hsü Chi-yü when he had trouble with the names of foreign countries in official documents.[7] From 1862 on he often received foreign visitors or officials, including Robert Hart, General Staveley, J. M. Brown, Anson Burlingame, and Halliday Macartney. To learn how to be modern, he put down in his diary the new Chinese terms for light, chemistry, electricity, magnetics, zoology, botany, and similar subjects.[8] Nevertheless, he remained personally conservative about foreign medicine. On May 8, 1871, he writes in his diary: "My wife's illness has daily become more serious. The children have invited a foreigner to treat her. In my mind I disapprove of it, but for the time being, I allow them to do so." [9] In his diary over a period of many years, he frequently describes his great suffering with chronic ringworm, the loss of the sight of one eye late in his career, and severe toothache. At that time, in both Shanghai and Tientsin, he could have obtained some relief from foreign physicians, had he been willing to consult them.

DOC. 12. EXCERPTS FROM TSENG'S LETTERS, 1862

During 1862, Tseng wrote to Li Hung-chang on various occasions as follows:

The barbarian affairs are fundamentally difficult to manage, but the basic principles are no more than the four words of Confucius: *chung, hsin, tu,* and *ching* — faithfulness, sincerity, earnestness, and respectfulness. . . *Hsin* means merely not to tell a lie, but it is very difficult to avoid doing so. We should start to work on the basis of this word. . . If today certain words were said definitely, tomorrow we should not, on account of a little advantage or harm to ourselves, change them. . .[10]

When you have contacts with foreigners, there are four important sentences to keep in mind, namely: your words must be faithful and sincere; your conduct must be earnest and respectable; you should coöperate with them in defense, but not in attack; and you should keep at a distance from them at first, but later on become close. . . This last phrase means that we must earnestly strive to make our military power adequate so that we can stand on our own feet. At first, by ourselves, let us suppress the rebels in one or two places where our sternness and bravery will not be ridiculed by foreigners, and then we can become close to them, and it still will not be too late. Although at present we may seem to be quarreling with the foreigners, if we use these few sentences as a basis for getting along with them, we shall in time certainly achieve harmony with them, and be mutually content. . . [11]

Confucius says, "If you can rule your own country, who dares to insult you?" If we are unified, strict, and sober, and if hundreds of measures are fostered, naturally they will not insult and affront us without reason. If we are not to be insulted and affronted, and if everywhere we are humble and modest, certainly we shall have no future anxiety. The way to win the hearts of people coming from afar lies in this, and the method of self-strengthening also lies in this. . .[12]

In your association with the foreigners, your manner and deportment should not be too lofty, and you should have a slightly vague, casual appearance. Let their insults, deceitfulness, and contempt for everything appear to be understood by you and yet seem not understood, for you should look somewhat stupid. This also is a good way of facing the situation. . .[13]

We should carefully watch and learn their superior techniques and also observe their shortcomings. We should not boast of, nor neglect our ceremonies. If they esteem sincerity and cultivate harmony, we should by no means open any frontier hostility with them; if they abandon good relations and break their covenant, we should then have the weapons to oppose them.[14]

DOC. 13. FOUNDING THE SHANGHAI ARSENAL

Tseng Kuo-fan's chief effort at Westernization was the Kiangnan Arsenal established by himself and Li Hung-chang at Shanghai in 1865.[15] Shortly after his transfer to the governor-generalship of Chihli in 1868, Tseng wrote a memorial to present a retrospective account of its founding. He first recalled that his memorial of August 14, 1861, had urged the building of steamships, and then continued: [16]

In 1862–63, when I was encamped at Anking [Anhwei], where I established a factory to try to make foreign weapons, I used Chinese exclusively and did not employ any foreign mechanics. Although a small steamboat was built, its speed was very slow. The knack of building it was not completely acquired. In the winter of 1863 I sent the expectant sub-prefect Yung Wing abroad to purchase machinery, since I intended to make a gradual expansion. Your minister, Li Hung-chang, now governor-general of Hu-kuang, had paid attention to foreign weapons since the beginning of his tenure of the governorship of Kiangsu [1862]. At that time Ting Jih-ch'ang was the taotai of Shanghai. Both he and Li discussed the strategy of resisting foreign aggression and the method of manufacturing weapons. In the fifth month [May 25–June 22] of 1865, I purchased a set of machines in Shanghai and sent the prefects, Feng Chun-kuang, Shen Pao-ching, and others to open a machine shop [lit., *t'ieh-ch'ang*, iron factory]. At this juncture the machines bought by Yung Wing, having also arrived at Shanghai, were combined with the others into one arsenal. At first, because it was at the height of the attack on and suppression of the Taipings, guns and cannon were made. Also, on account of the shortage of funds, it was difficult to start shipbuilding until the fourth month [May 4–June 1] of 1867, when your minister memorialized and requested the assignment of twenty per cent from the foreign customs revenue, using ten per cent particularly for the expense of building steamships. Fortunately we are indebted to the Sacred Empress for her acceding to the request. Thereupon both the funds appropriated and the materials purchased gradually became more abundant. . .

It has been learned that in building steamships the boiler, the engine, and the hull are the three most important parts. Formerly when the steamship was built by ourselves in the foreign factory at Shanghai the boiler and engine [p. 28] were both bought from foreign countries and brought to China to be fitted into the hull. There has never been a case where we ourselves designed the blueprint and made the whole set of heavy engine and boiler. This time, when we began construction, we employed our own ingenuity in the study of the blueprint. . . During the first ten days of the seventh month [August 18–27, 1868], the building of the first ship was completed. Your minister named her the S.S. *T'ien-chi* [lit., peaceful and auspicious], meaning that she will be in calm waves within the four seas, and the factory business will be secure and prosperous. Two parts, the boiler and the hull, were both made by ourselves in the factory, but the engine was an old one which was purchased and repaired. . .

[P. 29] The said arsenal was formerly at Hung-k'ou, Shanghai, where a foreign workshop was temporarily rented, located in the midst of Chinese and foreigners. This caused much inconvenience. Moreover, the number of machines had daily increased, so that the factory became too small to contain them. During the summer of 1867, we began to build a new arsenal south of the city of Shanghai. . .

In addition a school should be established in which to learn translation, because translation is the foundation for manufactures. Foreign manufacturing is derived from mathematics, all the profound mysteries of which can be discovered through diagrams and explanations. It is simply because the languages are mutually incomprehensible that, even though every day we practise on their machines, after all we do not understand the principles underlying their manufacture and operation. This year the commissioners in the arsenal have paid great attention to translation. At different times we have invited three persons, Wei-lieh-ya-li [Alexander Wylie] of England, Fu-lan-ya [John Fryer] and Ma-kao-wen [John MacGowan] of America, who have devoted their energies to selecting and carefully translating books which would be beneficial to manufacturing. . .

Tseng Kuo-fan's approach to foreign policy was on the basis of his own Confucian moral code. As with any leader of great moral earnestness, his faith in the efficacy of his own right principles gave him determination and courage. To foreigners who have not shared these principles, this faith has sometimes made him seem naive or moralistic. In 1867 the Tsungli Yamen circularized the high provincial authorities to secure their views on the proposed revision of the treaties of 1858 — a form of consultation which Peking found particularly useful in the post-Taiping period.[17] Tseng Kuo-fan's reply stressed so clearly and explicitly the application to foreign relations of the classical ethic of Confucianism that the document speaks for itself. Few Chinese statesmen after his time were able to speak with such simple and profound conviction. .

DOC. 14. TSENG'S VIEWS ON TREATY REVISIONS, 1867 [18]

In our relations with foreign countries, we should pay the greatest attention to faithfulness and righteousness, and especially should value determined resolution. What we cannot do, we should firmly resist from beginning to end, and we should never let ourselves be reversed by any difficulties. In what we can do, we should show our broad-mindedness and generosity and make an instant decision by a single word. We should absolutely never hem and haw [lit., half spit and half swallow], nor show the slightest sign of hesitancy, which gives them an opening for cunning argument.

Generally speaking, the foreigners in Europe have been annexing each other's territories for several hundred years, for no other reason than to seize the profits of the business people of the one country so that the ambitions of the attacking country may be satisfied. When the foreigners came to China, they set up ports of trade widely, for transporting and selling hundreds of their commodities. They also wished to apply the cunning scheme of exploiting and squeezing others so as to restrict the livelihood of our business people. Since the hostilities, the Chinese people have been for a long time in deep suffering, as if immersed in water or fire. In addition, the three (northern) and five (southern) ports [19] for international trade and the trade in the Yangtze River make their livelihood more and more difficult. The common people are impoverished, have no one to appeal to, and are as oppressed as if they were hanging upside down. Now if we allow the foreigners to transport [p. 2] salt, then the livelihood of the salt merchants who sell and transport it will be ended. If we allow foreigners to establish warehouses, then the livelihood of the storehouse owners will be ended. If we allow small steamboats to enter the inland rivers, then the livelihood of the boatmen and helmsmen of large and small boats will be ended. If we allow the foreigners to inaugurate and operate telegraph lines and railways, then the livelihood of the drivers of carts and mules and of the hotel porters will be ended. Of the various matters they have demanded [in the proposed treaty] we think that the only thing worth trying is the matter of coal mining, in which we shall borrow foreign tools for the operation of the mines to produce permanent benefit for China. . . As to other matters like steamships and railroads, etc., if they are to be carried out by foreigners, then the foreigners will take the profits from our interior; if they are to be carried out by Chinese who are attached to foreigners, then the rich and powerful people will usurp the profits of the poor people. None of these things should be done. . .

The main thing is to argue with the foreigners on the point of the livelihood of the common people. Actually this principle is so strong that it is indisputable. If the foreigners contest and argue endlessly, we may best tell them that even if the authorities in the capital complied with their demands reluctantly, your ministers in the provinces would still fight against them with all their might. Even if the ministers and officials complied with their demands reluctantly, millions of the common people of China when pushed to extremity would think of revolt and would regard them as enemies. This is also totally impossible for Chinese officials to forbid. China's princes and high ministers who plead for the lives of the Chinese people will not be worried for lack of expressions to put in their arguments. Even if, on account of this, we should incur hostilities, we shall have resorted to war to save the livelihood of the Chinese people and not be struggling for a superficial reason; thus we can face Heaven, Earth, and the spirits of all the emperors above and also the multitudes of the people within the vast country below. When we have nothing to fear in our minds, then there will be nothing to regret in the future. . .

[P. 3] As for the item of sending envoys abroad, since China and the foreign countries have already become friendly, to have relations with them is a normal matter. Some critics fear that our envoys may bring disgrace to their missions, and others are afraid that the cost will be enormous. These are words of overanxiety. It seems suitable to order the high ministers at the capital and elsewhere to look for men who could be envoys to distant countries and to mark their abilities for future use. Regardless of official rank, and with no definite time limit, whenever we have the person, we should send him, and if we have no man, we will not send anyone. . .

As for the expansion of missionary activities, we have found on investigation that at the beginning of Catholic missions in China, money and profit were expressly used to entice the people. In recent days foreign missionaries have been mostly poor. Their money is insufficient, so their theories likewise will not be believed. . . Catholicism had its beginning in Europe and yet today Protestantism has been separately established there as a reformed Catholicism. From this we can see that the religions of the heathen will decline at one time and be prosperous at others, and only the doctrine of the Duke of Chou and Confucius has never been worn out through all the ages. If China only cultivates her art of government and unifies her popular customs, making her education and religion enlightened, then even though the foreigners use hundreds of schemes to expand [p. 4] their religion, eventually there will be few who will believe in it. . .

Concerning these several items, of which the harm is rather slight, not only need we not dispute with them strongly, but also whatever they may demand may be immediately complied with. Only concerning the railroads, steamships, transportation of salt and opening of warehouses, and other matters which injure the livelihood of our people should we use all our energy to contend against them. We need not use words of rejection nor need we use any severe and stern language, but we should use polite words to make a plea and to move them by our sincere intentions. From beginning to end, we should not shift nor change our stand. We should make them understand that to have humane concern for our people in order to protect the nation is a constant principle of truth for emperors of all ages. It is also the family law of all emperors of our dynasty. In China today, where there are numerous troubles and where the foreigners are just expanding their influence, we cannot bend ourselves to the peace negotiations without any regard for the difficulties of the people in the interior. Even in the future, when China may become fully prosperous, and the foreigners may be in decline and weak, we shall also only seek to protect our common people, without any ambition to display our military power abroad. Even though they are stubborn and tricky, they must also understand that truth cannot be twisted, and the wrath of the multitude cannot be provoked. Probably they will be influenced by our extreme sincerity and accede easily to our conditions. These are my unworthy opinions; whether they are proper or not, I carefully offer my humble suggestions for your selection.

Although Tseng Kuo-fan's synthesis of Confucian principles and Western arms set a style for the succeeding generation, its efficacy as a basis for modern international politics was never proved in practice. In 1871, shortly before his death, we find Tseng arguing for the granting to Japan of the commercial privileges enjoyed by the West, in the following optimistic terms: [20]

We train soldiers to work toward self-strengthening, but from the beginning we have had no intention of displaying our power outside our own territory. We collect duties by following to some degree the foreign methods, but we have no ambition to accumulate and grasp a big profit. If all our measures are developed with enlightenment, if the Western foreigners and Eastern foreigners are treated equally well and we use both prestige and virtue to control them according to the proper time and make foreign nations understand that the Sacred Dynasty's control of peoples coming from afar is uniformly based on the great principles of justice, then a myriad states will unanimously appreciate our sincerity. . .

CHAPTER VII. LI HUNG-CHANG AND THE
USE OF WESTERN ARMS

Under Tseng Kuo-fan's aegis the most powerful official to emerge in the lower Yangtze provinces in the 1860's was Li Hung-chang (1823–1901), whose personality was to dominate much of China's foreign policy in the late nineteenth century (see Ch. X a, below). One of Li's first contributions was to take practical steps to secure Western arms, the need for which was now widely recognized.

The new Chinese view on this problem was illustrated by the censor Wei Mu-t'ing, who pointed out in a memorial of November 14, 1861, that firearms had originated in China under the Chin dynasty (A.D. 1115–1234) and had merely been improved upon by the Europeans. The Jesuits Adam Schall (1591–1666) and Ferdinand Verbiest (1623–1688) had cast cannon in China. Foreign arms should now be used to wipe out the Taipings.

Moreover I have heard that Russia formerly did not have a navy. After the Khan [i.e., the Tsar], Peter, came to the throne, he personally went to Holland in disguise to practice and learn about naval affairs and firearms. After several years he returned to his country where he immediately constructed warships. Step by step he enlarged his territory for several thousand *li*. Now in Europe the Russian troops are the strongest.[1]

A year later an imperial edict (Nov. 17, 1862) ordered the provincial authorities to train Chinese officers in Western military methods, so as to crush the Taipings: [2]

The rebellious bandits have been running away and disturbing the southeast, and have spread to Shanghai, Ningpo, and other ports where the government troops are not effective, and for the time being, we have to make use of foreigners to train our soldiers, as a scheme for self-strengthening. . . But to use foreigners to do the training is also to use foreigners to be the commanders; that is, they take the responsibility as instructors and also share the authority of commanders and generals. . . It would be better to select our own officers and order them to learn the military methods of foreign countries. . . Then not only can we save expenses, but also we shall not give foreigners any military authority. Let Tseng Kuo-fan, Hsueh Huan (1815–1880), Li Hung-chang, and Tso Tsung-t'ang (1812–1885) select ten or twenty officers of the rank of captain or lower whose talents merit such training, and order them to learn the military methods of foreign countries at Shanghai and Ningpo [p. 42]. . . If the newly trained officers after several months have accomplished something, then we can assign to their command the soldiers at Shanghai, Ningpo, and other places, where they are learning foreign military methods, and it will no longer be necessary to have them controlled by foreigners.

The difficulty of using foreign officers and instructors without being used by the foreign power concerned, a problem which so many weak countries have faced in the age of imperialism, was quickly perceived by Li Hung-chang. As governor of Kiangsu, he had to develop close working relations with Frederick Townsend Ward (1831–1862), "Chinese" Gordon (1833–1885) and other foreign commanders who successively led the mixed Sino-foreign force organized with Western arms to defend Shanghai.

DOC. 15. Li's LETTER TO TSENG KUO-FAN ON THE EVER-VICTORIOUS ARMY, FEBRUARY 1863 [3]

In my camp not a single day passes without foreigners coming to see me and I am really embittered by the trouble they cause. Nevertheless, on account of this, I am thoroughly in touch with them both in spirit and in person, and in the midst of all this there is no one who dares to spread rumors or coerce me to do anything. Because I do not care very much for ceremonies, they are also rather frank in pouring out their feelings completely; however, I have no time to return their visits one by one.

"In resorting to warfare it depends upon the man, not upon the weapons." This is certainly a profound idea. [Tseng had said in a letter [4] that if generals and soldiers are good, it does not matter if the weapons are poor]. . . . I have been aboard the warships of British and French admirals and I saw that their cannon are ingenious and uniform, their ammunition is fine and cleverly made, their weapons are bright, and their troops have a martial appearance and are orderly. These things are actually superior to those of China. Their army is not their strong point, yet whenever they attack a city or bombard a camp, the various firearms they use are all non-existent in China. Even their pontoon bridges, scaling ladders, and fortresses are particularly well prepared with excellent technique and marvelous usefulness. All these things I have never seen before. However, they cannot pitch a camp nor live in tents, and, in addition, when they approach enemies they are very cautious. Their courage is mostly insufficient. In these things they are inferior to good Chinese soldiers.

The rebel Chung [the Taiping Loyal Prince, Li Hsiu-ch'eng] hired some foreigners who are rascals and who also have no way to seek for or buy real cannon. . . The foreign chiefs unanimously say that the rulers of England and France do not allow their big guns and mortars [p. 47] to go to China. Formerly the English chief who managed the affairs of the Ever-Victorious Army with me said that if we did not permit his country to send an officer to lead the army jointly, he would immediately take back our foreign arms, and he fears that the Army will be rendered useless. . .

I feel deeply ashamed that the Chinese weapons are far inferior to those of foreign countries. Every day I warn and instruct my officers to be humble-minded, to bear the humiliation, to learn one or two secret methods from the Westerners in the hope that we may increase our knowledge. However, the able fighters Ch'eng Hsueh-ch'i (1829–1864) and Kuo Sung-lin (1834–1882) are firm and obstinate and for this reason they are unwilling to learn. Liu Ming-ch'uan (1836–1896) is more understanding and he is very anxious to ask for guns and mortars but is unable to get them. If we encamp at Shanghai for a long time, and cannot make use of nor take over the superior techniques of the foreigners, our regrets will be numerous!

The next document is remarkable both for its perception of the way China's social structure impeded Westernization and for its forecast of possible military developments in Japan and within China.

DOC. 16. Li's Recommendation of Western Military Methods, June 1863 [5]

[Li begins by describing how he devoted his attention to Western arms after he reached Shanghai, purchasing and studying foreign weapons and using the assistance of skilled mechanics in the effort to comprehend them. His detailed factual account of the process of casting cannon would indicate that he had gained a more thorough understanding than some of his colleagues such as Tseng Kuo-fan.]

[P. 8] Of all firearms presently in use, explosive shells [6] can best assure victory, and particularly effective are the long guns to fire them; but unless we use the whole set of foreign machines and employ foreign skilled workers, we cannot start making them. Both the long-range and short-range guns would be ineffective without foreign gunpowder. The various arsenals under my jurisdiction cannot yet try to cast the long guns but we have bought several tons of large and small guns from England and France. We cast our own shells to supply the endless need for them.

I have learned that when Western scholars make weapons, they use mathematics for reference and exert their energy in deep thinking to make daily increases and alterations. Consequently they can make different weapons every month and every year. Of the Chinese books on making cannon, the *Tse-k'o-lu* by T'ang Jo-wang [Adam Schall], and more recently, Ting Kung-ch'en's *Yen-p'ao t'u-shuo*,[7] "An illustrated explanation of artillery," are the most detailed, but both are superficial works which have been copied with misunderstanding and with the use of imagination. And yet our people all regard them as secret books (to be carefully guarded). No wonder the closer we seek the art of cannon making, the further we lose it! Generally, if a tool is inaccurate, it has no value. If a tool is not carefully used, then having an accurate tool is the same as being without it. When the cannon cannot be discharged, and the ball cannot be fired, this is the fault of the manufacturer [p. 9]. The long or short distance, and the quick or slow speed of the ball, the high or low elevation of the cannon and its slow or rapid discharge are the responsibility of the gunners. In all these respects there are definite and fixed principles which cannot be learned by smatterers.

Personally I think that "when a series of changes has run all its course, another change ensues," [8] and after change, things will proceed smoothly. Chinese scholars and officials have been indulging in the inveterate habit of remembering stanzas and sentences and practicing fine model calligraphy, while our warriors and fighters are, on the other hand, rough, stupid, and careless; so that what the scholars and officials use is not what they have learned, and what they have learned is not what they use. In peace time they sneer at the sharp weapons of foreign countries as things produced by strange techniques and tricky craft, which they consider it unnecessary to learn. In wartime then they are alarmed that the effective weapons of Western countries are so strange and marvelous, and regard them as something the Chinese cannot learn about. They do not know that for several hundred years the foreigners have considered the study of firearms as important as their bodies and lives . . . The foreign officials and workers in charge of manufacturing them are honored and admired by the whole country, and not treated as small artisans.

Everything in China's civil and military systems is far superior to the West. Only in firearms is it absolutely impossible to catch up with them. What is the reason? It is because in China the way of manufacturing machines is for the scholars to understand the principles, while the artisans put them into practice and do the work. In developing their learning the two do not consult each other, hence their achievements cannot keep abreast. The best of the artisans is limited to becoming a head craftsman. Foreigners, however, are different. He who can make a machine that can be used by the nation can become a prominent official and his family for generations can live on the trade and keep their position hereditary. Thus there are grandfathers and fathers who learn the same trade and cannot thoroughly master it, yet the son and grandson still practise it for generations, insisting upon mastering it before they stop. "If the Emperor above desires fish, the official would even dry up the valley to catch fish": if there is an offer of honor and profit, will no one exhaust his energy to seek it, exerting his strength day and night with the determination of not stopping until he has thoroughly mastered it?

Formerly England, France, and other nations regarded Japan as a foreign treasury, recklessly making demands upon her. The Japanese emperor and ministers exerted themselves to become strong, selecting brilliant sons from the imperial house and high ministers to learn various techniques in the factories of Western nations. They also bought the machines for making machines so as to practise manufacturing in their own country. Now they can navigate steamships, and make and use cannon. Last year the English people threatened them ostentatiously and brought up soldiers. And yet the superior techniques of the effective weapons which the British people have been relying upon [p. 10] for attacking and fighting had already been shared and mastered by the Japanese. Consequently, they remained steady and undisturbed; and the English in fact could do nothing against them. The Japanese of today are the "dwarf pirates" [wo-k'ou] of the Ming dynasty. They are farther away from Western countries but close to China. If we have some weapons with which to stand on our own feet, they will attach themselves to us, and watch the shortcomings or strength of the Westerners. If we have nothing with which to make ourselves strong, then the Japanese will imitate the Westerners and will share the Westerners' sources of profits. Japan, a tiny country overseas, can still change her course at the proper time and know what she should take as her model. Since we Chinese thoroughly understand the principle that when one reaches a point of exhaustion, one must reform and then one can go on smoothly, we should also greatly change our plans.

There is a further source of anxiety. China's remaining bandits have not yet been exterminated and the foreigners, whether they are officials or common people, are secretly selling them powerful weapons. Let us suppose that in some nook of the mountains or some corner of the sea there are worthless rogues who learn the Western methods under cover, secretly originate some new principles, and suddenly stop tilling the land, and show their superior ability in making new weapons. The weapons of our government troops are old-fashioned and handed down from the past. How can we resist them? Whenever I think of this, I cannot but be startled with fear and sadly emit a long sigh. . . Su Tzu-chan [1036–1101] says, "If you speak in a time of peace, it is a sufficient basis for taking action, but frequently the trouble is that no one will believe you; if you speak in a time of trouble, it may be sufficient to secure belief but it will be already too late." I think that if China desires to make herself strong, there is nothing better than to learn about and use the superior weapons of foreign countries. If we wish to learn about and use the superior weapons of foreign countries, there is nothing better than to look for the machines with which to make machines. We can learn their methods but need not necessarily employ their people. If we wish to seek machines which will make machinery, and the men who can make machinery, we might specially set up a course for students [from the civil service examinations]. If the students will commit themselves to this course for the rest of their lives, as a means of attaining wealth, rank, and reputation, then the trade may be established, the technique may be mastered, and the abilities may be concentrated. In Peking the artillery and musketry division should particularly learn first to make cannon and improve on them, so as to prepare to inspire awe in the empire and reject foreign encroachment. . . We must take warning from what has happened to prevent what has not yet happened. Furthermore, we must investigate thoroughly why it has been so.

This statement from Li Hung-chang was put before the throne by Prince Kung and the other ministers of the Tsungli Yamen, with some very interesting additional considerations, some of which we translate as follows:

DOC. 17. The Tsungli Yamen Memorial of June 1863 on China's Defensive Strategy [9]

It has been several decades since the foreigners first engaged in hostilities against us. Finally, in the period of Hsien-feng [1851–1861] domestic trouble and foreign insult came simultaneously. . . All commentators know that foreign countries such as England and France rely only on their solid ships and cannon to lord it overseas. But as to why their ships are solid and their cannon effective, this is put aside without discussion. Even if there were some who paid attention to this matter, there has been no way to learn about it because the foreigners keep secret this mechanical cunning, and are unwilling to teach others. . . But now all the foreign countries are willing to sell us foreign guns and cannon. . . and also willing to send people to teach us the manufacture of all sorts of arms. . .

In recent years, troops have been used in Kiangsu, where English and French officers have been hired to teach and drill our soldiers and militia. The foreign officers, then, import the victory-bringing firearms from their countries to the camps for our use, but charge us a big price. . . When we secure these weapons, they are sufficient to destroy strongholds and break open fortresses so that, wherever we advance, we are successful. All areas south of the Yangtze have been gradually cleared up. The promptness of this result has never been surpassed. . . At present the military campaign is still going on in Kiangsu and Chekiang. If we use this as a pretext, that our soldiers are to learn the manufacturing of weapons in order to suppress the bandits, we shall not reveal any traces [of anti-foreign intentions]. This is indeed an opportunity which should not be missed. If we begin to learn the manufacturing after the suppression of the bandits, then even if the foreign craftsmen would like to come for the high pay, the foreign officers must become suspicious and hinder them. . . Thus we should seize the opportunity, at a time when in the southern provinces our military power is in great ascendancy and foreigners are delighted to show us their superior techniques, to make a substantial study of all kinds of foreign machines and weapons in order to learn their secret completely. In times of disturbance they can be used to oppose aggression, and in times of peace they can show our prestige. . .

Your ministers frequently, in periods of leisure from public affairs, have thought and planned again and again: the friendliness or opposition of foreigners always depends upon the strength or weakness of China. Certainly Japan is not the only one to consider us in this way. If we can strengthen ourselves, then we can live peacefully with the others, and covertly deter them from undertaking their cunning and aggressive plans. Otherwise, we shall have nothing to depend upon. . .

[P. 3] After the battalions at the capital have learned to use these superb and secret weapons, learning to make them can be extended only to the banner troops stationed in the various provinces, because the bannermen have definite places to live in, which are comparatively easy to guard. In order to avoid other subsequent evils the common people should still be forbidden to learn about and use these weapons. It behooves us to request an Imperial decree to order the Division of Artillery and Musketry to select eight intelligent and dexterous military officers and forty soldiers from among those who have had some training in making firearms, to be sent to Kiangsu and placed under Governor Li Hung-chang for assignment. . .

CHAPTER VIII. INSTITUTIONS FOR LINGUISTIC AND SCIENTIFIC STUDIES (THE T'UNG-WEN KUAN)

To responsible officials on the spot like Tseng and Li, the undeniable need to make foreign arms entailed an equal necessity to study Western "mathematics," including its application in engineering. At Peking one of the first innovations to follow the Tsungli Yamen was the interpreters' college or T'ung-wen Kuan. Approved in 1861 at the same time as the Yamen, this college was set up first to produce diplomatic interpreters; but it soon expanded to include Western sciences taught by Western professors. For this forward step, as for so many others, the foreign customs inspectorate under Robert Hart (1835–1911) supplied steady financial support.[1]

The original argument for the T'ung-wen Kuan in 1861 (which was briefly quoted above in our condensed summary, Doc. 7) had been as follows: [2]

(5) We request Your Majesty to order Canton and Shanghai each to

send to Peking two men who understand foreign spoken and written languages to be commissioned and consulted. We note that in any negotiations with foreign nations, the prerequisite is to know their nature and feelings. At present, their speech cannot be understood and their writing can hardly be deciphered. Everything is impeded. How can we expect to make a suitable settlement?

Formerly with regard to the Russian language, a precedent was established by setting up a school (*wen-kuan*) for its study, and this showed a profound wisdom. Now after a long time, the regulations have become a pure formality and the language has not been thoroughly understood. Some kind of encouragement seems to be warranted here in order to call people's attention to it.

We have heard that among the Canton and Shanghai merchants there are some who are devoting themselves to the study of the written and spoken languages of England, France, and America. We request that Your Majesty order the governors general and governors of the two provinces to select bona fide and reliable men and send two from each province, altogether, four, to Peking, bringing with them [p. 25] the books of the various countries. At the same time, let four or five brilliant boys under the age of thirteen or fourteen be chosen from each of the Eight Banners to study under them. Those who are sent to Peking should be well paid, after the practice of the Russian school, and following two years of service their diligence or laziness should be appraised, and those who make a good record should be rewarded and promoted. When the students from the Eight Banners can all master the written and spoken languages we shall no longer invite Canton and Shanghai teachers.

As for the Russian written and spoken language, we still beg Your Majesty to order the school to discuss its regulations carefully and promote its work seriously. Among the men who learn the languages of various nations, those who thoroughly master them should be immediately reported with a request that they be encouraged so that this work will not be later neglected.

In 1863, Li Hung-chang supported the idea of the T'ung-wen Kuan in an eloquent memorial evidently drafted by his secretary, Feng Kuei-fen; some parts are lifted from one of Feng's essays (see Doc. 8 above), and we have therefore omitted duplicate passages in the following extract.[3]

DOC. 18. Li Hung-chang's Support of Western Studies, 1863 [4]

When China has contact with foreigners, we should first understand their ambitions, be aware of their desires, and thoroughly know their points of strength and weakness, their honesty and dishonesty, before we can expect to secure just treatment. During the last twenty years of trade relations there have been quite a few of their leaders who have learned our written and spoken language and the best are able to read our classics and history. . . Whenever we have a discussion between Chinese and foreign high officials, we depend entirely upon the foreign interpreters to transmit the ideas; it is difficult to guarantee that there is no such thing as prejudice or misinterpretation.

[P. 12] Your minister requests that we follow the example of the T'ung-wen Kuan by inaugurating at Shanghai another foreign language school, in which children from the vicinity below the age of fourteen, of brilliant ability and refined and quiet character, will be selected and taught by Westerners, and at the same time *chü-jen* and licentiates of excellent conduct and learning will be invited from the interior to teach them classics, history and literature. . . After the students show achievement in their studies, they should be sent to the governor-general and governor of the province to be examined and to qualify as district licentiates. . .

After the language students have become numerous, men of ability will emerge. . . Are Chinese wisdom and intelligence inferior to those of Westerners? If we have really mastered the Western languages and, in turn, teach one another, then all their clever techniques of steamships and firearms can be gradually and thoroughly learned. [Li then raises the question of a similar school at Canton.]

As a result of this proposal, a language school modeled on the Peking T'ung-wen Kuan was set up at Shanghai in 1863. Another one was opened at Canton in 1864 and a somewhat similar institution at the Foochow Shipyard in 1866.

On December 11, 1866, Prince Kung, representing the Tsungli Yamen, urged the emperor to develop the T'ung-wen Kuan by adding a scientific department of astronomy and mathematics and by admitting students of high attainment in Chinese learning. He repeated the stock argument that "the machinery of the West, its steamers, its firearms, and its military tactics, all have their source in mathematical science." He proposed to invite professors from the West. "What we desire is that our students shall get to the bottom of these subjects . . . for we are firmly convinced that if we are able to master the mysteries of mathematical calculation, physical investigation, astronomical observation, construction of engines, engineering of water-courses, this, and this only, will assure the steady growth of the power of the empire." [5] On January 28, 1867, Prince Kung submitted another memorial in which China's need of Western science was discussed in detail. This important document asserted that the natural sciences were the foundation of Western strength and stressed the point that officials like Tso Tsung-t'ang and Li Hung-chang who were conversant with foreign affairs all urged the adoption of Western learning and the manufacture of foreign weapons and machines as the method for China's self-strengthening. [6]

In spite of vehement conservative protests, the new department was set up and Hsü Chi-yü (see Ch. IV) became director of the school. Soon the T'ung-wen Kuan curriculum included astronomy, mathematics, chemistry, physics, biology, geography, geology, mineralogy, metallurgy, mechanics, anatomy, physiology, political economy, and international law. Putting all these subjects under the heading of "astronomy and mathematics" presumably represented an effort of Prince Kung and his colleagues to lessen the conservative resistance by camouflaging their innovations, since Western astronomy and mathematics were known to have been introduced into China and accepted as early as the seventeenth century.

In the full-dress debate touched off by this action, the conservatives were led by the Grand Secretary Wo-jen (d. 1871), a Mongol whose high scholarship had made him a tutor to the emperor, head of the Hanlin Academy, and president of several of the Six Boards in succession. A product of the orthodox philosophy of Chu Hsi, Wo-jen was in 1867 the recognized leader of the opposition to Prince Kung and Wen-hsiang, and he immediately memorialized against the establishment of Western studies in the T'ung-wen Kuan, inveighing openly against the Western influence on racial and cultural grounds.

DOC. 19. WO-JEN'S OBJECTION TO WESTERN LEARNING, 1867 [7]

Mathematics, one of the six arts, should indeed be learned by scholars as indicated in the Imperial decree, and it should not be considered an unworthy subject. But according to the viewpoint of your slave, astronomy and mathematics are of very little use. If these subjects are going to be taught by Westerners as regular studies, the damage will be great. . . Your slave has learned that the way to establish a nation is to lay emphasis on propriety and righteousness, not on power and plotting. The fundamental effort lies in the minds of people, not in techniques. Now, if we seek trifling arts and respect barbarians as teachers regardless of the possibility that the cunning barbarians may not teach us their essential techniques — even if the teachers sincerely teach and the students faithfully study them, all that can be accomplished is the training of mathematicians. From ancient down to modern times, your slave has never heard of anyone who could use mathematics to raise the nation from a state of decline or to strengthen it in time of weakness. The empire is so great that one should not worry lest there be any lack of abilities therein. If astronomy and mathematics have to be taught, an extensive search should find someone who has mastered the technique. Why is it limited to barbarians, and why is it necessary to learn from the barbarians?

Moreover, the barbarians are our enemies. In 1860 they took up arms and rebelled against us. Our capital and its suburb were invaded, our ancestral altar was shaken, our Imperial palace was burned, and our officials and people were killed or wounded. There had never been such insults during the last 200 years of our dynasty. All our scholars and officials have been stirred with heart-burning rage, and have retained their hatred until the present. Our court could not help making peace with the barbarians. How can we forget this enmity and this humiliation even for one single day?

Since the conclusion of the peace [p. 25], Christianity has been prevalent and half of our ignorant people have been fooled by it. The only thing we can rely on is that our scholars should clearly explain to the people the Confucian tenets, which may be able to sustain the minds of the ignorant populace. Now if these brilliant and talented scholars, who have been trained by the nation and reserved for great future usefulness, have to change from their regular course of study to follow the barbarians, then the correct spirit will not be developed, and accordingly the evil spirit will become stronger. After several years it will end in nothing less than driving the multitudes of the Chinese people into allegiance to the barbarians.

Reverently your slave has read the instruction to the grand councillors and officers of the nine government bureaus in the *Collected Essays of the K'ang-hsi Emperor*, in which he says, "After a thousand or several hundred years, China must be harmed by the various countries of Europe." The deep and far-reaching concern of the sage Emperor is admirable. Even though he used their methods, he actually hated them. Now, the empire has already been harmed by them. Should we further spread their influence and fan the flame? Your slave has heard that when the barbarians spread their religion, they hate Chinese scholars who are not willing to learn it. Now scholars from the regular channels are ordered to study under foreigners. Your slave fears that what our scholars are going to learn cannot be learnt well and yet will be perplexing, which would just fall in with (the foreigners') plans. It is earnestly hoped that, in order to maintain the general prestige of the empire and to prevent the development of disaster, the Imperial mind will independently decide to abolish instantly the previous decision to establish such studies in the language school. The whole empire will be fortunate indeed.!

DOC. 20. THE TSUNGLI YAMEN'S REBUTTAL, 1867 [8]

Your ministers have examined the memorial of Wo-jen: the principles he presents are very lofty and the opinion he maintains is very orthodox. Your ministers' point of view was also like that before they began to manage foreign affairs; and yet today they do not presume to insist on such ideas, because of actual difficulties which they cannot help. . .

From the beginning of foreign relations to the present there have been twenty or thirty years. At first the officials inside and outside the capital did not grasp the crux of the matter, and whether they negotiated peace or discussed war, generally there were empty words without effect; and so the incident of 1860 arose. At that time the foreign troops approached our city wall, and the gun-fire and flames illuminated the sky. The capital was in peril day and night. Scholars and officials either stood about, putting their hands in their sleeves, or fled away confusedly. Our deceased Emperor did not consider his ministers, I-hsin [Prince Kung] and others, to be unworthy, and ordered them to remain in Peking to manage the peace negotiations. Your ministers dared not imitate the vain and bitter cry of Chia I [201–169 B.C., a famous scholar who grieved so bitterly at the death of his prince that he died within the year],[9] . . . nor would they use empty words in perfunctory performance of their duties. . . It has been eight years since the conclusion of the [1860] treaty. The matters in negotiation between China and the West have been extremely difficult. Your ministers jointly have tried their best to maintain the situation, and in recent days the Westerners have been generally docile and agreeable. However [p. 2], while merely to get along with them for the time being is all right, it is not possible in this way to protect ourselves for several years or decades to come. Therefore your ministers have pondered a long-term policy and discussed the situation thoroughly with all the provincial officials. Proposals to learn the written and spoken languages of foreign countries, the various methods of making machines, the training of troops with foreign guns, the dispatching of officials to travel in all countries, the investigation of their local customs and social conditions, and the establishment of six armies in the area of the capital in order to protect it — all these painstaking and special decisions represent nothing other than a struggle for self-strengthening.

Moreover, the principal means which foreigners employ to secure victory is the use of steamships and firearms first of all. Formerly, because the Europeans in making firearms did not care how much capital they used and also because firearms have their roots in astronomy and geometry and are developed by trigonometry and mathematics, so that their guns can be cleverly discharged and marvelously hit the mark, the censor Wei Mu-t'ing requested that at Shanghai and other spots factories be established [see Ch. VII above]. . . Your ministers have also discussed this in correspondence with Tseng Kuo-fan, Li Hung-chang, Tso Tsung-t'ang, Ying-kuei, Kuo Sung-tao, Chiang I-li, and others. They all agreed that the clever methods for manufacturing must begin with mathematics. . .

We are afraid that the people who are learning these things will have no power of discrimination and are likely to be led astray by foreigners, as Wo-jen fears. Therefore we have deliberated and decided that those who participate in the examinations must be persons from regular scholastic channels. It is indeed those students who have read widely and who understand right principles and have their minds set upon upright and grand purposes — and the present situation is just what causes the scholars and officials to feel pain in heart and head — who would certainly be able to lie on faggots and taste gall [i.e., nurse vengeance] in order to encourage each other vigorously to seek the actual achievement of self-strengthening. They are different from those who have vague, easygoing, or indifferent ideas.

Wo-jen says that the barbarians are our enemies. Naturally this shows that he also has the intention of lying on faggots and tasting gall. But let us ask, is his nursing of vengeance in this way for the purpose of gaining a temporary fame, or is he going to seek actual results? If [p. 3] he says that he seeks results, then let us ask, should he seek results from the foolish and mean fellows, or should he seek them from among the scholars and officials? That is why your ministers' Tsungli Yamen has requested that only people coming from the regular channels take the examinations for the language school. Now upon reading Wo-jen's memorial, one gathers that he considers this action to be absolutely impracticable. The grand secretary has long enjoyed a flourishing reputation for Neo-Confucian studies. As soon as his idea is expressed, there will undoubtedly be a large number from among the scholars and officials who will agree with him. Ever since your ministers have managed foreign affairs, they have always hoped to get the opinions of others so as to use them for greater advantage in the handling of current events; they have never dared to cherish the slightest idea of avoiding such opinions. But this memorial of Wo-jen will not only inhibit scholars henceforth from going forward, but also, we are particularly afraid, will make those inside and outside the capital, who are sincerely performing their duties with no inclination to empty talk, become disappointed and discouraged. Then what your ministers and provincial officials have planned for several years will fail in one morning — this is indeed of great concern.

Your ministers have thought again and again and found that the foreigners who dare to come to China and act as they wish without any restriction do so because their minds have been made up and their designs have accumulated during the last several decades. The Chinese spoken and written languages, the important and unimportant geographic areas, and even a single word or a single action by us, they all know completely; whereas concerning the actions of their race, we do not know a thing. We merely continue our empty talk about moral principles and righteousness, and confusedly argue without end. Now the time for treaty revisions after a ten year period will soon come [i.e., in 1868]. Even if we plan and think about it day and night, it is already too late. If we remain contented with our ignorance, we are deeply concerned lest the situation will deteriorate like a stream running downhill every day. Yet as soon as we seek for some method of pursuing knowledge, then again public opinion will criticize us right and left. One mistake is enough; how can we bear to make another? . . .

Even though we run the risk of receiving the criticism of the empire we will not try to avoid it. But the grand secretary [Wo-jen] considers our action a hindrance. Certainly he should have some better plans. If he really has some marvelous plan which can control foreign countries and not let us be controlled by them, your ministers should certainly follow the footsteps of the grand secretary, exhausting their mean abilities in careful discussions with him, in order to show our harmony and mutual help, and to console your Imperial anxiety. If he has no other plan than to use loyalty and sincerity as armor, and propriety and righteousness as a shield, and such similar phrases, and if he says that these words could accomplish diplomatic negotiations and be sufficient to control the life of our enemies, your ministers indeed do not presume to believe it. . .

CHAPTER IX. TSO TSUNG-T'ANG AND THE FOOCHOW SHIPYARD

Tso Tsung-t'ang (1812–1885) was born into a poor peasant family of Hsiangyin and lived for a long time with his wife's family in Hsiangtan. (Tseng Kuo-fan, Tso Tsung-t'ang, and Mao Tse-tung were born and bred in neighboring districts of Hunan.) Being in straitened financial circumstances, Tso spent the first forty years of his life chiefly as a school teacher and gentleman farmer before he served in the army. In this period he associated with the scholar Ho Ch'ang-ling (1785–1848), who was the compiler, assisted by Wei Yuan (see Doc. 3), of the famous "Collection of essays by Ch'ing scholars of practical use to society" (Huang-ch'ao ching-shih wen-pien), and he participated three times (1833, 1835, 1838) in the metropolitan examinations but failed to get the chin-shih degree. After his third failure, Tso shifted his interest from memorizing Confucian classics for the examinations to pursuing knowledge for practical use. He read works on history and geography by early Ch'ing nationalist thinkers, such as Ku Yen-wu (see Ch. IIa), and also a large official work on the geography of Chinese Turkestan compiled in 1756–1782. This special study of works on Chinese topography and economics later proved helpful to his military campaigns and economic reconstruction work in the Northwest.

Tso was directly influenced by Lin Tse-hsü. When Lin passed through Changsha in 1849, Tso had a long talk with him and discussed all sorts of topics for a whole night. He was also fond of the Hai-kuo t'u-chih (see Doc. 3) and once urged a relative to make a special study of it; in 1875 he wrote a preface to a new edition. Finally Tso's plans for the Foochow shipyard were carried out by Lin's son-in-law, Shen Pao-chen (1820–1879). Tso served as tutor (1840–1848) in the family of his friend, T'ao Chu (1779–1839), a governor-general of Kiangsu, Kiangsi, and Anhwei. It was during this period that his talents were recognized by Hu Lin-i (1812–1861), a general and statesman of Hunan, who later became his patron. His personal connections with the great scholars and officials of his native province gave Tso some insight into state affairs, and he watched closely the development of events during the Opium War. His interest in the use of Western arms dates from this period.

In 1852 he was recommended by Hu Lin-i to fight against the Taipings. Due to his unusual ability, he was made governor-general of Fukien and Chekiang in 1864, and he recovered the latter province in the same year, with the help of French officers and soldiers, from whom he acquired a better knowledge of Western weapons. Like Tseng, he also directed the building of a steamboat by native mechanics, and tried it out on the West Lake at Hangchow. Since its speed was unsatisfactory, he sought the counsel of two French engineers in 1864. In his insistence on steamships as a means of China's self-strengthening, he was one of the first proponents of a modern Chinese navy. Later he became enthusiastic about torpedoes and wished to invite German experts to make them.[1]

But although Tso liked to employ foreign experts, he would not rely entirely on them. He wrote, "The method of self-strengthening should be to seek from among ourselves, not seek from among others. He who seeks the help of others will be controlled by others, and he who relies upon himself will have the situation under his own control." [2] Frankness and self-assurance were two of his chief characteristics.

Tso Tsung-t'ang was also an able administrator. As governor-general, he did a great deal toward the rehabilitation and reconstruction of Chekiang and Fukien after the suppression of the Taiping Rebellion. In Fukien, he selected a site for the shipyard at Ma-wei near Foochow (August 1866), and appointed two Frenchmen, Prosper Giquel (1835–1886) and Paul d'Aiguebelle (1831–1875), to serve as engineers and supervisors. He also planned a school, attached to the shipyard, to train young men to build and man ships. Some of the students of this school, such as Yen Fu (1853–1921, see Ch. XVI), later became famous. It is difficult to say whether Tso Tsung-t'ang was trying to develop a competitive program paralleling Tseng's Shanghai Arsenal; although Tseng and Tso, being leaders of the same province, were not on especially good terms, both were persistent in carrying out their plans. Document 21, below, indicates that Tso expected his plan for the Foochow shipyard to encounter many hindrances and criticisms from lethargic and conservative officials, who were quick in criticizing new undertakings but slow in presenting constructive proposals of their own. After submitting many memorials and receiving imperial approval, and after having put some of his plans into effect, Tso was transferred to Shensi, Kansu, and Sinkiang.

Tso's chief contribution was made in the barren area of the Northwest, where he spent more than twelve years (1868–1880). There he faced four great difficulties: money, food, ammunition, and transportation. To solve these problems, in a poor, thinly populated, culturally backward, politically corrupt, and rebellious area, far from the center of China, was a tough job. In order to save money and energy he aimed to complete the task according to a five-year plan which he reported to the emperor in advance. He ordered his soldiers, most or all of whom were originally peasants, to become military colonists, i.e., to raise their own food, improve irrigation, dig wells, and dredge rivers. They also planted thousands of trees for which travelers today, on the long shaded highways of Chinese Turkestan, are said to be still grateful. For the making of clothes, he attempted to transform the village handicrafts into a modern machine industry by encouraging cotton planting, improving sericulture, and opening woolen and cotton mills. For ammunition he established a manufacturing bureau in Shensi (1866) with an arsenal (1871) and a gunpowder factory (1875) at Lanchow. He employed Chinese, German, and other foreign mechanics to direct this work.

For money Tso reorganized the land, salt, tea, likin, and other taxes. He fought against greedy Manchu officials and abolished much red tape. His financial and supply operations for many years were handled by the famous treaty-port banker, Hu Kuang-yung, who maintained a depot at Shanghai and raised funds from foreign merchants. In 1867 Tso contracted such a loan for 1,200,000 taels, and thereafter he floated similar "foreign" loans four times (1868, 1877, 1878, 1881), totaling 15,750,000 taels.[3] His total expenditure in the Northwest is estimated to have been about one hundred million taels.[4] He cast coins and silver dollars and also attempted in 1878 to establish a modern bank and even to open gold mines.

For transportation Tso established his own system, running from Hu Kuang-yung's office at Shanghai through a provisions depot at Hankow, which gathered food and other local products from the interior, and a general transportation office at Sian. For cultural purposes, he established a printing office at Sian to print important books, and opened academies and free schools to educate the people. Although criticized for cruelty to the rebels, he worked hard on rehabilitation, provided effective famine relief, and prohibited the planting of poppy and smoking of opium.

His periodic fiscal reports, reproduced in his collected writings, are quite detailed (no such reports are included in Li Hung-chang's works). Tso was a diehard — advocating war against France, Russia, or any other foreign aggressor. He had a simple belief that in negotiation with a foreign power there were only three possible lines to follow: offense, defense, and peace; but one must be able to fight an offensive war before one could defend onself, and one must be able to defend oneself before a fair peace treaty could be obtained.[5]

Although the following document comes from an earlier and less successful phase of his official career, it shows Tso Tsung-t'ang's grasp of detail and vigorous imagination.

DOC. 21. Tso's Plans of 1866 [6]

The great advantage of southeast China lies on the water and not on land. From Kwangtung and Fukien, to Chekiang, Kiangnan, Shantung, Chihli, and Shenking around to the Northwest, the three sides of China are surrounded by vast seas. . . In time of peace, we could use ships for grain transport; then a thousand *li* would be as if at one's threshold; if we used them for trade, then hundreds of commodities would be gathered in the markets. . . When some incident occurs, steamships could be used for mobilization and then the forces of the hundred clans of Kwangtung could be concentrated into the three states of Korea. . . Since warfare has opened up on the sea, the steam warships of various European countries have come directly to Tientsin. Our national defense line has actually become fictitious. Their ships sail as rapidly as a shooting star or a whirlwind and we have no way to stop them.

Since foreign ships were permitted to carry away northern goods to be sold in the various ports, the prices of commodities in North China have been exorbitantly high. The great merchants of Kiangsu and Chekiang, who used to make sea transportation their profession . . . cannot reduce their prices to compete with the foreign merchants. . .

Hitherto, ministers within and without the capital have repeatedly discussed the purchase of steamships instead of building them, but no one has yet presumed to discuss the establishment of a plant to build them. The reasons are, first, the difficulty of selecting a place for the shipyard; second, the difficulty of finding and buying steamship machinery; third, the difficulty of engaging head mechanics; fourth, the difficulty of raising and accumulating a huge amount of funds; fifth, the difficulty that the Chinese [p. 2] are unaccustomed to navigation and that after the completion of the ships we would still have to engage foreigners; sixth, the difficulties of the numerous requirements of expenditures for coal, salaries, and wages after the ships have been completed, all of which would have to be paid every month, in addition to which from time to time the ships would have to be repaired. Seventh, in this unusual enterprise it is easy for slander and criticism to arise; one person initiates the plan, another carries it out, while a third is a mere bystander; and if the enterprise fails near its completion, then both public and private loss will result. With these several difficulties, it is no wonder that there is no man who cares to take the responsibility. . .

Your minister humbly believes that if we desire to prevent harm from the sea and, at the same time, to receive its advantages, we must reorganize our navy; if we wish to reorganize our navy, we must establish a plant, to supervise and build steamships. The Europeans are skilful but we Chinese do not have to be content with our stupidity. . . It is not impossible to get the machines.

As to the difficulty of engaging foreign head mechanics, we may first lay down the requirements in the contract and fix their salaries, and after they arrive at the machine shops, the office will select from the interior young and bright craftsmen in various lines, to learn from and practise with them. Those who have brilliant talent and clever ideas, regardless of whether they are officials, gentry, scholars or ordinary people, should all alike go to the plant for study and practice.

[P. 3] It is estimated that the building of the shipyard, the buying of machinery, and the recruiting of head mechanics must cost more than three hundred thousand taels; and that the starting of the work and gathering of materials, together with the payment of salaries to the Chinese and foreign mechanics, will require approximately fifty or sixty thousand taels each month. Figuring for a year, it will require a cost of more than six hundred thousand taels. . . .

We are concerned lest after the completion of the ships we have no qualified captains to watch the compass, control the helm, and the like, for all of which we shall have to hire foreigners. To obviate this difficulty, it should be distinctly indicated when the contract is first made that the teaching of shipbuilding will at the same time include navigation. As soon as a ship is finished, some Chinese will immediately be ordered to accompany the foreign mechanics to sea and sail to all the seaports. Regardless of whether they are soldiers, officers, or people in other fields, if any one of them has learned his job thoroughly and is able to become a captain, he will immediately be granted a military rank. . .

[P. 4] In an unusual enterprise, it is easy to incur slander or criticism. At the beginning people will worry about the lack of accomplishment; then they will criticize the expenditure as being too much, and will probably also say sarcastically that we have lost our national dignity. All this is imaginable and probably will happen. . . In the East, it was Japan that first bought a steamship, and then took it apart for examination and imitation. But they have not yet had any success. Recently Japan sent people to England to learn her language and study her mathematics as the basis for building steamships. Within a few years the steamships of the Eastern foreigners are certain to be successful. Only China, owing to the widespread fighting in recent years, has not yet had leisure to discuss this matter. . . Both Japan and China see the potential advantages on the high seas; Japan has something to rely upon and we alone have nothing. It is like crossing a river where others are rowing a boat while we are making a raft. It is like racing when others are riding on a steed while we are riding on a donkey. How is this possible? All of us are human beings, whose intelligence and wisdom are, by nature, similar; but in practice we cannot help being different. Chinese wisdom is spent on abstract things; the foreigners' intelligence is concentrated upon concrete things. Chinese take the principles of the classics as the foundation, and mechanical matters as the practical details; foreigners consider mechanical matters important, principles unimportant. Each of the two believes what it thinks right and neither can understand the other. . .

When the steamships are completed, the administration of grain transport will be prosperous, the military administration will be improved, the merchants' distress will be relieved and the customs duties will be greatly increased. The temporary cost will produce profit for several generations.

As for Chinese imitation of foreign ship construction, some people will probably think that we have lost our national prestige. This is still more wrong. [Tso here describes China's imitation of Western cannon in the seventeenth century.] Recently we have also been able to manufacture foreign guns, cannon and other weapons, whose foreign style China is imitating. If cannon can be imitated, why can ships alone not be imitated? How can this be considered a loss of our national prestige?

4

EFFORTS AT SELF-STRENGTHENING

1871–1896

CHAPTER X. THE PROBLEM OF LEADERSHIP:
PERSONALITIES AND INSTITUTIONS

The response of Ch'ing officialdom to Western military power seems to have gone through a curious cycle: the brief activity of the Opium War period was followed by the stagnant xenophobia of the 1850's, the promising innovations of the 1860's were followed by an apparent diminution of effort in the 1870's and 1880's. Thereafter, one might point to a renewal of creative effort after the defeat by Japan in 1895, as though China's attempted regeneration in each period had required the shock of actual foreign aggression and defeat to provide its stimulus. When the heat was off, the effort at reform cooled down. At any rate, the 1870's and 1880's appear to record a slowing down of the attempt at meeting the West by self-strengthening. Perhaps this impression merely reflects the fact that less research has been done on these decades: perhaps, on the other hand, self-strengthening as it proceeded met increasing opposition or obstacles which could not be overcome.

One key to this problem was in the realm of leadership. We therefore devote attention first of all to Li Hung-chang and his subordinates, as leaders in Westernization in the provinces, and then to the holders of power in Peking, particularly the Empress Dowager. The difficulties of Westernization can be seen in the projects for training students and setting up diplomatic legations abroad, and for building railroads and creating a real navy at home. All of these were essential developments for China, yet in every case there was at work against them a remarkable recalcitrance and inertia, which delayed their achievement for many years.

Behind these phenomena it should become apparent as serious research progresses that China's slowness in self-strengthening was due in part to the fact that the officials concerned were more interested in profit to themselves than in progress for their country. Li Hung-chang, for example, put his own men into the key positions from which China's modernization was supposed to be directed; most of them profited accordingly through the perquisites of power which these modernization projects carried with them.

a. *Li Hung-chang and his Subordinates*

Li Hung-chang (1823–1901), whom we have quoted already in Chapter VII, was born into a well-to-do family of Ho-fei, Anhwei. At the early age of twenty-four, he gained the *chin-shih* degree as well as an appointment in the Hanlin Academy. There he studied informally under Tseng Kuo-fan and this connection laid the foundation for his future career. From the age of thirty to forty-five (1853 to 1868), Li was in military service suppressing the Taiping and the Nien rebels, rising from a post as staff officer to independent command. As a military commander, he seems to have usually judged situations correctly and laid down careful plans well in advance. With the help of the foreign-led Ever-Victorious Army, organized before he was dispatched to Shanghai in 1862, Li recovered the province of Kiangsu within two years, which facilitated the final capture of Nanking; he was also able to wipe out the Nien rebels in 1868 after more than twenty other commanders had failed. His military success has been attributed partly to the influence of his patron Tseng Kuo-fan, who helped him organize the Huai (or Anhwei) Army, on the model of Tseng's own Hunan Army.

As an official, Li Hung-chang held many high posts, some of them concurrently: governor of Kiangsu (1862–1865), grand secretary (1872–1901), minister of the Tsungli Yamen (1896–1898), commissioner to the coronation of Tsar Nicholas II (1896) and governor-general of Liang-kuang (1900–1901). His principal post, however, was that of governor-general of Chihli from 1870 to 1895, the fateful decades before the defeat by Japan.

Li's position of leadership in China was in *yang-wu,* or "foreign matters." This term included the conduct of diplomatic relations and the borrowing of Western technology, two activities that were indeed aspects of a single problem, how to survive in the modern world. The foreign-style enterprises were begun mainly for military purposes and followed one another in a logical sequence. To suppress the rebellions and for coastal defense, there were, first, the establishment of arsenals and shipyards, and the building of forts and vessels. Secondly, technicians were needed to make these weapons and so schools were established and students and officers sent to study abroad. Since modern defense required modern communication and transport, the construction of telegraph lines and the organization of a steamship line were undertaken. Eventually, since modern defense also required money and material resources, a cotton textile factory was established, and coal, iron, and gold mines were opened.

Li Hung-chang understood that machinery was the dynamic of Western civilization and so he made use of it. But from the beginning he lacked an over-all plan to be carried out step by step and merely began one thing after another according to current needs. As for the modern schools and the sending of students abroad, the aim was not so much to promote academic studies as to meet military needs or diplomatic problems. To Li Hung-chang's mind, the wealth and power of the Western countries were derived entirely along these material lines; that was apparently the full scope of his *yang-wu* or "foreign matters." He did not recognize the value of European political and social institutions, much though he might pay them lip service.

On the contrary, Li seems to have thought that the Chinese political and educational systems and Chinese culture and customs were all superior to those of foreign countries — except for cannon, railways, and machinery, in which China was inferior. If China could learn to use these material things, then Li would have fulfilled his duty in the handling of foreign matters. The fallacy of this reasoning was conclusively revealed in 1894 when the Chinese army and navy were almost completely crushed in brief encounters with the Japanese forces.

To blame Li Hung-chang personally for the debacle of 1894 does not seem to be entirely fair. Among the scholar-officials of his day, he was certainly one of the ablest and he probably understood as much about the problems of modernization as any other Chinese in a responsible post.[1] The fact that he could hold his high position for almost a quarter of a century shows his political astuteness. His prestige among foreigners in China, though qualified, was quite unequalled. The failure of China's modernization program during this period should be attributed mainly to the anti-foreign conservatism of the Chinese educated class as a whole, and to the selfishness of the Empress Dowager and certain high officials at her court in particular. Whenever a new project based on a Western example was proposed, opposition would be voiced at once, mostly on ideological rather than factual grounds. These unrealistic outcries often influenced the decision of the court against a proposal and in some cases put a stop to programs already started. As Li frequently took the lead in proposing these modernization projects, he bore the brunt of the conservatives' onslaught. Regarding this problem, he once remarked: [2]

The present situation is one in which, externally, it is necessary for us to be harmonious with the barbarians, and internally, it is necessary for us to reform our institutions. If we remain conservative, without making any change, the nation will be daily reduced and weakened. . . Now all the foreign countries are having one reform after another, and progressing every day like the ascending of steam. Only China continues to preserve her traditional institutions so cautiously that even though she be ruined and extinguished, the conservatives will not regret it. Oh heaven and man! How can we understand the cause of it?

Other obstacles in the way of modernization were the traditional administrative practices and the personal ethics underlying them. Any official in charge of a public project would generally "milk" it as much as possible and use bribery to prevent the revelation of his malfeasance. Considering this circumstance, Li's accomplishments were actually rather remarkable. He was probably the least conservative high official of his day.

To undertake all the enterprises he initiated, Li Hung-chang was dependent on men of ability to assist him. Among the large number of his subordinates from 1870 to 1894 and after, some were men of proven integrity, most were given to extravagance, and a few were downright dishonest, but many were recognized for their abilities either in secretarial duties or as administrators. In addition to these two categories, there were under Li's direction army and naval officers, directors of education, and men in business or finance who were connected with his enterprises. There were also a number of Western advisers, some in his employ, some consulted occasionally, and some regularly, as in the case of the Tientsin Customs Commissioner, Gustav Detring.[3]

The staff members collected by Li Hung-chang compare favorably in intelligence with those of his teacher and predecessor, Tseng Kuo-fan, and those of his junior competitor, Chang Chih-tung. Tseng's staff seems to have included more men of character, used to simple living and devoted to studies; and under Tseng, men of talent, like Tso Tsung-t'ang and Li himself, perhaps, had more chance for individual development. Chang Chih-tung, however, insisted on doing everything himself, and very few of his subordinates went on to high position, although, on the other hand, none of his protégés was notorious for the accumulation of great personal wealth. Compared with these other groups, Li's lieutenants were more given to extravagant habits. Perhaps he used the chance of personal gain as bait to secure the services of able men. In any case, while his army and navy proved ineffective because of corruption and his industrial enterprises were of indifferent value to China, Li himself left a fortune, as did many of the men connected with his enterprises. This pattern did not disappear during the Republican period. Perhaps we can call it, without tangling with communist terminology, "official capitalism."·

Among the more prominent of Li's lieutenants were his personal secretaries, such as Hsueh Fu-ch'eng (see Ch. XV b), Chang P'ei-lun (1848–1903), Yü Shih-mei (1859–1915), and Wu Ju-lun (1840–1903); able administrators, such as T'ang T'ing-shu (1832–1892, founder of the China Merchants Steam Navigation Company and K'ai-p'ing Mining Corporation), Chou Fu (1837–1921), Sheng Hsuan-huai (1844–1916), and Yuan Shih-k'ai (1859–1916); and also men who had studied abroad, such as Ma Chien-chung (1844–1900, in France) and Yen Fu (1853–1921, in England).

Of the men mentioned above (out of a much larger number), one of those with the most influence on Chinese thought in the period ending in 1896, was Hsueh Fu-ch'eng. Hsueh had been a secretary on Tseng Kuo-fan's staff for eight years (1865–1872) before he joined that of Li Hung-chang in 1875. He served under Li until 1884, and later was concurrently minister to England, France, Italy, and Belgium for four years (1890–1894). We devote a later section to his essays on reform (Doc. 40).

b. *The Empress Dowager's Influence*

In the last decades of the nineteenth century, when China was in dire need of intelligent leadership under which to catch up with the West by modernization, the dominant figure at the court was not Prince Kung but a Manchu woman, the famous Empress Dowager, Tz'u-hsi (1835–1908).[4] A concubine of Emperor Hsien-feng, she had risen to the rank of Empress Dowager in 1861 when her son, Emperor T'ung-chih (1856–1875), ascended the throne at the age of five. She became co-regent with her late husband's principal wife, who was, however, only a figurehead. By allying herself with the deceased emperor's younger brothers, Prince Kung and Prince Ch'un, this able woman staged her first political maneuver and got rid of eight powerful but unpopular grand councillors who had themselves been plotting against her. Prince Kung then joined the regency and was made head of the Grand Council as well as of the Tsungli Yamen, in a position to act both for the throne and for the central government.

When in 1865 the throne had become fairly secure after the victory over the Taiping Rebellion, the Empress Dowager precipitated a quarrel with Prince Kung, removed him from the regency, and left him as head of the Grand Council. In other words, the prince was relegated to the level of a court official, albeit *primus inter pares.* In January 1875, when her son died without issue, the Empress Dowager adopted the son of Prince Ch'un and of her own sister, who was the prince's wife. Thus she resumed her power as regent, ruling for another child emperor, Kuang-hsü (1875–1908), and thereafter she never really relinquished that power. Except for a period of retirement from 1889 to 1898, she remained in effect the ruler of China.

Like most Manchu officials of that time, the Empress Dowager could read and write Chinese as her native language and learned a little Manchu just to get by in routine matters. She had a keen mind and, although not well educated, could grasp enough of the essentials of administration to meet her needs within the court and deal with the high officials, princes of the imperial family, and others serving within the palace, such as bannermen and eunuchs of the Imperial Household. With a dominant will and an understanding of human nature, she controlled high personages through forceful leadership, flattery, money, the delegation of authority, and unabashed power, as might be necessary, and generally succeeded in lining them up to support her. She could play the role of a helpless widow with a young child, and make it hard for men in the society of China to refuse her requests. Alternatively she could be ruthlessly insistent on her wishes and threaten the use of her authority to do away with any opponent.

Under her administration of the imperial bureaucracy, the provincial officials obtained much greater freedom of action than ever before in the dynasty. The more important governors general enjoyed unusually long tenures of office. There was a marked tendency among the Manchus to admit tacitly their own inadequacy and yield the important posts in the provinces to the Chinese. The Chinese officials who received this trust seem to have outdone one another in showing their loyalty to the throne, as of course their class had been sedulously trained to do for two centuries past. But possibly it is to the credit of the Empress Dowager that an atmosphere of Manchu-Chinese coöperation persisted so strongly in the Ch'ing dynasty, even during great crises in its period of decline.

In the realm of foreign affairs, although the Empress Dowager followed the general advice of her officials, there seemed to be always present in her mind a feeling of hatred toward the foreigners. Perhaps the only exceptions were those who worked for the Ch'ing government. It was the foreigners who had forced the court including herself to flee from the old summer palace (Yuan-ming yuan) near Peking in 1860 and who had sacked it in retaliation for mistreatment of allied envoys. The Empress Dowager apparently set her heart on restoring the summer palace and, in spite of opposition from many quarters, she cajoled and browbeat the high officials into rebuilding at least a part of it.

Another less publicized aspect of the Empress Dowager's conduct was her addiction to taking gifts or bribes from her officials. This had been done by every Manchu emperor before her and by almost all the officials throughout the dynasty, but she carried it to an extreme. In the old Chinese government, every superior expected something from his subordinates, while on the bottom layer the lowest officials made exactions from the people. The least corruptible officials — who were rather rare in this late period — were those who lived within their salaries and accepted just enough gifts or customary fees to meet their necessary expenses of office. Bribery, in the form of gifts, became an unwritten institution, and a minimum amount was customarily set for every kind of official transaction. At the pinnacle of officialdom, the Empress Dowager received some remuneration for every official audience, which by regulation was a necessary formality for all newly appointed or promoted officials and for high provincial officials who had held their posts for a number of years. A minimum sum was set for each rank and position, depending roughly on its lucrativeness to the incumbent. The Empress Dowager shared this income with her chief eunuchs and certain courtiers, usually the imperial princes who were supposed to officiate at the audiences. Although this debilitating practice was not new, under the Empress Dowager it had a marked growth in volume, much to the demoralization of the government service. In the case of Li Hung-chang, it is an interesting question how much his long tenure as governor-general of Chihli was due to his generous gifts to the Empress Dowager and her favorites.

Against this background, projects for modernization had to pay their way not only on the books, but in the purses of the officials. At the top, the ruler of China not only condoned "the system" but energetically applied it. The most notorious scandal of the period symbolized China's administrative problem:

millions of taels of silver accumulated for the purpose of building the modern navy were somehow turned over to the Empress Dowager to expend on the re-building of the Summer Palace (I-ho-yuan). Whether the Chinese navy could have defeated the Japanese in 1894, even if these millions had been spent on it, may still be open to conjecture. But misappropriation by the Empress Dowager, condoned, however unwillingly, by Li Hung-chang, certainly sealed China's fate. Today, the famous marble barge still stands in the Summer Palace lake as a reminder of this fiasco, its marble paddle wheels carved upon its sides.[5]

In 1874, during the Formosa incident, but twenty years before the dénouement with Japan, the aged Wen-hsiang emerged from retirement to speak plainly to the throne.

DOC. 22. WEN-HSIANG'S WARNING OF DISASTER, 1874 [6]

When the peace negotiations were completed [in 1860] everybody spoke of the necessity for self-strengthening, yet during the last ten years or more there has been little achievement [p. 13]. The reason is that those who look down upon and disregard foreign affairs merely have empty discussions without actual accomplishment, whereas those who are accustomed to the peaceful situation are content when nothing happens for fear that if anything is done it may arouse the suspicion of the foreigners. Even those who care-fully discuss defense measures are hindered by the insufficiency of funds, and nothing can be done or developed. Now the (Formosa) incident has al-ready taken shape, a war crisis is imminent. If we still do not pay attention to it and suddenly the great enemy (Japan) confronts us, what can we rely upon? It is humbly hoped that imperial orders will be sent to the Ministry of Revenue and the Imperial Household Department to raise plenty of the necessary supplies, to cut off lavish expenditures, to stop public works which are not urgent [i.e., the construction of the Summer Palace], and to plan for the most needed coastal defense; so that the ministers at the capital and in the provinces can all devote their energy to the scheme.

As for the way to make ourselves strong, it lies first in our readiness to accept advice in a humble manner in order to seek out the good and bad points of our administration. One should not take agreeable and soothing words as a source of pleasure and take straightforward and frank advice as distasteful. When Your Majesty is concerned to work diligently and alertly, then your ministers within and without the capital will be stimulated in spirit and not dare to follow their traditional dawdling habits. Otherwise they will remain accustomed to taking things complacently and will never think of reforms, in which case, I fear that internally and externally the country will fall apart, the people's confidence will be shaken, and the disaster will be unspeakable.

CHAPTER XI. TRAINING STUDENTS ABROAD

a. *The Educational Mission to the United States*

The traditional Confucian emphasis on human abilities and the enlisting of talented men in administration, which underlay the classical examination system, led inevitably to the idea of training Chinese in Western countries. As we have seen above, the incompetence and essential illiteracy of the Cantonese interpreters or "linguists," criticized by Feng Kuei-fen (see Doc. 8), and the importance of "foreign matters," especially the need for Western guns and ships, had brought the Chinese government to found the T'ung-wen Kuan, or College of Foreign Languages, at Peking in 1862 as a subordinate office to the Tsungli Yamen, and a school of Western languages and science in Shanghai in 1863, which was annexed to the Kiangnan Arsenal in 1869. A number of foreign instructors had been invited, but their faithfulness was suspected by some conservative scholar-officials, such as Wo-jen (see Doc. 19). As time went on it became increasingly obvious that if China were to master the secrets of Western technology it would be necessary for the Chinese government to send young men to Western countries for training.

Records of Chinese visitors to the United States go back to 1785; a great deal remains to be done in studying the American end of early Sino-American contact. On the Chinese side attention has been directed chiefly to the project promoted by Yung Wing (1828–1912), the first Chinese graduate of an American university — Yale in 1854 — by which one hundred and twenty Chinese students were brought to the United States in the decade 1872–1881.[1] Somewhat less attention has been devoted to the project which sent thirty Chinese students to England and France for technical training in 1876. Private ventures under missionary auspices and on the part of overseas Chinese may have played a more important role than has been realized — Sun Yat-sen is one such example. Yung Wing has had many successors in the persons of Chinese students in the United States. All in all, the latter have constituted the greatest movement of conscious acculturation in history.

Below we present the key memorial to the Tsungli Yamen, by which Tseng and Li finally got the educational mission of 1872 started; a series of letters dealing with its cessation; and an instructive report from one of Li Hung-chang's bright young men, Ma Chien-chung (1844–1900). (References to Pin-ch'un and other officials sent abroad are explained in the next chapter, on diplomatic missions.)

DOC. 23. THE PROPOSAL OF TSENG AND LI IN 1871 [2]

Last autumn when (I, Tseng) Kuo-fan was at Tientsin, Governor Ting Jih-ch'ang frequently came to discuss with me proposals for the selection of young and brilliant youths to be sent to the schools of various European nations to study military administration, shipping administration, infantry tactics, mathematics, manufacturing, and other subjects. It is roughly estimated that after more than ten years their training will have been completed, and they will return to China so that the Chinese can learn thoroughly the new techniques in which the Westerners are particularly strong, and then we can gradually plan for self-strengthening. In addition he says that the men who can take [p. 20] these young boys to foreign countries — Ch'en Lan-pin [a *chin-shih* of 1853], who is an assistant secretary of the Board of

Punishments, fourth rank, and Yung Wing, who is a sub-prefect of Kiangsu — are both competent for the job. . . After Pin-ch'un [3] and two other gentlemen, Chih-kang and Sun Chia-ku, had traveled in various countries by Imperial command, they saw the essential aspects of conditions overseas, and they found that maps, mathematics, astronomy and navigation, shipbuilding, manufacturing, and other matters all give assistance to military affairs. All those who have studied in foreign countries and have learned the superior techniques are to be immediately invited by academies after their return to teach the various subjects and to continue their own scholarly development.

Article VII of the treaty recently concluded with the United States [1868] says that hereafter, if Chinese wish to enter the higher and lower levels of American government schools in order to learn various kinds of literature and sciences, they will enjoy equal treatment with the people of the "most favored nation." It also says that Americans will be allowed to establish schools in China at the places assigned by Chinese for foreign settlement, and the Chinese can also do the same thing in the United States, etc., . . . [4] The foreign nations allow us to learn their superior techniques together with their own citizens; Chih-kang, Sun, and other gentlemen have already pioneered the way and report that to go aboard a steamer and cross the Pacific Ocean directly to America takes only one month or more. For these reasons it should not be a very difficult matter.

To establish arsenals for manufacturing and to open schools for instruction in China is just the beginning of the struggle to rise again. To go abroad for study, to gather ideas and the benefits of greater knowledge can produce far-reaching and great results. Westerners seek knowledge for actual use. Regardless of whether they are scholars, workers, or soldiers, they all go to school to study and to understand the principles, to practise on the machines, and to get personally familiar with the work. They all exert themselves to the utmost of their ingenuity, and learn from one another, in the hope that there will be some monthly difference and yearly improvement. If we Chinese wish to adopt their superior techniques and suddenly try to buy all their machines, not only is our power insufficient to do this, but also there is no way for us to master either the fundamental principles or the details of the profound ideas contained in these superior techniques, unless we have actually seen them and practised with them for a long time. The ancients said: "He who wishes to learn the Ch'i dialect should place himself in the midst of Chuang or Yü" [names of streets in an old city of Ch'i, modern Shantung] and another proverb says, "To hear a hundred times is not as good as to see once. . . "

But there are two difficulties in the trial period. One is the selection of human talent [p. 21], and the other is the raising of funds. . . Kuo-fan and Hung-chang are deeply aware of these two difficulties. But to make a hill we must begin with one basketful of earth after another, and to raise mugwort we have to wait three years. We lay plans for it now, so that in the future the number of students will steadily increase. . . We plan to send functionaries to Shanghai to establish an office for the selection of brilliant youths from all provinces. The number for each year will be thirty persons, and for four years there will be a total of one hundred and twenty, to be sent in annual groups aboard ships across the ocean to study in foreign countries. After fifteen years, they will begin to return to China in sequence, according to the year when they were sent. It is estimated that on their return to China all these young men will be in the neighborhood of thirty years of age. Their energies will then be at their prime; they will be able to render their services at their best time of life.

We have heard that, heretofore, the sons of people of Fukien, Kwangtung, and Ningpo also occasionally have gone abroad to study, but they merely tried to get a rough acquaintance with foreign written and spoken languages in order to do business with the foreigners for the purpose of making a living. This time, at the beginning of the selection, we shall be doubly careful; the students being taken to foreign countries will all be controlled by the commissioners. Specializing in different fields of study, they will earnestly seek for thorough mastery of academic knowledge. There will also be interpreters, and instructors to teach them Chinese literature from time to time, so they will grasp the great principles for the establishment of character, in the hope of becoming men of useful abilities. Although not all of them will necessarily become mighty instruments, yet out of a large number of talented men some extraordinary ones will certainly emerge from their midst. This is the theory of obtaining five out of the ten selected. . .

If your honorable Yamen considers this to be practicable, as soon as we receive your reply, our office will immediately submit a joint memorial. The required [p. 22] funds will also be conveyed under a memorial and an Imperial order requested to have them appropriated from the foreign customs duties at Shanghai. . .

Perhaps the most remarkable thing about the Educational Mission thus inaugurated (after ten years of agitation by Yung Wing) was the fact that it actually functioned, more or less as planned, for a decade (1872–1881), only to be summarily discontinued at the end of that time with nothing to take its place!

Some of the reasons for the recall of the Mission are stated in detail by Yung Wing, *My Life in China and America*, chapter 18. He puts the chief blame on Wu Tzu-teng, a *chin-shih* of 1852, a compiler of the Hanlin Academy, and a good mathematician, who worked for some time in the Chinese legation at Paris, before he was transferred to the United States as superintendent of students attached to the Chinese Embassy.[5] Wu was fond of display and prestige, and acted even more autocratically than the old-fashioned Chinese educational commissioners who had preceded him. No sooner was he installed in his new position than he summoned all the Chinese students to Washington to receive his instructions. When the students came for the interview they did not perform the kotow. One of the subordinates of the new superintendent, a Mr. Chin, became very angry saying, "All these students have forgotten their original civilization and disregard their teachers and elders. Even though they might have some success in the academic field [which was then still uncertain], still they could not be of any use to China." Mr. Chin, who turned out to be a favorite of a certain influential noble of the imperial family, prepared a memorial asking to have the students suddenly recalled to China, in 1881. Other staff members of the Chinese Educational Mission disapproved of this action but no one dared to say anything (according to Yung Wing) except Yung Wing, who argued strongly but to no avail. Huang Tsun-hsien, then consul-general at San Francisco, upon hearing of this incident was so affected that he wrote a long sad poem to describe it.[6]

Although Yung Wing says the conservatives in the Educational Mission sent many reports to the Chinese government, slandering the young students, it is difficult to trace any of their original letters or reports. Their positions were low and perhaps their writings were neglected by compilers. Below we present excerpts from Li Hung-chang's correspondence to show the points of view opposed to that of Yung Wing.

DOC. 24. LETTERS OF LI HUNG-CHANG CONCERNING THE END OF THE MISSION, 1880–1881

[To Commissioner Ch'en Lan-pin, Aug. 6, 1879] [7] The enterprise of sending young people to foreign countries has cost a lot of money and created numerous evils, but after all will have little actual effect. The criticisms of Chinese officials and scholars have been numerous. Recently I received a letter from Tseng Chi-tse [Tseng Kuo-fan's son, "Marquis Tseng"], who considers that since the sending of students from the Foochow Shipyard to England and France has had no great result, those students who have been in the United States likewise will not necessarily show great achievement. . . If all you gentlemen who are in charge of the task still cherish differing opinions and cannot control and manage it seriously, you have certainly failed in the first attempt which was inaugurated by Tseng Kuo-fan; and you and I will also be greatly criticized by public opinion.

[Another letter to Ch'en Lan-pin, May 10, 1880].[8] Yung Wing has come to see me, saying it is true the students have neglected their Chinese studies. It is due to Yung Wing's obstinacy in not desiring these students to learn much Chinese. Even during the summer when the schools were closed and it was just the time for them to review their Chinese, Yung Wing alone did not think so. . . I hope you will give him advice when it is convenient and not allow him to take too much charge of the Mission, which should be reorganized by Compiler Wu Tzu-teng, in order to concentrate authority so that in the future, when these children have finished their study and return to China, there will still be posts to which to commission them, and we shall not fail in the original idea of sending them to study abroad.

[Li Hung-chang's comment on the withdrawal of a portion of the students, March 29, 1881.] [9] In recent years there has been considerable criticism of Yung Wing, charging that he has laid too much emphasis upon Western knowledge, with the result that the young boys have neglected their Chinese studies. I have written letters to guide him, not once but many times. . . Two years ago after Wu Tzu-teng went to the office of the Educational Mission, he repeatedly wrote to me saying that there were numerous evils in the Mission's affairs and that it ought to be abolished quickly. . .

I have reviewed the case with a candid mind and feel that, since more than half the students were natives of Kwangtung who went abroad at an early age, it is probably hard for them to avoid indulging in foreign customs. Wu Tzu-teng disciplined them too severely and so compounded the trouble. Consequently he thought that all the students should be withdrawn, an opinion which seems to be too extreme. On a later occasion when he wrote me he said that those students who had deeply indulged in American customs and who were stupid by nature should be sent back to China, while those who had already entered the universities and whose graduation was near, and whose achievements were comparatively concrete, might be transferred to be under the control of the Chinese Legation [p. 8]. As for the general supervisor, Chinese instructors, interpreters, and other officials, they could all be dismissed. . .

Yung Wing has managed this Mission for a long time. He feels that it concerns his face or dignity and it is imaginable that he does not want to have the Mission cancelled. . .

On June 8, 1881, the Tsungli Yamen memorialized requesting the abolition of the Educational Mission and the return of the students to be employed according to their abilities. The request was granted.[10]

b. Students in Europe

The flow of Chinese students to Europe, while little studied, has been commensurate with that to the United States. The next item records the impressions of one of Li Hung-chang's protégés whom he later sent to Korea in 1882.

DOC. 25. MA CHIEN-CHUNG'S REPORT ON HIS STUDIES IN FRANCE, 1877 [11]

The last ten days of May were the examination period of the Political Institute. There were eight examination questions. . . The third was on the commercial proceedings of all nations, dealing with the basis of credit for commercial organizations and bank drafts. From this we know that the wealth of Westerners in the last hundred years has not come purely from the creation and development of machines but essentially from the protection of commercial organizations. . . Thus, even though the amount of capital required for railways, telegraph lines, steam engines, and mining is very great. . . and though there is a limit to gold and silver, there is no end to the use of money because, since the currency is represented by paper and guaranteed by credit, one coin may assume the usefulness of several hundred coins. . .

The fifth question was on the differences and similarities of administrative methods, government, and education in the three countries, England, the United States, and France, the methods by which the upper and lower classes coöperate, what are the advantages and disadvantages of each method, and what are the reasons for England being able to maintain herself so long without changing, for America not changing though having many defects, for France repeatedly changing and frequently getting worse. . .

The seventh one was on the similarities and differences of public administration in all nations, some of which are monarchies, some republics, and some partly monarchical and partly republican. The legislative, executive, and judicial powers are divided and are not given to one person. These three powers do not interfere with each other, and so the political situation is in good order, bright and presentable. The collection of taxes is not done by [police] officials, therefore bad officers have no way to fulfil their desires. The verdict for a crime is fixed by local juries; bad judges have no way to play on words. Everybody has the right to be independent, and seeks to be self-respecting.

The eighth question was on the levy of taxes and the amount of national debt. Western taxes are ten times heavier than those of China and yet the people are not resentful. The national debt is borrowed from the people and yet the people are not suspicious. Why?

For these eight questions the written examination took three days and I wrote more than twenty notebooks. . . I answered them one by one in detail, and all received good grades from the professors, and were announced in the newspaper. They say I have understood these subjects very thoroughly and have grasped the broad outlines. Those who are merely bookworms cannot be compared with me. This praise is also caused by the fact that Westerners have had little contact with us Chinese and usually are scornful of us. Therefore, whenever there is a Chinese student who knows a little and understands half of what he has studied, he is praised as being extraordinary. This "being extraordinary" [as an individual] is just a sign of being despised [as a race]. I can only study hard, with strong determination. How dare I become proud of a little progress?. . .

[P. 2b] I have been in Europe for more than a year. When I first came here, I thought that the wealth and power of all European nations lay exclusively in their fine manufacturing and strict discipline of troops. But when I worked on their laws and antecedents, and read their writings, I realized that their pursuit of wealth is based on the protection of commercial concerns, and that those who seek power consider it important to win the hearts of the people. When they protect commercial concerns, then taxes can be increased and their savings will naturally be more adequate. When popular support is won, then loyalty and patriotism will be doubled, and the people can be expected to unite against a national enemy. Other good things are the increase in the number of intelligent students after the spread of schools, and the communication of the opinions of the lower classes after the establishment of parliaments. As for manufacturing, the army and navy, and these various large items, they are all but unimportant details.

Thus, I thought the government of all Western nations was perfect. When I went to listen to the lectures in the Political Institute and discussed these things forwards and backwards with scholars and officials, I began to realize the truth of the statement [p. 21] that "It would be better to be without books than to give entire credit to them." England has a king and besides has an upper and lower house. It seems that all policies must originate there, but we know that the king only gives an endorsement and the upper and lower houses merely have empty discussions, the handle of policy is wielded by the premier and two or three chief ministers. Whenever they have to face a difficult matter, they use the parliament as a cover. The president of the United States is elected by the people themselves, and this seems to be just, without being selfish, but whenever it is time for an election, bribery is publicly practised. When the president is changed, the whole list of government personnel is changed, and all officials are members of his party. How can they expect good administration? France is a republican nation where it appears that those who become officials need not come from aristocratic families, but we know they organize political factions among themselves, and except for those scholars such as Tien-yeh [Adolphe Thiers, 1797–1877, President of the Third French Republic, 1871–1873] and others whose wisdom and ability are outstanding, it is very difficult for men who do not belong to the same faction to find a good job or get into a fine position. . .[12]

CHAPTER XII. DIPLOMATIC MISSIONS ABROAD

Considering the efficiency and skill of many Chinese diplomatic representatives in the twentieth century, it seems amazing that the Ch'ing dynasty should have delayed so long in dispatching envoys abroad. The first semi-official venture in this direction was the mission chaperoned by Robert Hart in 1866. Headed by "an elderly Manchu official of low rank," Pin-ch'un,[1] this mission of investigation included three students from the T'ung-wen Kuan. It visited nine European countries, but had little effect on its return. The famous "Burlingame mission," which visited the United States and Europe in 1868–1870, appeared to the West to be primarily the achievement of the former American minister at Peking, Anson Burlingame, but the Chinese records make it clear that two Ch'ing officials, Chih-kang and Sun Chia-ku, were sent as his co-envoys with equal status. The Tientsin massacre of 1870 necessitated the sending of a special mission of apology to France, under the Manchu Ch'ung-hou; but this still did not constitute the establishment of a regular diplomatic legation. After much discussion and some false starts, a mission was finally established in England only in 1877; even then its immediate occasion was to present China's apology for the murder of a British representative, A. R. Margary, on the Burma border in 1875. The first Chinese legation in the United States was established in 1878 by Ch'en Lan-pin and Yung Wing, who had been in charge of the Educational Mission. Legations were also established in Germany (1877), France (1878), Russia and Spain (1879), and Peru (1880).

The following chapter presents first an account of the Tsungli Yamen's discovery of the efficacy of international law — a Western device of considerable value for defense against the West. This is followed by a long analysis (Doc. 27) written by the first envoy in London, Kuo Sung-tao (1818–1891), a highly competent, respected, and orthodox Chinese official who nevertheless called spades "spades" as soon as he saw them in England and later did not mince words over China's ineffectual handling of her relations with France. Marquis Tseng's dialogue with the Empress Dowager (Doc. 28) is the nearest thing to a press conference recorded from this period.

DOC. 26. PRINCE KUNG'S DISCOVERY OF INTERNATIONAL LAW, 1864 [2]

Your ministers have found that the Chinese spoken and written language is learned with care by foreigners in China without exception. Among them, the cleverest go even further and immerse themselves in studying Chinese books. When a case is argued or discussed, they can usually base themselves on Chinese legal codes. . . Unfortunately the regulations of foreign countries are all written in foreign languages and we suffer from being unable to read them. And it will still take some time for the students in the T'ung-wen Kuan to master the foreign languages thoroughly.

We have learned that there is a book called *Wan-kuo lü-li*,[3] "Laws and precedents of all nations." Yet when we wanted to seek it directly, and entrust its translation to the foreigners, we were afraid that they might wish to keep it confidential and not have it shown to us. At this juncture, the American minister P'u-an-ch'en (Anson Burlingame) came and told us that various countries have had the *Ta-ch'ing lü-li* ("Laws and precedents of the Ch'ing dynasty") translated into foreign languages. Also he said that in foreign countries there are laws and by-laws in general circulation which recently have been translated into Chinese by a scholar named Ting-wei-liang [W. A. P. Martin, later president of the T'ung-wen Kuan], and which are worthy of reference. Shortly thereafter, in October of last year, Martin was brought for an interview and presented four volumes of the *Wan-kuo lü-li*, saying that it should be read by all countries having treaty relations with others.[4] In case of dispute it can be taken for reference and can be quoted. But his style is not very smooth or clear, and so he asks us to do some editing for him, in order to have it printed. Your ministers forestalled his attempt to get us to follow the book, by telling him at once that China has her own laws and institutions and that it is inconvenient to consult foreign books. Martin, however, points out that although the *Ta-Ch'ing lü-li* has now been translated by foreign countries, China has never compelled foreign countries to act by it. It cannot be that when a foreign book is [p. 26] translated into Chinese, China should be forced to follow it. Thus he has pleaded repeatedly.

Your ministers think that his purpose is two-fold, first to boast that foreign countries also have laws, and secondly, to imitate men like Matteo Ricci in making a name in China. Upon examination, the book seems to deal generally with treaties, laws of war, and such matters.[5] Particularly there are laws that govern the mutual controls and restrictions imposed on each of the belligerent parties at the outbreak of hostilities. Unfortunately the wording was in disorder and unless he had explained it to us personally, it would not have been clear. . . We dispatched four secretaries of the Yamen . . . to discuss his translation carefully with him and edit it. . . During the past half year the draft manuscript has been finished. Martin regrets that there is no money to publish it, and he says if he could get five hundred taels he would be able to complete the project.[6]

Your ministers find that the contents of this book of foreign laws do not entirely agree with the system in China, but there are occasional passages which are useful. For instance, in connection with the case this year of the Danish ship captured by Prussia outside of Tientsin, your ministers used as arguments some sentences from this book without expressly saying so. The Prussian minister immediately acknowledged his mistake and said nothing further. This seems conclusive.[7] Your ministers have deliberated and decided jointly to grant Martin five hundred taels of silver according to his request. It is agreed that after the book has been printed, he will present 300 complimentary copies to your ministers' Yamen. Thereafter a copy will be distributed to each of the treaty ports. In this book there are laws which can to a considerable extent control the foreign consuls, and this is certainly a useful thing. The amount of silver will be paid by your ministers' Yamen out of the three per cent received from the customs funds. [Vermilion endorsement:] "Let it be as proposed."

The following letter from Kuo Sung-tao to Li Hung-chang reports his personal observations while head of the Chinese legation in London. It gives a comprehensive summary of the political and social development of England, which we largely omit, and draws a sharp contrast between Chinese conservatism and the rapid changes in Western society.

DOC. 27. A LETTER OF KUO SUNG-TAO FROM LONDON, 1877 [8]

Here in England the circumstances of administration, education and the social customs are changing every day. To trace the whole history of the nation — at first the king and the people struggled for political power and slaughtered one another. Great confusion lasted for several decades or a hundred years until the time of Jo-erh-jih [i.e., George I, 1714–1727] when the situation became settled. Originally there was no time-honored accumulation of absolute virtue and excellent education (as there had been in China). . . Their attainment of wealth and strength really began only after the Ch'ien-lung period (1736–1795). Steamships were first built at the beginning of the Ch'ien-lung period, but at first they were not very profitable. Then in 1801 they began using them on the ocean. The method was again followed in the building of locomotives, which had its beginning in 1813. Thereafter the study of electricity was pursued. Letters and messages were transmitted by a machine of magnetic-iron, until in 1838 a telegraph was first established in their national capital. . . From the beginning of England's rise, it has been only several decades; while China was weak and declining they covered a distance of 70,000 li in the wink of an eye. . . Chinese scholars and officials are presumptuous in their sanctuary and are trying to obstruct the changes of the universe; they can never succeed.

After several months here, I have actually seen the convenience of the railway train. A round trip of 300 or 400 li takes only half a day. In this country the local gentry strongly advise China to build railways; they say that the power and might of England are really based on them. At first they were also suspicious [like the Chinese populace] and tried to stop their construction [p. 2]. To speak first of the road between London and the seaport of Southampton — the coach transportation back and forth formerly used more than 30,000 horses, and the people concerned were afraid that this railroad would be detrimental to their livelihood. But when the railroad was opened as many as 60,000 or 70,000 horses were used. This was because the convenience of the railroad daily attracted more traffic and, since the train could run on only one route, those who were several tens of li away and came to take the train had to make use of more horses.

Last winter when I passed through Shanghai I saw a railroad map in the Academy of Natural Sciences [9] on which there was shown a railroad from India directly to Yunnan; a branch . . . going eastward to Canton, etc., . . . Upon seeing it I was greatly surprised, saying that no sooner had trade relations with Yunnan been opened than the routes of railroads were immediately planned. . .

When the Japanese minister saw me, he said that the natural resources of the universe can be developed by Westerners. They do the hard part — we do the easy part; can we waste more time in idleness? The vastness of China's territory and the number of her people are envied by all nations, but he has learned that until now not a single thing has been developed in China, which is a great pity. I was so embarrased that I could make no reply. . .

The foreigners' power is daily becoming more oppressive, and we suffer increasingly from their disturbances. We should investigate carefully their entire history and itemize [p. 3] the actual causes of their becoming rich and strong and uncover their ambitions. . . I have had a plan to compile a book and submit it to the Tsungli Yamen for distribution among the schools of the empire. . . But, when I reached the capital, I was frustrated by the clamorous opinion there and I refrained from expressing myself.

Personally I think there is something in the minds of the Chinese which is absolutely unintelligible. Among the injuries that Westerners do us there is nothing more serious than opium. Even the British gentlemen feel ashamed of having used this pernicious thing as a pretext for hostilities with China, and they are making a strong effort to eradicate it. Yet Chinese scholars and officials are willing to indulge complacently in it, without any sense of remorse. For several decades it has been the national humiliation, it has exhausted our financial power and poisoned and injured the lives of our people, but there is not a single person whose conscience is weighed down by it. Now clocks, watches, and toys are owned by all families, and woolen and cotton cloth and the like are prevalent in poor districts and the isolated countryside. The practice in Kiangsu and Chekiang even goes as far as to put aside the national currency for the exclusive use of foreign bank notes. . . Nevertheless as soon as these people heard of the building of railroads and telegraph lines they became sorely disturbed and enraged, and arose in multitudes to create hindrances and difficulties. There are even people who regard foreign machines as an object of public hatred. Tseng Chi-tse, on account of a family funeral, took a small steamship [instead of walking home with a sorrowful face, according to custom] from Nanking to Changsha; this caused a great uproar among the local officials and gentry that lasted for several years. All this means they are willing to accept the harm from others and let the latter squeeze the marrow from their bones, but they use their whole strength to choke off the source of profits. I do not know what is in their minds. There have been foreign relations for thirty years, but the provincial authorities are entirely ignorant of them. They impose their ignorant ideas on the Court under the guise of public opinion. The latter encourages them to do this and itself uses "public opinion" as a gloss for its own purposes.

[P. 4] There are more than 200 Japanese learning technology in England, scattered in all the seaports. There are ninety of them in London. I have met more than twenty, and all can speak English. There is one by the name of Nagaoka Ryōnosuke who was originally a feudal lord governing a kingdom by himself; he is now degraded to be a noble of hereditary rank and is studying law here. . . The telegraph office which was established in Japan was also first learned from London; as soon as the technique was mastered, a telegraph office was set up to provide the same service. There are very few who are studying military methods, probably because military science is but a practical detail, whereas the establishing of various kinds of institutional systems is the foundation for establishing the nation. The Grand Secretary [Li Hung-chang] is just now advocating military strengthening; therefore he is devoting his mind to the investigation of military methods. As far as my humble observation can reach, there is absolutely no reason to reorganize the military system in the various provinces. As for the recruiting of soldiers, it is impossible to keep it up constantly. For several decades to come we should not worry about the West taking up arms against us but simply try to decide everything with them by reasoning and by the force of circumstances. . .

[P. 5] There is a Mr. [Sir MacDonald] Stephenson here who says that all countries are building more railroads. He particularly and indefatigably advises China to do this with dispatch. Herewith I carefully submit to you the general plan which he has drafted.[10]

However, my idea is that if everything must be done by foreigners it cannot last long. We should first make the Chinese thoroughly familiar with their methods. The state of Egypt is in Africa, and when she builds railroads she first sends some people to England to study and then build them by imitation. This is the best example. . .

There is nothing more urgent than to plan earnestly for better domestic administration, in order to lay a foundation of wealth and strength. . . The area of China is more than 10,000 *li*. The postal transportation to a distant place takes several tens of days. . . If the two things (railways and telegraphs) are carried through, then 10,000 *li* will be like the hall or threshold of one's house. If suddenly one morning there were a flood, or news of drought or a bandit uprising, the Court could be informed in the evening. Then there would be no anxiety over treacherous people's secretly starting an outbreak of rebellion. This is the first advantage. The condition of the Chinese officials and people is that they are too distant from each other; in addition, both are trying to cover the eyes and ears of the Court in order to facilitate the pursuance of their selfish purposes. For this reason the people's ideas are frequently and miserably suppressed and never reach the Emperor. If the two things (railways and telegraph) are widespread. . . [p. 6] there will be no anxiety over having covetous officials suppress the opinion of the people or carry on their mischievous work for gain. This is another advantage. . .

The critics merely say that wherever the machines of foreigners reach, the local geomantic harmony [*feng-shui*, lit., "wind and water"] is injured. This is a great error. Railways and telegraph lines are always built on level ground following the state roads. There is nothing to dig up or to destroy. As for the machinery used in opening coal mines and pumping water, it is for the purpose of making the mine deeper. The deeper one digs the better the quality of coal. When Chinese dig coal they like to penetrate from the sides; when foreigners dig coal they like to get it in depth. Both are opening the mine. The shallow method and deep method actually have the same result. What harm is there? Take for instance the natural resources in Hunan: the iron mines are mostly in Pao-ch'ing and the coal mines mostly in Heng-chou, and yet the people who are famous in passing high literary examinations are particularly numerous in these two districts. . .

After several decades foreigners will arrive and then they will gradually build railways and develop (natural resources) for us. Their influence will be sufficient to control the people and the profit will be enough to bribe the wicked, the unruly, and the trouble-makers, who will be employed in their service. Then both the ownership and the profits will fall into the hands of foreigners and China will have nothing to depend upon. Mencius says: "when heaven produced these people, it made those who know beforehand teach those who know afterward, and those who perceive earlier inspire those who perceive later." The responsibility for foresight and perception must lie in the great ministers of the Court.

Another able and outspoken Chinese envoy was Tseng Kuo-fan's son, Tseng Chi-tse (1839–1890), known to the West as "Marquis Tseng," who had some grasp both of Western science and of the English language. He has usually been considered a good diplomat, not so much because he was minister to England and France in 1878–1886, as because he signed on February 24, 1881, the Treaty of St. Petersburg by which Russia was obliged to return to China certain strategic territory in the Ili region, after it had been ceded by Ch'ung-hou's ill-advised signature of the Treaty of Livadia in 1879. While Tseng's success on this occasion was partly due to Tso Tsung-t'ang's military victory in Sinkiang and the bellicose support of Tso and others during the negotiations in Russia, it was also due partly to Tseng's quick-witted disputation with the Russian authorities.[11]

After living in Europe, Marquis Tseng became not only a zealous advocate of Westernization, but a practitioner of Western ways, devoted to foreign clothes, utensils, and medicine, for all of which he was criticized by Chinese conservatives.[12]

In 1878 he was appointed to succeed Kuo Sung-tao as minister to England and France. Before he sailed from Shanghai on November 22, 1878, he had an interview with the Empress Dowager Tz'u-hsi at Peking, after which he recorded in his diary the naive and interesting conversation translated below. (Her declarative sentences were recorded as imperial decrees.)

DOC. 28. TSENG CHI-TSE'S ACCOUNT OF HIS AUDIENCE WITH THE EMPRESS DOWAGER, 1878 [13]

On August 25, 1878, I received a decree granting me the privilege of wearing the peacock feather and appointing me Imperial Commissioner to England and France. . . On the 26th, at the beginning of the *ch'ou* period [1–3 a.m.],[14] I went to the Court. . . At the beginning of the *mao* period [5–7 a.m.], I entered the Ch'ien-ch'ing gate and sat for a long time in the room for intracourt interview. At the beginning of *ch'en* [7–9 a.m.] the grand councillors came out from their audience and the throne summoned me to the eastern apartment of the Yang-hsin Hall, which I entered by lifting up the curtain. I knelt on the ground to give thanks for celestial grace. I took off my hat and kotowed. Then I was ordered to put on my hat and stand up and to proceed to the front of the cushion where I knelt to listen to the sacred instruction. The Empress Dowager Tz'u-hsi asked, "When do you plan to start the trip?" The Empress Dowager Tz'u-an also asked the same question.[15]

I replied, "Because there are public and private affairs that your minister must prepare well in Shanghai, it is necessary for him to leave the capital earlier. Now he plans to start the journey on the 29th of September."

Question: Are you going by way of Tientsin?

Answer: It is necessary to go via Tientsin and also to stay for some ten days to discuss various matters with Li Hung-chang.

Decree: [16] Li Hung-chang is familiar with foreign affairs. You may take up the various matters with him in detail.

Answer: Yes.

Question: Are you going to spend some time in Shanghai?

Answer: It's a long way to go abroad. All the arrangements and all the things to be taken along must be well prepared in Shanghai. Moreover, the retinue which your minister is going to take along cannot be appointed until he has arrived at Shanghai, and therefore he will spend a considerable time there; probably he will have to stay for more than a month.

Question: Will you memorialize again about the staff members you are going to take along, after you have arrived in Shanghai?

Answer: Of your minister's retinue, some of them are going to travel with him from the capital, some are going to be transferred and appointed from the provinces outside the capital. As to the latter who are going to be appointed from outside provinces, whether they can go or not cannot be known in advance. [P. 2] He has to wait until the assignment is made and then he will assemble the information and submit a memorial for your approval.

Question: How many days will it take to go from Tientsin to Shanghai?

Answer: The speeds of the vessels of the China Merchants Company are not the same. The fastest from Tientsin to Shanghai takes only three and a half days.

Question: Are you going to England first or to France first?

Answer: Your minister plans to start the journey from Shanghai on November 22 aboard a French ship for Marseilles, where he will go ashore to take a train for Paris. Paris is the capital of France. When the French see the arrival of a Chinese minister they will certainly have someone perform ceremonies of welcome and entertainment. If your minister goes straight on without taking a look at Paris it will not be proper. He intends to send a telegram from Shanghai to Kuo Sung-tao asking him to come to Paris and hand him the seal. Your minister will receive the seal in Paris, and will immediately present his credentials to France first. Then he will go to London to present his credentials to England. London is the capital of England.

Question: Have the credentials been prepared and given to you?

Answer: He has already received them.

Question: How are you going to decide upon your living quarters?

Answer: Kuo Sung-tao has rented a house some time ago. When your minister goes there everything will be the same as before. Recently he has discussed with the princes and great ministers in the Tsungli Yamen whether in the future, if we have sufficient funds, it may be necessary to purchase a house in each country to be used as an embassy. The houses of foreign ministers in China are all purchased or built by themselves. It is indeed not a long-term plan for China's ministers to live in rented houses. Moreover, the rent is exorbitant and in the long run it is not economical.

Decree: The things which you have to attend to abroad should be discussed with the princes and high ministers from time to time.

Answer: Yes.

Question: After you are abroad how will you send us memorials and reports?

Answer: In regard to important matters which should be memorialized and explained, Kuo Sung-tao has been sending them in care of the Tsungli Yamen. As for ordinary affairs, about which he should consult the Tsungli Yamen, either in the form of an official dispatch or as a letter, they were all sent through the Office for the Transmission of Government Correspondence in Shanghai. Your minister plans to handle the matter in the same way as before. . .

Decree: The members of your retinue should all be carefully controlled and not allowed to cause trouble in foreign countries and thus incur the contempt [p. 3] of foreigners.

Answer: Your minister will reverently obey the sacred instruction and be particularly careful in regard to the matter of his retinue. At present it is not easy to find those who are familiar with foreign affairs and who can be deeply trusted. He has no candidates in mind. It would be best for your minister to make a selection from scholars whom he has known for a long time, who are clear-minded and careful in everything. . . Now the second councillor, Ch'en Yuan-chi, who is to be taken along, is the brother-in-law of your minister. Your minister dares to follow the precedent of the ancients who "did not avoid the use of relatives in their intimate employment" and take him abroad, because the duties and responsibilities are extremely heavy. Were he not an intimate friend of your minister, who knows his background thoroughly from former days, your minister would not take a chance on appointing him. . .

Question: How old is this relative of yours?

Answer: Thirty-six years old.

Question: Can you understand a foreign written and spoken language?

Answer: Your minister reads a little English and understands a little spoken English. He learned it from books and so it is comparatively easier for him to read the language but more difficult for him to understand it, because his mouth and ears are not accustomed to it.

Question: Is the common language English or French?

Answer: English is a commercial language. Foreigners stress business, therefore the people of the various countries can speak English. As for the language of France, it has been handed down for generations; therefore, in documents and official dispatches among various nations French is frequently used. For instance, the international treaties, ratifications of treaties, and so on, are often written in French.

Question: Since you understand both the spoken and written language, it is much more convenient. You do not need to rely on the translations of interpreters [do you?].

Answer: Although our minister can understand and read a little, he is not very familiar with it and he still has to depend upon interpreters. . . Understanding of a foreign written or spoken language and management of foreign affairs are two entirely different things [p. 4]. It is essential for those who manage foreign affairs to be familiar with treaties and with official procedures. It is not essential for them to concern themselves with the duties of interpreters. In the future when your minister discusses official business with foreigners even though he understands the language he still would wait for the restatement by the interpreter, partly because the procedure of the Court ought to be so, partly because during the interval of restatement by the interpreter he can take advantage of the pause to give thought to the language with which he should answer. The British Minister, Thomas Wade, can understand the Chinese written and spoken language. When he discusses official business he has to use interpreters to convey the meaning to him. That is the same idea.

Question: I have learned that Wade is going to come here soon. Have you heard about it?

Answer: During the summer your minister read a newspaper which said Wade would start his trip in the autumn; since then no exact news about him has been heard.

Decree: Wade is a very cunning person.

Answer: Wade can understand the Chinese written and spoken language. As a person he is very cunning and his temperament is very harsh. Foreigners also say that he is bad tempered.

Decree: It is very difficult to manage foreign affairs. I have heard that in Fukien there are again cases of the burning and destruction of churches and houses; in the future, there will be trouble again.

Answer: The difficulty in handling diplomatic affairs lies in the fact that foreigners are unreasonable, while Chinese are ignorant of current events and circumstances. Chinese ministers and people usually hate foreigners, as goes without saying, but we must plan gradually to make ourselves strong before anything can be done. The destruction of one church or the killing of one foreigner by no means avenges our grievances or wipes out our humiliation. At present many Chinese do not understand this principle and so there has been the Margary incident in Yunnan [Feb. 1875],[17] which caused the Empresses Dowager and the Emperor work and worry day and night.

Decree: It is true indeed. How can we forget our grievances for a single day? But we must gradually make ourselves strong, as you just stated very clearly. The killing of one person or the burning of one house definitely cannot be considered as having avenged our grievances.

Answer: Yes.

Decree: Very few persons understand this idea. If you manage such matters for the nation, there are bound to be times when people will scold you. You, however, should bear the toil and blame.

Answer: When your minister formerly studied the classics and came to the sentence, "To serve the ruler one must be able to offer one's life" [p. 5], he thought that a loyal minister would have reached the extreme point of loyalty if he devoted his whole life to it. After observing the recent situation and the course of negotiations between China and foreign countries, he has found that sometimes it is necessary to consider his life a secondary matter; and in the last analysis he even has to risk considering his reputation unimportant, before he can make the general situation secure on behalf of his country. For instance, at the time of the former Tientsin incident [June 1870] [18] your minister's father, your deceased minister, Tseng Kuo-fan, before he started his trip from Pao-ting, was then on his sickbed and immediately he wrote his last will and testament to bid his family make arrangements as though he had already discarded his life. After he arrived at Tientsin and saw that the matter was so serious that it could not be satisfactorily concluded even by [the sacrifice of] his life, he made concessions and secured the best arrangement to obtain a peaceful settlement. At that time many scholars and officials in the capital condemned him. Your minister's father accepted the responsibility and blamed himself. In sending letters to his friends he frequently wrote the eight characters: "Outwardly I am ashamed of public criticism and inwardly I cannot live with my conscience." This shows how he struggled to protect the general situation by disregarding his own reputation. As a matter of fact, at that time there was no other way to deal with the case, apart from what had been done by Tseng Kuo-fan.

Decree: Tseng Kuo-fan was really a just and loyal man who took the nation into consideration. (Note: I took off my hat and kotowed, but did not make any reply.)

Decree: It is also bad luck for the nation that before long Tseng Kuo-fan departed from the world. Now there are many great officials in various places who are cowardly.

Answer: Li Hung-chang, Shen Pao-chen, Ting Pao-chen and Tso Tsung-t'ang are all loyal and sincere ministers.

Decree: All of them are good but all are old troopers. The new ones all fail to equal them in ability; they have not kept abreast of new ideas.

Answer: Kuo Sung-tao is certainly an upright and straightforward person. This time he also risked damage to his reputation in order to manage affairs for the nation. In the future it is hoped that the special grace of the Empresses and the Emperor will protect him in every respect.

Decree: Up above [*shang-t'ou*, i.e., by the rulers] it is thoroughly understood. Kuo Sung-tao is a good man. Since his mission abroad he has managed many affairs but he has also received plenty of scolding from people.

Answer: Kuo Sung-tao is vexed by the fact that China cannot become strong immediately and he has frequently argued with people and therefore he has been scolded. After all he is a loyal minister. Fortunately the Empresses Dowager and the Emperor understand him. Even though he has lost his reputation in the fight, still it is worthwhile. [p. 6]

Decree: We all know him. The princes and great ministers also understand him.

Answer: Yes.

Question: Are you now living in the Tsungli Yamen?

Answer: The affairs of the Tsungli Yamen must be kept confidential. Formerly your minister and others dared not participate. Now, since he has received the order to go abroad on a mission, he must thoroughly investigate the old and new documents in cases concerning England and France, and he must jot down some essential points. Even though the complete cases are now in the hands of Kuo Sung-tao, yet when your minister is on his journey, there are certain to be some foreigners who will meet and entertain him. If during the course of conversation he is ignorant of the facts of the case, it will be somewhat embarrassing.

Decree: You are really quite careful in handling public affairs. (Note: Reverent silence, no reply.)

Question: Are you going to take some students along from the T'ung-wen Kuan?

Answer: Your minister is going to take an English interpreter, a French interpreter, and a clerk. This will be reported when he reaches Shanghai.

Question: Are all of them good?

Answer: Your minister understands English only slightly. The English interpreter, Tso Ping-lung, your minister knows can be employed. The French interpreter, Lien-hsing, has not yet been carefully investigated by your minister, because your minister does not understand French. . .

Question: Will the date for presentation of credentials be decided by you or by the foreigners?

Answer: We must wait until (your minister's) arrival in their country; then both sides can discuss the matter and deal with it.

Question: Is there also a Tsungli Yamen in foreign countries?

Answer: In foreign countries it is called a *Wai-pu* [or ministry of foreign affairs]. The matters it deals with are the same as the public business of the Chinese Tsungli Yamen. I have heard it said that recently England also changed the name to Tsungli Yamen, but in reality the name in a foreign language is entirely different; it is called neither "Wai-pu" nor "Tsungli Yamen." Only, if the work they do is the same, it is the same office.

Question: When can you arrive there?

Answer: If the Empresses Dowager and the Emperor wish him bon voyage [*I-lu-p'ing-an*] and if there are no delays en route, he should be able to reach the capital of France near the end of the year.

Question: You have never been in foreign countries. I presume you must have heard about these routes and their circumstances.

Answer: Some information has been obtained by consulting books [p. 7] and maps and some by inquiry.

Question: Is your ship going to cast anchor at Hongkong or not?

Answer: Your minister is going to board a French Company's steamship. The steamship must have cargo to be loaded or unloaded, passengers to embark or disembark, and so on. There will be delay in every harbor throughout the journey, but everything will be decided by the captain.

After a long pause there was a

Decree: Now you kneel for greetings. (Note: I withdrew to my original position, knelt and said) Your minister Tseng Chi-tse kneels and prays for the good health of the Sage.

Raising the curtain I withdrew. It was already the *ch'en* hour [9:00 A.M.].

CHAPTER XIII. PROBLEMS OF THE
INDUSTRIALIZATION EFFORT

From preceding sections it is evident that Chinese thinking on the problem of defense against the West went through a progression from the idea of "using barbarians to control barbarians" and employing Western arms, to the realization successively that Western arms must be made in China, that they must be produced by Chinese, that Chinese must be instructed to make them, and that therefore Chinese must be trained in Western sciences in general and that institutions must be established for their training and for the practice of the new skills so acquired. All these successive ideas stemmed from the basic desire for defense, which certainly continued undiminished as a dominant motive in the 1860's.

As the 1870's wore on, both Li Hung-chang and other provincial authorities sought to establish industrial enterprises and the transport facilities to accompany them. This involved them in the problems of balanced industrial development already familiar to the West. For example, the China Merchants Steam Navigation Company, founded in 1872 to compete with British shipping in China, needed a Chinese coal supply independent of foreign imports. The Kaiping coal mine, forerunner of the Kailan Mining Administration north of Tientsin, was opened to meet this need in 1878. The earliest surviving railway in China was later built to connect with the Kaiping mine.[1]

Li Hung-chang expressed the new recognition that China's strength must rest on industry: "In the various European countries mineralogy is the basis on which they can fight for supremacy. England, as a nation, is established on three islands in the sea, where the natural resources are not very abundant, and yet her annual production of coal and iron is very prosperous, and so her wealth and power are the first in the world." [2]

In 1872 it was found that the original plan to build sixteen steamships at Foochow in five years for three million taels had produced only half the number of ships (six built and three building), but had more than exhausted the funds. The ships completed were still inferior to foreign ships. Some officials suggested abandoning the enterprise, to which Li Hung-chang replied in the following vigorous memorial.

DOC. 29. LI HUNG-CHANG'S DEFENSE OF BUILDING STEAMSHIPS, 1872 [3]

We have seen with admiration the Sacred Emperor's vigorous striving for self-strengthening and for laying down broad far-reaching plans. Our admiration is beyond telling. Your minister has been thinking that the various European countries in the last several decades have advanced from India to the southern oceans, from the southern oceans to the northeast, and have invaded China's frontiers and interior land. Peoples never [p. 45] recorded in previous histories, who have had no contact with us since ancient times, have come to our points of entry (*kuan*) to ask for trade relations. Our Emperors have been as generous as the sky and have made treaties with all of them for international trade in order to control them. People from a distance of ninety thousand *li*, from the cardinal points of the globe, are gathering together in China; this is the greatest change during the last three millennia and more!

The Westerners particularly rely upon the excellence and efficacy of their guns, cannon, and steamships, and so they can overrun China. The bow and spear, small guns, and native-made cannon which have hitherto been used by China cannot resist their rifles, which have their bullets fed from the rear opening. The sailing boats, rowboats, and the gunboats which have been hitherto employed cannot oppose their steam-engined warships. There-fore, we are controlled by the Westerners.

To live today and still say "reject the barbarians" and "drive them out of our territory" is certainly superficial and absurd talk. Even though we wish to preserve the peace and to protect our territory, we cannot preserve and protect them unless we have the right weapons. They are daily producing their weapons to strive with us for supremacy and victory, pitting their superior techniques against our inadequacies, to wrangle with and to affront us. Then how can we get along for one day without weapons and techniques?

The method of self-strengthening lies in learning what they can do, and in taking over what they rely upon. Moreover, their possession of guns, cannon, and steamships began only within the last hundred years or so, and their progress has been so fast that their influence has spread into China. If we can really and thoroughly understand their methods — and the more we learn, the more improve — and promote them further and further, can we not expect that after a century or so we can reject the barbarians and stand on our own feet? Japan is just a small nation. Recently she has begun to trade with Europe; she has instituted iron factories and built many steamships. She has changed to the use of Western weapons. Does she have the ambition to plot to invade the Western nations? Perhaps she is merely planning for self-protection. But if Japan seeks only self-protection, she is nevertheless oppressing and looking down on our China. Should not China plan for herself? Our scholars and officials have confined themselves to the study of stanzas and sentences and are ignorant of the greatest change of the last several thousand years; they are accustomed to the temporary security of the present, and so they forget why we received the heavy blow and deep suffering of twenty or thirty years ago [the Opium War], and how we can obtain domestic security and control the foreigners within several centuries. That is how this talk of stopping steamship construction has originated.

Your minister humbly thinks that all other expenditures of our nation can be economized, but the expenses for supporting the army, establishing defense measures, drilling in guns and cannon, and building warships should by all means never be economized. If we try to save funds, then we shall be obliged to neglect all these defense measures, the nation will never have anything to stand upon, and we shall never be strong. . . The amount which has already been spent will, in turn, become a sheer waste. Not only will we be a laughing stock to foreigners, but we will also strengthen their aggressive ambitions. . .

[The rest of the memorial explains why the expenditure has surpassed the original estimate — because it was roughly estimated by Frenchmen who were not experts, and because the price of machinery subsequently and unexpectedly rose. The progress of English and French warships is described, and a small type of warship for defense purposes is suggested. According to Li, China has "more land than water; it is more urgent to train an army than a navy." (p. 47b) Li also discusses the difficulty of converting warships to commercial use, but he recognizes the need of commercial vessels for grain transportation and commercial competition with foreigners. Then he continues (p. 49):]

Furthermore, the building of ships, cannon, and machinery will be impossible without iron, and then we shall be helpless without coal. The reason for England's power and influence over the Western lands is only her possession of these two items (iron and coal). The various arsenals in Foochow and Shanghai daily need a huge amount of imported coal and iron, because the Chinese product is most unsuitable. Even foreign ships coming to our ports have to carry foreign coal. Suppose there is a time when the points of entry to China are closed by boycott; then not only all our iron factories would have to suspend work and stand distressingly in idleness, but also the steamships which have been built would be unable to move a single inch without coal. What deserves more anxious thought than this! . . .

[P. 50] Recently Westerners have frequently requested permission to open coal and iron mines in the Chinese interior, pointing out that it is a great pity that China's natural resources cannot be developed by herself. We have heard that now Japan is adopting Western methods of opening coal and iron mines to gain a great profit, and this has also helped her shipbuilding and machinery. . . If we can really make plans to persuade the people, by means of the system of "government-supervision and merchant-operation" [kuan-tu shang-pan], to borrow and use foreign machines and foreign methods only, but not allow foreigners to do the whole job on our behalf, then these articles of daily necessity, when produced and processed by proper methods, must have a good market. A source of profit will naturally be opened. Taking the surplus funds from the new source we can even use it to maintain our ships and train our soldiers.

In 1880, through military necessity, Li Hung-chang also recognized the importance of the telegraph: "In mobilizing troops," he writes, "speed is of the essence. . . A telegram from Russia to Shanghai takes only one day, whereas from Shanghai to Peking. . . a Chinese mail steamer requires six or seven days. . . In 1874, when Japan invaded Taiwan, Shen Pao-chen and others repeatedly spoke of the advantage of the telegraph and an Imperial decree was issued to institute it, but the matter was only perfunctorily carried out and thus far there has been no achievement." [4] Accordingly, Li urged the construction of two telegraph lines: from Nanking to Peking, and from Hankow to Peking. Trunk railroad construction still remained suspect, however, partly on the ground that it would enable foreign invaders to penetrate the interior too easily — as the Japanese were to demonstrate in a later generation.

Textile production had less obvious strategic value and moved more slowly. Tso Tsung-t'ang had set up a woolen mill in Lanchow, Kansu, in 1878 with the help of German technicians and machinery, but it did not flourish after his death. In 1882, Li Hung-chang planned to establish a cotton mill at Shanghai, and called for merchants' share-capital to help finance it. He proposed to exempt its products from transit or *likin* taxes en route from Shanghai to other parts of the country, which would have set a precedent for giving special protection to "national goods." His plan, however, was not carried through until 1891, and the new Shanghai cotton mill, the first in China, burned down in 1893 after one year of successful operation. Li soon reorganized it on a larger scale. At Wuchang, Chang Chih-tung also established a cotton mill in 1891, and another one in 1894.[5] Li set up a paper mill in Shanghai in 1891; a cement factory was attached to the Kaiping coal mine; and a match factory and flour mill were also opened.

Heavy industry got started even more slowly. Chang Chih-tung opened the Ta-yeh iron mine and the Hanyang Iron Works in Hupei in 1890, employing German technicians, but these projects never developed into the big industrial complex that their founder had hoped for.

The variety and yet the ineffectiveness and slow development of some of these projects, many of them sponsored by Li Hung-chang, may be indicated in a list:

1863 A foreign language school was established at Shanghai.

1865 The Kiangnan Arsenal was established at Shanghai, with a translation bureau attached.

1867 The Nanking Arsenal was established.

1870 A machine factory, first established by Ch'ung-hou in 1867 at Tientsin, was enlarged.

1871 A foreign-style fort was planned for Taku, outside Tientsin.

1872 Students were sent to study in America.
Officers were sent to Germany to learn military sciences.
The China Merchants Steam Navigation Company was organized.
The opening of coal and iron mines was requested.

1875 A plan was made to build steel warships.

1876 A request was made to open a bureau to study foreign sciences in all provinces; also to add a new subject on foreign affairs in the civil service examinations.
Students and apprentices from the Foochow shipyard were sent to study in England and France. Seven army officers were sent to Germany for advanced training.

1878 The Kaiping coal mine was opened.

1879 A telegraph line was opened from Taku to Tientsin.

1880 A plan for a modern navy was launched, beginning with a program to purchase warships from foreign countries.
A naval school was established at Tientsin.
Telegraph land lines were requested and sanctioned.

1881 Li supported Liu Ming-ch'uan's request to build railways.
North of Tientsin the T'angshan railroad (about six miles) was completed.
The first telegraph line, Shanghai-Tientsin, was opened and merchants were invited to develop the telegraph service in all provinces.

1882 A dockyard was built at Port Arthur (completed in 1891).
A cotton mill was planned at Shanghai.

1885 A military preparatory school (an army school) was established at Tientsin.

The navy yamen was inaugurated.

1887 Mints were established at Tientsin and Paoting.

1888 The Peiyang Army was organized.

1889 The Mo-ho gold mine, in Kirin, was planned.

1891 The Lung-chang paper mill was founded at Shanghai.

A review of the new navy was held at Port Arthur.

a. *The Principle of "Government-supervision and Merchant-operation"*

The explanation of this poor record, compared to contemporary developments in other countries, lies only partly in the pressure of commercial competition exercised by the imperialist powers in China. The real key, as we have suggested in Chapter I, lies in the nature of Chinese society — its "oriental" features, whereby merchant capital was not easily available for industrial investment except under the wing of official patronage. This close merchant-official connection was exemplified by the system called "official-supervision and merchant-operation" or management (*kuan-tu shang-pan*), under which many of the early enterprises were set up. While it is beyond our scope to analyze the economic and social characteristics of this system, it is plain that it met China's needs quite inadequately: officials unversed in business held the whip hand over managerial personnel of inferior social status, who were, therefore, in no position to use modern entrepreneurial methods of capital accumulation and reinvestment.

The *kuan-tu shang-pan* system was an adaptation of a traditional Chinese device in economic administration; it seems in fact to have been patterned after the Chinese government salt monopoly, in which the government appointed official overseers but the production, distribution, and retailing of salt were farmed out to different groups of salt merchants. A number of enterprises were set up on this new basis: merchants contributed part of the share-capital, but the manager usually had official status as an expectant taotai or magistrate who could deal with the local government to secure exemption from taxes or other facilities. At the same time he was the business manager. Sometimes there were two managers: one to deal with the government and the other to look after the business. The function of the manager was thus half-official and half-commercial, and his enterprise as a whole was also halfway between the two. While the original purpose of the system was to raise funds from the public, in practice the officials invested money in the government-sponsored enterprises under the names of merchants, and placed their relatives in charge as managers in order to make a great profit. For example, Sheng Hsuan-huai was summoned by Li Hung-chang to manage the China Merchants Company, which bought its ships from the American firm of Russell and Company for 2,200,000 taels of silver. Sheng on behalf of Li Hung-chang asked the governor-general of Liang-chiang to contribute one million taels from official funds and he made up the rest by calling for public purchase of capital shares.[6] At the beginning of 1880 a memorial impeached the company for spending money lavishly and for "squeezing" official funds to fill the pockets of its officers, who had been appointed by the government.[7] Li Hung-chang, the sponsor of the company, was ordered by the emperor to investigate this charge. The result was a complete whitewash.[8]

The evils which resulted from the mixing of Western commerce and industry with Chinese bureaucratism were vividly described by a scholarly compradore, Cheng Kuan-ying, who wrote an influential and eloquent book on China's problems.

Cheng Kuan-ying was a man of obscure origin, but from his own writings we gather that he started his career by working as a compradore in foreign firms (Dent & Co., and Butterfield and Swire) for about thirty years. He joined the enterprises of Li Hung-chang in 1882 and served in various directorial capacities in the Chinese Telegraph Company, the China Merchants Company, and Li's cotton mill company. From 1892 to 1902 he was associate director and then director of the China Merchants Company and traveled widely in China and East Asia. During the Sino-Japanese war he served concurrently as a government purchasing agent for ammunition. For a brief period in 1896 he became the manager of the newly reorganized Hanyang iron foundry.

During the 1890's Cheng became a patron and enthusiastic reader of the *Wan-kuo kung-pao*, a journal sponsored by foreign missionaries which contained articles on science, history and social problems, and had wide influence. According to Timothy Richard, Cheng bought a hundred copies of the translation of Mackenzie's *Nineteenth Century* (*T'ai-hsi hsin-shih lan-yao*) and distributed them to his Peking friends. The book which he wrote, "Warnings to the seemingly prosperous age" (*Sheng-shih wei-yen*), had a vogue before 1898 and merits attention.[9] Eventually this "warning" was presented to the Emperor Kuang-hsü, who ordered the Tsungli Yamen to publish and distribute it to officials. It was popularly read in the decade after its publication, although its influence on the 1898 reform movement was probably limited by the fact of the author's compradore background.

According to the communist writer Hsiao San, *Sheng-shih wei-yen* was one of the books Mao Tse-tung liked to read in his boyhood;[10] Mao has not mentioned Cheng in his own writings, where he writes of K'ang Yu-wei and Yen Fu.

As a compradore-scholar with wide contact among foreigners and an acquaintance with missionary writings, especially those of Timothy Richard, as well as with contemporary Chinese literature, Cheng Kuan-ying was in a position to advance ideas. He demanded a higher public status for the merchant class and argued that if greater freedom were given them in their commercial activities, it would be an effective defense against foreign exploitation of China. Accordingly he urged that merchants should be admitted to the civil service examinations at the local level, and should have access to the officials.

One amazing thing about Cheng's book is its humanitarian sentiment — not only his thesis that the government is for the people, but also his moving descriptions of the social abuses of the time. He was especially grieved by the inhumanity of penal practices and prison conditions, by the suffering of women from footbinding, and by the general misery of the countryside. He therefore offered many suggestions for reform, relief for the poor, agricultural improvement and the like, including the idea of using an alphabet for writing Chinese so that "all the people could read and write."[11]

DOC. 30. THE CRITICISMS OF CHENG KUAN-YING, C. 1892 [12]

In recent days, although the court has ordered the governors-general and governors to develop commerce and open all kinds of manufacturing bureaus, and has authorized the inviting of merchants to manage them, yet the officials and merchants have habitually been unable to get along together and have distrusted each other for a long time. Even though the officials are capable and brilliant and willing to protect them [p. 8], the merchants are afraid, since it is unpredictable whether their successors will be wise or not. . . Who would like to have his interests and rights taken away by officials? For this reason, rich merchants and great businessmen who have undertaken many affairs, although they understand clearly that there are profits to be made, nevertheless hesitate to accept the invitation to manage government enterprises. Even if some accept the invitation, they still fear that the officials will deceitfully entrust affluent merchants with the charge of certain enterprises, while actually having some other selfish scheme in mind. During the last ten years or more, there have frequently been bad officials who allied themselves with cunning merchants. The latter either ask the authorities to give them charge of tax collections in certain lines (Note: The tax for building forts, contributed by all trades in Kwangtung province, was handled by inviting merchants to collect it), or they imitate Western methods of inaugurating enterprises; in order to secure more shareholders they may falsely claim that a certain amount of stock has been sold and a license received, before they even establish an office. Thus they work for their private ends on the pretext of a public enterprise. They are neither affluent merchants, nor have they any special training. Such enterprises can hardly be successful, and many people have suffered by involvement in them.

According to Western custom, a bureau is established by the government to handle state affairs, while a company is established by respectable merchants to conduct a business. No matter who establishes it, a business company need only act entirely according to the company law drawn up and enacted by the state. The chief manager is elected by the trustees of the shareholders and the affairs of each branch are decided by the chief manager. If the chief manager is not thoroughly familiar with commercial affairs, nor versed in the advantageous and disadvantageous aspects of business, even though he has many shareholders and holds high official positions, he is not allowed to venture carelessly into an undertaking. . .

Now in China when companies are founded through a petition to the higher authorities, even though the shares are sold to merchants, they are called bureaus. The chief managers, whose duties are only slightly concerned with government matters, are appointed and given orders by high officials, who disregard whether they are competent or not and look only for men whose rank is comparatively high and who suit their own ideas. Then they are considered qualified to fill the posts. Consequently, most of the chief managers of the various bureaus are people with the rank of taotai (Note: What they have learned cannot be used for what they are doing, and that is always ridiculed by Westerners). After the official seals and stationery have been received, item by item, then the business is carried on entirely in an official [i.e., bureaucratic] manner. Those whose positions are dignified and who have great authority can dominate the business and can achieve their private ambitions at the cost of the public enterprise. Those whose positions are low and who have little authority generally take orders and dare not say much. If a surplus or profit is made by the company, all the local officials request some contribution and overstep their proper duty to meddle in the company's affairs. The managers of small companies, even though they have not been appointed by high officials, also indulge in embezzlement and malpractices; the shareholders are afraid of their power and, on account of the lack of commercial law, they dare not appeal to higher courts. Therefore, during the last several decades there have been few shareholders who have made a profit, and many who have lost their capital. . .

Now if we wish to reorganize our commercial affairs, we must imitate the Western practice and compile a commercial code quickly. . . [P. 9] All those who organize a commercial company ought to state in a petition who the trustees of the shareholders are, how large the capital is, and what business they are going to do, and they ought to send these details for registration with the local government. If a company is not registered, the official will not take care of it when anything happens. Thus . . . the officials will not dare to squeeze the merchants and the latter will not practice fraud. As to the people employed by the company, whether in high or low position, they must be thoroughly familiar with the business before they are given employment. The authorities should not recommend people to the company at random; all the old inveterate malpractices should be entirely wiped out.

In another passage, Cheng Kuan-ying gives an eloquent summary of the injustices and humiliations suffered by Chinese at the hands of foreigners in Shanghai:

The Westerners frequently take advantage of the differences in language and in law to profit themselves at the cost of others, and do as they please without regard for reason. . . . When a foreign ship collides with and destroys a Chinese boat, the latter, contrarily, is blamed for being slow in avoiding the collision or is falsely charged with having a dim light on its mast. . . When a foreign stagecoach hurts a Chinese, the latter is, contrarily, charged with not knowing how to yield the right of way, so that he incurred the disaster himself. Even if the driver is taken to court, he only pays a small fine. Furthermore, Chinese employed by foreign companies or as sailors on foreign ships frequently have their wages cut on some pretext or are even beaten to death. Cunning Westerners ally themselves with local rascals to kidnap and sell the foolish country fellows, whose grievances and miserable lives are like those of the dark ages. Again, for example, when a Chinese merchant owes money to a foreign merchant, as soon as he is accused his property is confiscated and his relatives and friends are disturbed; whereas when a Westerner is in debt to a Chinese, even though he has abundant private savings, by following the regulations for declaring bankruptcy, he is entirely free from obligation. . .

[P. 48] Our treatment of Westerners has been so magnanimous, and their treatment of the Chinese so poor. Where is justice and where is humanity? Their steamboats sail as fast as if they flew through our harbors, and their stagecoaches rush along our thoroughfares, they carry weapons in time of peace, they reduce the wages of their employees, they speculate and go bankrupt, they protect Christian converts, they control the customs duties, they kidnap and sell our people — all these various kinds of wrongdoing should be forbidden by Western law and not tolerated by international law. . .[13]

To make his complaint specific, Cheng lists ten grievances: (1) the Shanghai foreign settlement is taking over land outside its boundaries; (2) Chinese stagecoaches are differently taxed and not allowed to pass foreign stagecoaches; (3)

Chinese are fined for hunting out of season; (4) Westerners go hunting as they please at any time; (5) the paper chases of Western horsemen destroy the fields without compensation; (6) the Mixed Court at Shanghai issues blank warrants which are misused by the municipal police who prey upon the populace; (7) no Chinese representatives are allowed in the Shanghai municipal council; (8) Chinese are excluded from the Shanghai public park and race course, although they pay sixty or seventy per cent of the taxes to the municipal government; (9) Chinese are excluded from the park along the river; (10) land for roads is expropriated from farmers without proper compensation.[14]

b. *The Debate over Railroads*

The term *t'ieh-lu* (lit., "iron road") for "railroad" probably first appeared in Chinese literature in 1864 when an English engineer, Sir MacDonald Stephenson, traveled to China by way of India. He suggested that a railroad be built from Shanghai to Soochow, but there was no response from Chinese circles. In the following year an English merchant built a short railroad of more than one *li* outside the Hsuan-wu Gate of Peking and tried to run a locomotive on it. This appears to have been the first introduction of the railroad in China,[15] but because the spectators were greatly alarmed, the railroad was soon removed. In 1866 British merchants, including Jardine, Matheson and Co., again began to build a railroad by preparing a carriage road thirty-eight *li* in length between Shanghai and Wusung. In May of 1876, rails having been laid, service was formally opened. However, because it was built by foreigners and the Chinese populace were greatly irritated by the new invention, local public opinion turned against it. After a Chinese soldier was killed on the railway, and officials and people had become more clamorous, Shen Pao-chen, then governor-general of Liang-chiang, in September 1876, negotiated with the British consul-general, Thomas Wade, purchased the railroad, and had it destroyed in 1877. The superficial reason for this destruction lay in superstition and conservatism of the type that had also appeared in England and the United States at the beginning of railroad construction — such as the idea that the roaring locomotives would startle the cattle and prevent them from grazing in safety, that hens would not lay, that the poisoned air from locomotives would kill the wild birds and destroy vegetation, that farm houses would be ignited by sparks, etc.[16] Behind this lay the real reason, that the British merchants had built the Shanghai-Wusung railroad without the consent of the Chinese government, which was averse to foreign control over so powerful an instrument of economic exploitation.

After this incident it took some time for Chinese leaders to promote the construction of railways in China. Among these promoters Feng Kuei-fen, Li Hung-chang, Liu K'un-i, Tso Tsung-t'ang, Liu Ming-ch'uan and others wrote long memorials to call the attention of the court, as well as the populace, to the need of railroads both for defense and for commerce.[17] Li Hung-chang and Liu Ming-ch'uan in particular conducted vigorous campaigns for the introduction of railways, while T'ang T'ing-hsing, Wu T'ing-fang and Sheng Hsuan-huai became the chief supervisors and administrators of railroad construction.

DOC. 31. SHEN PAO-CHEN'S PURCHASE OF THE SHANGHAI-WUSUNG RAILWAY, 1876 [18]

We have found that during the spring of this year the British merchants in Shanghai built a railroad without authority, in the leased territory, and on it ran a locomotive train and directly reached Wusung. Your ministers

Shen Pao-chen and Wu Yuan-ping sternly ordered the customs taotai to communicate with the British consul-general in order to stop it. Consul-General Meadows adamantly refused. We also wrote to the Tsungli Yamen to send a communication to stop it. The envoy of the said country, Wade, was also very obstinate and he put it off for several months. . . The British envoys at first wished to have the railroad operated jointly by Chinese and foreigners, each side contributing some money. Then they wished, after the purchase of the railroad by China, to have it still managed by foreign merchants. . . We immediately explained in detail that in Chinese territory foreigners should not build a railway without authority. We accommodated them with a price, which is already a special consideration. If there is still more trouble, then it is not China's fault but the Westerners'.

After repeated discussions between the (Shanghai) customs taotai and others, an agreement has been reached on October 24 that China has full freedom to buy the line, to stop operation, and to take other action concerning the railroad. Foreign merchants have no right to make further inquiries. But during one year, until the purchase price has been entirely paid, the foreign merchants shall manage it. They are only permitted to take passengers back and forth and not to take goods, as it is against the regulations. In addition, they cannot purchase more land for extending the railroad. . .

DOC. 32. HSUEH FU-CH'ENG'S SUPPORT OF RAILROAD BUILDING, 1878 [19]

Now all the European countries are competing with one another for wealth and strength and their rise to prosperity is rapid. What they rely upon are steamships and railroads. The manufacture of steamships has been imitated by China with visible effect. I think if the system of railway trains is not used [p. 10], China can never be rich and strong. . . In England railways have been studied and steadily improved and a large amount of profits has accrued. The price of coal and iron has been reduced three-fourths. Accordingly, England could exert her power in manufacturing and expand into other matters, and thereby become the strong leader of Europe. Shortly afterward, the railroad was extended to Russia, France, Germany, Austria, the United States, and other large countries.

The United States is a newly created country, and forty years ago there was no railway. Now a general estimate of the whole country shows the railroads, spreading out on all sides, amount to as many as twenty-one hundred thousand *li* [*sic.*, i.e., 70,000 miles?]. Wherever a new city is founded or untilled land is opened, railroads are always built to lead the way, and as soon as the population becomes numerous and business prosperous, then the railroads are increased to improve things still further. The nation has been established only a hundred years, its daily progress is like rising steam, and it is almost an equal of England and Russia. I have heard that from San Francisco in America to New York by train the distance is eleven thousand *li*, and the journey does not exceed eight days; that is, ten thousand *li* takes the same time as several hundred *li* in China. The traveling expense is but little more than a hundred dollars; that is, the cost of ten thousand *li* is like the cost of one thousand *li* in China. Thus, if China should adopt the railroad, then distant areas could be brought near, the stagnant could be made to flow, expense could be saved, and the scattered could be concentrated. . .

[P. 11] The new tasks on which China is now trying to make a start are numerous, yet all must have railroads to relieve their difficulties. Why?. . . The more goods are imported or exported, the more extensive will be the transportation and trade by steamship. This shows that railroads and steamships are mutually helpful [lit., like outside and lining]. Coal, iron, and other mines far away from a river can use a railway for transportation, and then the capital expense will be lightened and sales will be facilitated. When distribution is easier, the mining industry will become more prosperous, and thereafter coal and iron mines will be more extensively opened, and accordingly the cost of building and managing railways will be further reduced. This shows that railroads and mining are mutually helpful. The speed of a train is more than a thousand *li* a day, and the velocity is double that of the fastest horse of the military post stations. Thereafter, official dispatches will be speeded up, and regulations will be established for people to send mail by Western methods, so as to make the mail an appendage of the railroad company. . . This is the railroad's help to the postal administration.

CHAPTER XIV. THE ATTEMPT AT A POSITIVE FOREIGN POLICY

In the latter half of the nineteenth century, China's foreign policy and the modernization movement were both geared to foreign aggression. When a Japanese expedition to Formosa, sent to punish the murder by Formosan savages of shipwrecked Liu-ch'iu islanders, revealed China's military incompetence in 1874, Li Hung-chang had already realized that China's backwardness in the matter of armament, communications, and modern machinery placed the country at the mercy of stronger powers. Hence, in 1872, as we have noted above, the China Merchants Steam Navigation Company had been formed. In 1880, Li Hung-chang vigorously supported the resumption of railway construction, and he recommended the establishment of the first telegraph lines in China. In addition, he sponsored a number of schools for technological training. The French naval destruction of the Foochow shipyard in 1884 further stimulated the Chinese government to carry out its plans for a modern navy. Li was made Associate Controller of the Board of Admiralty, and he was able to secure enough funds to build a number of ships. Unfortunately, the new Chinese army and navy, which represented the result of a generation of effort at modernization, were crushed by Japan in the war of 1894–95. After this fiasco, Li Hung-chang almost gave up hope for rebuilding a strong China, with modern industries and communications, that would be able to fight against Japan. Instead, he sought an alliance with Russia, thus continuing China's traditional foreign policy of using one barbarian to fight another.

China's foreign relations were handled in considerable part by Li Hung-chang in the period after he became governor-general of the metropolitan province of Chihli in 1870, and particularly after the Empress Dowager removed Prince Kung from the Tsungli Yamen in 1884. The study made thus far of late Ch'ing foreign affairs reveals that there were various policies at different times, but no overall strategy. Since Li formed at least one principal center of policy formation, his writings have special interest.

In general, Li Hung-chang seems to have kept his eye on Japan as China's major foreign threat, rather than on Russia. In his view the Restoration of 1868 in Japan and her aggression in Formosa in 1874 were both a menace and a stimulus. Wen-hsiang had been one of the earliest officials to recognize Japan's probable ambitions, and Li Hung-chang had a similar foresight. In 1872 he wrote to a friend:

In Japan the emperor above and the people below have identical minds. They believe in the Western countries — in machinery, guns, artillery, warships, railways, and everything. They have patterned all these after France, England, and the United States. Hereafter Japan will certainly be a source of anxiety for China, as near as elbow and armpit. While our own weakness remains chronic, our strong neighbor daily becomes a threat to us. What technique can we employ to cope with her? [1]

One of Li's memorials, written on December 10, 1874, reads:

Japan recently has changed to the practice of Western military methods, has imitated the West in building railways, setting up telegraph lines, opening coal and iron mines, and coining foreign-style currency, all of which is not without benefit to her national polity and to her people's livelihood. She has also sent many students to foreign countries to acquire learning and practice in the use of machinery and technology; she has raised many foreign loans, and has secretly made an alliance with England. Her power is daily expanding, and her ambition is not small. Therefore she dares to display her strength in eastern lands, despises China, and takes action by invading Taiwan. Although the various European powers are strong, they are still seventy thousand *li* away from us, whereas Japan is as near as in the courtyard, or on the threshold, and is prying into our emptiness or solitude [i.e., weaknesses of our defense measures]. Undoubtedly she will become China's permanent and great anxiety. [2]

After the settlement of the Formosa incident, Li Hung-chang wrote a very serious letter to Shen Pao-chen, part of which reads:

Hereafter I hope our Emperor, officials, and the upper and the lower classes alike will "sleep on firewood and eat gall," to seek vigorously for methods of self-strengthening. . . As an earlier letter of the Tsungli Yamen says, "When something happens, we hurriedly plan to make up our deficiencies; but after the incident, we again indulge in pleasure and amusements." [3]

Li recognized the administrative ability and statesmanship of the great Japanese leader, Itō Hirobumi (1841–1909), about whom he made a secret report to the Tsungli Yamen in 1885. Itō, he says, "has traveled long on the continents of Europe and America and is strongly imitating them. He really has the ability to govern his country. He pays particular attention to these policies: to encourage trade and to be harmonious with neighboring nations, to enrich the people and strengthen the troops. . . In about ten years, Japan's wealth and power will be considerable. She is China's future disaster, not our present anxiety." [4] Obviously Li's prophecy was all too accurate. (For the conversation between Li and Itō in 1895, see Doc. 35.)

Over Russian expansion in Central Asia, Li had fewer misgivings than the bellicose group of high officials represented by Tso Tsung-t'ang. Li at least was more painfully aware of China's genuine weakness. In 1880 while Tso was demanding war, Li wrote to a subordinate:

Ili was seized by Russia, who took advantage of the Mohammedan rebellion. The local people really do not wish to return to our jurisdiction. To me this seems to be an extremely distant encroachment on our frontiers, and it may be unnecessary to request the return of Ili immediately. Those within and without the capital who are in charge of national plans suddenly feel boastful and take pleasure in meritorious deeds; again and again they have urged the recovery of Ili. Our key officials [of the Tsungli Yamen and the imperial court], without consulting the opinion of many persons, suddenly chose a weak and ignorant individual [Ch'ung-hou, who signed the unfavorable treaty of Livadia in 1879] and granted him authority. Again, suddenly, the whole country shouts madly like the barking of dogs to rescind the treaty which has already been signed. Can we say this is fair?

After the suppression of the Taiping and Nien rebellions, the demobilization of [Chinese] officers and soldiers has caused further exhaustion of the sources of provisions, because every year we have to supply six or seven million taels to the Western-style troops [to take their place] and there is no time limit to this expense. After the Formosa incident [of 1874] we began to deliberate about costal defense, for which the nominal appropriation was four million. Actually, the amount given each year is less than one million. The appropriation for the Peiyang coastal defense is only three or four hundred thousand. When there is no money, there are neither crack troops nor effective weapons. The subsidies for the Huai Army have also been reduced forty per cent. Last year I received the decision of the Ministry of War ordering me to disband more than ten thousand soldiers and the remaining force still has to defend the two oceans in the south and in the north. In our military forces, can we be said to be strong? [5]

During the negotiations with Russia in 1880–81, China mobilized many troops in the north to back up her envoy, Tseng Chi-tse, in St. Petersburg. Li Hung-chang doubted the soundness of Tseng's judgment; in a reply to him on April 12, 1880, Li wrote:

You also say . . . that the Russians, in their own country, fear a rebellion by the people and, abroad, have to defend themselves against invasion by the English, so that they are not in a position to start a large-scale frontier war with China. Your estimation of the enemy is certainly very clear and thorough; however, although you say that the English would not permit the Russians to fulfill their ambitions in China, have you really a fundamental basis for this assertion? If the Russians are to fulfill their ambitions in China, the first place of invasion must be in Sinkiang, next in Heilungkiang and Kirin. All are areas beyond the reach of the power of the British people. If there is harm to England, then the English may create some obstruction.

If there is no injury to England, then the English merchants will take advantage of the situation to plan for profit. Can they really show sincerity in rendering help to us Chinese? [6]

After Tseng Chi-tse's rearrangement of the Ili settlement in 1881 (usually considered a great success because it compelled Russia to disgorge territory she had already swallowed), Li remained unimpressed. To a friend he opined that the settlement gave "after all, no actual advantage to China, while the Russians have fulfilled their desires. The stupidity and confusion of our scholar-officials, and the lack of men of ability in the court are really ridiculous." [7]

Kuo Sung-tao was another diplomat who remained sceptical of warlike policies on the part of China. During the protracted and confused course of the fighting and negotiation with France in 1884, he submitted the following summary of his views.

DOC. 33. KUO SUNG-TAO ON THE FUTILITY OF A WAR POLICY, 1884 [8]

The European countries have concentrated on trade relations. . . The areas they have occupied are as far away as several tens of thousands of *li*, all occupied on the pretext of commerce. At first they had no intention of resorting to war, but after [the local people] had repeatedly gone back on their promises, the foreigners inevitably took offense and so used military force. Nor had they any preconceived idea of fighting for territory; but the more they fought, the further they advanced and thereupon they took the opportunity to usurp territory. The various islands in Southeast Asia are almost completely invaded and occupied, and all by this process. Therefore, in negotiating with the European nations on commercial affairs, we can use reason to overcome them but should absolutely not resort to force in a dispute; we can inspire their confidence by sincerity and good faith, but should by no means gloss things over; we can make use of their power to plan to make ourselves strong, but we must not on any account be envious of their strength and so seek to challenge them.

Your minister once held that, of the requests the Europeans have made, whether trifling or serious, large or small, with hundreds of variations and changes, there is none that cannot be settled by compromise according to reason; whereas, if war is resorted to, then they will not be easy to settle. This is because . . . [p. 38] their purpose is no more than to trade with us for profit; they cherish no hatred or grudge in their hearts. We have noticed that they do not speak lightly of war but argue with us back and forth, leaving themselves ample leeway to seek in each instance some advantage. If, on account of the fact that they do not speak of warfare easily, we goad them into acting with outrageous violence, then there will be a great deal of harm. Once warfare has been resorted to, the military expense they incur will eventually be sought from us as an indemnity. This is the principle by which the various European countries try to dominate one another. We simply have no argument with which to deny their request. They may eventually suffer a defeat and run away under full sail, but . . . after a year or two they will be sure to come again. They may overrun us as arrogantly as they like and the catastrophe they bring will be even more serious. Wars among the European countries last ten and sometimes twenty years. In each battle the cannonading on both sides may not cease for several days. . . China's coastline is 8,000 or 9,000 *li*. By what means can we oppose them?

This is why your minister has said that the various European countries are surrounding and gathering together against China so that she has no chance to fight, no power to fight, and simply no reason to fight. The French barbarians have frequently made private treaties with Annam exclusively for the purpose of trade with Yunnan. After the British initiated trade at T'eng-yueh [Yunnan], the French were even more fearful of being left behind and cherished the idea of competing with them. This is seen in the book by T'e-la-ko-erh, *T'an-ti-chi* [Doudart de Lagrée, *Investigation of the Routes*, 1865]. The ambition they cherish has been long and deep. . .

When the French barbarians caused trouble in Annam we should have sent an envoy to the capital of France and should also have sent an envoy to Saigon to investigate the opportunities and observe the changes in the situation, and yet we sent no one. When the French caused trouble in Annam, one place it started was in Saigon. In the Saigon area were more than 300,000 Chinese [p. 39] and a consul should have been established there to take care of their affairs, and yet it had not been possible to do so ahead of time. Important strategic opportunities of this sort have been idly lost!

At first the French barbarians thought that if they had 500 soldiers stationed at Saigon, these would be more than enough to overrun Annam. When they were assaulted on the flank by Liu Yung-fu [1837–1917, leader of the "Black Flags," Chinese irregulars], they were surprised at the unexpected attack and were in a dilemma. We might have taken advantage of this situation to settle the dispute, but again we lost this opportunity.

Of all the officials in and outside the capital, there is not a single one who is versed in foreign affairs. All they do is cautiously watch the intention of the court and show their zeal for war. The officials in charge of frontier troops are also accustomed to the old habits of military camps and make falsely exaggerated reports, which are all mere fabrications that avoid mentioning defeat but report success without a single sentence that can be verified. . .

When the French barbarians had caused trouble in Annam and had not yet reached China, the ministers at court favored war to resist them. . . When they came, our troops had withdrawn beforehand. When they withdrew, a retaking of the place was reported. . .

The cost of the shipyard at Ma-wei, Foochow, and the installation of machinery amounted to several millions. Whenever a battleship was built the maximum for one ship was a million and several hundred thousand dollars. Even the minimum was several hundred thousand. In a single engagement [with the French, 1884] all have been entirely destroyed. The loss is ten or twenty million. Thus we ourselves vainly destroyed our only ships and manufacturing machinery in order to make the warmongers happy. . .

During the last two or three years, since the start of the border war,

Western merchants have withdrawn their capital in China and ceased to trade; our coastal merchants have all become bankrupt and their original strength has been greatly drained; the populace in turn are moving away [p. 40] and becoming vagrants — in one day they may be frightened several times without being able to protect their own lives. Our merchants have suffered even more. In this war we merely cause ourselves trouble . . .

At present the number of levies and transfers of funds, and the broad extent of conscription, far exceed those of the period of Hsien-feng [1851–1861] when military force was used to quell the rebels. We are showing off our military might in places where it cannot be applied and are seeking to do battle with an enemy who is not responsive [to our strategy]. Along the several thousand *li* of our coastline, defense works are laid out everywhere, merely to the exhaustion of our own strength, and yet there is no end to it. . .

Your minister has heard that since ancient times in fighting foreign wars it has been necessary first to make secure the domestic administration. The Westerners have occupied our seaports and have penetrated deeply into the interior. There is therefore nothing for us to say about fighting a foreign war, but we should instead quickly attend to security within the country. If military action is taken everywhere and the frontiers are disturbed, we shall lose control on both fronts — neither expelling the foreigners nor having security within the country. . .

These divergent views on policy and the inefficiency of China's projects for self-strengthening are both illustrated in the case of the continued Chinese efforts at naval development.

a. Building a Modern Navy

The old-style naval and marine forces in the Ch'ing Dynasty, as part of the territorial Chinese "Army of the Green Standard" (*Lü-ying*), were traditionally divided into provincial commands. The land-minded Manchus had not paid much attention to the development of a navy and used their "water forces" only to patrol the coasts and certain commercially important inland waterways. Except in the 1680's, during the conquest of Formosa, and in the years 1795 to 1805, during the suppression of large pirate fleets off the South China coast, the programs of shipbuilding and naval training had been perfunctorily maintained as matters of routine.

During the Opium War the English fleet, using artillery of superior fire power and auxiliary steam-powered gunboats, played havoc with the Chinese fortifications and war junks all the way from Canton to Nanking, and practically destroyed everything that confronted it. Yet the Chinese officials of the day, as we have seen, developed no real doctrine of sea power. In spite of some discussions about the purchase of foreign war vessels for coastal defense, the Kwangtung squadrons of war junks were rebuilt along the same old lines as before. The new naval force which resulted was no match even for the pirates that became rampant in the late 1840's in the Canton estuary and along the waterways into Kwangsi. Some of these pirates later joined the Taiping rebels and manned their boats on the Yangtze when the Taiping horde overran Hunan and Hupei and descended on Nanking. It was mainly to deal with the Taiping fleet that Tseng Kuo-fan began to build up his Hunan militia army (*Hsiang-chün*), a large part of which was a marine force transported on long boats powered by oars. Foreign-built steamers were bought and rented in increasing numbers for use against the Taipings in the lower Yangtze valley after about 1853.

In the early 1860's, the value of Western-style gunboats in Chinese waters was signalized by the famous Lay-Osborn flotilla project, under which a powerful fleet was built for China in Britain, only to be disbanded in 1863 following a dispute over the manner in which Chinese official control of the squadron was to be exercised.[9] The subsequent shipbuilding efforts of Tseng Kuo-fan at Shanghai and Tso Tsung-t'ang at Foochow have already been noted (see, respectively, Doc. 13, Ch. IX, and Doc. 29), but it was not until 1867 that an organized Chinese navy was proposed, when Li Hung-chang, accepting the suggestion of Ting Jih-ch'ang (1823–1882), memorialized urging the appointment of three admirals who would take charge of the northern, central, and southern squadrons, respectively. In 1881 Hsueh Fu-ch'eng drafted regulations for the northern squadron and in 1882 a dockyard was begun at Port Arthur by Li Hung-chang. In 1884 Tso Tsung-t'ang memorialized proposing the establishment of a modern navy, and at the same time Chang P'ei-lun (1848–1903) submitted the memorial translated below, which urged the establishment of a central office in charge of the navy. As a result the Hai-chün Yamen, or Naval Office, was created on October 13, 1885. Prince Ch'un (1840–1891) was appointed controller of this board and Li Hung-chang was made one of the associate controllers.[10]

In the Naval Office, Li Hung-chang and Tseng Chi-tse were the responsible policy makers, but they were unable to keep the Empress Dowager from using the money originally appropriated for the development of the Chinese navy to rebuild the Summer Palace.[11] Although the northern squadron was organized in 1888 to consist of 28 ships of various sizes, it was a navy only in form, its organization and equipment being poor [12] — a situation which forecast the disaster of 1894. Near the end of the dynasty the naval administration was reorganized, but even in the twentieth century China has failed to develop a navy on Western great-power lines.

DOC. 34. Chang P'ei-lun's Proposal of 1884 [13]

The reason for the European countries' overrunning the seas and the difficulty of contending against them lie in their possession of solid ships and effective guns. During the last twenty years, trade relations between China and foreign countries have been established and treaties concluded. . . The intentions of these nations, standing like birds of prey and covetous as wolves, with watering mouths and eyes staring at Asia, are understood by everyone. Even if our nation, right now, greatly develops its navy, we fear that we cannot rival them. If we are again hesitant, wondering what to do, and do not work on the fundamental plan for self-strengthening, I really fear that the menace from the sea will be unlimited. . .

After the suppression of the Taiping and the Nien rebels, China gradually built shipyards and bought machines to establish a new navy with steam warships. That was the beginning of our navy. Funds were insufficient, men of ability were not forthcoming, flood, drought and other catastrophes frequently occurred, and opinion within and without the capital was not unified; so, until now, the old regulations for naval ships in the outer seas have not yet been changed, nor has a definite system yet been established for a steamship fleet of all the provinces. When there is no alarm, the funds for the southern and northern squadrons are never delivered in full by any of the Maritime Customs offices; when there is an alarm, every province retains for its own use the subsidy for the navy. If this situation continues without change and we still wish to have a coastal navy sufficient for attacking or coming to the rescue, or to be adequate for offensive war as well as for defense, it will obviously be very difficult. . .

[P. 3] Your minister has studied the European military systems. Concerning their navies, they all establish a special ministry of the navy with very great powers. The Englishman Robert Hart has made a suggestion to the Tsungli Yamen regarding the establishment of a bureau in general charge of coastal defense. We have seriously considered the plans of two or three veteran statesmen and consulted the new systems of five or six sea powers. We can see the advantages and disadvantages in the proposal that the naval forces should be combined in one unit, not divided and scattered. Thus, if we wish to seek a method to control our enemies, we cannot do it unless we create a navy with steam warships for the outer seas; and if we wish to accomplish the overrunning of the seas, we cannot do it unless we establish an Office (ya-men) of the Navy. The important functions of the navy are in general four: namely, the investigation of coastal topography, the training of officers of ability, the building of naval vessels, and the study of various operations. Coastal defense is of concern to the governors general and governors, but since there are boundaries between provinces, they cannot entirely disregard each other's spheres of jurisdiction. If we have an important minister take full charge, then the relative importance of all seaports along the entire coast line can be distinguished; also where iron ships should be anchored, where forts should be built, where shipyards may be prepared, and where mines may be laid; the generals and the admirals will be like one family, the water and land defenses will be well coördinated. . .

b. *The Failure at Self-Strengthening*

The collapse of the Chinese empire is as complex a subject as the decline and fall of ancient Rome. A similar multiplicity of factors contributed to the general debacle and many years of study will be necessary before we can generalize about it, or compare China's failure with Japan's success in a few well-chosen words.

One thing is worth noting, however. While many writers in contemporary China now stress the deleterious impact of Western imperialism upon the old Chinese state and society, the Chinese leaders of the nineteenth century maintained a rather different view of their problem. Through all their writings, as noted above, runs a constant emphasis upon the need for men of ability (*jen-ts'ai*, "human talent") who could deal with the crisis. This concern stemmed from the ancient ethnocentric assumption that the Chinese empire's foreign relations were only a subsidiary function of domestic administration — of the twin evils, "internal rebellion and aggression from without" (*nei-luan wai-huan*), the former was assumed to open the door for the latter. A dynasty that could handle its domestic problems need have little fear of foreign aggression.

Whether or not this analysis took adequate account of the bite of modern imperialism, it at least threw the moral blame for the failure at self-strengthening upon the Chinese leaders, not upon foreign imperialist scapegoats. This traditional Chinese concept that government is indeed a personal matter, that history is made by the ruler and his ministers, not by impersonal social and economic "forces," may well have contributed to the demoralization of Chinese officials who saw things going steadily from bad to worse.

Li Hung-chang's awareness of the Meiji reforms in Japan has been evidenced in many preceding documents, as well as his specific recognition of Itō Hirobumi as the great protagonist of Japan's self-strengthening. In 1885 the two men had negotiated the Li-Itō convention to stabilize the Sino-Japanese rivalry in Korea. A decade later, after China's complete and sudden defeat and the destruction of Li's plans and hopes of many years, they met again to negotiate the Treaty of Shimonoseki. Part of their conversation on March 20, 1895, was as follows: [14]

DOC. 35. LI HUNG-CHANG'S CONVERSATION WITH ITŌ HIROBUMI, 1895

Li Hung-chang: In Asia, our two countries, China and Japan, are the closest neighbors, and moreover have the same language. How could we be enemies? Now for the time being we are fighting each other, but eventually we should work for permanent friendship. If we are enemies endlessly, then what is [p. 262] harmful to China will not necessarily be beneficial to Japan. Let us look at the various European countries which, even though their military forces are strong, do not lightly start hostilities. Since we Chinese and Japanese are on the same continent, we should also imitate Europe. If the diplomatic ministers of our two countries mutually and deeply understand this idea, we ought vigorously to maintain the general stability of Asia, and establish perpetual peace and harmony between ourselves, so that our Asiatic yellow race will not be encroached upon by the white race of Europe.

Itō: I am very much pleased with the idea of the grand secretary [Li Hung-chang]. Ten years ago when I was at Tientsin, I talked about reform with the grand secretary. Why is it that up to now not a single thing has been changed or reformed? This I deeply regret.

Li: At that time when I heard you, sir, talking about that, I was overcome with admiration, and furthermore I deeply admired, sir, your having vigorously changed your customs in Japan so as to reach the present stage. Affairs in my country have been so confined by tradition that I could not accomplish what I desired. At that time you advised me and said, "China is large and populous, the reform of various policies ought to come gradually." Now in the twinkling of an eye ten years have gone by, and everything is still the same. I am even more regretful. I am ashamed of having excessive wishes and lacking the power to fulfill them. The soldiers and generals of your honorable country are excellently trained on the model of Western methods; in all kinds of policies and administration, you are advancing daily to newer and more prosperous planes. This time, when I went to Peking and talked to scholars and officials, I found that some of them have also thoroughly realized that our country definitely should undergo reform before we can stand on our own feet.

Itō: "The providence of heaven has no affection, except for the virtuous." If your honorable country wishes to exert itself to action, Heaven above would certainly help your honorable country to fulfill its desires. It is be-

cause Heaven treats the people below [i.e., mankind] without discrimination. The essential thing is that each country should do its own best.

Li: Your honorable country, after it has been so reorganized by you, sir,
is very admirable. . . [The conversation then turned to other topics.]

c. *The Alliance with Russia*

As Lin Tse-hsü and Wei Yuan had pointed out more than fifty years before,
the barbarian menace could be met partly by borrowing the superior military
methods of the Western powers or, alternatively, by using one power against
another. For a whole generation, from 1860 to 1894, China's leaders had aimed
at self-strengthening with Western help, chiefly the help of Britain in the customs
administration as well as in the naval program. By 1895, Japan had blown this
program to pieces. British opinion had suffered disillusionment over China and was
beginning the shift that led eventually to the Anglo-Japanese alliance of 1902,
while the other powers, especially Germany, were developing the tendencies that
soon led to the scramble for concessions and the threatened partition of China in
1898. In this situation China turned to Russia as a potential ally to check Japan.
Without attempting to explore the complex diplomacy of the period, we quote
memorials of two influential provincial leaders and present also the text of the
secret treaty of 1896, which has not been widely available in English. While Li
Hung-chang performed the act of "inviting the Russian bear into the parlor" in
China's northeastern provinces, it is apparent that other high officials, not of his
camp, supported the step. Thus the Chinese people's potential base for future industrial development was drawn irrevocably into the vortex of power politics.

DOC. 36. LIU K'UN-I'S SECRET PROPOSAL, JULY 1895 [15]

Liu K'un-i, Imperial Commissioner and Governor-general of Liang-
chiang, submits a secret report of a great plan to ally with Russia for opposing Japan, in order to consolidate the defense of the second capital [Fengtien,
whither the Court had fled] and to strengthen the whole situation:

Your minister notes that diplomatic relations between Chinese and foreigners have continued for thirty years until the present day, when the
matter is even more difficult to handle. China's use of hard and soft policies
should stress their modification according to the times. The chances of all
countries being friendly or hostile to us are guided by circumstance. After
the war in Annam, when China failed to handle the issue properly, we were
considerably despised by all countries. This time, when we negotiated peace
with Japan, we made too many compromises which encouraged the gradual
inception of a waylaying policy — glaring at us like tigers, all the various
powers seek to find a plump spot to bite into us. We estimate that our
power is inferior to theirs, so we must quickly make an international
alliance as a means of seeking assistance.

According to your minister's humble understanding, the impending
disaster from other countries is still slow in coming, but that from Japan is
imminent. This is because she is close to us; after she has obtained Taiwan
and Liaotung, the way for her entrance will be even more convenient, as if
her army could start directly from our pillow and mat — it can invade any
part of our territory at will. . . But Russia does not want Japan to be strong,

and Japan's invasion of our Three Eastern Provinces [Manchuria] makes Russia even more jealous. Thus, by the Sino-Japanese peace treaty [of Shimonoseki] we had already ceded Liaotung to Japan, but Russia, France, and Germany compelled her to return it to China. Is Russia doing this especially for us? She is, at the same time, working for herself. If we take this opportunity to establish close relations with her, for mutual assistance, and also give her some concessions, Russia will surely be glad to comply. Even though this move cannot protect our various coastal provinces, Japan certainly will not dare to covet the territory of the Three Eastern Provinces, which are close to Russia. . . If these provinces were lost, how could the dynasty maintain its foundation, and how could our Emperor face his ancestors? That is why, whenever your minister thinks of this, he cannot keep his heart from palpitating and his muscles from twitching.

Some people say that Russia is adjacent to the widest stretch of Chinese territory and that in the future she will certainly do harm to China. Heretofore, your minister was also of the same opinion. Now he is inclined to think that this statement is wrong. It also depends upon how we are going to console or control her. Russia's territory is already very large and, moreover, she is well known for her good faith and righteousness. She has had good relations with us for two hundred years and several decades, during which time there was no war at all. This is really a rare thing in all times. Formerly [1881] she returned Ili [p. 21] to us, and this time she coöperated with France and Germany to struggle against Japan for the return of Liaotung to China, an even greater favor than before; and yet some suspect her of having other ambitions, and would no longer associate with her in sincerity. That is, the nation which is coöperative with us, we keep at a distance; and toward the nation which is magnanimous to us, we are stingy. Soon they will say that it is not worthwhile to help China, and our position will become even more isolated. . .

As long as Sino-Russian relations are permanently solid, Japan and other countries will have scruples and will not go to the extreme of considering China non-existent, and cunningly seek to start trouble. . .

DOC. 37. Chang Chih-tung's Memorial of August 1895 [16]

To save the critical situation today, nothing is better than the conclusion of a secret treaty of alliance with a strong power for assistance. From ancient times, whenever nations have opposed each other, as if with horns, they usually have used the policy of allying with a distant country to attack an enemy nearby. With regard to the Sino-Japanese situation today, this policy is even more suitable. China's power today [p. 36] can never oppose simultaneously all the nations in the East and West. . .

I understand that the tendency of foreign countries in recent years has been to establish particularly close relations with one or two others among all the countries which have general relations. In time of peace they make secret treaties in advance, and in wartime they aid one another with military provisions and armaments. If there is no secret treaty, then when something happens they remain neutral and will not interfere.

Now if we wish to make a treaty, and to have a bond for mutual assistance, naturally Russia is most convenient for us, because England uses commerce to absorb the profits of China, France uses religion to entice the
Chinese people, Germany has no common territorial boundary with us, and
the United States does not like to interfere in others' military affairs. It is
difficult for all of these nations to discuss an alliance with us. It is known
that Russia, as China's neighbor, has kept treaty agreements with us for
more than two hundred years, and that she has never embarked on hostilities; she is different from other countries who have frequently resorted to
warfare with us. Moreover, her behavior is grand and generous, and cannot
be compared with that of the Europeans. For example, in the church case
at Tientsin in 1870, in which all the countries were busy making a clamor,
Russia did not participate; and in the treaties over Ili [1879 and 1881] our
nation completely refused and then modified the eighteen articles, and
Russia generously consented. This time she has demanded the return of
the territory of Liaotung for us; although she did it for the sake of the general situation in the East, yet China has already actually received the benefit.
Japan's spearhead has been slightly blunted by this. In comparison with
other countries who acted as bystanders, putting their hands in their sleeves,
and covertly planning for commercial profits, Russia shows a great difference.

It is just the right time for us to take this opportunity and work vigorously for an alliance, deepening our friendship and making a secret treaty
with her. In everything concerning Russian commercial affairs and boundary
matters, we should make some compromises. If Russia resorts to warfare in
the East, we should aid her navy with coal and food, permitting her war
vessels to enter our dockyards for repairs. On land we must permit her to
use our roads, supply her with resources, food, vehicles and horses; in accordance with her reliance on our supplies we should offer her coöperation and
subsidy according to our means. But we should have it settled in the contract
that in case China is attacked, Russia will have to help us with armed
forces, of which the most important is the navy. We must also make a decision during our conference with Russia concerning the method of compen-
sating her, because Russia is very suspicious that England dominates the
situation in the East. If China and Russia form an alliance, English influence
will be considerably curbed; and Russia would be willing to accommodate us.

After all, it is not easy for China to train a navy. If we have the Russians
to aid us, in the future, regardless of what country may start hostilities with
us, after a few weeks several tens of Russian warships could be sent to
patrol the Eastern seas. Thus we can prepare only the strategy of war on
land, and our enemy cannot plan to invade the interior deeply. This is the
crucial point in our international relations and the most important policy for
saving the critical situation.

With regard to the foreign countries, China has always treated them on
the same level. Thus, during the last time [presumably, the Sino-Japanese
War of 1894] there was no one to help us. Such matters must be prepared
in advance [p. 37] during days of peace, and at present our plan for alliance
should absolutely not be delayed. It behooves us to request an Imperial

decree to order the princes and high ministers to deliberate secretly and conclude the matter carefully. But by no means should we ever let Robert Hart [the British Inspector General of Chinese Imperial Maritime Customs, 1863–1908] hear of it, lest he be jealous, impede us, and spoil the matter. Reverently memorialized, August 8, 1895.

The treaty concluded by Li Hung-chang on his visit to Russia to attend the coronation of Tsar Nicholas II was reported at the time by British correspondents, evidently on a basis of rumor. In 1922 its content was briefly announced by the Chinese delegation at the Washington Conference, but we have not found an exact translation of the Chinese text in previously published works. Judging by the memorials of Liu and Chang just quoted, China got the military agreement they desired, but at the price of strategic, if not indeed territorial, concessions which set an almost disastrous pattern for the future.

DOC. 38. TEXT OF THE SINO-RUSSIAN SECRET TREATY OF 1896 [17]

His Imperial Majesty the Emperor of China and His Imperial Majesty the Tsar of Russia, desiring to maintain the present situation of peace in the Far East, and to prevent future aggression by other powers upon the territory of Asia, have determined to conclude a treaty of mutual assistance. Therefore, His Imperial Majesty the Emperor of China has specially appointed His Excellency Li Hung-chang, Imperial Commissioner and Plenipotentiary of the first class, Grand Tutor of the Heir Apparent, Grand Secretary of the Wen-hua Palace, Stern-and-resolute Earl of the first rank, and Superintendent of Trade for the Northern Ports; and His Imperial Majesty the Tsar of Russia has specially appointed Prince Lobanov, Imperial Commissioner and Plenipotentiary, Foreign Minister, member of the Cabinet and of the Imperial Council and Privy Councillor, and (Count) Witte, Imperial Commissioner and Plenipotentiary, Finance Minister, member of the Cabinet and Privy Councillor, as their respective plenipotentiaries, who, having exchanged and examined their credentials and found them in proper form, agree to the following stipulations:

Article I. In the event of a Japanese invasion of the territory of Russia in Eastern Asia, or the territory of China, or the territory of Korea, the present treaty shall be considered as having been involved, and measures shall be taken according to the treaty. In such an event both contracting powers promise to dispatch all the military and naval forces that can be mobilized for mutual assistance; they shall also supply each other with munitions and provisions as far as possible.

Article II. Having entered into the present treaty of mutual defense, neither contracting power can conclude a separate peace agreement with the enemy without mutual consultation.

Article III. Should an emergency arise during the war, Russian warships shall be allowed to enter all ports on the coast of China; in case of need, the local authorities shall give aid to the best of their ability.

Article IV. In order in the future to facilitate the rapid and safe transportation of Russian troops for opposing the enemy, and for the supply of munitions and provisions, the Chinese Government agrees to let Russia construct a railway through the territory of Heilungkiang and Kirin to connect with Vladivostok. However, the construction of this railway is not to be used as a pretext for the infringement of Chinese territory, or for encroachment on the lawful rights and privileges of H. I. M. the Emperor of China. The Chinese Government will entrust the Russo-Chinese Bank with the management of the (railway) matter. The Chinese Minister to Russia and the Bank shall consult on the spot and decide upon the terms of the contract.

Article V. When Russia is engaged in the defensive measures against the enemy provided for in Article I, she may use the railway as provided in Article IV for the transportation of troops, provisions, and munitions. In peace time Russia may also use this railway for troops and provisions in transit. Apart from temporary stops due to changes of trains, they shall not be allowed to stop over for any other reason.

Article VI. The agreement shall be effective for fifteen years, beginning with the date on which the contract mentioned in Article IV shall have been ratified and put into effect. Six months before the expiration of this treaty, the two contracting powers shall negotiate for its extension.

Special provision: The plenipotentiaries of both contracting powers agree that the Sino-Russian treaty concluded on this day [18] shall be rendered into the Chinese and French languages in duplicate copies, to be signed and have seals affixed. The Chinese and French copies have been compared and found to be without error. In case of dispute the French text shall be the decisive version.

Concluded on the 22nd day, 4th month, and 22nd year of Kuang-hsü, which is May 22, 1896 (o.s.) [June 3, 1896], at Moscow.

5

THE REFORM MOVEMENT

THROUGH 1900

CHAPTER XV. PROMOTERS OF INSTITUTIONAL CHANGE

The decade preceding China's defeat in the Sino-Japanese war of 1894–95 is perhaps the least studied in the whole century of China's modern history. No doubt this is partly because Western rivalry and attention did not center on China or the Far East in this period, in contrast to the succeeding decade from 1895 to 1905, and accordingly less has been written by Westerners. During these years British influence and British trade were dominant in Ch'ing foreign relations — this was the heyday of the British treaty system in China, the period of pay-off when the British "opening" of China for commercial exploitation had finally become effective in terms of imports and exports facilitated by the Customs Service under Robert Hart. Meanwhile, the rivalry of foreign powers had not yet reached a stage of more-than-commercial exploitation of the Chinese empire. In domestic affairs, the leaders who had come into power with the suppression of the Taiping Rebellion were likewise at the height of their careers — Li Hung-chang and his colleagues were cautiously inaugurating new and lucrative enterprises in the treaty ports while the Empress Dowager was established in her domination of the court at Peking. One has the impression that this was a period when the old order was able to coast along, in the benevolent shadow of Victorian Britain.

Across the water in Japan, on the other hand, it was during these years that vigorous leaders were actually carrying out changes which had been only talked about in China. Whatever the complex historical background of this amazing contrast, it is plain that the leaders of the Meiji Restoration had more opportunity for effective action than their contemporaries in China. With foreign help they were feverishly trying to telescope the whole process of the industrial revolution, with its attendant changes in social, economic, and political life, into the time span of one generation. In China this startling achievement of the Japanese people was known but did not call forth similar action. Meanwhile, knowledge about Europe and America was being accumulated from missionaries in China and from Chinese officials who went abroad, but the process was slow.

a. *The Missionary Influence*

Missionaries in China have been the most immediate channel of Western influence in human and personal terms. China's idea of the West has been formed in great measure from their activity, yet the work of the missions has thus far been studied more from the Western side of organization and personnel than from the Chinese side of publications, sermons, and doctrines presented to the Chinese people in their own language.

The Protestant missionaries, from the beginning of their work in China in the early nineteenth century, had been interested not only in converting the Chinese heathen in order to "save their souls" for Christianity but also in helping them improve their way of life in this world through useful knowledge. The pioneer Protestant missionary, Robert Morrison (1782–1834), reached Canton in 1807, learned Chinese, compiled a dictionary, and brought out a Chinese version of the Bible which was later used by Hung Hsiu-ch'üan and so influenced the early Taiping religious documents. One contribution of Morrison and the early English missionaries from the Chinese point of view was the founding of a school for Chinese converts and a Chinese printing establishment at Malacca in 1814. Yung Wing (see Ch. XI a) was one of its students.

The early American missionaries, David Abeel (1804–1846) and E. C. Bridgman (1801–1861), who arrived at Canton in 1830, founded a school, and Bridgman and S. Wells Williams (1812–1884) maintained a valuable monthly periodical, *The Chinese Repository* (1832–1851). Peter Parker (1804–1888) of Yale started the first American missionary hospital and medical school at Canton, which has been in operation ever since. After more treaty ports were opened, and inland missionary work became legalized by treaties in 1858–1860, there was a tremendous expansion by both Catholic and Protestant workers. The Jesuits resumed their work at Zicawei (Hsü-chia-hui), a village in the suburbs of Shanghai named after Hsü Kuang-ch'i's family (see Ch. II b), establishing there a school, a library, a meteorological station, and a printing plant. The various Catholic orders, like the Protestant denominations, agreed among themselves upon the allocation of areas for their work.

By degrees an increasing number of English and American Protestant missionary scholars worked seriously on the problem of interpreting the West to China and vice versa. It was these men who did most of the composing of Chinese tracts and translations of Western works in history, science, technology, and other subjects. Their translations, worked over by competent Chinese assistants, were readable and so had a great deal of influence among the scholar class. Foremost among these pioneers in cultural relations were the Englishmen William Muirhead (1822–1900), Joseph Edkins (1823–1905), Alexander Wylie (1815–1887), and James Legge (1815–1897); and the Americans, W. A. P. Martin (see Doc. 26), S. Wells Williams, John Fryer (1839–1928), and Young J. Allen. The last two were especially prolific: Fryer, at the translation bureau of the Shanghai Arsenal, produced many valuable compilations and translations which became the textbooks for Chinese students interested in scientific subjects. Allen's Chinese periodical, the *Wan-kuo kung-pao* ("The Globe Magazine"), published in Shanghai from 1875 to 1907, had the avowed aim of being "devoted to the extension of knowledge relating to Geography, History, Civilization, Politics, Religion, Science, Art, Industry, and General Progress of Western countries." [1]

Perhaps the most influential missionary who advocated reform was Timothy Richard (1845–1919). He came to China in 1870 and ten years before the war with Japan he was already warning Chinese officialdom that it was to China's advantage to pursue a policy of peace, as the less costly course of action. He predicted that unless China introduced institutional changes at once, including modern schools, disastrous consequences would be near at hand. In 1890–91, on the invitation of Li Hung-chang, Richard served as the editor of the *Shih-pao*, a daily newspaper, at Tientsin. He used the editorial section as a pulpit for preaching his ideas of institutional and technological reform, hoping to make the Chinese official class realize the impending danger. He also spent much time seeking interviews with high officials, and associated himself with many young Chinese scholars, some of whom became leaders of the reform movement. In 1895, after the Sino-Japanese War, Richard brought out a volume of essays entitled *Hsi-to* ("The Warning Bell from the West"), which he had written during the preceding fifteen years. In them he had exhorted the officials and scholars of China to follow the example of Japan in establishing modern schools and beginning other institutional reforms. His prestige was enhanced by the fact that history had proved him right.

Important as the missionaries were in planting ideas of reform in the minds of Chinese students, their positive influence was limited mainly to a few coastal cities and reached a rather small percentage of the gentry-scholar-official class. The majority of the latter resented the increasing prestige of the missionaries and felt that the foreigners threatened their own positions as teachers and upholders of Chinese tradition. The missionaries were also disliked by the gentry-officials because of their interference in lawsuits on behalf of their converts, a practice followed especially by the Catholic missionaries. The anti-missionary movement was particularly serious in the late 1880's along the Yangtze and, although suppressed by the officials, sometimes half-heartedly, it was not rooted out until after 1900. One factor underlying it was the difficulty experienced by the gentry and lower Chinese officials in distinguishing between Western religions and other aspects of Western civilization. They might willingly have accepted the latter without the former, had they seemed distinct. This inability to comprehend the difference between Christianity and the rest of Western culture was quite universal, from the court down to the coolie class, as the Boxer Uprising was to demonstrate. No doubt it resulted from the fact that the Western missionaries had consciously used medicine and other forms of good works as vehicles for proselytism. The result was that Chinese resentment against foreign evangelism in China became unreasoningly attached to Western ways generally, and so, in fact, retarded the process of learning from the West.

b. *Early Chinese Advocates of Reform*

Among the writers who prepared the way for institutional reform in China, one of the most interesting and quixotic was Wang T'ao (1828–1897),[2] a gifted journalist whose bicultural experience and personal opportunism fitted him to be an effective cultural intermediary and conveyer of ideas, even though he was not an official and represented no particular group. He took a post under the Ch'ing, deserted to the Taipings, later betrayed them and worked in the treaty ports. He had been in contact with Westerners in Shanghai and Hongkong from 1848, and formed a close association with the leading British missionary sinologues Walter H. Medhurst (1796–1857), William Muirhead, and James Legge, eventually assisting the latter in translating several volumes of *The Chinese Classics*. It is interesting to note that shortly after Ito Hirobumi's return from England to Japan, Wang T'ao was invited by Legge to Scotland, in late 1867. He spent two years in the British Isles and Europe, where he saw something of the Franco-Prussian war and wrote a book on it. He had a scholarly correspondence with the French sinologue Stanislas Julien (1799–1873), and gave a lecture at Oxford in 1868, pre-

sumably with Legge as his interpreter. Returning to Hongkong with a large library in 1870, he soon became well known as an editorial writer. In 1879 he
visited Japan, where he was enthusiastically received by Japanese who had read
his writings and with whom he had much correspondence.

Wang T'ao had begun his journalistic work shortly after he escaped from
Shanghai to Hongkong in 1862. He served as editor of the *Hongkong News*,
which was established under foreign auspices, and in 1873 founded in Hongkong
his own newspaper, the *Tsun Wan Yat Po* (*Hsün-huan jih-pao*), in which he
wrote his most famous editorials. His son-in-law, Ch'ien Cheng, was an editor and
for some time editor-in-chief of the Shanghai *Shun Pao* (*Shen-pao*), to which
Wang was a frequent contributor. In 1882 his editorials were collected and published.[3] They are written in an elegant style and contain much interesting information.

Under foreign protection in Hongkong and Shanghai, Wang T'ao was bold in
his attacks on the corrupt Chinese administration of the day. He was also an ardent
advocate of a domestic reform program. About 1870 he wrote three essays on
"Reform and Self-strengthening" in which he advocated four reforms affecting the
selection of scholars, the training of troops, the school system, and the legal code.[4]
A few years later he wrote an editorial, "To Get Rid of Abuses," advocating
clarification of the qualifications for official position, weeding out of sinecure posts,
replacement of Manchu bannermen in office, discontinuance of river conservation,
elimination of extravagant expenditures, and abolition of the *likin* tax.[5] In another
essay, "To Promote Profit," Wang T'ao discussed the utility of opening mines for
coal, iron, and other metals, setting up textile mills, and building steamships.
About 1878 he urged the training of a navy,[6] as well as the installation of telegraph
lines, and the building of railways.[7] He was one of the first Chinese to propose the
abolition of extraterritoriality,[8] and demanded the return of Macao from the control of Portugal.

As a diplomatic strategist, Wang T'ao anticipated about 1879 that Russia's
ambition was for territorial expansion and annexation, and "if she is not successful
in Europe, she will make a disturbance in China." [9] Therefore he suggested a
containment policy by proposing to set up two barriers against Russia. In Europe
the six countries, England, France, Prussia, Austria, Italy, and Turkey should unite
to resist Russia, otherwise they would be conquered one by one, just as the Ch'in
had conquered the six states of ancient China in the third century B. C. and built
the great Ch'in Empire. In Asia, Wang T'ao suggested an alliance of China, Japan,
Annam, Siam, and Burma to prevent Russia's expansion.

In his cultural outlook Wang T'ao shared the optimism of Victorian England
and prophesied the unification of nations through the conquest of distance by the
new inventions of science. The first entry in his collected editorial writings is on
"The origin of truth," in which he says, "The truth of the world is only one. . .
It begins by proceeding from identity to divergencies and it ends by proceeding
from divergencies to identity." [10] In his view the steamship and railway would
help people to reach every corner of the earth. These inventions which "the Western powers are now using for their encroachment upon China are the very things
which the sages of a future age will utilize as the means for the unification of all
nations." [11]

As a result of his trip to Europe, Wang warned China against her effort to
learn only the superficial, external mechanics of the West. He praised the Western
system of law and justice, popular elections and constitutional government, and
discussed the three forms of state in Europe: the ruler-governed state (*chün-chu
kuo* or monarchy), the people-governed state (*min-chu kuo* or democracy), and
the ruler-and-people jointly-governed state (*chün-min kung-chu kuo* or constitu-

tional monarchy). Of these three, he favored the constitutional monarchy of England.[12]

While Wang T'ao was keen in observation and better versed in Western conditions, he adhered essentially to the same pattern of thought as Feng Kuei-fen and Chang Chih-tung. He wanted Chinese civilization to remain the foundation on which gradual reforms might be superimposed.[13] In fact he was pitifully ignorant of ancient Western history and political institutions, and shared the naive rationalization that China had been the early home of Western culture.[14] While on the one hand he regarded the United States as the most powerful country of the West, on the other hand he said, "Recently in the United States of America most women in the state of Massachusetts have preferred to get concubines for their husbands" — this from one of the leading "old Western hands" of his day!

DOC. 39. WRITINGS OF WANG T'AO

A Refutation of the Idea of Using Barbarians Against Barbarians
(from a letter written in the period 1858–1860 to a private friend) [15]

Formerly it was said, "The Europeans who have trade relations with China are more than one country; it is better to use them to attack each other, or use them so that they make compromises with each other, or use them so as to separate them from each other." These three statements all seem to be calculations based on profound deliberation and far-reaching thought. And yet nowadays I am afraid that they are impracticable. Why? Because all the European countries have the intention of keeping China on the outside. How can they be utilized by us? Even though there were one country which was willing to be utilized by us, all the other nations would undoubtedly ridicule her. As for two countries which engage in a prolonged struggle against each other, with the issue not yet decided, the practice in Western countries is to persuade them to make peace. If the advice is not taken, then assistance is given the weak party to attack the strong, just as England and France helped Turkey to attack Russia in recent years. . . But the practice in the West is, after all, not a sufficient rule to be applied to China. The most tractable Western country is the United States of America. Nevertheless she still takes the victory or failure of England as her own glory or disgrace [p. 22]. . . Thus there have been occasions for her to assist England, but there has never been an occasion for her to assist us and attack England. As to her relations with us, though she has never made unreasonable demands on us, yet she has shared all the benefits gained by England and France. . . If she sincerely wants to give us support, how could she act in this way? . . .

If, suddenly, the Westerners seized an opportunity to attack us, how could we resist them? Our soldiers are inferior to theirs, our finances are inferior to theirs, our weapons are inferior to theirs, and our military strategies are also inferior to theirs. They already thoroughly understand the hostile actions which we on our side may take, whereas we are as yet incapable of knowing what hostilities they may commit. We excuse ourselves by saying that it is because they are too far away from us. Yet with all the publication of daily newspapers and the spread of postal communications, can we not make some inquiries and obtain some information? During the last hundred years or more, America's revolt against England and France's assault on England were both occasions of peril to her. Recently the mutiny [of 1857] in India and the violation of treaties by Persia were both incidents which she had to cope with. The occurrence of such incidents is sporadic. The essential thing is for us to be good at forecasting them.

On Reform [16]

If Confucius were born today we may be certain that he would not stubbornly believe in antiquity and oppose making changes. . .

First, the method of selecting civil servants should be reformed. The examination essays up to the present day have gone from bad to worse. . . And yet we are still using them to select scholars. . .

Secondly, the method of training soldiers should be reformed. Now our army camps and water forces have only names registered on books, but no actual persons. The authorities consider our troops unreliable, and then they recruit militia, who can be assembled but cannot be disbanded. . . This is called 'using the untrained people to fight,' which is no different from driving them to their deaths. . .

Thirdly, the empty show of our schools should be reformed. Now district directors of schools and sub-directors of schools are installed, one person for a small city, and two for a larger city. It is a sheer waste. . . Such people are usually degenerate, incompetent, and senile and have little sense of shame. They are unfit to set the example for scholars. . .

He who rules the empire should establish the foundation and not merely mend the superstructure. . . [P. 15] Formerly we thought that the foundation of our wealth and strength would be established if only Western methods were respected or adopted and that the result would be achieved immediately. . . Now in all the coastal provinces there have been established special factories to make guns, bullets, and ships. Young men have been selected and sent to study abroad. Seen from the outside, the effort is really great and fine. Unfortunately, however, we are still copying the superficialities of their methods, getting the terminology (of Western civilization) but little actual substance. The ships which were formerly built at Foochow were entirely based on old methods of Western countries, beneath contempt, to those who know. As to things made in other places, for the trick of moving a machine or valve we must rely on the instruction of Westerners. Yet, if we watch the bearing of the Chinese manufacturers, they already feel noisily pleased with themselves. They usually believe that their thinking and wisdom are sufficient to match those of the Westerners, or that they have even surpassed them.

In general (the advantage of) guns lies in the fine technique of discharging them, that of ships in the ability to navigate them. . . The handling of effective weapons depends upon the people. . . But the so-called able minds of our people are not necessarily able, and the so-called competent ones are not necessarily competent. They are merely mediocrities who accomplish something through the aid of others.

Therefore, the urgent problem of our nation today lies primarily in the governance of the people; next in the training of soldiers; and in these two matters the crucial thing to aim at is the accumulation of men of ability. Indeed, superficial imitation in practical matters is certainly not as effective as arousing genuine intellectual curiosity. The polishing and pounding in factories is definitely not as important as the machining of peoples' minds. . .

[P. 16] Let us now talk about the conventional examination subjects. The themes on classics in the second examination ought to be replaced by some practical knowledge . . . so that the candidates can understand the body politic and can transfer their knowledge into actual practice. . . After four or five examination periods, the eight-legged essays can also be abolished.

On Domestic Administration [17]

[P. 25] For flood control, there is no good method in China or the West. This is because the river sand daily accumulates, the river basin daily rises, and the dikes must be built higher to prevent a break. Such methods have been handed down from dynasty to dynasty without any attempt at change. People who live near the river are as though living in the basin of the river. When after a long drenching rain the water breaks through the dikes and flows out horizontally, they have the fear of becoming fish and turtles. Now it is better to adopt the Western method, to dredge the sand, to comb and scrape, and make the water flow, to get rid of the banking up of sand and then open many small branches in order to reduce the force of the water. . .

As for the handling of foreigners, the difficulty is not in the conveying of our instructions overseas; the foremost trouble is in the managing of the foreigners in the interior of China. . . If the Western merchants, missionaries, and others were contented with their lot, law abiding, and willing to obey our jurisdiction, then even though they went everywhere, there would be nothing to worry about. Unfortunately among the Westerners who travel in China there are frequently many who rely on their power to insult our people. The gentry and the people of our country in turn despise them, and do not care to associate with them, so incidents daily grow up which merit serious thought. The practice in the West is that when a foreign merchant comes to the territory of a nation, if he violates the law, he is judged by the officials of the nation. This practice cannot be applied in China because the Western governments dislike China's frequent resort to torture in examining a case. According to the Chefoo Convention, hereafter when there is a legal suit between Chinese and Western merchants, the accused will be handled by the officials of his country. . . But the Chinese law is severe, and Western law clement. There are many Western officials who understand Chinese law, and there are few Chinese officials who know Western law. Even if both sides can make inquiries and give just decisions, it is difficult to guarantee that the litigants will have no resentment. . .

A Note on the British Government [18]

England is in a remote spot overseas, three islands which stand like mountains off the northwest of Europe. . . In view of the fine quality and strength of her armament and soldiers, the richness of her revenue and the abundance of her natural resources no European country dares to be stiff-necked with her. . . In recent years she has maintained her prosperity and preserved her state of peace and has been so cautious in resorting to arms that unless there is no other way out she never carelessly starts a military expedition. . .

The real strength of England, however, lies in the fact that there is a sympathetic understanding between the governing and the governed, a close relationship between the ruler and the people. . . My observation is that the daily domestic political life of England actually embodies the traditional ideals of our ancient Golden Age [lit., the Three Dynasties and earlier].

In official appointments the method of recommendation and election is practised, but the candidates must be well known, of good character and achievements before they can be promoted to a position over the people. . . And moreover the principle of majority rule is adhered to in order to show impartiality. . . In their treatment of the people the officials never dare to use severe punishments, heavy fines, or tyrannical and excessive taxation. Nor dare they accept any bribery . . . or squeeze the blood and flesh of myriads of people in order to fill up their own pockets. The English people are likewise public spirited and law-abiding; the laws and regulations are hung up high (for everyone to see), and no one dares violate them. He who violates the law goes to the court only to have his confession taken; when the real truth has been obtained, then a verdict is made, and he is imprisoned. There has never been such cruelty as torturing and beating him by bamboos and clubs so that his blood and flesh spread all over. In prison the convict is supplied with food and clothing, so that he may not be hungry or cold. He is taught to work and not allowed to become idle. He is visited every seven days by preachers to make him repent and live a new life. He is never maltreated by those in charge of the prison. The excellence of the prison system is what China has never had since the Golden Age. . .

An important question is jointly discussed in the upper [p. 18] and lower houses of Parliament, and all must agree before an action can be taken. If there is a proposal for a military expedition it is necessary to make a universal inquiry of the whole nation. When the multitude of the people desire to fight, then there is a war; and when the multitude desire to cease, then a truce. . .

The expenditure of the British ruler is a constantly fixed amount for every year; he does not dare to eat myriads of delicacies. His palaces are all very simple; he does not care for extravagance, and he has never had separate mansions and distant palaces linked with one another over scores of *li*. The king has only one queen, and besides her there is no concubine, and there has never been a multitude of three thousand beautiful women in the harem. . .

While Wang T'ao as a pioneer journalist was reaching a newspaper-reading audience in the treaty ports, the former secretary of Tseng and Li, Hsueh Fu-ch'eng (see Ch. Xa), was writing memorials and essays which had a more limited but also more influential circulation. In 1879 he compiled a volume called "Rough discussion of the management of foreign affairs" (*Ch'ou-yang ch'u-i*), which contained fourteen essays on current problems — how to handle Russia and Japan, how to secure "intelligence about the enemy," prevent the loss of China's "vassal states," carry out "institutional reform" (*pien-fa*), assert China's sovereignty, revise the treaties, and the like. Hsueh first submitted these essays to Li Hung-chang, who laid them before the Tsungli Yamen, and later Tseng Chi-tse distributed several dozen copies.

Hsueh Fu-ch'eng's proposals were strengthened by the fact of his own experience of state affairs. After joining Li's staff he had assisted in negotiating the Chefoo Convention (1876), drafted the regulations for a modern Chinese navy in 1881, and been the one who suggested the timely dispatch of a Chinese force to Korea following the riots in Seoul in 1882. It is true that Hsueh never took a higher degree than that of Senior Licentiate of the Second Class (*Fu-kung-sheng*, 1867) nor held a higher post in China than that of an intendant (taotai) in Chekiang, where he rendered good service in coastal defense against the French attack in early 1885. His prominence as a reformer came from his four years' diplomatic service in Europe, mainly in London and Paris, about which he left a very instructive "Diary of a mission to the four countries of England, France, Italy and Belgium" (*Ch'u-shih Ying Fa I Pi ssu-kuo jih-chi*) covering the period from January 31, 1890, to April 8, 1891. It was published in 1892, and a supplement covering the period from April 9, 1891, to July 1, 1894, was published in 1899. These diaries reveal his favorable response to Western civilization. He comes to the conclusion that only through modernization can China save herself, and cites Siam and Japan as two examples to follow.[19]

As with Wang T'ao, Hsueh Fu-ch'eng's appreciation of Western ways is by no means limited to material things. The parliamentary governments, especially those of England and Germany, seem to him the best form of political organization. He visits the British parliament and writes a detailed description of its system.[20] He attributes the prosperity and strength of European nations to the development of science, the system of compulsory education for boys and girls, rich and poor and from all walks of life, the encouragement given commerce and industry by the governments, and the use of machinery to produce wealth and so feed the people.

He does not blindly admire everything European, however, and criticizes the Western religions, especially Catholicism. He insists that although the freedom to propagate the faith in China is permitted by the treaties, priests should be forbidden to interfere in Chinese internal politics or to attack Confucianism.[21] Nor does he like the Western type of social relationship between the rulers and the people, parents and children, husbands and wives. He notes that state ministers occasionally compel a ruler to abdicate, and that boys and girls under twenty-one claim the right to arrange their own marriages without asking for instruction from their parents; after the wedding they live separately and divide their property, without having much social contact with their parents. When a son beats a father he will only be imprisoned for three months. "The Western custom honors women, looks down on men. When a woman has an outside paramour, even if she is a duchess or marquise, she often deserts her husband or remarries, and it is not considered strange. If a husband meets a girl outside, his wife can complain before the judge and have him punished. . . Girls before marriage have many boy friends and even though they have borne children, they will not be despised. . . This is quite contrary to the doctrine of our sage." [22]

In foreign policy Hsueh viewed the Chinese migration overseas as an important outlet for relieving China's population problem. He worked hard to establish consuls general in Singapore and other places to protect Chinese living abroad, and believed that Chinese diplomats could accomplish a good deal through patience, sincerity, and skillful tactics.[23] Unfortunately, just as with Kuo Sung-tao and Tseng Chi-tse, there was no chance for this man of ideas to carry on practical administrative work in China. Hsueh Fu-ch'eng died in Shanghai only 20 days after he returned from Europe in 1894.

In the following essays we can see at work that process of harmonizing Chinese and world history which K'ang, Liang, and later reformers were to pursue for so long, and which Marxism in China is now attempting in its own way to complete. The chief device used by Hsueh and later reformers like Liang Ch'i-ch'ao was to make an interpretation of China's past in terms of which the modern adoption of Western institutions could be sanctioned. If China had had previous periods of institutional reform, or if China had given the original impetus to the growth of science, which the West had merely carried further, then China could now justifiably learn from the West without giving up the essential Chinese way. All these arguments, historical references, and interpretations thus had a psychological aim — to convince the leadership of China that Westernization was consonant with China's ethnocentric culturalism. The hectic days of 1898 merely carried this process of thought to a higher and more explicit point.

DOC. 40. Essays of Hsueh Fu-ch'eng

On Reform (1879) [24]

I have said that from the origin of mankind down to the present is approximately no more than ten thousand years. How do I know this? I know it from the urgency of social change (shih-pien); according to the way of heaven, there is a small change once every several hundred years, and a great change once every several thousand years. [Hsueh then recounts the main periods in traditional Chinese history, to show that changes both great and small periodically occur as a matter of course, including barbarian incursions from neighboring lands.] As we reach the present day, the European nations suddenly arise overseas by means of their knowledge of machinery and mathematics. . . In ninety thousand li around the great globe there is no place where they do not send envoys and have trade relations. Even though Yao and Shun [the legendary emperors] were called upon to face this situation, they would not be able to close the doors and rule the empire in isolation. . . Therefore the empire has to be changed from a divided world, in which the Chinese are segregated from the barbarians to an integrated world in which China and foreign countries are in close connection. When social change is small, the laws governing society accordingly will undergo small change; when social change is great, the laws governing society [p. 21] will also be greatly changed. . .

Only a sage can pattern himself after another sage, and only a sage, too, can change the law of another sage. The reason for their making reforms is not because they like to do it, but that they are obliged by the circumstances of the time. . .

As for the various European countries, they rely on intelligence and energy to compete with one another. When China wishes to stand with them on an equal level, our commercial policy and mining affairs should be planned; and if no reform is undertaken in these lines, they will be rich, and we poor. Our study of technology and manufacturing of machinery should be accurate; without reform on our part, they will be clever and we will be stupid. Steamships, trains, and telegraphs should be adopted; if not, they will be quick and we shall be slow. The advantages and disadvantages of treaties, the competence or incompetence of envoys, and the improvement of the military system and strategy should be discussed; without reform in these lines, they will be coöperative, we will be individualists; together they will be strong, alone we shall break easily.

Formerly Ch'ih-yu [a legendary leader of savage tribes] made military weapons and invaded the territory of the feudal lords; the Yellow Emperor began the making of bows, arrows, and the compass to overcome him. . .

Now if we really take over the Westerners' knowledge of machinery and mathematics in order to protect the doctrines of our [Emperors] Yao, Shun, Yü, and T'ang, [Kings] Wen and Wu, the Duke of Chou and Confucius, and so make the Westerners not dare to despise China . . . I know that if they were alive today they would probably work on these pressing tasks, and their doctrines would also be gradually spread to the eight bounds of the globe. That is what is called using Chinese influence to reform the barbarians.

Some may say that in practicing reform one should aim to surpass others and not to pursue them. Now the Western methods are superior to ours, and if we run after others with our worn-out knowledge, what can we do, it may be asked, when there is no way to surpass them? This view is not correct. In general if we wish to surpass others, it is necessary to know their methods before we can reform, but after reform we may be able to surpass them. We cannot expect to excel others merely by sitting upright in a dignified attitude. Now we see that some people are ahead of us; and if we say contemptuously that we do not care to run after them, later we shall not be able to move even half a step. Moreover, they have concentrated the ability and energy of several million people, have spent millions of dollars through prolonged years and generations before they acquired their knowledge. If we wish to excel them within a single morning, is it possible or impossible? In general a large river may begin from the overflow of small bogs, and a lofty hill may be based on overturned baskets of soil. Buddhism came from India and yet it flourished in the East. Mathematics had its beginning [p. 22] in China and yet it has reached its highest development in Western lands. Comparing the ability and wisdom of the Chinese with those of the Westerners, why are we not able to surpass them? . . .

Indeed, social changes are endless; and likewise the methods of the sages in controlling these changes are also limitless. To be born in the present generation, but to cling stubbornly to traditional methods, is to be like one who lived in the age of Shen-nung [who invented cooking] and still ate hides and drank blood [i.e., ate uncooked food], or like one who lived in the age of the Yellow Emperor and yet, in opposing the savage action of Ch'ih-yu, struggled against him with bare hands. Such a one would say, "I am observing the methods of the ancient sages". . .

An Essay in Praise of the United States (A diary entry of May 1, 1890) [25]

Formerly Kuo Sung-tao frequently praised the merits of the governmental administration and popular customs of the West, which caused him to suffer criticism and ostracism from scholars who like to criticize others. I was also slightly surprised at the exaggeration of his words, which I checked with Ch'en Lan-pin. . . who said that his statement was correct. This time when I came to Europe and traveled from Paris to London I began to believe that the statements of Kuo Sung-tao could be verified in the parliaments, schools, prisons, hospitals, and streets.

Among my associates some talk about the honesty and magnanimity of the people of the United States. I think the Western countries today are at the pinnacle of their prosperity, which is caused by their good fortune in natural resources. At the beginning of the nation, the population of the United States was not very large, and these natural resources had not yet been unearthed. By nature the people are open and generous. This is because the development of America was later than that of Europe, and the development of Europe was later than that of China. Among the various European countries, again, some were developed later and some earlier; and accordingly the customs are good and bad. America is like the time of the Golden Age of Ancient China [lit., the time of Yü and Hsia]. Russia is like the time of Shang and Chou. England and Germany are like the two Han dynasties of China. France, Italy, Spain, and Holland are probably like Chinese T'ang and Sung. As for the inconstant and excitable spirit of the French, with their perpetual struggles among political factions, they resemble the age of the former Ming dynasty.

Some say the Irish (*Ai-li-shih*) people in the United States are outrageous in the jealousy and violence with which they oppress and expel the Chinese people living there; where is the good old spirit? My answer to this is that, in the time of the Three Dynasties, the notorious tyrants [26] . . . Chieh, Chou, Yu and Li [27] also caused periods of disorder. How can we (expect everybody to) follow the same path?

Science Makes Europe Prosperous (A diary entry of May 19, 1890) [28]

The secret of the sudden rise of the various nations in Europe and America lies in the fact that day by day their knowledge progresses and their industry and commerce increase in prosperity. But the pivotal implements have all developed in the last hundred years. As for the means by which they cross the globe with no hindrance, the Westerners rely on steamships, trains, telegraphs, and the like, all of which were invented during the last sixty or seventy years. It is the same with other matters.

Nowadays some Chinese critics are either surprised at the strength and prosperity of other countries and praise them too much; or else hold that great China should not imitate Westerners, should reject their inventions, and condemn them severely. I think both are narrow-minded.

In general the Westerners' commercial administration, military methods, shipbuilding, machine manufacturing, agriculture, fishing, husbandry, mining and all such matters, are indeed developed to a high point of excellence, and yet all are derived [p. 12] from studies of steam, light, electricity and chemistry, by means of which they have obtained the methods of controlling water, fire, and electricity. These result from the ingenuity of the inventors, and there is no reason to expect that they can be kept secret for a long time. Famous experts of the West have been particularly entrusted with demonstrating them. The way revealed is one that belongs to all the universe; it is not a monopoly of the Westerners. The intelligence and energy of Chinese scholars are not necessarily inferior to those of Westerners. Unfortunately the energy of their youth has been mostly wasted on eight-legged essays, examination papers, and the calligraphy of small model characters. They are not like thousands and millions of Westerners who exert their intelligence and wisdom in pursuing their study of special subjects and so can at once achieve the best and finest. Certainly we should not deny this fact, and why, likewise, should we confine ourselves to what we are?

In ancient times inventions were concentrated in China. As spiritual sages arose in succession, they invented ploughs, hoes, boats and carriages, bows and arrows, fishing nets, clothes, and writing. At the time of primeval chaos and uncultivation, there suddenly arose this civilization. If we compare it with the European inventions today, was it not even more marvelous? But people are accustomed to our old civilization and do not realize this. As for the fixing of the four seasons in the chapter "Yao-tien" [of the *Book of History*] and the teaching of mathematics through the book, *Chou-pi* [see Ch. II above], Western astronomy and mathematics may have been derived from both of these. How can we know that they have not patterned other matters useful to their nation and people after those of China? In antiquity, when there was not yet any invention in the universe, Chinese sages had observed what was above them and examined what was below and gradually Westerners imitated them. In modern times, Westerners have followed the inventions of Chinese sages, stepped after them, and elaborated upon them. Why should China not follow Westerners now? If we are afraid that they are ahead of us, and so do not want to reveal our shortcomings, that would be to conceal one's illness because of hating to see the doctor. If you say that it is not easy to follow in their steps and you fear that eventually you cannot overtake them, that is like stopping to eat on account of choking. In general, blue is distilled from indigo, but it is bluer than indigo; and ice is frozen from water, but it is colder than water. Wu Ch'en taught the Wu kingdom to make the Ch'u weak.[29] King Wu-ling adopted barbarian clothes and later wiped out the barbarians. Learning from others does not necessarily mean that there is no chance to surpass them. How can we know that after several thousand years the Chinese cannot carry further the knowledge of Westerners and develop once more the genius of creators, so that the Westerners will be astonished and dazzled by us?

Education Makes European Countries Strong (A diary entry of Feb. 11, 1891) [30]

There have never been more laws governing the education of the people in various European countries than there are today. If boys and girls of eight years or older do not go to school, their parents are punished. Certainly there is not a single boy without education; there is not even a single girl without education; even the disabled, the deaf, the blind and the dumb, all receive education. There are free schools to educate people who are without means and the parentless orphans. In country districts there are country schools. In every county and state in the national capital, schools stand like a forest and there are universities, high schools and grade schools. For those just beginning to study, those who have acquired some knowledge, and those who can do advanced graduate work, definite stages of work are all provided. . . Not only do scholars have schools, but also soldiers, workers, farmers and merchants all have schools. . .

During the last several decades the schools in Germany particularly have flourished and all other large nations are trying to equal her. Most German soldiers have had some schooling and thus in fighting they are always victorious. . . The system of popular education as evident today is probably the origin of the rise of the various European countries.

Use Machinery to Promote Wealth and to Feed the People (1892) [31]

Generally when people use things they seek good quality and cheap prices. This is certainly the tendency of human nature. . .

Machinery can make what cannot be made by human power. . . The work of a hundred men can be done by one man with the help of a machine, and the amount of goods produced will necessarily be increased. Yet when the work of a hundred men is done by one man with a machine, the cost is reduced to that of the work of ten men. Then all the people around will try to buy the commodity. If the cost is again reduced to that of the work of two or three men, then everyone will try even more to buy it. . .

The population of China is ten times [p. 9] that of all the European countries. Critics say that if machinery is extensively used, it will take away the livelihood of the poor people. . . In the West an intelligent use of machines is a means of feeding the people, whereas China considers the restriction of machines to be a means of supporting the people. If the latter theory is carried through, there will necessarily be some articles which other people can make but which we cannot. Moreover, the cost of work done by one person would certainly be included (in the price of the goods). . . Thus it is clear that our articles will not be able to compete with Western goods. . . Hereafter Chinese products not only cannot be sold to other nations, but cannot even be sold in their own country. Hereafter the Chinese people will not only be unable to support themselves, but further, when they realize that the use of their energy profits them little, they will not exert themselves. Hereafter the Chinese people will not only be unable to produce much to compete for profit with Westerners, but also will try to buy Western goods to supply their own needs, and thereby grossly increase the profits of the Westerners. In these circumstances, how can our commerce fail to decline, the people's livelihood not suffer and the national power not deteriorate? . . .

In general, if we use machinary to produce goods, then the profits will accrue to rich Chinese merchants; if we do not use machinery to produce goods, the profits will accrue to Westerners. When the profit is gained by rich merchants, it is still in China, and the surplus can still be shared in order to support our poor people. When the profit is gained by Westerners, the situation is like water gradually drying up and the rice plant naturally withering away, or like oil which is gradually consumed, whereupon the light will certainly go out. The future catastrophe will be beyond description.

CHAPTER XVI. K'ANG YU-WEI AND SOME OF HIS ASSOCIATES

The written record of China's response to the West in the last few years of the nineteenth century is so voluminous, and so replete with items of literary excellence, that it is difficult even to make a representative selection. This was the time when the carefully trained masters of the Chinese classical style, as yet unadulterated by the new terms and expressions of the modern vernacular style, could turn their fine literary gifts to the truly epic theme of China's extinction or survival. The defeat by Japan in 1894–95 was a shattering blow to the pride and complacency of the scholar-official class, and the threatening encroachment of Russia, Germany, and the other powers in 1897–98, in their "scramble for concessions," seemed to foreshadow not only the end of the dynasty but the extinction of the Chinese state itself. Both the reformers of 1898 and their opponents were fully conscious that three thousand years of Chinese history and culture looked down upon them. They all knew their classical texts and argued still by quotations from the sages. Since the sayings of the sages by this time included a number of very pithy utterances, the result is good reading.

The political corruption of the late Ch'ing period as well as the foreign encroachment of the time gave added vigor to the demands of Chinese intellectuals that the government make reforms. The ministers of England and the United States at Peking and missionaries like Timothy Richard and Young J. Allen had also for some time been urging political and social changes after the pattern of the West. Chinese scholars had published warnings [1] and a distinct trend had set in among the scholar class; by degrees, as they gained more understanding of the West, they had moved from the appreciation of Western weapons to that of ships and railways, and thence to an admiration of Western political and social institutions. Perhaps it is worth noting that many leaders of reform and revolution were Cantonese, who had had direct contact with Westerners in Hongkong and Shanghai. Without attempting to summarize the full sweep of the philosophical issues with which K'ang Yu-wei and his contemporaries were now dealing, we present some brief notes on them followed by passages from their polemics.

K'ang Yu-wei (1858–1927). K'ang's most important work in political theory was a treatise on "the cosmopolitan society" (*Ta-t'ung shu*, A book on the universal commonwealth). Having read widely in Confucian, Buddhist, and Western literature (in translation), K'ang developed his idea of utopia from the *Ta-t'ung* section of the *Book of Rites*. Among other things, he diagnoses the suffering of mankind as due to nine barriers: between nation and nation, between race and race, between territory and territory, between men and women, between one species and another, etc. Were these barriers removed, all would be well. The existence of nations is a source of wars and evils. K'ang proposes a world government under which all national states and armies shall be abolished, while a universal language, calendar, and units of weight shall be used. The governors of the world government shall be elected by the world citizens. In the commonwealth, men and women shall be born free, equal, and independent. There shall be no family restrictions: men and women who have lived together for only one year may renew the relationship or find new partners. Children shall be cared for and educated by the state. There shall be no private property and no class distinctions. All farms, factories, and business enterprises shall be owned and operated by the public. All natural resources shall be scientifically developed. In short, K'ang's utopian universal state is to be a true liberation from national boundaries, from distinctions of class, race, sex, family, property, profession, and species, and free from all injustice and unhappiness. This iconoclasm indicates the vigor of K'ang's thinking, which was more powerful because combined with high scholarship.

When he was twenty-seven, K'ang Yu-wei, although lacking official status, had attempted to submit to the throne his first memorial urging reform. He was looked upon as insane and his memorial was not presented. After the Sino-Japanese peace treaty of 1895, however, K'ang and his student Liang Ch'i-ch'ao, who were taking the metropolitan examinations at Peking, secured some 1300 signatures from among the candidates and presented to the throne the famous "Letter of ten thousand words" (*Wan-yen shu*). The gist of this long memorial, which was subsequently called "The memorial presented by the examination candidates" (*Kung-ch'e shang-shu chi*),[2] was to reject the peace treaty, transfer the capital, and carry out reforms. It also suggested the relaxation of the strict traditional qualifications in favor of men of ability, the increase of salaries to foster integrity and honesty, cessation of sales of official rank, elimination of sinecure offices, reform of the civil service examinations, promotion of more schools and more translations of Western books for the training of men of ability, bestowal of rewards or medals to encourage new inventions, the establishment of agricultural and business schools so as to help the production of wealth and enrich the people, revision of the laws for local government, and promotion of a benevolent policy for protecting the people. The memorial also discussed public health, poor relief, repair of roads, printing of bank notes, the inauguration of shipping lines, transfer of poor people to better regions, study of mineralogy, introduction of insurance for the people, increase of the opium tax, discontinuance of the *likin* tax, construction of more railways and warships, and a number of other topics. K'ang had broad interests.

When Germany compelled China to lease Kiaochow Bay in 1897, K'ang Yu-wei, now a second-class secretary of the Board of Works, wrote another memorial urging the emperor to take as his model the Meiji Emperor of Japan and Peter the Great, decide upon a national policy of reform, and allow provincial authorities to initiate reforms in the areas under their jurisdiction. His associates in the Board disliked K'ang's candid statements and did not present this memorial to the throne on his behalf. In the early part of 1898, however, K'ang managed to have an audience with the Emperor Kuang-hsü and eventually persuaded the young man to issue a decree announcing a national policy of reform on June 11. This date is usually regarded as the beginning of the Hundred Days of reform, although some reform decrees had been issued before (see Ch. XVI).

K'ang Yu-wei was a follower of the "modern-text" (*chin-wen*) school of classical scholars. He liked to speak rather cryptically of *t'ung san-t'ung*, "going through the three periods of unity," by which he meant that the three ancient dynasties of Hsia, Shang, and Chou were different from one another and reforms should have been made from time to time during them. He was also fond of speaking of *chang san-shih*, "the displaying of the three epochs," by which he referred to a progression from the existing epoch of disorder, through a peaceful epoch to the epoch of world peace. The more reforms were made, the faster would be this progress.[3]

Without trying here to expound K'ang's interesting political philosophy, it may be pointed out that his veneration of Confucius was at least in part a political device. In his startling book on "Confucius as a reformer" (*K'ung-tzu kai-chih k'ao*), he used his scholarship to show that Confucius had actually created the theory of a golden age in the past so as to persuade contemporary rulers to make reforms as the ancient sage-kings had done. Thus it followed that if Confucius favored change, all Confucianists, patterning themselves after him, should by no means object to it.

Huang Tsun-hsien (1848–1905). Huang first gained fame as a young poet. He went to Hongkong in 1870 and recorded his miscellaneous impressions of the good municipal government and of the foreigners' aggression against China. In 1877 he went to Japan and worked as a secretary in the Chinese legation for six years, learning Japanese and associating with Japanese scholars. He was consul-general at San Francisco from 1882 to 1885, in a period when the anti-Chinese labor movement in California left him with a bad impression of the United States. After he returned to China he spent a few years of leisure writing his "History of Japan" (*Jih-pen kuo chih*), in which a preface and commentary to almost every chapter express his admiration of the Japanese reform movement as well as his hope for a similar development in China. Some of his ideas were advanced and some conservative; he did not admire Western social life, especially the relationship between husband and wife, father and son, and the like. From 1890 Huang was Chinese consul-general at Singapore for a few years and in this period he traveled in England and France.

In 1894 he was called back to China, where the repeated defeats in the Sino-Japanese War inspired him to write many emotional poems.[4] In 1896 Huang made the acquaintance of Liang Ch'i-ch'ao and they became fast friends. In the early fall of the same year he had an audience with the emperor and the latter asked him in what respects the European governments were superior to that of China. Huang's reply was, "The strength of Europe is entirely due to reforms. When I was in London I heard the British gentlemen say that a hundred years ago their government was still inferior to that of China." The emperor, it is said, was at first surprised, and then smiled.[5]

In the following year, after Germany declined him as Chinese minister, Huang was appointed judicial commissioner of Hunan. The governor was Ch'en Pao-chen (1831–1900), a liberal-minded and efficient administrator. Huang and the governor started a reform program and invited Liang Ch'i-ch'ao, T'an Ssu-t'ung, and others to run a school called the "College of current affairs" (Shih-wu hsueh-t'ang). They made public speeches, promoted reform ideas, purchased steamers for the rivers, and planned to build a railroad between Kwangtung and Hunan. At the same time their activities caused much protest from the local conservative scholars. While Huang was in Hunan he presented his "History of Japan" to the emperor, who liked it so much that he asked for another copy. In the summer of 1898 he retired from his post on account of poor health, and recuperated in Shanghai.

Huang's career as a poet indicates how the reformers of the 1890's contributed to the later literary revolution. He was a nationalist, writing in a persuasive emotional style, in order to inspire patriotism, and was probably the first modern poet to introduce Chinese slang into his poems. He also described the landscape of foreign countries and inserted a world viewpoint and Western ideas into his verse, which was classical in phraseology, but had a free form of expression. He said, "I use my hand to describe my mouth [i.e., I write the way I speak], without being restricted by the traditional style." [6]

Yen Fu (1853–1921). Yen Fu, although not formally an associate of K'ang, was a significant figure. He studied at Greenwich Naval Academy, and Ku Hung-ming (Ku T'ang-sheng, 1857–1928) at Edinburgh; both worked under Chang Chih-tung, and eventually taught at the Peking University. In their day they were probably the two Chinese scholars most thoroughly learned in Western philosophy and social science. Both admired the West at first but in the latter part of their lives they became conservatives, despised Western civilization, and honored their own. Ku Hung-ming's writings were mostly in English [7] and there are studies of him in that language.[8] Yen Fu, however, is best known as a translator of Western books into classical Chinese, and his main contribution was that he introduced Western political, social, economic and philosophical thought to the Chinese society of his time.

When Yen Fu was fourteen years old, he was a student in the naval school attached to the Foochow Shipyard. After his graduation in 1876 he was sent to England for further training in the navy. He was proficient in mathematics and at the same time he took an interest in logic, sociology, jurisprudence and economics. Returning to China, he served as a teacher at the Foochow Shipyard and taught in the naval school at Tientsin. Later on he was for some time the president of Peking University.

In 1897 Yen Fu coöperated with Hsia Tseng-yu (1865–1924) to start a periodical, the "National news" (*Kuo-wen pao*; later called *Kuo-wen chou-pao*), at Tientsin. This journal, issued every ten days, had an unusually wide coverage of materials translated from the Western and Japanese press and helped to spread reform ideas.[9] In 1898 Yen published in book form his translation of Huxley's *Evolution and Ethics*, which went through numerous editions. The doctrines of the struggle for existence and survival of the fittest caught the imagination of the Chinese literati and soon became common expressions in the mouths of orators and in the writings of journalists. Yen also translated John Stuart Mill's *On Liberty*, Mill's *Logic*, Spencer's *Study of Sociology* and Adam Smith's *Wealth of Nations*. While these translations served to introduce the modern thought of the West, they constituted only a very feeble beginning, and were little understood by the general public.

After the revolution of 1911, Yen Fu became a councillor of President Yuan Shih-k'ai. In 1915 he participated in Yuan's campaign to become emperor and was one of the sponsors of a society working for that purpose, for which he was harshly criticized by his republican contemporaries.

While K'ang Yu-wei developed his thought from Chinese studies, Yen Fu had his intellectual roots in Western works, although his grasp of Chinese was also excellent. The scope of Yen's thinking was at least superficially broader than that of K'ang and in his earlier years he discussed all sorts of reforms with fluency.

In this period, when he favored reform, his criticism was that the reform leaders did not sufficiently understand the West. He said:

Chinese understanding of the necessity of learning Western methods did not begin until after the defeat of China by Japan in 1895. Since the lifting of the ban on Western merchants coming to China by sea, there have been quite a few developments: (1) the Tsungli Yamen; (2) the T'ung-wen Kuan; (3) the Foochow Shipyard; (4) the educational mission to send students to study abroad; (5) the China Merchants' Steam Navigation Company; (6) manufacturing; (7) the navy; (8) the Ministry of the Navy; (9) foreign military drill; (10) the opening of schools; (11) the dispatch of Chinese envoys abroad; (12) the opening of mines; (13) the establishment of telegraph and post offices; and (14) the building of railways. If we count everything, there are more than ten or twenty items. Most of these things have served as the foundations on which Europe became rich and strong, but when we applied them in China, they were like a good orange tree on the bank of the Huai River which, after it was transplanted, produced thick-skinned oranges. The tree looks as if midway between life and death and we do not get the fruit we sought. What is the reason? [10]

I think the greatest difference between China and the West, which can never be made up, is that the Chinese are fond of antiquity but neglect the present. The Westerners are struggling in the present in order to supersede the past. Chinese consider a period of order and a period of disorder, a period of prosperity and a period of decline, as the natural course of heavenly conduct of human affairs; while Westerners consider that daily progress should be endless, and that what has already been prosperous will not decline, and that when things are well governed, they will not be in disorder again — all of which they take as an absolute law of academic thought and political ideas.[11]

Yen Fu also criticized the idea made famous by Chang Chih-tung (see Doc. 45) — "Chinese culture for the foundation and Western culture for practical use." He says:

The foundation [t'i] and the use [yung] mean the same thing. The body of an ox should have the use of carrying heavy things; the body of a horse should have the use of carrying something to a distance. I have never heard that the ox is the body or the foundation, while the horse is for use. The difference between Chinese and Western knowledge is as great as that between the complexions and the eyes of the two races. We cannot force the two cultures to be the same or similar. Therefore, Chinese knowledge has its foundation and function; Western knowledge has also its foundation and function. If the two are separated, each can be independent; if the two were combined, both would perish. . . If we consider that science consists of techniques, then the Western techniques are actually the foundation of Western government. If we say that science does not consist of techniques, then the two things, government and techniques, are both derived from science like the left and right hands. I have never heard that the left and the right hands can be considered, respectively, as the foundation and the superstructure.[12]

It is interesting to note how Yen, like many of his generation, eventually reversed his admiration of the West. In his earlier period he had favored a thorough reform but a gradual or evolutionary one, not a sudden change. He desired to have good relations with foreign nations, to have the emperor win the hearts of the people, and to break the political monopoly of the conservatives. He advocated the encouragement of the people's power, the cultivation of their knowledge, and the revival of right conduct on their part. In later years, after 1911 and especially after the European war, Yen Fu's ideas changed sharply. He then considered that the Chinese governmental system and Chinese learning were both better than those of Europe. He said, "The culture of Western countries since this European war has been corrupted completely. . . I feel that the three centuries of progress of their races have only accomplished four things, that is, to be selfish, to kill others, to have no integrity, and to lose the sense of shame. When we recall the doctrines of Confucius and Mencius, they are really as broad as heaven and earth and their influence is extended to the people all over the globe. This is not what I alone say; even Europeans who have good minds also gradually have got such notions." [13] Thus Yen Fu wound up a conservative who preferred to keep his queue and criticize the New Culture movement.

Amid the great variety of ideas put forward in the 1890's by cultural intermediaries like Wang T'ao and Yen Fu and by reformist scholar-officials such as

Hsueh Fu-ch'eng and Huang Tsun-hsien, it required a particularly vigorous personality to take a definite stand and assert leadership. The following is one of K'ang Yu-wei's early calls to action.

DOC. 41. K'ANG YU-WEI'S STATEMENT FOR THE "SOCIETY FOR THE STUDY OF SELF-STRENGTHENING," 1895 [14]

The Russians are spying on us in the north and the English are peeping at us on the west; the French are staring at us in the south and the Japanese are watching us in the east. Living in the midst of these four strong neighbors, and being the Middle Kingdom, China is in imminent peril. How much more so will it be when there are more than ten nations who are sharpening their teeth and watering at the mouth, desiring to share the surplus? The Liao-tung peninsula and Formosa are in confusion, the Mohammedan rebellion is disturbing us, the popular mind is perturbed and the situation seems hardly supportable.

Formerly, India was a celebrated nation in Asia, but she preserved her traditions without changing and so during the time of Ch'ien-lung [1736–1795] the British people organized a company with one hundred and twenty thousand gold as capital to carry on a trade with her and subjugated the five parts of India. Formerly, Turkey was a large Moslem nation. Her territory extended over three continents, Asia, Europe, and Africa, but she was conservative and made no changes; so her government was seized by six nations, her territory was partitioned, and her ruler was banished. Of others, such as Annam, Burma, Korea, Liu-ch'iu, Siam, Persia, Afghanistan and Baluchistan, as well as those established in Africa and on the islands of the Pacific Ocean, the general number may be estimated at several hundred or one thousand. Actually the (territories of these conservative states) have been either reduced or annexed, and among all the conservative nations on the globe there is probably not a single one which has been kept intact.

Our enfeebled China has been lying in the midst of a group of strong powers and soundly sleeping on the top of a pile of kindling. In adminstration she cares only to prevent evils but does not care to develop sources of profit. Her officials know only how to be law-abiding, but do not know how to judge the trends of the time. Her scholars specialize in the study of antiquity, not in the understanding of the present. Her people can defend their immediate surroundings but cannot go far afield. Mencius said, "A state must first smite itself, and then others will smite it." The defense of the Mongolian leagues, Fengtien, Kirin, Ch'inghai, Sinkiang, Tibet, the native tribes and the frontier guards is all a defense of alien waste land. The fertile soil of Chihli, Shantung, Fukien, Chekiang, Anhwei, Hunan, Hupei, Kwangtung, Szechwan, Kweichow, Yunnan and Kwangsi has become entirely a bandits' granary. It will not be long until we become Turks and Negroes.

Westerners are very strict about races and they look upon other races as enemies. When the French obtained Annam, the way for the Annamese to become rich and ennobled through civil service examinations was cut off, and the former prominent officials have now become silk merchants. England conquered India more than a hundred years ago, but it was not until 1889 that an Indian was elected a member of Parliament. Other native peoples are treated like cattle and horses. If we do not plan in advance, but suddenly are divided among ourselves. . . then, alas, the fate of our sacred race will be unspeakable, utterly unspeakable!

For China, on the great earth, has had a ceaseless succession of sacred emperors and the country has been very famous. Her principles, institutions, and culture are the most elevated in the world. The vastness of her territory is ranked third among myriads of states, the number of her people is rated the first; her climate is in the temperate zone, her people are intelligent and accomplished, and her soil is rich and productive. Among all countries on earth none is her equal. Only because her customs are unenlightened and because of a dearth of men of ability, she is passively taking aggression and insult. Formerly Tseng Kuo-fan discussed academic problems with wise scholars like Wo-jen and others in Peking, and he deliberated on the method of militia training with various eminent officials like Chiang Chung-yuan and Lo Tse-nan in Hunan; eventually he achieved the merit of suppressing the Taiping Rebellion. In Prussia there was a society established to make the nation strong [ch'iang-kuo chih hui] and then she was revenged on her enemy France. In Japan there were people who advocated respect for the Emperor and the rejection of the barbarians and hence they accomplished their reforms. Generally, knowledge can be achieved by means of discussion, and men of ability can be produced by encouragement. When the talent and power of many people are combined, then it is easy to assemble the books; and when the minds and thinking of many people are combined, then it is easy to exchange information. The *Book of Changes* says, "Superior men discuss problems with friends." The *Analects* of Confucius say, "Mechanics have their shops to dwell in, in order to accomplish their work. The superior man learns, in order to reach the utmost of his principles." The water in the ocean is bubbling and boiling. In our ears and in our dreams the noise of artillery is roaring. All you gentlemen, how can you avoid the grief of being ruined and (becoming) subject to the rule of a different race? Are we trying to avoid slander? O you closed-door scholars, are some of you coming to the point of speaking about respecting the emperor and rejecting the barbarians? If you do, not only the teachings of the sacred Ch'ing dynasty, the two emperors, the three kings, and Confucius, but also the four hundred millions of the people will have something to rely upon.

Liang Ch'i-ch'ao (1873–1929). Among all of K'ang Yu-wei's associates the most influential in later years was his student and coadjutor, Liang Ch'i-ch'ao, whose writings will be quoted again below (see Ch. XXII and Ch. XXVIII). Liang was one of the most widely learned scholars and one of the best known writers of modern China. His career may be divided into three stages: from 1890 to 1911 he campaigned for the reform movement and constitutionalism, from 1912 to 1919 he campaigned for republican government, working part of the time as a governmental official, and from 1919 to his death he was a professor at Tsing Hua University. Throughout all these years he produced newspaper articles, research studies, and essays on a voluminous scale.

When he was nine years old, Liang was regarded as a precocious child, and could write long, fluent, classical essays. When he was eighteen he read the

Ying-huan chih-lueh of Hsü Chi-yü (see Doc. 6 above) and began to take an interest in Chinese translations of Western works. He became a student of K'ang Yu-wei and a friend of T'an Ssu-t'ung; and was much influenced by K'ang's *Ta-t'ung shu* and T'an's *Jen-hsueh* (see below).

Liang began to participate in the political reform movement in 1895. In the following year he edited at Shanghai the newspaper *Shih-wu pao*, in which he wrote a series of ten articles on "A general discussion of reform" (*Pien-fa t'ung-lun*), some of which are translated below. Chang Chih-tung was impressed and offered him a job, but he declined. He accepted, instead, an invitation of the Hunan governor, Ch'en Pao-chen, to be the dean of the new "College of current affairs." In Hunan he also joined with Huang Tsun-hsien and T'an Ssu-t'ung in organizing the "Reform association of South China" (Nan-hsueh-hui). They published a newspaper, *Hsiang-pao*, advocating the people's rights (*min-ch'uan*), protection of the nation and the race, and the like. The following extracts indicate the persuasive reasoning by which the reformers of 1898 sought to stand on China's past and yet face modern times.

DOC. 42. LIANG CH'I-CH'AO ON REFORM, 1896 [15]

I. *Preface.* Why is it necessary to reform? In general, there is nothing in the universe which does not change. The change between daytime and evening makes the day; the change from winter to summer makes the year. . . When the purple or red blood circulates in the body, when second by second carbon is breathed out and oxygen is breathed in, and a thousand changes take place in a day, thus the living person is formed. . . In ancient China the method of tribute and assistance was changed into the system of land, labor, and poll taxes; the latter three were changed into semi-annual taxes, which again were changed into a unified annual tax. . . Throughout the span of one thousand years there was not a single time without change, and not a single thing without change. . .

Those who advocate no change frequently claim, "We follow the ancients, follow the ancients." Do they know that from prehistoric, ancient, medieval and modern times down to the present day, there have been many hundreds of thousands and myriads of changes? . . I have investigated this tendency from ancient times, when one family received the mandate to make laws and establish systems and have them followed for several generations, and yet what their descendants had to obey and put into effect was inevitably different from what their ancestors did. Nevertheless the prince and the people, the upper and lower classes always stubbornly thought that "our laws today were used by our ancestors to rule the Empire, and it was well governed." They obstinately observed them, following tradition without discrimination. Gradually as time moved on the tradition changed from bad to worse, everything became neglected and finally was so rotten that it was beyond repair. If the one who rose to replace the former rulers examined their defects and reformed them, he would be the new ruler. If the original dynasty's descendants understood this idea, examined the defects themselves and reformed them, then this was called a restoration. The restoration periods of Han and T'ang were like that. The *Book of Odes* says, "Although the Chou [p. 2] is an old kingdom, its life has been renewed." That means that to rule an old country, it is necessary to use new laws. . . Those who insist that there is no need for reform still say, "Let us follow the ancients, follow the ancients." They coldly sit and watch everything being laid waste by following tradition, and there is no concern in their hearts. . . The *Book of Changes* says, "When there is exhaustion, there should be change; after a change there is cohesion; when there is cohesion things will be long-lasting." I Yin says, "Make use of the new, dispose of the old, then the illness will not stay. . ."

II. *On the Harm of not Reforming.* Now here is a big mansion which has lasted a thousand years. The tiles and bricks are decayed and the beams and rafters are broken. It is still a magnificently big thing, but when wind and rain suddenly come up, its fall is foredoomed. Yet the people in the house are still happily playing or soundly sleeping and as indifferent as if they have seen or heard nothing. Even some who have noted the danger know only how to weep bitterly, folding their arms and waiting for death without thinking of any remedy. Sometimes there are people a little better off who try to repair the cracks, seal up the leaks, and patch up the ant holes in order to be able to go on living there in peace, even temporarily, in the hope that something better may turn up. These three types of people use their minds differently, but when a hurricane comes they will die together. . . A nation is also like this. . .

India is one of the oldest countries on the great earth. She followed tradition without change; she has been rendered a colony of England. Turkey's territory occupied three continents and had an established state for a thousand years; yet, because of observing the old ways without change, she has been dominated by six large countries, which have divided her territory. The area of Africa is three times larger than Europe and in the interior, except in the desert zone, there are everywhere luxuriant plants and abundant flocks. The native people could not achieve civilization and therefore they meekly handed over their land to strong enemies. Poland was a famous country in Europe. Her political institutions were not developed, internal struggles arose daily. Russia, Prussia, and Austria made mutual agreements and divided her as their meat. The Moslems in central Asia have usually been well known for their bravery and skill in warfare, and yet they observe the old ways without changing. The Russians are swallowing them like a whale and nibbling them as silkworms eat mulberry leaves, almost in their entirety. Annam, Burma, and Korea obeyed and belonged to China. Gradually, they learned bad habits from China and followed corrupt ways of administration, drifting along without change. Now of the dignity and the manner of Chinese officials, nothing remains there.

Russians settled in a land of bitter cold, suffered the yoke of the Mongols and the tyranny of former emperors; the people were so downtrodden that they thought they could not last out another day. After Peter the Great traveled in various countries and learned their techniques, he returned and carried out reforms. [Liang then cites examples from the history of Prussia, Japan, Spain and Holland] [P. 3] Siam lies between Burma and Annam, as thin as a piece of silk, and yet she was roused to action and proudly she still stands. The *Book of Rites* says, "If one knows not the future, one should look at the past." Also it says, "When the cart in front is overturned, the cart behind it should take it as a warning." Among all nations on earth during the last century the cause of their being strong and prosperous has always been the same, and the cause of their being weak and overthrown has also never varied. The crucial difference is as dreadful as that.

The age of China as a country is equal to that of India and the fertility of her land is superior to that of Turkey, but her conformity to the defective ways which have accumulated and her incapacity to stand up and reform make her also like a brother of these two countries. . . Whenever there is a flood or drought, communications are severed, there is no way to transport famine relief, the dead are abandoned to fill the ditches or are disregarded, and nine out of ten houses are emptied. . . The members of secret societies are scattered over the whole country, waiting for the chance to move. Industry is not developed, commerce is not discussed, the native goods daily become less salable. . . "Leakage" [i.e., squeeze] becomes more serious day by day and our financial sources are almost dried up. Schools are not well run and students, apart from the "eight-legged" essays, do not know how to do a thing. The good ones are working on small researches, flowery writing, and miscellaneous trifles. Tell them about the vast oceans, they open their eyes wide and disbelieve it. . . [Liang next expatiates on a theme developed by K'ang, that China has all the resources of greatness but is held back by her old political institutions.]

[P. 4] My critics may say that the political system of today is not modern but old; it is what the five emperors and the three kings have handed down. . . and it has been followed from generation to generation for a great number of years. . . But this dynasty alone has been particularly good at making changes in the fundamental laws for the benefit of society. At the beginning when the Manchus entered Shanhaikwan, they immediately issued orders to shave the hair in the front of the head, to wear peacock feathers and the riding-jacket. Such things did not exist in ancient times and thus they have changed the official costume. They employed Dahai [d. 1632] to create the national script, borrowing Mongolian letters to indicate the Manchu pronunciation, and thus they changed the system of writing. They employed Adam Schall von Bell and Jacobus Rho to make a calendar, using European methods to improve the traditional calendar. Thus they changed the calendric system. . .

[P. 5] All these examples show that this dynasty changed the laws or systems of preceding dynasties, making them better and better. . . (Among the European countries) industry is promoted and commerce is protected, because they fear the sources of profits may be captured by others, and the country on account of that may be impoverished and distressed. Generals must have knowledge, soldiers must be literate and must drill day and night as if approaching a great enemy; their ships [p. 6] and weapons are up to date, and they really compete in maneuvers, because they feel that if they show the slightest military weakness they will be defeated, probably never to rise again. Other administrative measures are all like this. They make comparisons among themselves and every day stimulate each other. Therefore the talents and the wisdom of their people are learned by emulation, and the prosperity and strength of the countries are always sufficient to enable them to fight against each other. . .

But this so-called independent or isolated country, China, has never seen great enemies. Proudly she regards herself as high and mighty, and says no one is her equal. . .

T'an Ssu-t'ung (1865–1898). Liang Ch'i-ch'ao's friend, T'an Ssu-t'ung, became a martyr to the Reform Movement of 1898 at the age of thirty-three. He was a precocious and ingenious thinker, and an emotional and heroic young man of high principles. He appears to have had an unhappy family life, owing to maltreatment by his stepmother, but he read widely and intelligently. Both his poems and his prose are written in a delicate style, and the expression of his philosophical ideas in his book, "A Study of Benevolence" (*Jen-hsueh*), written from 1896 to 1898, may be compared stylistically with classical works. He has generally been viewed as a philosopher and given a prominent position in the history of modern Chinese philosophy.

T'an Ssu-t'ung's ideas were derived from Confucianism, Buddhism, and the Western sciences as well as from K'ang Yu-wei, whom he respected as a teacher. The main tenets of his philosophic thought are contained in his *Jen-hsueh*, in which he recommends for every person the freedom that would be possible were there no boundaries between nations. When the world has no national boundaries, "wars will cease, jealousy will disappear, secret plans will be abandoned, the distinction between you and me will be lost, equality will result, there will be neither noble nor mean, rich nor poor, the world will be really cosmopolitan." The reason human beings cannot reach this kind of society is that numerous restrictions or ties stand in the way. If we wish to bring human beings into a cosmopolitan world, we must necessarily break through these numerous bonds, such as those of profits and emoluments, those of classical studies pursued by silly scholars, those of rulers, of the human relationships, of heaven, of Buddha, etc., etc. After all these bonds have been broken, society will be as vast as the sky or ocean; it will be free from restrictions and thus real freedom will be secured.

T'an Ssu-t'ung's desire to break the bond of allegiance to the ruler may have been influenced by Huang Tsung-hsi's essays on "The Ruler" and "The Minister" (cp. Ch. II). Unlike K'ang Yu-wei, T'an wished to break the restrictions set up by the alien Manchu rulers as well as those set up by the aggression of foreigners. He subscribed to the idea of China's self-salvation by means of reform. With reform the people would be intelligent, rich, strong and rejuvenated. The method of reform is to create four *t'ung* or "good connections": between the upper and lower classes, between China and foreign countries, between male and female, between oneself and others. When these four lines of connection are not barred, then the way to freedom will be open and the whole globe will be unified.

Because of this fundamental idea, T'an Ssu-t'ung disapproved boycotting or blockading trade with foreigners, nor did he approve of forbidding Chinese to go overseas. He believed that Western trade was beneficial to China — a revolutionary idea which may have reflected the Western view. When he made a study of the *Hai-kuo t'u-chih*, he criticized Wei Yuan's policy of using one barbarian to control another barbarian (see Doc. 3 above). T'an said that this was a foolish policy by which China had suffered repeatedly, as in the T'ang, Chin, and Sung dynasties. He admired the far-sightedness of Lin Tse-hsü who said that China's disaster would come from Russia.[16]

T'an Ssu-t'ung considered that Chinese politics during the preceding two thousand years had been a system for bringing the nation to ruin by hypocrites.

The best way to struggle for existence and self-salvation was to get rid of the traditional political regulations entirely and adopt a Western system. He considered that the strong points of the West lay not merely in its material civilization; the effectiveness of its ships and cannon was actually based on good government. These ideas seem close to those of Kuo Sung-tao, and more advanced than those of Chang Chih-tung and K'ang Yu-wei. T'an believed that human nature is the same everywhere and that it is fundamentally good, regardless of whether it is Chinese or foreign. Therefore, what Westerners can do, Chinese should also be able to learn, if they make up their minds to do so. Almost alone in 1898 he favored China's "complete Westernization" (*ch'üan-p'an hsi-hua*), and the abandonment or remaking of Confucianism and the traditional culture. The following excerpts are from one of T'an's long letters to a friend.[17]

DOC. 43. T'an Ssu-t'ung on the Need for Complete Westernization

Your letter says that the technique of studying foreign affairs has not yet been very good, and asks, shall we reform our institutions to provide for better government? Or among the doctrines of the Chinese sages are there some which should not be discarded completely?

Ssu-t'ung thinks that there is no doubt about the doctrines of our sages. It is impossible for us to discard even a little, so how can we do it completely? But the so-called *tao* ("doctrine") is not empty words. It must be accompanied by something [tool or machine] before it can be seen. . . Without *tao* there will be no *ch'i* [tool or machine]. . . and without *ch'i* there will be no *tao*. . . Without the bow and arrow there will be no *tao* for archery; without the carriage and horse there will be no *tao* for charioteering. [T'an goes on to explain that the *tao* or moral conception varies according to the *ch'i* or means of production — a considerable modification of the old Neo-Confucian idea. When the means of production is changed, he says, the *tao* must be changed accordingly. He then discusses the Western family and social relationships between father and son, husband and wife, etc., and finds them good, although most other Chinese of his time thought differently.]

(In the Western relationship) between husband and wife, from the ruler down to the common people, there is never a precedent for taking a concubine and marriage is arranged out of the desire of the two parties. Hence, the couple are devoted to each other, and there is no trouble over jealousy [between wife and concubine]. Among their children also there is no suspicion and envy owing to one's being the son of the wife or of the concubine. Among their friends they honor manners and righteousness; they cultivate sincerity and foster harmony. They share their financial hardships together. The rules of their schools and academies result in the teachers and disciples having clearly marked friendships and duties to each other, which is entirely different from the corrupt conditions of Chinese academies. . .

[P. 21] Those who slander the foreigners say that they have done all kinds of inhuman things such as gouging out the eye-pupils and hearts (of Chinese children), but who has seen it? If it is really true, why have we never heard of such things being done in their own countries?. . . No intelligent person would believe this rumor.

[P. 22] Your letter says that during the last several decades Chinese scholars and officials have been trying to talk about "foreign matters" (*yang-wu*), but that they have achieved absolutely nothing and, on the contrary, they have been driving the men of ability in the empire into foolishness, greed, and cheating. Ssu-t'ung thinks that not only do you not know what is meant by "foreign matters," but also that you are ignorant of the meaning of discussion. In China, during the last several decades, where have we had genuine understanding of foreign culture? When have we had scholars or officials who could discuss them? If they had been able to discuss foreign matters, there would have been no such incident as we have today [the defeat of China by Japan]. What you mean by foreign matters are things you have seen, such as steamships, telegraph lines, trains, guns, cannon, torpedoes, and machines for weaving and for metallurgy; that's all. You have never dreamed of or seen the beauty and perfection of Western legal systems and political institutions. . . All that you speak of are the branches and foliage of foreign matters, not the root. . .

We have more than one arsenal, and those at Tientsin, Shanghai, and Nanking are the oldest; but at the time when we need guns and cannon, there are no guns and cannon. We have more than one shipyard, and those at Port Arthur and Foochow are the largest; but at the time when we need ships, there are no ships. Helplessly we have to purchase these things from foreign countries. But the foreigners know that China has no machinery to test the quality of ships and weapons, and no way to distinguish between good and bad, so they sell to China, for an exorbitant price, weapons which have already been abandoned. . . And Chinese diplomatic envoys in foreign countries seek a share of the profit. When they receive a remittance and dispatch the officers to make the purchase, they ask for a fee. Consequently, the higher the price, the poorer the weapons. . . In this way China has wasted several decades. Yet you still consider Chinese scholar-officials to be learning about foreign matters. Are you not overestimating the various authorities and wishing to wash off their blame?. . .

[P. 26] We should extend the telegraph lines, establish post offices to take charge of postal administration, supply water, and burn electric or gas lamps for the use of the people. When the streets are well kept, the sources of pestilence will be cut off; when hospitals are numerous, the medical treatment will be excellent. We should have parks for public recreation and health. We should have a holiday once every seven days to enable civil and military officials to follow the policy of (alternation between) pressure and relaxation. We should thoroughly learn the written and spoken languages of all countries so as to translate Western books and newspapers, in order to know what other countries are doing all around us, and also to train men of ability as diplomats. We should send people to travel to all countries in order to enlarge their points of view and enrich their store of information, to observe the strengths and weaknesses, the rise and fall, of other countries; to adopt all the good points of other nations and to avoid their bad points from the start. As a result there will be none of the ships and weapons of any nation which we shall not be able to make, and none of the machines or implements which we shall not be able to improve. We should be exact about our units of measure, examine our legal system, and unify our moral standards and customs. When our legal system is established, our culture will be kept intact. . .

[P. 30b] Your idea of despising our enemies arises because you think that they are still barbarians. This is a common mistake of the scholars and officials of the whole empire and they must get rid of it. A proverb says, "Know yourself and know your enemy" ["and in a hundred battles win a hundred victories"]. We must first make ourselves respectable before we despise others. Now there is not a single one of the Chinese people's sentiments, customs, or political and legal institutions which can be favorably compared with those of the barbarians. Is there any bit of Western culture which was influenced by China? Even if we beg to be on an equal footing with the barbarians, we still cannot achieve it, so how can we convert them to be Chinese? . . . [p. 31b] Hereafter, Ssu-t'ung will seek more and new knowledge and will not confine himself to what has been mentioned above. If you do not scorn me as crazy, I have even better policies which I would like to explain to you in full. The first is how to raise funds for reform. . . The big mansions and the high buildings (of temples or monasteries) can be made into parliaments, schools, and other public offices. . .

[P. 32] Secondly, how to increase the usefulness of reform. The use of machines depends only on coal and petroleum for power. The consumption of fuel is great and naturally the sources will be exhausted someday. In Western countries, some are trying to collect heat from the earth and from the sun to operate steamships, also to use electricity to operate the railways. The power of the heat from the earth and the sun, however, is very small, and the capital needed for electricity is very large. . . If we seek the greatest and most unlimited power, we should do better to make use of the tides of the sea. According to astronomers, the power of the tide is governed by the sun and the moon, and it could make the earth leave its orbit temporarily, so that after a long time there would be a difference in the number of days in the year. Now we let it rise and ebb naturally and do not think of making use of it. . .

Thirdly, how to strengthen the protection of reform. [Under this item T'an Ssu-t'ung states his ambition to improve all the new weapons — including motor boats and balloons — so that China could get ahead of the West.]

Fourthly, how to seek men of ability for reform. In the preceding lines, I have talked about seeking men of ability through change in our school system and in the civil service examinations, and yet the most valuable thing is to have men to shoulder the responsibility at the beginning of the reform. There is nothing better than to urge the gentry leaders of all counties, prefectures, and districts to promote the ideas of abolishing temples and monasteries or of gathering stockholders to open mines or of installing machinery, etc., . . . Anyone who is outstanding in achievement or in any type of service or in any economic enterprise which will yield a profit shall be given special honors and ranks, or be allowed to become a member of parliament, and be subsidized and protected by the officials in order to bring his work to a successful conclusion. . . .

Wang K'ang-nien (1860–1911). Another of the reformers of 1898, Wang K'ang-nien was a secretary of the Grand Secretariat and is now known as a pioneer in Chinese journalism. After the Sino-Japanese War he became a leading advocate of modernization and reform and in 1896 started the famous newspaper *Shih-wu pao*, published in Shanghai with Liang Ch'i-ch'ao as editor, while he himself served in the capacity of manager. Wang K'ang-nien was an advocate of the people's rights and of their participation in government under a constitutional monarchy. He makes a cautious but persuasive appeal, not for a sudden full democracy, but for a partial adoption of democracy, in terms remarkably suggestive of more recent decades.

DOC. 44. Wang K'ang-nien on Democracy [18]

Chinese who discuss governmental systems speak only in terms of governing the people by a ruler. In the West, however, there are democratic countries and also countries governed jointly by the ruler and the people. Chinese scholars are surprised and consider it strange. Nevertheless what is strange about it? In ancient times all who discussed government always gave consideration to the people below. Thus the chapter "Hung-fan" of the *Book of History* says "to deliberate with the common people," and the chapter Lü-hsing" says, "The emperor frankly consults the people below him." In the *Rites of Chou* it is stated that the official in charge of the provincial administration brought the multitude of people together to ask their opinion. . . Mencius says, "When the people of the nation unanimously say that someone is capable, then he may be employed; when the people of the nation unanimously say that he is incapable, then he may be removed; and when the people of the nation unanimously say that he may be killed, then kill him." Other such references appearing in the classics are too numerous to be counted on the fingers. This shows that in ancient times those who governed the nation were not without the desire to govern it together with the people.

Nevertheless, there are some people who are apprehensive that power may be shifted downward. They do not know that in a nation governed jointly by the ruler and the people, when there is an important national issue, it is sent to the parliament for discussion and decision, which is then executed by the ruler. If the ruler has a different opinion from the officials, it may be discussed again. If the discussions do not result in a decision, the members of parliament may be changed. That is, the highest power is still held by the ruler.

Some critics say that if the people have rights, then the cruel and the crafty will be ambitious, the violent and unprincipled will act in an overbearing manner, and there will be endless confusion. They do not know that it is in the people's power to elect only the superior and the wise to the parliament, where they cannot carry out their own ambitions without control. Parliamentary members can only discuss a matter and cannot undertake its execution. How can they act outrageously and overbearingly?

Some people say when authority lies in the emperor, it is concentrated; when it lies in the people, then it is divided, and when it is divided a nation cannot be a nation. They do not know that, even though the number of parliamentary members is great, the election is very carefully conducted, and even though the discussions may be complicated, the majority opinion must be followed. When the election is carefully conducted, then there will be few absurd opinions. When the majority opinion is selected, then there will be many who are willing to carry out the decision. This proves that all three arguments are insufficient to cause us worry.

Moreover, at a time like the present, three great advantages will result from the partial adoption of democracy. Formerly in Europe the authority of the emperor was too great, but with the increase of the power of the people the authority of the emperors slightly declined. In China the ruler's power has been gradually lost and it is necessary to have the people's power restored before the emperor's authority can be upheld. Why? Because, although China's governmental systems and laws were said to be initiated by the ruler, yet the rulers in preceding dynasties greatly feared that their descendants might be ignorant of state affairs and might do illegal and cruel things. They therefore repeatedly explained that everything should be patterned after the preceding dynasties, and that no one was to be permitted to make any changes and, thus, all actions were decided upon by precedent. All great officials followed the routine procedure of the documents and all other officers in charge depended entirely on old custom to make their decisions. Then those clerks who were thoroughly familiar with the by-laws and precedents could privately shift matters around. Therefore, the great power of the nation did not rest with the emperor above, nor with the officials in the middle, nor with the people below, but was controlled merely by the clerks, whose purpose was to obtain money to hand down to their posterity. From the beginning they had no great ideals. Therefore they merely sought profit and worked for their selfish purposes, causing evils as numerous as the hair on one's head. The good laws and fine ideas were confused and gradually destroyed.

Not only that; when the emperor stands alone, above the hundreds of officials and millions of people, then his perception cannot reach those below, and his personal power again is insufficient. For this reason when there are omissions in financial accounts, he does not know it. When there are misjudgments in judicial affairs, he is unaware of them. When the work is poorly and corruptly handled, he is not informed. Repeatedly he has warned his people against favoritism and yet his inferiors still resort to their personal connections as before. Repeatedly he has ordered them to keep themselves pure and yet his inferiors are greedy for bribes as before. Repeatedly he has commanded them to observe the law and yet his inferiors cheat as before. His decrees are severe and earnest, and his officials in appearance seem to be in awe, but actually they make not the slightest change in their bad habits. Can it then still be said that the emperor has authority? If only democracy ["the people's rights" or "people's power"] is partially used, then there will be thousands of ears and myriads of eyes which cannot be covered or beclouded. And when a thousand persons point to one object, it is impossible to avoid seeing it. Whether an order should be put into execution or a prohibition be carried out, everything will be followed according to the emperor's wish. Therefore even though one may say that the people's rights [or people's power, democracy] are partially used, there is no better way than this to carry through the emperor's authority.

Moreover, when the people have no power, they do not realize that the nation belongs to all the people, and they keep at a distance from the emperor. When the people have some power, then they will realize that the nation is their own concern, and they will be drawn close to the emperor. This is probably because close relationships among human beings come from mutual discussions of important matters, from contacts and feelings, and from exchange of ideas. If the emperor majestically appears as Heaven, and the people are humbly looked down upon as grass and weeds, they will think that the empire and the four seas are all properties of the emperor, and that they are merely his slaves and servants. In time of peace, they are indifferent to political affairs and activities. When faced with catastrophes, they will desert the emperor, one and all. They merely blame him for not being able to protect them, but they do not exert their minds and energy in the smallest degree for him. If the emperor governed the nation jointly with the people, then the latter would have contact with his voice and feelings, and affections would naturally grow up. Thus when the people of Western countries see their rulers, they take off their hats to show their respect; whenever they drink wine, they toast the ruler's health; and whenever there are great affairs of state, they all gather to make plans. The reason is that it is necessary to make the people enjoy themselves together with the emperor, so that they can take pleasure in his enjoyment; and to make the people share his worry, so that they take it as their own concern. That is a matter of course.

Considering the national situation in which we find ourselves today, it is even more urgent for us to apply the people's power (to the conduct of public affairs), because when only the emperor's power is employed to fight against the foreigners, he is weak and easily controlled by foreigners. When the people's power is used to stand against the foreigners, then the force is strong and it will be easier to advance our arguments. The Westerners doing business in China often exploit the power of our emperor in order to control our people. If China desires to oppose the foreigners, her power is insufficient; if she wishes to use the objection of the people as an argument, then, because for a long time her people have had no power, no pretext can be derived from them. For this reason, treaties were revised or made without the people's being consulted. When concessions were demanded, and indemnities requested, these were again granted without consulting the people. Other requests, which were detrimental to the nation and to the people, were also unhesitatingly granted as the Westerners desired, in echo-like response. The officers in charge would receive the orders and follow their instructions to carry out the transaction, fearing only that they could not do it soon enough. Thereupon, while the people hated the Westerners, they also turned their hatred against the officials.

In general, when the power of the empire comes from one person, it is weak. When it comes from millions of people, it is strong. That is positively true. Moreover, if people of all provinces are united to plan for a thing, then the spirit of the nation is integrated; otherwise, divided. If the scholars, merchants, and common people can all feel concern about the dangers and difficulties of the nation, then the people will be intelligent; otherwise, ignorant. Therefore, unless we rely on the people's authority, it is impossible to change our disunited spirit to one of concentration and our ignorance to wisdom. What harm would there be? I can only see that if our ancient system is restored, then our sovereignty will be respected and our national position consolidated.

In another essay on "Methods to make China strong," [19] written about 1898, Wang K'ang-nien repeats his demand for the consolidation of public opinion and restoration of confidence in the administration — specifically, by setting up a parliament and cabinet government, followed by councils at local levels, simplification of the written language, and a multitude of legal, economic, military and other reforms.

CHAPTER XVII. THE REFORM PROGRAM OF
CHANG CHIH-TUNG

Students of modern Chinese history are familiar with the slogan *Chung-hsueh wei t'i, Hsi-hsueh wei yung*, which may be translated, "Chinese learning for the fundamental principles, Western learning for practical application," and which became for a generation the main theme in the debate over China's cultural policy (see above, Ch. Vb). In 1898 it was made famous by Chang Chih-tung (1837–1909), who was both a liberal official who worked for reforms and a conservative scholar who objected to parliamentary government. Some of his industrial efforts have been noted above (Ch. XIII). Because of his significance throughout the decade before and after 1900, we pause here to look briefly at his career and opinions as a whole, out of their chronological sequence.

Chang was born into an official family and received a superb classical education. Shortly after he obtained the *chin-shih* degree in 1863 he began to write memorials to the throne, and by this means made himself famous. He served as governor-general of Kwangtung-Kwangsi for five years (1884–1889), and of Hunan-Hupei for eighteen years (1889–1907), with some interruption as acting governor-general at Nanking. This service enabled him to become an indispensable consultant on all the pivotal affairs of the late Ch'ing government, one feature of which was that the initiative in formulating domestic and especially diplomatic policies was largely exercised by the governors general, through the medium of their memorials. Eventually, after the death of Li Hung-chang (1901), Liu K'un-i (1902), and Jung-lu (1903), Chang Chih-tung was to become the leading elder statesman in the capital, serving as grand secretary and grand councillor in special charge of supervising the new Ministry of Education (see Ch. XXb). The actual power of his last posts, however, was not great and he could not do much to help the tottering dynasty, which survived him by only two years.

Chang Chih-tung's essential ideas of reform were presented in his widely read book, "Exhortation to study" (*Ch'üan-hsueh-p'ien*).[1] Written in 1898, this work followed some thirty-eight years after Feng Kuei-fen's essays, *Chiao-pin-lu k'ang-i* (see Ch. Vb). As we have pointed out, Chang's famous slogan was plainly derived from Feng. The two scholars had the same pattern of thought, but Chang, a generation later, had more information, not only about Western technology, but also about Western governmental institutions (*Hsi-cheng*) including the school system, financial management, taxation methods, military preparedness, laws and statutes, and the encouragement of industry. Chang did not esteem Occidental philosophy or political theory. His ideas may be briefly summarized under three headings:

(1) *To save the Manchu dynasty by a revival of Confucianism.* Like Tseng Kuo-fan, and on a similar basis of philosophical conviction, Chang Chih-tung was thoroughly loyal to the Manchu regime. As a high official under three generations of emperors, Chang felt grateful for their magnanimous government, their remissions of taxes, and other benevolent acts toward the people, which he emphatically eulogized, one by one. He tried to prove that Manchus and Chinese were of the same race,[2] that therefore, to preserve the Chinese race, it was necessary to preserve the Manchus also.

Chang emphasizes Confucianism as the heart of Chinese civilization. He criticizes the translations of the Chinese classics into English, because to him they seem based on the interpretations of vulgar scholars. He himself stresses the "three bonds" (*san-kang* — the relationships between prince and minister, father and son, husband and wife) and the "five constant virtues" (benevolence, justice, politeness, wisdom and faithfulness). He says, "If one recognizes the importance of the bond between prince and minister, the doctrine of democracy is untenable. If one recognizes the importance of the bond between father and son, the theory that both the father and the son may be equally guilty [instead of the conception that the father is always right] and the abolition of funeral and sacrificial ceremonies is impracticable. If one recognizes the importance of the bond between husband and wife, then the doctrine of equal rights between men and women is impracticable." [3] Thus he strongly attacked the institutions of democracy, constitutional monarchy, and Western-style personal liberty, in order to protect the Manchu rulers against revolution. In 1900 he actually suppressed an uprising at Hankow and executed twenty reformers or rebel leaders.

Chang usually adopted a strong, even belligerent, attitude against foreign aggression. This was repeatedly expressed in his memorials against Russia in 1879–1880, against France in 1882–1885, against Japan in 1894–1895, and against Russia again in 1901 during the post-Boxer negotiations in Manchuria. In the latter case his severe criticism of Li Hung-chang roused the court.[4]

At Peking, Chang Chih-tung was considered the leader of the Northern Faction, while Weng T'ung-ho (1830–1904) headed the Southern Faction. In Chang's chronological biography (*nien-p'u*), he is said to have regretted he had no steady partisans. Compared with Weng, Chang was rather liberal and certainly more farsighted. He advocated a program of gradual modification based on education rather than the rapid changes which the emperor and K'ang Yu-wei were attempting in 1898. He sharply criticized K'ang's work and favored, instead, a synthesis of Confucianism with Occidental technology and governmental methods (as opposed to governmental institutions). "Chinese learning is the inside knowledge; Western learning is the outside knowledge. Chinese learning is to control the body and soul (of the people); Western learning is to be applied to their mundane affairs." [5] Thus he formulated variations of his famous slogan.

(2) *To save China by education. Chiao-yü chiu-kuo,* "Save the country by education," was a popular slogan in the 1920's. Upon reading Chang Chih-tung's writings, however, one must be impressed by the extent to which he had been working on that principle several decades earlier. He founded academies in Chengtu (1875) and Canton (1887) and was the patron of publications. With the help of his assistants, he compiled a handbook on study and composition and a selected bibliography of basic Chinese works (*Shu-mu ta-wen*) which is still useful.

Later on he recognized that education was a barometer of the power and prosperity of a nation. He says, "Since ancient times, for the brightness or darkness of the fate of the world, and for the prosperity or decadence of men of ability, the external reason has lain in government, the internal reason has lain in education." [6] "The strength of Western countries lies in the strength of their schools." [7] He asks, "How can a race be preserved?" and answers his own question: "With possession of knowledge it is preserved." [8] "In order to save the current situation we must begin with reform, and reform must begin with the changing of the civil service examinations." [9]

Chang recommended the establishment of colleges and universities in Peking and in the capital of each province, middle schools in all prefectures, and elementary schools in all districts (*hsien*). The funds of guilds and clan organizations should be spent for the support of elementary schools. Buddhist and Taoist temples should be transformed into school buildings (a very radical idea at that time). In a memorial of 1893 Chang proposed to found a "self-strengthening" (*tzu-ch'iang*) academy and it was established in Nanking in 1896. Foreign professors were invited to teach diplomacy, agriculture, industry and commerce. In December 1895, he also planned to train a "self-strengthening" (*tzu-ch'iang*) army.[10] The Tzu-ch'iang Academy and the Tzu-ch'iang Army formed the culmination of a generation of the self-strengthening movement. In the following year Chang sent forty students to study in England, France, and Germany, following the precedent of Tseng Kuo-fan's educational mission of 1872.[11] In the early twentieth century he sent many students to Japan. When they returned he questioned them about foreign countries in great detail; the educational scheme Chang drew up for China when he was minister of education was patterned mainly on that of Japan, and based on information supplied by students returned from that country. Although Chang recognized the importance of education, he was ignorant of educational psychology. His curricula stressed the classics and loyalty to the emperor.

(3) *To save China by industry*. Chang Chih-tung was a pioneer in the modernization of Chinese economic life. In 1889 he opened China's first modern mint in Canton. In 1895 his Tzu-ch'iang Army was moved to Wusung near Shanghai, to form the nucleus of a modern military force industrially supplied and drilled by German instructors. Probably his best known project was the Han-Yeh-P'ing iron and steel works centered at Wuhan, where he also sponsored cotton mills, silk factories, and tanneries. He introduced bicycles, loading cranes, and other machines to the Wuhan cities, earning for that area the sobriquet of "Chinese Chicago." An ardent advocate of railroad construction, he personally supervised the building of the Peking-Hankow railway. He encouraged the establishment of a merchants' association in each city, and urged the improvement of the tea, silk and other productive industries.[12] Finally, although his life was so eventful and fruitful, he died a poor man.

His *Ch'üan-hsueh-p'ien* was well received by the throne in 1898 and forty copies were ordered distributed to the high provincial officials for reproduction. Extracts of the more important chapters are translated below.

DOC. 45. SELECTIONS FROM CHANG'S "EXHORTATION TO STUDY," 1898

Rectification of Political Rights [13]

Nowadays scholars who hate the customs of the times are angry at the foreigners for cheating and encroaching upon us, at the generals for being unable to fight, at the great officials for not carrying out reforms, at the directors of education for not developing schools, and at numerous officials for not investigating industry and commerce. Therefore they promote discussion of the people's rights [*min-ch'üan*, the term used above by Wang K'ang-nien and later used by Sun Yat-sen: "democracy"] in order to get the people to unite and exert themselves. Alas, why use such words that incite disorder!

The doctrine of people's rights will bring us not a single benefit but a hundred evils. Are we going to establish a parliament? Among the Chinese scholars and people there are still many even today who are content to be vulgar and rustic. They are ignorant of the general situation of the world, they do not understand the basic system of the state. They have not the most rudimentary ideas about foreign countries — about the schools, the political systems, military training, and manufacture of armaments. Even supposing the confused and clamorous people are assembled in one house, for every one of them who is clear-sighted, there will be a hundred others whose vision is beclouded; they will converse at random and talk as if in a dream — what use will it be?

Moreover in foreign countries, in such affairs as raising funds [levying taxes] and other financial matters, the emphasis is on the lower house; in other (important) legislation the emphasis is on the upper house. In general one must have moderate wealth in his family to get to be a member of parliament. Nowadays Chinese merchants rarely have much capital; the Chinese people, moreover, are lacking in farsighted long range ambitions. When an important proposal for raising funds is to be discussed, all of them make excuses and keep silent. So their discussion is tantamount to non-discussion. This is the first reason why there is no use (in having a parliament). [The author goes on to state three more reasons, which we omit.]

[P. 24] Nowadays China is indeed neither impressive nor powerful. Nevertheless, the populace are still content with their daily work because the laws of the dynasty hold them together. Once the doctrine of people's rights is advocated, foolish people will assuredly be delighted; unruly people will rise up; the laws will not be carried out; great disorder will arise on all sides. . .

Furthermore, the towns will certainly be plundered and churches burned or destroyed. I am afraid that certain foreign countries will be sure to take the protection of their nationals and properties as a pretext and send their gunboats with land forces to penetrate deeply and occupy our territories. The whole country then will belong to others with our acquiescence. Thus the doctrine of people's rights is just what our enemies will like to hear about. . .

Formerly in France, after a succession of harsh regimes under tyrannical rulers, the people of the whole country were resentful and furious, the higher and lower orders attacked each other, and then she was changed into a republic [*min-chu chih kuo*, lit., a state where the people are the masters]. Our dynasty has been profoundly magnanimous and generously beneficent; and there has been no harsh government. Why bother to urge these steps (which can only result in) disorder and bring woe both to oneself and to the empire as well? . . .

An investigation of the origin of the doctrine of people's rights in foreign countries merely reveals the idea that a state should have a parliament where the people can express their general opinion and communicate their group feelings. It is only desired that the people should be able to explain their feelings; it is not desired that they wield any power. Translators have altered the wording to call it "people's rights," which is a mistake. (Note: Americans who have come to China have themselves spoken of the defects of their public elections. The people below usually cherish selfish plans and those above play favorites, which has caused great trouble. Those Chinese who praise it are all talking without thorough investigation.)

In recent days those who have picked up some Western doctrines have even gone so far as to say that everybody has the right to be his own master [tzu-chu]; this is even more absurd. This phrase is derived from their religious book. It means that a man is endowed by God with his nature and soul, that every person has wisdom and intelligence, and that all are capable of doing usfeul work. The translators eventually interpret it to mean that every person has the right to be his own master. This interpretation is a still worse blunder. . . [P. 25] Each Western state definitely has a government, and a government has laws. Officials have administrative laws, soldiers have military laws, workers have labor laws, and merchants have commercial laws. The lawyers learn them, and judges preserve them. Neither the ruler nor the people can violate the law. What is suggested by the executive may be argued by members of parliament, and what is decided by the parliament may be dissolved by the ruling dynasty. To say that nobody has the right to be his own master is correct, but how can we say that every person is his own master?

In general the uproar of a market must certainly cease in the end; and in a group of bandits there must be a chief. If people are all their own masters, every family will be selfish for itself, every village will be selfish for itself, every scholar will want to sit and eat, every farmer will want exemption from his tax, every merchant will want a monopoly, every worker will want a higher wage, poor people without an occupation will want to rob or plunder, the son will not obey his father, the pupil will not respect his teacher, the wife will not obey her husband, the lowly will not submit to the exalted, and the weak will be the prey of the strong. There will be no end until mankind is entirely extinct. Certainly there has been no such government among the myriad nations of the earth, nor any such custom among aboriginal and barbarous tribes.

In foreign countries today there are liberal [tzu-yu, "freedom"] parties — the western word actually sounds li-po-erh-t'e [liberty] — which means that everything must be just and of benefit to the multitude. The name may be translated "public opinion party," but to translate it "freedom" [tzu-yu] is wrong.

As for the policy of strengthening China to resist foreign countries, the only way is to use the principles of loyalty and righteousness in order to summon and unite the moral vigor [hsin] of the empire, and to exert the majestic spiritual power of the court toward uniting the strength of the entire country.[14] These are fundamental principles of the universe, which do not change either in ancient or in modern times, either in China or in foreign countries.

Following the Proper Order [15]

Now if we wish to make China strong and to preserve Chinese knowledge, we must study Western knowledge. Nevertheless, if we do not use Chinese knowledge to consolidate the foundation first and get straight in our own minds what our interests and purposes are, then the strong will become rebellious leaders and the weak will become slaves of others [i.e., of the foreigners]. . .

Scholars today must master the classics first, in order to understand the purpose underlying the establishment of education by our ancient Chinese sages and teachers. They must study history, in order to learn the rise and fall of succeeding dynasties of China, and the customs of the empire. They must glance over the philosophical works and belles-lettres in order to become thoroughly familiar with Chinese academic ideas and exquisite writings. And then they can select and make use of that Western knowledge which can make up our shortcomings, and adopt those Western methods of government which can cure our illnesses. These, then, will be beneficial and harmless. As one who is recuperating must first get some energy from rice, and then be offered all sorts of delicacies. . . [p. 28] so the acquisition of Western knowledge must follow after Chinese knowledge.

In all schools in foreign countries the Bible of Jesus Christ must be read every day to illustrate their religion. In grade schools Latin must be learned first to ensure the preservation of antiquity. The map of their own country must be familiar first, before the map of the whole globe is examined, to show that there is a proper order. . . A Chinese scholar not versed in Chinese knowledge resembles a man who does not know his own surname, or a riding horse without a bridle, or a boat without a rudder; the more profound his Western knowledge the more severe will be his contempt for China. Even though there are such scholars, who have a broad knowledge of things and are equipped with many abilities, how can the country make use of them?

To Remove the Poison [16]

Alas, the harm of opium is the "great flood and fierce beasts" of today, and yet it is even worse. The harm of the "great flood" lasted no more than nine years and the harm of the "fierce beasts" did not extend beyond the capital of the Yin dynasty. But the perniciousness of opium has been spreading for more than a hundred years and gradually expanding to the twenty-two provinces. Millions of people have suffered from this perniciousness, yet there is still no end to its insidious influence. (Opium) has ruined men of ability, weakened the morale of soldiers, and wasted money. . .

According to the Confucian Analects: "The Master said, 'If discipline of the people is sought by means of punishments, they will try to avoid the punishments, but feel no shame. If they be disciplined by rules of propriety, they will have a sense of shame and therefore will become good.'" [17] That is to say, when law cannot govern, the ming [reputation or honor] can bring good results. (Note: Ku Yen-wu says: "To use law to rule the people is not as good as to use *ming* to rule them.") The chapter "Hsüeh-chi" [Record on the subject of education, of the *Book of Rites*] says, "If a superior man wishes to transform the people and to perfect their manners and customs, must he not start from the lessons of the school?" [18] That is, when the government cannot transform people, education is able to transform them. Why?

The beginning of opium smoking by the Chinese starts from laziness. Laziness comes from having nothing to do, which again comes from the lack of knowledge, which again is derived from the lack of information. The knowledge of scholars is taken from classical commentaries and examination papers. The knowledge of officials is taken from case work. The knowledge of soldiers is taken from dull weapons and archaic positional warfare; they are content with these. . . In general everything can be obtained without exertion, profound thinking, wide acquaintance, or distant traveling. [P. 39] Ignorance produces stupidity in a man; stupidity produces slowness; slowness produces a leisurely easiness; leisurely easiness produces wastefulness. Thereupon the addiction to opium will hit him. These are all caused by lack of learning.

If learned societies [study groups?] are widely organized, people either in the city or in the country, either noble or mean, can learn civil and military theories and techniques. The weak will learn how to read a newspaper, and the strong will learn from traveling. The superior men will harbor the knowledge of the five continents. The humble men will wish to try hundreds of techniques. They will even desire to measure the distances of the stars in the sky and to investigate the earth below, and to search for the southern and northern poles on the horizontal. How could there still be any who turn the day into night and spend the rest of their lives on a bed beside an opium lamp? Even if they were tempted they would not do it. How much less will it be necessary to forbid them?

Therefore I say, the development of education is the medicine to use for the suppression of opium. . .

On Reform [19]

Reform [*pien-fa*, lit., a change of statutes] is the duty of the court. Why should it be discussed with scholars and the people? . . . The decision as to whether our system should be changed rests with the state, but actually it is determined by the wishes and discussions of scholars and the people.

Let us review events: when Tseng Kuo-fan was a vice-minister, he once submitted a memorial pointing out the defects of examining the Hanlin scholars in small-model writing and in the composition of poetry and the *fu* verse. After he was successful and became a state minister, if he had kept up [and taken action on] this criticism, he would have produced many men of ability in the Hanlin Academy during the last thirty years. Yet nothing more was heard about the matter. Why? Because after the great rebellion had been suppressed, he became fearful lest he be vilified by the contemporary scholars.

Wen-hsiang once opened the T'ung-wen Kuan and published various books on international law and the natural sciences. If he had kept on promoting these things, he would have been able to obtain many men qualified to be sent to distant countries and thoroughly familiar with current affairs. Nevertheless, those who are careful about trifles and feel self-conscious warned one another against entering the T'ung-wen Kuan or taking the examinations for secretaries of the Tsungli Yamen. Among the capital and court officials those who can discuss new knowledge are silent and unheard. Why? Because they were impeded by the erroneous ideas of all the absurd and narrow-minded scholars. Thus, even a meritorious minister [Tseng] and a venerable statesman [Wen-hsiang], though celebrated for their virtue and great authority, still cannot avoid being hindered by the criticism of those who are accustomed to using the wrong to overcome the right, and so no good effect can be seen. This is pitiful and lamentable!

Again, Tso Tsung-t'ang established a shipyard near Foochow and an arsenal and a woolen mill in Kansu; Shen Pao-chen set up the shipyard administration, opened schools, and consulted with Li Hung-chang in establishing the China Merchants' Steam Navigation Company; Ting Pao-chen instituted arsenals to make foreign guns and bullets in both Shantung and Szechwan — these were famous ministers who were known at the time to be honest, upright, and orthodox Confucians. Nevertheless, the things they undertook were all this kind of enterprise. At that time it was in the middle of the T'ung-chih period [1862–1874] and the first years of the Kuang-hsü period [1875–1908], when the nation was quiet and at ease. Unfortunately, current opinion caviled at many points, and those who followed (the men mentioned above) were again lacking in knowledge. They either let their establishments go to waste or operated them in a reduced form. None of them could achieve any expansion. Therefore the effect was not great.

In general, that which should not be changed is our human relationships and fundamental principles, not the system of laws; it is our sage's way, not instruments; it is the principle of the mind, not technology. Let us find evidence from the classics.

When all alternatives are exhausted, one has to make a change — change and accommodation to make the most of an advantage; change and accommodation to suit the time. The method of diminution and increase [of the statutes] should be used to keep abreast of the times. That is the idea of the *Book of Changes*.[20]

"In instruments we do not seek old ones but new." [21] That is the idea in the *Book of History*. "Knowledge exists among the four barbarians." That is the idea in the *Commentary on the Ch'un-ch'iu*.[22] The Five Emperors did not follow the old music and the Three Kings did not copy the old ceremony. "The timely ceremony is the most important." That is the idea of the *Book of Rites*.

"He cherishes his old knowledge and is continually acquiring new [23]. . . When I walk with two persons, they may serve as my teachers; I select their good qualities and follow them." That is the idea of the Confucian *Analects*.[24]

"When he employs (these virtues) they will be in accordance with right." That is the idea of *The Doctrine of the Mean*.[25] "When one has no sense of shame for not being equal to others, what will he have with which to be an equal of them?"; that is the idea of Mencius.[26]

Let us find evidence from the histories. . . . In the successive dynasties the most conspicuous reforms are these four: King Wu-ling of Chao [*ca.* 300 B.C.] reformed the traditional military system (from foot soldiers) to mounted archers, and by means of this the Chao frontier was made secure. King Hsiao-wen [A.D. 467–499] of Northern Wei reformed the traditional system toward a more civilized one, by means of which the Wei kingdom was well governed. These were gains from reform. . . Shang Yang reformed the traditional system [359 B.C.], casting off filial piety, younger brotherhood, benevolence and righteousness. The Ch'in state remained strong for a time and then fell into distress. Wang An-shih (1021–1086) conducted a reform by devoting himself to harassing the people. The Sung dynasty was thereby involved in disorder. These were losses from reform. The error of Lord Shang and of Wang lay in the cruelty of harassing the people. It was not because the reform should not have been made, but because these particular reforms were improper. (Note: In Western political systems two things, the elimination of punishments and the feeding of the people, are matters of priority.). . . There have been many changes (in the Ch'ing dynasty). Even when steamships and telegraph wires were first introduced, there was much criticism. But at the present time, if anyone wished to discard them, would there not be people who would bare their arms and fight against the proposal?

Now those who reject reforms generally belong to three categories [p. 20]. One consists of the narrow-minded scholars who are ultra-conservative; the defects of ultra-conservatism are easy to understand. Another consists of the vulgar officials who like to take improper ease. For reform we must tax our thinking, must collect funds, must select people, and must do actual work. These are all inconvenient to the selfish plans of those who are confused and lazy, and who like to shirk work, to be influenced by favoritism, or to take the easiest tasks. Therefore, under the cover of bookish and conservative talk, they gloss over the subterfuges of slippery officials who take improper ease. Such are their true feelings. When asked about their academic ideas and the governmental principles of the Chinese traditional system, all is revealed to have been neglect and sham on their part. They have not done a single thing. This is what they [the critics] mean by "follow the ancients." Is this sound? The third kind consists of the talkative scholars who like to be captious. Actually, in recent years there have been some imitations of Western methods which bore no fruit.

There are, however, four reasons for this. The first is, all people care for their selfish purposes, and so they plan only for themselves and no progress is made — for example, the various officials in charge of factories and the various people who went abroad. This is a defect of the people, not the defect of the reform. The second is the inadequacy of funds. From this comes a deficiency of money on all sides which prevents superior products, such as the shipyards. This is a defect of the times, not the defect of reform.

Third, there is no fixed policy at Court. A new thing may be suddenly taken up and then suddenly suspended, with nothing accomplished, such as the sending of students abroad and of officials from the capital to travel in foreign countries. This is the defect of unfounded reports [as to their behavior], not the defect of reform. Fourth, there are instruments but no personnel to handle them. When we had not yet learned mechanical engineering, we bought machines; when we had not yet trained captains or admirals, we purchased a fleet — such were our navy and the various factories. This is the defect of having the wrong sequence in what should go first or later, not the defect of reform. Nevertheless, there is the idle talk of people not on the scene, who do not trace the causes of the [following] unfortunate results: the fluctuations of national policy, the carelessness in employing people, the decentralization of responsibilities, the insufficiency of funds, and the half-hearted effort in our studies. But they cavil at trifles and reproach us for producing little result. They are even worse than the person who "looks at a crossbow and immediately expects a roast dove before him; or who sees an egg, and immediately expects to hear it crow." [27] When schoolhouses are just being built, they demand accomplished men of ability. When a mine has not yet been opened, they demand that it pay a profit. There is no fixed standard in handling matters and no fixed aim in personnel. When some state affair is urgent, then everything is taken up; and when things have slowed down, then everything is again put aside. One digs a grave, the other fills it up. How could we expect any success?

Condemnation of Attacks on Missionaries [28]

Attacks of different religions upon each other have always occurred since the time of the Chou and Ch'in dynasties. The Confucianists and the Mohists attacked each other. . . In the T'ang [618–907] the Confucianists and the Buddhists attacked each other. In the later Wei [386–535] and Northern Sung [960–1279] the Taoists and the Buddhists attacked each other. . . By the present day right and wrong have been greatly clarified. . . Now the essential thing to do for the disciples of our sages who fear the decadence of the sacred doctrine, and who desire to protect it and enlarge its influence, is to cultivate good administration and not struggle against other religions. This is the difference in circumstances between ancient and modern times.

Since the beginning of large-scale communication between China and the West, Western churches have spread all over China. Missionary work has been permitted by treaties, and the burning and destruction of churches again have been clearly forbidden by Imperial decree. Recently Germany took the incident of missionaries being killed in Shantung as a pretext, and occupied Kiaochow. All the other countries also took this opportunity to make demands. A crisis for China becomes daily more imminent. Purposeful scholars should work hard to gain knowledge, and should stimulate their sense of loyalty and righteousness, in order to clarify the great duty of respecting parents in China, and should discuss the important methods of making China wealthy and strong. When our national power becomes daily stronger and the Confucian influence increases accordingly, then the foreign religions will be merely like the Buddhist monasteries and Taoist temples, which we may leave to their natural fate. What harm can they do us? But if we remain decadent and self-indulgent, and cannot put the academic principles and governmental techniques of Confucius and Mencius into actual practice; if our knowledge is inadequate to meet the needs of society, and our talent and strategy are insufficient to extend our national prestige; and if we merely seek for victory by cursing others, what is the good of that? Not only is there nothing to be gained by it, but also if scholars advocate this idea, then foolish people will respond to it, disloyal people will take this opportunity to rise, and rebels of secret societies and disbanded soldiers will find some opportunity to loot or plunder and start turmoil for no reason. . . [p. 51].

Not only that, but also our knowledge about the sea [i.e., about overseas countries] is gradually becoming more intimate, and the barriers between China and the West are gradually vanishing. When foreigners travel in the interior, ignorant men and children, upon noting their Western costumes, follow them with clamorous shouts and try to drive them away by stoning them with pebbles. They all arise in an uproar, no one knowing what the matter is, nor do they ask whether the foreigners are missionaries or non-missionaries, Europeans or Americans. In general, to curse and attack people without reason is impolite. Europeans are not of one kind. Some of them are employed by the customs office; some are employed by a government office; some are travelers and some are missionaries. To be blind and make no distinction, to get angry against them all is ignorant and foolish. To disobey the Imperial decree is unlawful. To attack one or two persons with a crowd of several hundred people is unchivalrous. To be timid in public war but courageous in private strife is to be destitute of shame. Therefore foreigners frequently say that China is uncivilized. When our people are crazy like this, how can we excuse ourselves?

As for the popular rumor that in churches there are frequently cruel actions, such as that the pupils of human eyes are gouged out, to be mixed with chemicals to make corrosive acids, or to transform lead into silver, these are all false rumors. . . Were there such things, then the peoples of the Western nations would have been entirely destroyed by the churches long ago. . . If we say that they do not injure Westerners but harm only the Chinese people, then where did they get their medicine, their corrosive acids and their silver bars, for the one thousand years or more before they had contact with China? Moreover, the amount of medicine and corrosive acids which are needed by all foreign countries and the silver bars which they import each day are already innumerable. Even though there are churches in all Chinese provinces, how can they kill several myriads of their converts every day, and daily pick out several myriads of eyeballs to supply the demand? A proverb says, "A stray bullet stops on an entrenchment, and an unfounded rumor stops with the wise." The gentry class and learned scholars all have the responsibility of inspiring and leading the foolish and the ignorant. We must carefully avoid the covert ridicule of our ignorance by foreign people.

CHAPTER XVIII. THE FAILURE OF 1898

The repeated memorials of K'ang Yu-wei and others and K'ang's books on reform in Russia and Japan, which were presented to the court in the spring of 1898, raised the issue of reform among some liberal officials, and, most important, in the mind of Emperor Kuang-hsü himself, who then enjoyed much greater power than he had ever had since he attained his majority in 1889. On June 11, 1898, the emperor issued his first reform decree, recognizing the need for a change. On the same day, a reader of the Hanlin academy, Hsü Chih-ching, recommended to the throne that K'ang Yu-wei, Liang Ch'i-ch'ao, Huang Tsun-hsien and others be appointed advisors to the emperor in the promulgation of the proposed reforms. K'ang was given the privilege of a personal audience with the emperor on June 16, and he was subsequently appointed secretary of the Tsungli Yamen and granted the privilege of submitting his memorials directly to the throne. Emperor Kuang-hsü and the reform leaders were all ideologists inexperienced in politics, and they issued scores of reform decrees hastily, without studying the political and social scene to see whether the new reforms could be effective. These decrees dealt with important scientific studies, the adoption of Western military drill, the improvement of agriculture and education, the abolition of the eight-legged essay in the official examinations, the promulgation of a public budget, the dismissal of conservative officials, and the abolition of sinecure positions, etc. They evoked strong opposition from officials entrenched in lucrative posts and from students whose chief training was in the eight-legged essays. The conservatives urged the Empress Dowager Tz'u-hsi to suppress the reform movement, lest even her own position be endangered. On September 21, the emperor was imprisoned by order of the Empress Dowager, who resumed the regency. The conservatives and anti-reformists now held full sway, advocating policies which were eventually to culminate in the Boxer Uprising. First, let us present the complicated situation within the court, and then describe the even more complicated and kaleidoscopic ideas of the conservative scholars.[1] Since K'ang and Liang had risen to power from the status of commoners only a few months earlier and had the self-righteousness of reformers, they stirred up violent objections from the conservatives.

a. The Court and the Emperor

Within the struggle for reform subordinate struggles went on between conservatives and liberals, between Manchus and Chinese, between England and Russia, and, most important, between an autocratic aunt, the Empress Dowager, and her nephew, the emperor. The Empress Dowager cared for little but her family's fortunes. If she had been somehow placed at the head of the reform movement, in the most prominent position, her opposition might have been lessened. Yet in any case there would still have been a struggle because the power of Tz'u-hsi was built on her favorite eunuchs and on the conservative officials whom she protected, while the emperor was the actual head of the reform movement. Without removing the Empress Dowager's people, the reformers could not carry out their policies, while if she accepted their proposals, her power would collapse. The reform effort threatened her directly and also endangered the positions of the high conservative officials who were its main object of attack. If the emperor, as a reformer, wielded real power, the conservatives including the Empress Dowager could not maintain their privileges. The top Manchu military commander, Jung-lu (1835–1903), was entirely dependent on the Empress Dowager and opposed reform to protect his own position. Hsü T'ung (1819–1900), an associate grand secretary, was another conservative minister. The emperor disliked him so much that he had been summoned for only one interview during the long interval between 1887 and 1898. But because he was trusted by the Empress Dowager, he had not been dismissed.

In this period there were Southern and Northern Factions in the court. The Empress Dowager favored the Northern Faction headed by Hsü T'ung and Li Hung-tsao (1820–1897), a sub-chancellor of the Grand Secretariat. The emperor favored the Southern Faction led by his tutor, Weng T'ung-ho (1830–1904). Kang-i (d. 1900), another favorite of the Empress Dowager, tried his best to block the reforms and strongly advocated deposing the emperor. Needless to say, the notorious eunuch Li Lien-ying (d. 1911) was a staunch opponent of any new elements in the government. Jung-lu, Kang-i, and Li Lien-ying banded together to fight reform.

Among the high provincial officials, only the Hunan governor, Ch'en Pao-chen, carried out the reform decrees effectively. Others, like the governor of Shantung and the governor-general of Szechwan, were partisans of Jung-lu. Pretending to observe the orders, they actually disobeyed them. The governors general at Canton (T'an Chung-lin) and at Nanking (Liu K'un-i) also took their lead from Jung-lu. When the emperor urged them to enforce the reform edicts, Liu made the excuse that the official documents had not yet been received, while T'an at Canton did not even bother to reply.

Among the censors, those who criticized the reforms all had connections with conservative ministers. Even if he had not had such contact before, as soon as a censor criticized the reformers, he was immediately patronized by the conservative leaders. For instance, there was a provincial graduate, Tseng Lien, who presented a memorial requesting that K'ang Yu-wei be killed. His motive was not clear, but Hsü T'ung was so pleased that he immediately invited Tseng to his house, treated him as an honored guest, and soon after recommended him to a post as prefect. Among the courtiers, Weng T'ung-ho was basically a conservative, and had been the most trusted tutor of the emperor for a long time. When Weng saw that the emperor now trusted K'ang Yu-wei and others more than himself, he was very jealous and afraid that his own position might be jeopardized.

When orders were initiated to dismiss sinecure officials and abolish offices such as the Supervisorate of Imperial Instruction, the Transmission Office, the Banqueting Court, the Court of State Ceremonial, the Court of the Imperial Stud, the Court of Judicature and Revision, the three governorships of Hupei, Kwangtung, and Yunnan, and other government posts, many high officials faced the immediate loss of their jobs. Many provincial and metropolitan graduates were confronted with the loss of their opportunity to become officials. The idea of transforming monasteries or temples into school buildings seemed deceptively simple; yet at that time the higher class of monks and nuns usually had contact with the eunuchs in the Forbidden City and had direct or indirect associations with the Empress Dowager. When the monks whispered to the Empress Dowager's eunuchs that the temples or monasteries might be torn down or used for other purposes and that all eunuchs might be dismissed, the latter tried their best to persuade the old lady to stop the reform movement as soon as possible.

In general, the reform leaders were mostly, if not entirely, Chinese and the objectors to reform were in large part high Manchu officials. Kang-i said that reform was for the benefit of Chinese at the cost of the Manchus. Another Manchu accused K'ang Yu-wei of distinguishing between loyalty to the throne and patriotism toward the country, and of desiring to protect the four hundred million Chinese by putting the Manchu dynasty aside. In July of 1898 the wife of a board president wept before the Empress Dowager, saying that all Manchus would be dismissed; this charge is said to have affected the Empress Dowager so much that she decided to take ruthless action against the reformers. With the help of her old friend, Jung-lu, she carried out her decision by the famous *coup d'état* of September 1898. Six reform leaders, including T'an Ssu-t'ung, were eventually executed and the emperor was imprisoned for the rest of his life. When it came time for the old lady to die in 1908, her hapless nephew preceded her by one day.

The following interview between Emperor Kuang-hsü and K'ang Yu-wei took place on the crucial date of June 16, only five days after the emperor had embarked upon the famous Hundred Days. Since the account was written by one of K'ang's students after his death, K'ang is referred to as "our late teacher" (*hsien-shih*). Presumably this represents the "Modern Sage's" own version of the conversation.

DOC. 46. K'ANG YU-WEI'S CONVERSATION WITH THE EMPEROR, JUNE 1898 [2]

Early on June 16 our late teacher entered the Court anteroom, where he happened to meet Jung-lu. With Jung-lu he discussed informally the matter of the governmental reforms. When Jung-lu entered and had his audience with the Emperor, he personally attacked our late teacher for using sophistry to disturb the government. After Jung-lu withdrew our late teacher went in for his audience. After the Emperor had asked about his age and his qualifications, the teacher said, "The four barbarians are all invading us and their attempted partition is gradually being carried out: China will soon perish."

The Emperor said, "All that is caused by the conservatives." The teacher reverently said,[3] "Your Majesty's sacred intelligence has thoroughly understood the root of the illness; and since Your Majesty has understood the root of the illness, the medicine is right there. Since Your Majesty knows already that the conservatives have caused the disaster and failure, then unless we change the old institutions entirely and make them new again, we cannot make ourselves strong."

The Emperor said, "Today it is really imperative that we reform." K'ang said, "It is not because in recent years we have not talked about reform, but because it was only a slight reform, not a complete one; we change the first thing and do not change the second, and then we have everything so confused as to incur failure, and eventually there will be no success." The Emperor agreed with him.

Our late teacher again reverently said, "The prerequisites of reform are that all the laws and the political and social systems be changed and decided anew, before it can be called a reform. Now those who talk about reform only change some specific affairs, and do not reform the institutions." He also requested that a bureau be opened first of all to study the various systems. The Emperor gave his consent.

The teacher again reverently presented his views: "With regard to the matter of reform, your minister [K'ang] has traced the causes of the reforms in all nations and their multiple functions, in order to ascertain which may be adopted and applied in China, and he has considered and modified them to prepare a complete set of rules and regulations. If Your Majesty has made up his mind to reform the institutions, it may serve him for reference." The Emperor said, "Your reform program is very detailed." The late teacher then replied, "Your Majesty's sagacity has already noted it. Why not vigorously carry it through?"

The Emperor glanced outside the screen and then said, with a sigh, "What can I do with so much hindrance?" The late teacher understood that the Emperor had difficulties and so he continued to present his views, saying, "According to the authority which Your Majesty is now exercising to carry out the reforms, if he works on only the most important things, it will be sufficient to save China, even though he cannot make a complete reform. Nevertheless, today most of the high ministers are very old and conservative, and they do not understand matters concerning foreign countries. If Your Majesty wishes to rely on them for reform, it will be like climbing a tree to seek for fish."

The Emperor said, "All of them are inattentive to their work." The late teacher replied, "These high officials are not inattentive. Unfortunately they have been transferred and promoted by the traditional system of qualification, and when they come to high positions, their spirit and energies are already declining [p. 27]. Moreover, they hold concurrently many positions and actually they have no leisure time, nor have they any way to acquire new knowledge. Really, they cannot help it. If Your Majesty wishes reform, the only thing to do is to promote and make use of the lower officials, increase the channels by which they are recommended, summon them to audience, and employ them without following tradition. Now the Grand Council and the Tsungli Yamen are both using such officials on commissions. If we use the directors and sub-directors of the ministries and the censors to take care of the domestic and foreign commissions, everything could be managed. As for the old officials, let them stay on for the time being. But they are conservative in every way, and so I request that Your Majesty issue more decrees to make them aware of your real intention. All reform matters should be proclaimed by special decrees and then they will have no way to refute or criticize them. . . Since the ceding of Formosa [1895] the people have been alienated from the government. If we wish to stir up the determination of the officials and consolidate the minds of the people, nothing can accomplish it unless Your Majesty issues a decree filled with grief and pathos." The Emperor said, "Yes."

Our late teacher again presented his views: "The trouble today lies in the non-cultivation of the people's wisdom, and the cause of the non-cultivation of the people's wisdom lies in the civil service examinations based on the eight-legged essays. The eight-legged essay writers do not read the books written since the Ch'in and the Han, nor do they investigate the facts about all the nations on the globe. Nevertheless, they can be enrolled as officials, and eventually reach high positions. Today, among the numerous array of ministers none of them can adapt himself to circumstances, because all of them achieve high positions through the eight-legged essay examinations." The Emperor said, "It is so. Westerners are all pursuing useful studies, while we Chinese pursue useless studies. Thus the present situation is brought about."

Our late teacher replied, "Since Your Majesty is already aware of the harm of the eight-legged essay, could we abolish it?" The Emperor said, "We could." Our late teacher replied, "Since Your Majesty already considers that it can be abolished, may I request that Your Majesty immediately issue a clear decree, which should not be sent down for discussion by the ministries. If it is sent down to be discussed by the ministries, the ministers would refuse to put it into effect." The Emperor said, "Yes."

The Emperor said, "Today our anxiety is over poverty and how to raise funds." Our late teacher briefly remarked that everywhere in China there are mineral resources and means of producing wealth. We should simply find ways to open up the material resources, and then we need not worry about the insufficiency of our financial resources. Our late teacher again presented his views in detail on the translation of books, the sending of students to study abroad, the dispatching of high officials to travel abroad, and such matters. After he had finished one topic, he would pause for a time to await the command of the Emperor. When the Emperor still did not order him to arise, he again discussed the employment of the right persons and the execution of administrative affairs. Finally he spoke about promoting ideas of reform in society in order to inspire [p. 28] the wisdom of the people and to encourage their spirit. He also talked about inviting surrender from and pacifying the rebels in the secret societies. He took this opportunity to express his gratitude for the Emperor's favor in affording protection when the *Pao-kuo-hui* ["Society for protecting the nation"] was accused. The Emperor nodded and said, "Yes." After a long time the Emperor nodded and said, "You should withdraw and take a little rest." And again he said, "If you have something more to say you may prepare memorials to state your suggestions in detail and send them here." Our late teacher then arose and went out. The Emperor's eyes escorted him to the door.

The Manchu attendants (*su-la*) met K'ang and asked him questions because there had never been so long an audience — more than five hours [*shih-k'o*, presumably "ten quarters" of the two-hour period then used as the chronological unit].

The repeated references to the example of Japan, in the writings of the reformers already quoted, indicate how after 1895 Chinese hatred of the recent enemy had gradually become mixed with admiration. Some Chinese thought of studying in Japan, and Japanese Restoration leaders were welcomed in China. Among them was Itō Hirobumi, who visited Peking in the autumn of 1898. On that occasion, a number of Chinese officials suggested making use of Itō's ability to assist the Chinese reform movement, and also to consolidate the bond between the two countries. Fu K'uei, a *chü-jen* of Kweichow, urged that he be made the chief minister of the Chinese government in order to carry through the new reforms. Since Itō was so highly esteemed by various officials as the rebuilder of Japan, and since the emperor had been remaking his own administration, on paper, for three hectic months, he granted an interview to Itō on September 20, 1898, when the Reform Movement was just about to come to an end.

DOC. 47. Itō's Conversation with the Emperor, September 1898 [4]

Itō memorialized saying [p. 273], The alien minister (Itō) Hirobumi on this occasion has come to your honorable country for the purpose of travel. Today he is given this audience of Your Majesty; it is a great honor for him indeed. He sincerely hopes that Your Majesty will reform your former institutions, and energetically plan for the wealth and strength of the country.

It goes without saying that this will have an important bearing on the maintenance of the existing situation of peace in Eastern Asia. Hirobumi's traveling is at an end, and he is returning to his country to report to His Majesty the Emperor; His Majesty will necessarily be heartily pleased. Hirobumi reverently hopes Your Imperial Majesty will live ten thousand years!

After Itō had presented his memorial, [Emperor] Kuang-hsü bade him sit down, and then the conversation went on as follows:

Kuang-hsü: We have heard of the great reputation of your Excellency for a long time. To have this chance to see you unexpectedly today is indeed a great pleasure.

Itō: That today Your Majesty should not be ashamed to grant me this interview, so that I may come to within a few feet of your Imperial countenance — for me there is really no greater honor than this.[5]

Kuang-hsü: Have you been safe and comfortable on your trip?

Itō: Under the great blessing of Your Majesty, I have been very safe and comfortable on my trip.

Kuang-hsü: Is His Majesty the Emperor of your honorable country well?

Itō: This time after I had decided to take this trip, I entered the palace to have an interview and found that his Imperial person was very well.

Kuang-hsü: The government of your honorable country after its reforms has been praised by all nations. The contribution of your Excellency to your fatherland has been really admired by all people.

Itō: This is too generous a compliment, an honor which I by no means deserve. Your alien minister was merely considering the august model set by His Majesty, the Mikado, and performed the duty of an official.

[p. 274] *Kuang-hsü:* The two countries, yours and ours, are geographically situated on the same continent [Asia] and are the nearest to each other. At the present time reform is pressed upon our country by necessity. We are willing to hear an opinion expressed by your Excellency, and we request your Excellency to tell our princes and great ministers of the Tsungli Yamen in detail the process and methods of reform, and give them advice.

Itō: I have reverently received your decree. If your princes and great ministers will make inquiries, your alien minister, in accordance with what he has actually seen, will certainly sincerely explain to them whatever is beneficial to your honorable country.

Kuang-hsü: To coöperate constantly and whole-heartedly with your honorable country, and to continue perpetually the close relations between the two countries is our most earnest hope.

Itō: The august intention of His Majesty, the Mikado of my country, is truly the same. If this intention could widely prevail among the peoples of the two nations, then it would be really an easy matter for our relations to become closer daily. . .

The remaining conversation is conventional and without great significance. After the interview, Itō was honored by a banquet.

b. *The Conservative Opposition*

The opponents of the reformers of 1898 offered little new in the way of theory or ideology. They contented themselves mainly with the invocation of traditional principles, in the effort to combat change. Nevertheless, their arguments were often both learned and ingenious, and they form an instructive part of the record.[6]

In their political ideas, the anti-reformers may be divided into two large categories. The first consisted of conservatives who unconditionally objected to change. They thought that China should be governed as of old, by men and by virtue, and maintained that ancestral institutions should never be abrogated under any conditions. The second category were not so absolute in their objections: some believed that Chinese ways were simply better than Western ways, so that no change was needed. Others recognized certain superior qualities in Western institutions, but believed they were not suitable to Chinese society. The most they would grant was that some Western methods and governmental policies might be imitated, although K'ang's reform program as a whole would bring only harm. The most serious harm would be to corrupt the minds of the common people, for the superior quality of Chinese institutions lay in government by the superior men of virtue — wang-tao, the "kingly way" — while the Westerners cared only for money and their government was by law and by power politics.

Wang Hsien-ch'ien (1842–1918) was a leading scholar, best known today as the compiler of part of the Tung-hua lu, a condensation of imperial documents. Both he and Yeh Te-hui (1864–1927), a famous bibliophile, believed that the evils in China lay in the moral state of the people, not in the legal or political systems; rather than try to change the institutions, it would be better to talk about changing the minds of the people.[7] Wang went a step further and declared that, while the national character of Westerners was public-spirited, that of the Chinese was selfish, so that democracy could hardly apply to China. He wrote: [8]

Generally what is called self-government arose from the fact that, in the old days, Western countries had originally no government or education. Their people were unbearably poverty-stricken and the lower classes were separated from the upper and it was out of this situation that self-government developed. In China for several thousand years sacred emperors and enlightened kings have been exerting their minds and energies to be good princes and teachers and to acquire experience in planning; their consideration has been very careful and they have been particularly vigilant in preventive measures. Our fundamental idea of establishing a nation has been different from that in the West. Nevertheless, the difference between the public spirit of the West and the selfishness of the Chinese also comes from this. . . Among Westerners each one uses his right of self-government to join and submit voluntarily to the control of congenial organizations. What they plan to do at home is for the public benefit, and what they go out to discuss is also for the public. Political commands are for public [not private] purposes. Property is for the public. Territory is also for the public. (Note: For example, India was seized by a company but given to the nation.) Thus it is natural that the king above should not appear quarrelsome and insecure, and that the people below should have no idea of neglecting their duty and being idle spectators, because they have formed the public-spirited habit.

Since the Yellow Emperor, and Emperors Yao and Shun, the Chinese people have respected the emperors as Heaven and regarded them as gods, and in addition they have been delighted with the emperor's benevolence in allowing them to have a little more than mere subsistence, and in other matters they were glad to be independent of him. . . Since the first emperor of the Hsia dynasty regarded the empire as his family property, the people in turn regarded themselves as his children, and each generation tries to be selfish. The emperor and the people all kept their individual purposes and thus the egotistical pattern was formed. . . Now it would be definitely unsuitable to use the selfish minds of the Chinese to adopt the self-government policy of the Westerners.

Ch'u Ch'eng-po thought the first step was to reform the people's minds; in 1898 he wrote: [9]

In our society today the trouble is not that we lack institutions for good government, but that we lack upright minds among the people. If we seek to reform institutions we should reform our minds first. . . At the beginning of the T'ung-chih period [1862–1874] Tseng Kuo-fan, Tso Tsung-t'ang, Li Hung-chang, Shen Pao-chen and others, on account of the fact that foreign aggression had become very serious, greatly admired Western knowledge. . . These reformers said from the beginning that, even though the Chinese imitated the superior techniques of Westerners, eventually they would get ahead of the Westerners. But since their reforms have been carried on perfunctorily up to the present, the island pirates [the Japanese] have suddenly invaded us and the whole situation of the nation has collapsed. . . The real mistake was that we did not secure the right persons to manage the new institutions. . . Could the various workers in the shipyards and the arsenals really fulfill the original plan of Tso Tsung-t'ang, to do the work entirely in Chinese factories? . . . Among the students sent abroad by Li Hung-chang were there any who had learned excellently and could exert their loyalty to ward off aggression from the nation? . . . Could we train a navy by ourselves, as was originally expected by Shen Pao-chen? Arguing from these analogies, we can see that it will be all the same with other things. . . Usually there was a good start but no finishing. There was much talk, but little action. . . The most far-reaching plans were ruined by our putting up an ostentatious façade while behind it all is hidden covetousness and selfishness. . . Formerly, the Tsungli Yamen in planning for coastal defense said: "If we cannot secure the right men everything will turn out to be a sheer waste of money. The mistake will be in the employment of improper (unsuitable) persons, not in the weakness of our system." . . .

Some Chinese conservatives, after comparing Western governments with their own, arrived at the conclusion that the Westerners knew only things mechanical and mathematical and nothing else, while the Chinese had long ago discovered the real and eternal way of governing people by virtue. With such moral force behind her, China was surely going to achieve the unification of the whole world and have all the barbarians at her feet. One of these critics, Huang Jen-chi, wrote: [10]

If we say that Heaven, the earth, the people and the animals can all be controlled by mathematics, this would suggest that in foreign countries they should have order, with no disorder; prosperity with no decline; life, with no death; and wealth, with no poverty. How, then, are the foreign countries not able to control the course of order and disorder, prosperity and decline, life and death, existence and extinction, wealth and poverty? This is probably because in mathematics there is also a moral principle which serves as the controlling power. The foreigners merely know how to investigate one period of time or one subject, but the Chinese knew long ago how to investigate one hundred generations or one thousand years ahead, that is, we Chinese have had sages and the foreigners cannot expect to have such people. . .

In foreign countries they emphasize material profits, but they also live up to the word "sincerity"; the upper and lower classes are of the same mind and the prince and ministers have the idea of being one body with the people. Although their nations are rich and strong, ultimately the feelings of the multitudes cannot be unified. We Chinese unanimously stress righteousness and at the same time live up to the word "benevolence." Because we are not all of the same mind, we, on the contrary, appear to be declining and weak. Nevertheless, the doctrine of cultivating virtue, unifying our families, governing the nation and pacifying the empire, is all actually inferred from these (principles of righteousness and benevolence). The foreigners expressly follow the numerical system and at the same time they promote techniques in which everything is fixed numerically. Hence they entirely neglect the theory of relations between ruler and minister, father and son, husband and wife, elder brother and younger brother, good and evil, chastity and licentiousness, good luck and bad luck, misfortune and good fortune. Chinese, however, in addition to the numerical system, also talk about moral principles. . .[11]

Pursuing this line of thought, many scholars and officials acknowledged the superiority of the West in the techniques of producing wealth and power, all of which they felt might be adopted on condition that they be modified to suit the Chinese environment. The famous phrase, *Chung-hsueh wei t'i, Hsi-hsueh wei yung,* had various connotations. As Professor Wilhelm has pointed out,[12] the antithesis *t'i* and *yung* was an ancient one in Chinese thought, going back to the "within" and "without" of Mencius. In Chu Hsi these two terms might be translated, roughly speaking, as "substance" and "function." They could also be taken as parallel to the famous dichotomy of "principle" (*li*) and "manifestation" (*ch'i*), within the general framework of Neo-Confucianism. It is noteworthy that Chang Chih-tung, the most famous exponent of the slogan, was steeped in Chu Hsi and his philosophy, so that it was perfectly natural for him to divide all studies into two categories — "take the old learning as substance and the new learning for function." When applied to the realm of political theory, this doctrine was taken to mean that a government by virtue should be the main principle, but with the addition of a certain amount of government by law. Some, harking back to the ancient idea of law as a punitive tool of the ruler, interpreted this as allowing room for some *pa-cheng* ("power government" or rule by force) within a framework of *wang-tao* ("the kingly way" or rule by virtue and benevolence). The adoption of some Western methods might be expedient for the needs of the time, but the permanent guiding principle of Chinese government should still be a government by benevolence, righteousness, truth and virtue. Thus the slogan meant: to model the state after the classics and to respect the emperor as its foundation, but to accept some barbarian ideas and take in some elements of "power government," so as to make the country rich and strong in its practical functions. The scholar Wen-ti wrote:

If we wish to receive the benefit of Western methods, we must first acquire a knowledge of Confucius, Mencius, Ch'eng and Chu [i.e., Neo-Confucianism], and keep it as the foundation to make people thoroughly familiar with filial piety, younger-brotherhood, loyalty, sincerity, ceremony, righteousness, integrity, a sense of shame, obligations and the teachings of the sages and moral courage, in order to understand and demonstrate the foundation, before we can learn the foreign spoken and written languages for some practical use.[13]

A number of travel diaries indicate how easily this moral attitude could be associated with an aversion to the strangeness of Western ways. In a book by Yuan Tsu-chih "Personal point of view after travelling to foreign countries" (*She-yang kuan-chien*), there is an interesting passage which reads: [14]

China has all four seasons and the climate is proportionally distributed. In parts of the West the heat and cold are unseasonable, the winter and summer change their normal order, and there are spots that from ancient down to modern times have never had frost or snow. . .

As to human affairs, China emphasizes human relationships and honors benevolence and righteousness. In the West, on the contrary, a son does not take care of his father, a minister cheats his emperor, a wife is more honored than a husband; thus the bond of the three relationships is broken. Because the proper relationship between husband and wife is not cultivated, the marriage ceremony is neglected. As soon as a girl is twenty-one years old she is permitted to find a husband whom she likes, and there are those who make many selections or trials before they make a match. They do not consider sexual relations preceding marriage as a shame. Beautiful young girls are seeking for males everywhere; the hoary-headed and the widows can invite male companions as they like. The customs are bad to such a degree! . . .

As to other customs, the residence of the emperor is the same as that of ordinary people except that it is a little larger, and it lacks an awe-inspiring appearance and dignity. The pictures of the emperor and empress are hung up at random in the markets for sale and people can purchase them as toys. Thus there is no distinction between the noble and the mean. . .

Speaking about official costumes, except in one country, Turkey, where the costume is strange, all other nations are the same. The noble and the mean use the same style, which makes it difficult to tell who is honorable and who is lowly. In summertime there is no linen or silk to make their bodies comfortable, and in winter there are rarely furs or padded coats to dress their bodies. They have to go to the trouble of taking a carriage or a horse, but do not have the comfort of sedan chairs. The skirts of their women are seven feet long, only good for sweeping dust. The bed curtain is hung ten feet high but it is hard to keep mosquitoes away.

As for food, there is no difference between winter and summer; they always sip cold water and juice. They cannot appreciate the culinary art, but like butter and mutton ribs. The amount of food served at meals is small, and they use many different kinds of utensils [p. 470b] to cause servants a good deal of work. The kinds of soup are very limited. Delicious things are completely lacking.

In government, their taxes since antiquity have been unprecedently heavy and numerous. There is actually a levy of taxes of certain amounts according to the value of commodities. If smuggling is detected, the tax on the smuggled article is increased ten or a hundred times as a fine. In some places there is a land tax. Some have a poll tax, or property tax, or tax on trademarks. The government takes money from the people insatiably. How can the people bear it? Moreover, they worship their unorthodox religion and allow the Christian clergy to overrun the country, exhausting all the people's money in building churches, thus spending useful funds for a useless purpose.

As for the law, it has no articles for punishing adultery; a wife can have a concubine [i.e., a lover] and can accuse her husband. This is even more ridiculous. Apart from these there are other things which they improperly turn upside down. Their prisons, for instance, are as comfortable as the Kingdom of Heaven. It is not very easy for people to maintain their living, because the cost of food and utensils is as high as that of precious jewels. The five relationships are not cultivated, the five kinds of grains are incomplete, hundreds of herbs are unknown to them and hundreds of grasses or flowers are not fragrant. . .

The first Chinese vice-minister to England, Liu Hsi-hung, in his "Diary of a mission to England ' (*Ying-yao jih-chi*) says: [15]

Their practical knowledge consists entirely of the details of miscellaneous crafts, the use of which can make a machine or an instrument; but it is limited. . . If we pursue only these miscellaneous skills to make trains and ships for profit, to make firearms for killing people, and to struggle for more such productions and for clever designs, considering these as wealth and strength; can these really be called useful knowledge? . . . After all, we forbid people to make strange weapons so as to prevent rebellion, and proclaim benevolence and righteousness, so as to establish the fundamental doctrine for our government.

Another line of attack on Western materialism was to argue that the stagnation of China's material civilization was due to the fact that the Chinese people preferred lofty principles to material things. For example, Liu Yueh-yün (1849–1917) says: [16] "The technique of the barbarians is merely that of a worker, of which a gentleman would not care to speak and which a scholar and an official would despise . . . We despised (mechanical civilization) and did not try to develop it. Instead we seek for larger and higher purposes."

Others were less proud and more pessimistic. Some Chinese maintained that Western material civilization was so far ahead that it would be absolutely impracticable for the Chinese to try to learn the Westerners' methods in order to control them. Therefore Westernization should be avoided, and another method for self-preservation should be sought. One of the prescriptions given by a famous scholar, Yü Yueh (1821–1907), was a kind of Taoist passive resistance: [17]

Then how can we overcome them? The answer is, two pieces of steel cannot overcome each other. That which can overcome steel is softness. Two sharp (knives) cannot overcome each other. The one can overcome the sharpness of the other by dullness. Well, then, two clever persons can hardly control each other. But the way to control the clever is by stupidity. [P. 6b]

Even if we have to determine our fate on the battlefield, their weapons could only hurt several scores or several hundred of our people. Yet if our system of reward and punishment is well observed and our orders are very strict, then our people should form groups of several hundreds or one thousand and push ahead like a wall — what can they do [p. 7] against us? Therefore, I say, only the stupid can control the clever. Using great stupidity to overcome great cleverness is the method of achieving an assured victory.

Finally there were several arguments specifically against Western machines: (1) That Chinese human labor and experience can achieve better results than machines. Shen Ch'un wrote: [18]

A Chinese helmsman by looking at the sun's halo and the clouds' vapor knows when there will be wind or rain; by observing the wrinkles of the water and the appearance of sand, he knows where there are hidden rocks; and by looking at the shape of a mountain and the color of the water he knows where he is on the sea. One day's experience like this serves him for a life time. Other things like . . . the ornamental pillars at Peking, the ivory sculpture of Kwangtung, the pillars and beams of the old palaces in Egypt, and the stone sculpture in Italy — none of them was made by machinery. When foreigners see them, they usually stroke them with their hands and gaze at them a long time in admiration, but without knowing how such marvelous objects could be made. . . Why should we think of making a change when we see something strange, and why should we use the barbarian culture to change Chinese culture?

(2) That since the Chinese population is already too large, if machines are used, many laborers will be out of jobs and the order and peace of Chinese society will be seriously affected. This is cogently explained by a scholar, Chu I-hsin (1846–1894): [19] "In Western countries the territory is large, the population is thin, therefore they even use machines for agriculture. If China employs them, one person's agricultural work may take away the livelihood of ten others. These ten others, if they do not want to sit down and wait for death by starvation would choose a risky road (i.e., become bandits)."

Chang Tzu-mu also says: [20]

The farmers in the south, the miners in the northern mountains and those who are pulling carts and manning boats, all these several thousand or million people have been working all their lives at hard labor and if this is suddenly replaced by machines they will lose their way of making a living. Would they not gather together to cause disorder or start a rebellion? This is probably the reason that, following the widespread adoption of machines in Europe less than a hundred years ago, great revolutions have repeatedly occurred.

(3) That the natural resources of the world are limited, but production by machines is limitless. When the natural resources are exhausted it will not be easy for human beings to make a living, and therefore one should object to the use of machines. Yü Yueh says: [21]

The Europeans only know how to exhaust what exists in the universe to supply their needs. A proverb says: "If you fish by drying up the water, then next year there will be no fish." I have heard that they use coal without limit, and the places where coal is produced are becoming fewer day by day. . . Inferring from the one thing, coal, we know that if everything is consumed without limit there must be a time of exhaustion. . . Day by day the essential materials are being exhausted and I fear that the earth will become so barren that it will no longer be able to maintain human life.

CHAPTER XIX. THE BOXER UPRISING

The blow dealt to the Reform Movement of 1898 and the resumption of power by the Empress Dowager did not work out as well as the conservatives had expected. The threatened disintegration of the empire into areas of foreign control, and the rising tide of Chinese antagonism towards Manchu rule made more and more people realize the necessity of institutional reform. Yet the Empress Dowager could not initiate reform herself without seeming to confirm the Emperor Kuang-hsü's decrees of 1898 and thus condemn herself in the eyes of the world. She would have preferred to achieve a position as arbiter between the reformers and the conservatives. By 1900, however, incensed by the expressions of public opinion against her, particularly those from foreigners who had openly sympathized with the reformers, she finally chose to throw her lot with the conservatives, who tried to channel all economic, social and political discontent against the foreigners, their converts to Christianity, their churches and their railways.

The upshot was that in June 1900 thousands of Boxers, inspired by superstition and encouraged by the conservative officials, joined in an uprising which spread over Shantung, Chihli, Shansi, and southern Manchuria. They burned churches, destroyed telegraph lines and railways, and killed many Chinese Christians and foreign missionaries. On June 20, when the Manchu regime declared war on the foreign powers, they laid siege to the foreign legations and a Catholic cathedral in Peking. They cut rail communications between Peking and Tientsin and obliged a British relief force of some two thousand men to retreat. The half-hearted siege ended on August 14, when the allied forces of eight nations (Japan, Germany, England, France, the U. S. A., etc.) reached Peking. In 1901, the Boxer protocol exacted an indemnity which amounted to some $333,900,000.

So great a disaster to the Manchu fortunes could have been precipitated only by leaders profoundly ignorant of the West, even granting the fact (which we have not emphasized) of great foreign provocation.

Among the leaders of the die-hards were several princes of the imperial family. Since the 1860's, the school for princes had been discontinued and their education neglected. Brought up in relative ignorance, yet accustomed to being obeyed, these princes easily fell victims to certain popular superstitions of the day. Hence, when the Boxers in Shantung claimed to be invincible to bullets through the aid of certain popular deities, they were actually believed by these princes and perhaps even by the Empress Dowager herself. The Boxers were thought of as loyal supporters of the dynasty, available for use in a showdown against the foreigners. All their irrational acts of violence — the killing of Christian converts and foreigners and the destruction of anything with a foreign connection — were regarded at the time as patriotic acts against foreign invaders. The mad situation in and near Peking in the summer of 1900 was thus a product of ignorance, superstition, and mob hysteria.

As to the origin of the Boxer movement, there are several theories. Chinese sources are represented by Lao Nai-hsuan (1843–1921), who believed that a secret society called the *I-ho-ch'üan*, and known to have existed in 1727 and 1808, had maintained its existence uninterruptedly down to the end of the nineteenth century. As to its name, the word *ch'üan* refers to the Chinese form of calisthenics for personal defense, or "boxing," and the term *I-ho-ch'üan* refers to the type of defensive art practised by a kind of fraternal order called the "Harmonious Brotherhood." ("Righteous and Harmonious Fists" is a crude and misleading translation.) In short, this group originally seems to have been a society teaching the methods of one school of boxing. Because the government ordered the people of Shantung to organize militia forces, *t'uan-lien*, against the German encroachment in that province, the society in different localities gradually changed its name to *I-ho-t'uan*, "Righteous and Harmonious Militia," thus adopting the status of a semi-official military force. Some Western scholars (e.g., Dr. G. N. Steiger in his *China and the Occident*) have consequently followed the more strict and literal view that the Boxers actually came into being after the Empress Dowager's *coup d'état* of 1898, as a legal militia recruited in response to imperial command, but more recent research has made this view untenable.

Of the three documents of the Boxers translated below, the first is reminiscent of circulars or handbills that had appeared from time to time in China's history as far back as the Han Dynasty. Such warnings were put out sometimes as a prank, but also at times by serious plotters of disorder as a way to cause unrest among the ignorant and superstitious. The other two documents are typical of Boxer proclamations during the period from April to August 1900 in North China villages, where the elders tried to restrain the youths from excesses, but themselves believed in the claims of the Boxers.

In these three short statements there is no direct attack on foreigners, but there are appeals to Taoist, Buddhist, and other superstitions. The first document, especially the part of it about the "ten disasters," appeared in many places.

DOC. 48. PROCLAMATIONS OF THE BOXERS [1]

1) *A Boxer Circular*

Statement by the Saintly Emperor Kuan-kung during his visitation at our divining altar: This year seventy per cent of the population will die. Lives can be saved by praying to Bodhisattva Kuan-yin for her mercy and kindness. Circulate this statement and disaster can be avoided — one sheet for yourself, three for your whole family. To refuse to circulate it and to tell lies about it will cause condemnation by the gods and an increase in the disaster.

Those who do good will be safe, those who do evil can hardly escape. If you do not believe, you will see that in the seventh and eighth months of this year countless people will die. These gods and saints have always been watching for the good and evil deeds among you mortals. Heaven now fears ten disasters. The first is about how the world is going to be in a turmoil. The second is about everything in Shantung being wiped out. The third is that flood will cover Hupei and Hunan. The fourth is that wars will come to Szechwan. The fifth is that Kiangnan is to suffer from a big famine and uprising. The sixth is about the deaths of more than half of the population. The seventh is that members of the Righteous and Harmonious Boxing Order [*I-ho-ch'üan*] are too weak. The eighth is about the foreigners disturbing Chihli. The ninth is that there will be clothes but no one to wear them. The tenth is that there will be rice but no one to eat it.

A disaster, however, may be turned to a blessing, for destiny is in charge.

One who copies this out for somebody else will have his whole family exempted from suffering the calamity.

On the 19th day of the sixth month, and the 26th day of the seventh month, make sacrificial offerings towards the south and you will be exempted from suffering the calamity.

2) A Boxer Notice

The Ma-lan Village in the Ch'i-chia police magistrate's precinct of the district of Wan-[p'ing] in the prefecture of Shun-t'ien, Peking, on the occasion of piously setting up the sacred I-ho Society, makes the following declaration of instructions and strict advice to our fellow villagers and neighbors! The Catholics since the Hsien-feng period (1851–1861) have conspired with foreigners, have caused China trouble, wasted our national revenue, broken up our monasteries, destroyed Buddhist images, and seized our people's graveyards. All these myriad acts of evil should be bitterly resented. This has affected people's trees and plants so as to make them suffer from the catastrophes of locusts and drought almost every year. Our nation is deprived of peace and our people of security. This has angered the Court in Heaven.

Now by the grace of the great deity in Heaven, all the spirits have descended to set up an altar in the wall in order to teach our young men their magic boxing so they can support the Ch'ing, extinguish the foreigners, and enforce right principles on behalf of Heaven. When we exert our energy for the nation in order to bring peace to the land, when we help the farmers and protect our villages, this is an omen that prosperity is coming after misfortune has reached its limit.

Nevertheless, we are afraid that some ignorant people and vagabonds may rely upon the foreigners' power in acting contrary to reason, and cling to the strong in order to oppress the weak. They should be reported to the village head and the chief of the society, who will handle public affairs justly and sentence them according to law, and who are not allowed to be influenced by selfish purposes. If they indulge in private favoritism, the eyes of our spirits like lightning will pierce through them without discrimination, and will not let them get away with any deviation from the just punishment. Because some persons use foreign religion and tricky techniques to deceive the people, Heaven above is angered and is sending many sages to descend to earth and come to the divining altar to initiate our youths into the I-ho Society. I means kindness, and ho means politeness; kindness and politeness will make town and countryside peaceful and harmonious. Our people should take right principles and virtue as their foundation and should devote themselves to agriculture as their profession. They should follow and obey Buddhism. They are not permitted to resort to public accusations for avenging a personal grievance, to use poverty as a pretext for oppressing other poor people, to rely on strength to maltreat the weak, or to regard the right as wrong.

Prepared by Group K'an [the second of the Eight Trigrams] of the I-ho Society, Ma-lan Village, Ch'i-chia police precinct, at Chai-t'ang. . .

3) *Another Boxer Notice*

Attention: all people in markets and villages of all provinces in China — now, owing to the fact that Catholics and Protestants have vilified our gods and sages, have deceived our emperors and ministers above, and oppressed the Chinese people below, both our gods and our people are angry at them, yet we have to keep silent. This forces us to practise the I-ho magic boxing so as to protect our country, expel the foreign bandits and kill Christian converts, in order to save our people from miserable suffering. After this notice is issued to instruct you villagers, no matter which village you are living in, if there are Christian converts, you ought to get rid of them quickly. The churches which belong to them should be unreservedly burned down. Everyone who intends to spare someone, or to disobey our order by concealing Christian converts, will be punished according to the regulation when we come to his place, and he will be burned to death to prevent his impeding our program. We especially do not want to punish anyone by death without warning him first. We cannot bear to see you suffer innocently. Don't disobey this special notice!

Prepared by the *I-ho-ch'üan.*

In opposition to the hysteria of the Boxer movement, only a few individuals at court had the courage to stand forth. Among them were Hsü Ching-ch'eng (1845–1900) and Yuan Ch'ang (1846–1900). Hsü, a *chin-shih* of 1868, had served the Chinese government as minister to Japan (1880), as minister to France, Germany, Italy, Holland and Austria (1884–87), and as minister to Russia (1891–98). Yuan Ch'ang, a *chin-shih* of 1876, had been a secretary in the Tsungli Yamen for over ten years (1883–94). In September 1898, he was appointed lieutenant-governor of the province of Chihli and, pending his assumption of the post, was given the rank of a third grade official so as to serve as one of the ministers in the Tsungli Yamen. He regarded the Boxers as wholly undependable, and he considered China's declaration of war against several other nations to be suicidal, and the attack on the legations to have been a grave violation of international law. When both Hsü and Yuan, who were good friends and both from the province of Chekiang, advocated strong measures to suppress the Boxers, they were accused of being pro-foreign traitors, arrested on July 26, and executed two days later.[2] The following three memorials attributed to these courageous ministers give a general idea of the background and progress of the Boxer uprising as seen from Peking at the time.

DOC. 49. MEMORIALS OF ANTI-BOXER MARTYRS, 1900

The first memorial of Hsü Ching-ch'eng, Senior Vice-president of the Board of Civil Office, and Yuan Ch'ang, Director of the Court of Sacrificial Worship, strongly urging the suppression of the Boxer bandits in order to prevent a great disaster (June 1900) [3]

We find that, according to an imperial decree of the seventh month, 1808, there had been bandits in the area of Shantung and Honan, establishing organizations called "The Eight Trigrams Society" (*Pa-kua-chiao*) and the "Righteous and Harmonious Boxing Order" (*I-ho-ch'üan*); they were really descendants of the "White Lotus Society" (*Pai-lien-chiao*). A severe decree was proclaimed to arrest every single one of them and to punish them severely. Last year [1899] Lao Nai-hsuan, magistrate of Wu-ch'iao, wrote a book[4] in which he investigated their origin in the greatest detail. In the last month Yuan Shih-k'ai, governor of Shantung, in making a report according to imperial decree, said "On no account is there any reason to summon the Boxers and reorganize them as regular troops." He spoke most candidly and plainly. When the former governor of Shantung, Yü-hsien, handled the case of heretical bandits in P'ing-yüan, he said that the bandit chief Chu Hung-teng claimed to be a descendant of the Ming dynasty, to be using magic spells to arouse the masses, and that people everywhere responded to him. Fortunately he was arrested by government troops and executed on the spot. He had absolutely no magic to enable him to avoid the bullets of guns and the cutting of a sword or axe. This is clear evidence. . . To save the present situation we must clean up the bandits in the Inner City of Peking in order to pacify the minds of the people and soothe the feelings of the foreigners, so we can stop their troops, which are being continually summoned. It is necessary that China suppress the Boxers by herself if we are to avoid having foreign soldiers help us in their suppression. . .

The second memorial of Hsü Ching-ch'eng and Yuan Ch'ang requesting protection for the Legation Quarter in order to maintain the general situation (July 1900) [5]

After the German Minister von Ketteler was shot to death on his way [to the Tsungli Yamen] on June 20, the Boxers attacked the Legation Quarter of all nations. The Kansu troops under Commander-in-Chief Tung Fu-hsiang were particularly responsive to the power of the Boxers, all being in collusion for seditious purposes. . . Now more than twenty days have passed; only a few foreign soldiers have been killed; but the bodies and skeletons of the bandits are scattered everywhere around the Legation Quarter. . . Where is the magic now? . . .

[P. 13] According to the principles in the *Spring and Autumn Annals,* when two countries engage in warfare, they should not kill diplomatic envoys. According to Western international law, it is also particularly provided that the minister is an important official of a nation, and he who despises her minister also despises the nation. Now if we let these bandits attack and burn the Legation Quarter and kill all the diplomatic envoys, all countries will take it as a great insult and will form an alliance in order to avenge themselves to the death. The foreign troops in the capital are limited but the foreign troops who will continue to come are limitless. It is your ministers' humble opinion that, with one nation fighting against all nations, it will not be merely a matter of victory or defeat for China but will actually be a question of survival or ruin. Our country has had trade relations with all the European countries for about sixty years and we have allowed them to spread religion in all our provinces. In ordinary times the converts who rely on the foreigners' influence have exploited the rural people as their fish and meat, and have regarded the foreign missionaries as their protectors. It was unavoidable that the local officers, perhaps hoping to conclude the matter cursorily, also have oppressed the common people. The people have been resentful, and they have regarded the converts with antagonism. All this was

due to the mismanagement of Chinese officials. . . When the bandits saw
the missionaries wearing foreign clothes and speaking different languages,
they called them all *mao-tzu* ["hairy ones"] and took pleasure in extermi-
nating them. . .

Your ministers request that the Legation Quarter be protected as a measure to pave the way for a compromise in the future. On the one hand, a strict
imperial decree should reprimand the Commander-in-Chief, Tung Fu-
hsiang, and order his Kansu troops to get out of the city entirely. . . and,
on the other hand, in order to avoid a most imminent crisis, we should ask
the Grand Secretary, Jung-lu, to take the responsibility for driving the
Boxers completely out of the city within a definite time.

The third memorial of Hsü Ching-ch'eng and Yuan Ch'ang, which caused their execution (July 28, 1900) [6]

It has been little more than one month since the Boxer bandits caused
trouble. The people of the Imperial capital and the whole Empire have
been disturbed. War has broken out and disaster has occurred. The whole
globe is involved. It is an extraordinary thing which has never happened
before in all the ages of Chinese history, and will result in a catastrophe such
as has never been experienced in all ages. . . [p. 19] When the Boxers
first raised their standards they had neither effective guns and cannon, nor
had they any training on the battlefield. They merely displayed the characters "support the Ch'ing and exterminate the foreigners" (*Fu-Ch'ing mieh-
yang*) to summon the undisciplined masses to mob violence. If we had had an
able local governor or military officer, he could have suppressed them with
ease. The former Shantung Governor Yü-hsien fostered the cancer at first;
the Chihli Governor-general Yü-lu courteously welcomed them later, and
gave them weapons; it was like giving wings to tigers. . . Moreover, Yü-lu
invited the chiefs of the Boxer bandits and treated them as distinguished
guests. The rural rascals would also assemble as many as one thousand
people, hold up a visiting card with the three characters, *I-ho-t'uan*, and they
would be immediately invited into the governor-general's office to talk with
him as if they were equals. Is this not contempt of the Court and a shame to
the scholars of contemporary times? . . .

[P. 20] The Grand Secretary Hsü T'ung is muddle-headed and is unaware of what is advantageous and disadvantageous. The Grand Councillor
and Assistant Grand Secretary, Kang-i, who associated with the traitors
and flattered the bandits, is obstinately reactionary by nature. The Grand
Councillor and Minister of Rites, Ch'i-hsiu, who is bigoted in his own ideas,
is stupid, but would like to be independent. The Grand Councillor and
Minister of Rites, Chao Shu-ch'iao, whose mind is very cunning, is an accomplished sycophant. At the time when the Boxers had just come to
Peking, the officials within and without the Court, from the princes on
down, had the honor to be summoned and consulted about the policy of
suppressing or pacifying them. Some of your ministers offered the statement that the Boxers are not patriotic, that they cannot be relied upon to
resist our enemies, and that we should not carelessly challenge all foreign

countries without reason. Hsü T'ung, Kang-i, and others actually dared to scorn these as rebellious statements in front of the Empress Dowager and the emperor. . . Now even in some [p. 20b] of the mansions of princes and other high dignitaries, the Boxers' altars are established. The Boxer bandits are not only foolish themselves, but they also lead Hsü T'ung, Kang-i, and others into folly; Hsü T'ung, Kang-i, and others are not only foolish, but they also lead princes and other dignitaries into folly. That is to say, Hsü T'ung, Kang-i, and others are the pivotal figures fomenting the disorders. . .

At the beginning, when the bandits arose, how did they dare reject the Imperial decree, to insult the officials, and to destroy government properties? How did they dare to take up weapons and burn houses, plunder and kill the populace? Since Hsü T'ung, Kang-i, and others praised them as patriotic, the power of the Boxer bandits increased still more, the confusion of the common people became worse, and the gathering of rascals became greater. . . Had Hsü T'ung, Kang-i, and others not called them patriotic people, the bandits would not have dared to commit their atrocities in arson, plundering and massacre. When we trace the origin of these breeders of mischief, we find that these officials are to blame. It behooves us to request an Imperial decree to punish first Hsü T'ung, Kang-i, Ch'i-hsiu, Chao Shu-ch'iao, Yü-lu, Yü-hsien, and Tung Fu-hsiang according to the severe criminal code; others who improperly gave protection to the Boxer bandits, and who made the same mistake as Hsü T'ung and others, should receive such punishment as they deserve. We should not take into consideration membership in the nobility or Imperial family as a reason for reducing their punishment. Then all nations will suddenly understand that those who formerly and purposely allowed the bandits to start hostilities were all these reactionary and stupid officials, that it was not the original idea of our nation. They may give up their hatred in order to seek good terms with us and our ancestral temples will be spared. Then Your Majesty can kill us to redress the imbalance in the deaths of Hsü T'ung, Kang-i, and the other ministers. Even though we die, we shall go to the next world with smiling faces. We cannot help shedding tears in preparing this memorial and we cannot overcome our extreme grief and anxiety.

[After this memorial was submitted, the two memorialists were executed.]

6

REFORM AND REVOLUTION

1901–1912

CHAPTER XX. THE CONSERVATIVE REFORM MOVEMENT

With the collapse of the Reform Movement of 1898 and the Boxer Uprising of 1900, there had occurred a profound split within the ranks of the Chinese scholar-official class, whose response to the West is our main topic in this volume. From that time dates the clear divergence between the dynasty and an important and growing group of the upper-class leadership. The latter was further split into two groups who carried on their arguments in their party papers: the revolutionists, headed by Sun Yat-sen, and the constitutional monarchists, led by K'ang Yu-wei. The reform program carried on by the Ch'ing government in the 1900's was designed to make amends for its previous conservatism, but this was only one of the channels of change, the other consisting of the anti-Manchu agitation carried on by groups inside and outside the country, with their main base among the Chinese students in Japan.

Under the official reform program there were a multitude of paper documents and some accomplishments. The broad sweep of the reform effort is indicated in the basic statements prepared by Chang Chih-tung and Liu K'un-i in 1901 (Doc. 50). In the documentation which follows, we touch upon only a few of the major developments: abolition of the age-old civil service examination system (Doc. 51), which was followed by an extensive proliferation of modern and semi-modern educational institutions; the movement for constitutionalism (Doc. 52), which led to unforeseen political developments in the provinces and paved the way for the revolt of 1911; the building of a "modern" army, which injected a heightened element of military force into a political situation in which civil government was fast losing its grip. These important lines of change were paralleled by significant developments in the fields of law, industry and communications, banking and finance (see Ch. XXI), journalism, and social custom generally, all of which might be further illustrated here if space permitted. In law, for instance, a special bureau under the direction of Shen Chia-pen revised the imperial code in the period 1902–1907 and began drafting a modern civil code and codes of procedure — a development which continued under the Republic.[1]

The classical metaphor for describing the dilemma of the Ch'ing government in the 1900's is that it was in quicksand. It could only sink deeper the harder it struggled to save itself. Thus the reform program as outlined by Chang Chih-tung and others stressed the training of personnel, but this meant a modern type of education, to be found only outside the country, and this in turn led to the growth of patriotic anti-Manchu revolutionary sentiment among the student class. By giving modern education to its prospective official class, the dynasty reared its own executioners, dug its own grave, and signed its own death warrant. Essentially this was because the dynasty, as an alien monarchy, was itself incapable of becoming "modern." Support for this view is found in its increasing inability to meet the problems of government in China in the later 1900's. How much the failure was one of institutions and how much one of personnel ("human abilities," as Chang Chih-tung had feared) cannot be said offhand; perhaps the two are by definition indivisible, outmoded institutions inevitably producing retrograde leadership.

a. *The Post-Boxer Program*

By the time of the court's flight to Sian in 1900, most of the ultra-conservatives who had been prominent in the Boxer Uprising were either dead or banished. The old Empress Dowager learned a bitter lesson from her rough, cold, and hungry trip across country by cart and chair from Peking to Sian. For her these months of intimate contact with the villagers and local officials of the hinterland must have been instructive in many ways. Possibly upon the advice of her close friend and counselor, Jung-lu, who was the only top Manchu official with her, she issued a series of decrees in the name of Emperor Kuang-hsü in which he blamed himself, requested public criticism, and, most important of all, announced a reform policy, so as to indicate tactfully the court's repentance, and thus gloss over its responsibility for the Boxer Uprising.

On January 29, 1901, a reform decree was issued in which the instruction of the Empress Dowager was quoted: "Adopt the strong points of foreign countries in order to make up China's shortcomings." This decree denies that she had ever hindered reform. It goes on to state the criticism that "those who have recently been learning Western methods have limited themselves to the foreigners' written and spoken languages and to the manufacturing of machines. These are the skin and hair of Western technology, but not the fundamental source of Western government." All high officials in and out of Peking were accordingly ordered to express their opinions fully and item by item as to what should be reformed and what should be newly introduced.[2] Accordingly, a number of memorials were submitted to the court.

On April 21, 1901, an "Office in charge of governmental affairs" (*Tu-pan cheng-wu ch'u*) was instituted to examine the memorials dealing with reform. This new organization was staffed by Jung-lu, I-k'uang (1836–1916), and others, while Liu K'un-i and Chang Chih-tung were made associate members directing its affairs from a distance.[3] At that time the most influential governors general were Li Hung-chang, Yuan Shih-k'ai, Liu K'un-i and Chang Chih-tung. But Li Hung-chang was now an old man in his last days. Soon after performing his final and most humiliating service, the negotiation of the punitive Boxer Protocol of 1901, he died. Meanwhile Yuan Shih-k'ai was fully occupied with rehabilitation work in the Tientsin area, in the effort to secure an early withdrawal of the allied occupation forces. Liu and Chang were thus left in a leading position to outline the reform plans in their three famous memorials, which were submitted on July 12, 19, and 20, 1901, respectively.[4] Their recommendations were pronounced, in a decree of October 2, to be "mostly practicable," and orders were given that the important recommendations be selected and enforced at once.[5] Indeed, a decree of August 29 had in the meantime ordered the abolition of the eight-legged essay, beginning in 1902, and of the military examinations as a whole. On September 16, another decree approved and encouraged the sending of students to study abroad from Kiangnan, Hupei, Szechwan, and other provinces.[6]

These significant memorials of 1901 outlined reforms which were in large part carried out only after the Russo-Japanese war, when many students were sent to Japan. Thus China's real and large-scale modernization effort under government leadership did not really get started until the present century, and was some forty years behind that of Japan, on which so much of it was modeled.

DOC. 50. THE JOINT PROPOSALS OF LIU K'UN-I AND CHANG CHIH-TUNG, 1901

1) A Memorial in Compliance with Your Majesty's Decree to Plan and Discuss (a Reform Program), to Show that in Political Reform the Primary Consideration is Human Ability [7]

We admire our emperor who warns us and guards us against numerous difficulties, and who strongly desires to wipe out longstanding abuses in order to relieve the current hardships. After being moved to tears, we feel both ashamed and aroused. Your ministers once heard that, according to the *Book of Changes (Chou-i)*, "The Way of Heaven changes or transforms itself, hence the movement of heavenly bodies is continuous. This is a great demonstration of self-strengthening" [that is to say, a human or political body should also keep on moving or changing as a heavenly body does, in order to achieve "self-strengthening" (*tzu-ch'iang*), a phrase derived from the *Book of Changes*]. We have also learned from the *Works of Mencius* that "men for the most part err, and are afterwards able to reform. They are distressed in mind and perplexed in thoughts and then they arise to vigorous reform. Thus their mind is stimulated, their nature hardened, and their incompetencies supplied." That is the principal reason why he who lives a sorrowful and anxious life (will die in comfort) [8] . . .

We presume to say that China is poor not in natural resources but in men of ability; she is not weak in troops but in morale. The dearth of men of ability is due to our limited knowledge and unsubstantial learning. The weakness of morale is due (partly) to those who care for temporary security and lack far-reaching plans for coping with danger and for saving the nation from extermination; and (partly) to those who are self-complacent and wanting in the power of persistence in studious pursuits. Without men of ability there is no means for the protection of the nation and for bringing about good government. Carefully we first consider the major aspects of the training of men of ability and the establishment of schools; by taking into consideration both ancient and modern methods and both the civil and military examinations, we have planned and now propose four items: (1) to establish civil and military schools; (2) to reform the civil service examinations to a considerable extent; (3) to abolish the military examinations; and (4) to encourage students to study abroad. Let us reverently explain them for our sacred ruler:

(1) *To establish civil and military schools* [The authors survey the school

and examination systems from ancient to modern times and then continue, p. 11b:] The T'ang adopted the Mohammedan calendar, the *Sui* (*History*) bibliographic section collected many works on dialects. . . During the K'ang-hsi period of our dynasty Westerners were employed both in astronomy and in the casting of cannon. The maps in the palace adopted the longitude and latitude of the Western method. . . The demarcation stone at Nerchinsk was inscribed in three languages. . . [p. 11] The old practice of our ancestors is really adequate to be the model for ten thousand generations. Even now the school systems of all European countries still have ideas (which seem as if) handed down from our Three Dynasties. To say that we can recover our forgotten ceremonies from abroad is not wrong.

[Then the authors give a detailed description of foreign school systems, with special attention to Germany and Japan. The various grades and levels of schools, subjects, extra-curricular work, military drill, etc., are reported in detail (pp. 12–20). They suggest the establishment of primary schools in all districts of the empire (p. 14) and the abolition of the eight-legged essay. Employment for scholars trained to write in this style is also discussed so that such essayists will not have to worry about getting jobs (pp. 20–22)].

(2) *To reform the civil service examinations to a considerable extent.* This is a matter of crucial importance in our self-strengthening and search for talent. . . During the last half year we have consulted officials, gentry and scholars, and in all our discussions reached agreement. . . The general idea of the change in regulations is focused on the pursuit of useful knowledge while never neglecting the classical works. We wish that the case could be considered and managed according to your minister Chang Chih-tung's memorial of 1898 regarding changes to be instituted in the civil service examination, which was approved by an Imperial decree. . . The general scheme was to have three examinations. . . The first one was to be on Chinese political and historical events, the second on politics, geography, military systems, agriculture, industry, mathematics and the like, of all countries, and the third was to consist of a treatise on the classical meanings of the Four Books and the Five Classics. . .

Now we propose that some slight changes be made in the old regulations of the civil service examinations, and that they be continued parallel with the new schools and without conflict [p. 24].

[The other two points, to abolish the military examinations and to encourage students to study abroad, are explained in memorials quoted below.]

[P. 28b] These four items are matters of chief concern in seeking men of ability for the realization of a better administration. Among them the facts and reasons are mutually related and mutually auxiliary. That is why we first submit to Your Majesty these four proposals. This is because unless ability is trained, it is impossible to strive for national survival; unless schools are opened, it is impossible to train ability; unless the civil and military examinations are reformed, it is impossible to open schools, and unless students study abroad, it is impossible to remove our deficiencies in opening schools. An investigation of today's current situation shows that there is no alternative and no time for delay. . .

2) *A Memorial in Compliance with Your Majesty's Decree to Prepare a Discussion on Reform, Carefully Proposing Twelve Items for the Reorganization of the Chinese (Political) System* [9]

Your ministers have planned and proposed four items for developing education and nurturing ability, which have been jointly memorialized and are on record. . . In general there are three important factors in building a nation: good administration, wealth, and strength. . . The reorganization of the Chinese political system is to serve as an instrument for bringing about better administration. The adoption of Western methods is for the purpose of attaining wealth and strength. We have carefully considered those aspects of the Chinese system which ought to be reorganized and reformed, and make proposals under twelve heads: (1) to honor frugality, (2) to break down customary formalities [red tape], (3) to stop the contributions or payments for official rank, (4) to examine the officials and increase their emoluments, (5) to remove the useless clerical staff, (6) to weed out the government servants and messengers, (7) to lighten punishments and imprisonments, (8) to reform the method of civil service examinations, (9) to plan for the livelihood of the Manchu Bannermen, (10) to abolish the military colonies and garrisons, (11) to abolish the Army of the Green Standard [*Lü-ying*] and (12) to simplify the documents and laws. These are reverently prepared for the Court's selection and adoption. . .

[Since these headings are almost self-explanatory, we do not translate the arguments one by one. Their conclusion is as follows, p. 32]: The above twelve items are concerned with the causes of China's chronic weakness, which makes her incapable of exerting herself. They are particularly the hooks on which foreign countries hang their criticisms and abuse of us. Of the plans proposed by your ministers, some are for cultivating the peoples' strength, some for cleansing official circles, and some for arousing the scholars' spirit. Many people had discussed these matters before. But because they had such mistaken notions as that among evils one should remove only the worst, and because they were afraid of being criticized for changing everything, all the statutes, orders, documents, and notices have remained mere paper documents. They may have achieved something but they have lacked long-term and far-reaching plans.

Now foreign aggression is becoming daily more serious. Those who like to follow tradition and devote themselves to cheating and glossing things over always say that the peoples' minds are solidly united. They do not know that popular feelings are not the same as thirty years ago. The people admire the wealth of foreign countries and despise the poverty of the Middle Kingdom. Seeing the strength of foreign soldiers, they are sick of the timidity of their own government's troops; delighted at the fair play of the Maritime Customs Service, they hate the *likin* (transit tax) offices which purposely cause them trouble; praising the stern orderliness of the foreign concessions and settlements, they are tired of the disorder caused by our official clerks. Therefore our people believe in the foreign religion, merchants display foreign flags, and schools register in the names of foreign nationals. All has resulted in a disunited and disillusioned national morale.

Insurgents are slowly emerging, and they take this opportunity to spread subversive doctrines. This concerns the very foundation of the nation. We cannot overcome our anxiety and apprehension. We must first entirely wipe out the various defects mentioned above before we may expect a permanent unification of the popular mind. Then we may speak of being affectionate to our superiors, dying for our elders, opposing humiliation and resisting aggression. We humbly beseech your sacred enlightenment to decide with discrimination and to put these proposals into practice, and use them as the foundation for self-strengthening.

3) *A Memorial to Plan Reform and to Adopt Western Methods* [10]

Your ministers have planned and proposed four items for developing education and nurturing ability, and twelve items for reorganization of the Chinese political system, which have been put on record as two joint memorials. . . Now all countries on the globe are undergoing changes every day and becoming more prosperous every month. . . On investigating their political systems and academic training we find that they are mainly the product of several hundred years of research and of thousands of persons' modifications. After its effectiveness has been demonstrated, the system is imitated by each nation in turn. The Americans adopted some from Europe, and the Japanese also adopted some from the West. . . Now we have received the favor of a specially proclaimed decree in which the failure of previous events has been taken as a warning. Absurd discussions have been put aside, and Western methods are to be adopted to make up for the deficiency of Chinese methods. Your Majesty's humility and broad-mindedness are universally respected by people within and without the Imperial realms. They are raising their heads and wiping their eyes to see the realization of a policy of self-strengthening. The outlines or essentials of Western methods are, however, innumerable. Your ministers carefully take the most important and easily practicable methods and group them together under eleven items: . . . The essential thing is that all reforms should be carried out under the guiding principle of not losing their proper sequence. . .

(1) *The extensive dispatch of travelers abroad.* The strong and prosperous countries of Europe and America have watched and waited for an opportunity to invade us for a hundred years. . . There has been no instrument, however, by which to make ourselves strong, and no method of dealing with them. . . All this has arisen from the handicap of limited information and a narrow point of view, blind ignorance of the territory, politics, literature, and military preparations of all countries. Although in the latter part of the T'ung-chih period travelers were dispatched, resident ministries instituted, and students sent abroad, yet ignorant, absurd, and blundering people denounced as nonsense the words of those who had been in foreign countries, and whenever the latter saw the officials in the Tsungli Yamen they were spitefully treated like dirt. Thereupon, they warned one another against the discussion of foreign affairs, considering it taboo. Even last summer [1900], among the great officials in and out of the capital there were still some who said that foreigners could not walk on land [i.e., be-

cause their knees could not bend, a bit of folklore current in 1839 or earlier],
and others said that since the legations and churches had been burned,
foreigners would never appear again. It is indeed painful to think that such
stupidity and conservatism should be the cause of our country's present
danger. . .

The only way to find a method of quick relief is to dispatch travelers
abroad. They are to observe the national power of other countries, to examine their administrative affairs and academic achievements, to investigate
the major issues in their relations with our country, and the condition of
their relations with other nations. After their return to China they can re-
count what they have experienced and seen to their relatives and friends,
by whom it can be spread to others. By a natural process our group ignorance will be suddenly awakened to prompt consideration of reform. . .
Hereafter all newly appointed members of the Tsungli Yamen, secretaries
of the Grand Council, superintendents of customs, ministers to foreign
countries and their aides must be selected from those who have been sent
abroad. . . Those who have never been abroad will not be allowed to fill
posts of assistant police magistrate, censor, metropolitan minister or
taotai. . . [p. 4b] We have found that the prosperity of Western countries
has been preceded by travel. . .

(2) [P. 5] *The practice of foreign military drill.* . . Emperor K'ang-hsi
used the Westerner Nan Huai-jen [Ferdinand Verbiest], to cast the red-bar-
barian cannon, and up to the present on these cannon the name of Nan
Huai-jen is still inscribed. . .

[P. 8b] In training soldiers there is one further important point, in all
the capitals of foreign countries, great ministers are appointed to take
special charge of controlling and planning military affairs. In England,
France, Germany, and other countries, the name for such a functionary is
Chief of Staff [*Tsung-ying-wu ch'u*], and in Japan the office is called the
Imperial General Staff [lit., "Headquarters of Strategic Counsellors," *Ts'an-
mou pen-pu*], which has approximately the same significance as the Privy
Council [*Shu-mi-yuan*] of the Sung Dynasty. It has special charge of the
whole country's naval and military system: the rate of wages and rations,
maps and books, the code of military drill, the purveyance and storage of
military provisions, the preparation of carts and ships for transportation,
diplomatic affairs, intelligence and other matters. . . [P. 9] If China wishes
to train crack troops we must establish this office. For its regulations please
order the minister Li Sheng-to [in Tokyo] to obtain a copy from the
Japanese government, and to have it translated and sent to you for your
selection and adoption. But to the office of the chief of the military staff
must be appointed one who has a profound knowledge of military affairs
and who has been promoted through the ranks of the troops. We should
not employ only those who have the qualifications of nobility or Imperial
blood. . .

(3) *Enlargement of military supply.* Although the peace treaty [1901]
has been settled, military preparations must not be neglected. If we have no
weapons, then peace cannot be maintained. Military instruments must be
manufactured in spite of the lack of funds; otherwise our officers and

soldiers will never know what modern warfare is. Naturally it is difficult to set up many large arsenals. We must, however, make an effort to open small factories. . . [P. 10b] It would be particularly advisable to send people to Japan and other countries to study modern weapons.

(4) *Improvement of agricultural administration.* China is founded on agriculture. . . In recent years some progress has been made in both industry and commerce, but agricultural affairs are quite stagnant. There has been retreat but no progress. . . If we wish to improve agricultural administration, we must first promote agricultural studies. We have learned that among the foreign countries making a pursuit of agricultural knowledge, France and the United States are considered the finest, but the translations of their books are still few. Recently, however, dozens of Japanese books on agriculture have been translated, and they are succinct and easy to understand. Moreover, the products and customs of Japan are similar to those of China, and there are many ideas which can be imitated and put into practice. Among these books there are some, previously translated from Western agricultural works, in which are stated all the advantages and disadvantages of various products, the fitness of the soil, new methods of improving fertilization and the effect of giving advice and encouragement to farmers.

It has been learned that in the ninth month of 1898 a decree was received ordering all provinces to establish bureaus of agricultural affairs. We wish to request that such a public decree be re-issued, earnestly charging all provinces to take the matter seriously. Since the Han and the T'ang dynasties there has always been a special officer in charge of agriculture. We further request that in the capital, a minister of agricultural administration be particularly appointed to take charge of the study and promotion of agricultural matters. . .

(5) *The promotion of industry.* People usually say that the wealth of Western countries lies in commerce, but they do not know that it actually lies in industry. This is because merchants handle the completed goods, while industrialists make things out of raw materials. . . When there is industry, there are commodities, and merchants have goods to trade with. . . Foreign countries are abundant in wealth; China is richest in men [p. 16]. Today, if those Chinese who are looking for ways of enriching the country wish to compete with European and American countries in commerce, that is impossible for us; but if we compete with these countries in industry, that we certainly can do.

There are three methods of promoting industry: (a) to establish schools of technology, in which factories are set up; . . . (b) to open industrial exhibitions [p. 18]; and (c) bestow official rank on skillful workers as a reward. . . As for those who can create new methods of producing any kind of commodities, they should be given a license allowing them a monopoly for a number of years. All manufactured goods should be charged a specially light rate of *likin* tax, and innovations should be exempt from the *likin* for three years. This is also an important measure for encouraging industry. In short, if we wish to feed the poor and to check the increase of barren land, there is nothing better than to encourage hundreds of handicrafts; if we wish to stop financial leakage and to resist the foreigners, there is nothing better to depend on for enriching the country and the people than the production of native goods. Thus we should worry only about our population not being numerous; why should we worry about its daily becoming more numerous?

(6) *The making of mining laws, transportation laws, commercial laws, laws of negotiation and penal codes.* China's mineral resources are abundant, hidden and not yet excavated, and her railway rights are laid out in a connected pattern, but we have been hesitant and have not yet built the railways. These two things have been coveted by foreigners for a long time [p. 9]. In the last few years, all countries have been busy gathering capital and coming to China, where they know that in regard to these matters we have as yet no definite regulations, and as to foreign conditions we are still not well informed. They take this opportunity to fool us, to usurp our profits, and invade our rights. Sometimes on the pretext of opening a mine they grab a railway, and sometimes on the pretext of operating a railway they open mines. . . In recent years, France in Yunnan and Kweichow, Germany in Shantung, England and Italy in Shansi and Honan, all have made agreements with China. The regulations are complicated and not uniform and we are afraid that they are not wholly safe and suitable. . . [Various types of legislation are then discussed.]

(7) *The use of the silver dollar.* There are three advantages to the silver dollar. One is that the weight and value are so uniform, the paying and receiving so clear-cut that official clerks cannot indulge in graft and extortion, and the officials and people (involved in a transaction) will not suffer from having to make up a deficiency [as was the case in using ingots of silver]. Second, its use in commercial exchange will make transactions simple and straightforward, and the brokers will have no chance to cheat; and so it is not only beneficial to travelers but also convenient for remittance. Third, the collection and distribution of official funds will be entirely in the silver currency for which the larger coin [dollar] will be used as a unit, and the smaller coins as sub-units. . . After the expenditure for the workers and the mint, there will still be a surplus [p. 22] . . .

(8) *The use of the stamp tax.* We have learned that the policy of taxing commodities in foreign countries, apart from tobacco, liquor, and opium, is that generally there are no internal duties but a huge income comes solely from the stamp tax. All deeds, bills or documents which have to do with money and property must have affixed on them a stamp obtained from an official bureau. The general idea is to levy a tax on the money value, not on the commodity [p. 23]; to levy a tax on the goods sold, not on those unsold, and to collect a tax from all the four kinds of people [scholars, farmers, craftsmen and merchants] and hundreds of other professions which have an income, not only from merchants and traders. Therefore Westerners explain the meaning of the stamp tax by saying that this is a tax on money-income. Today in raising funds this method should probably be imitated and practised. . .

(9) *Promotion of the postal administration.* [P. 25] It has been learned that in all foreign nations, the postal administration is a big source of gov-

ernment income; in general the annual income is often several tens of millions of taels, and the delivery of mails is very rapid. Chinese military postal stations are a big item of wasted money; the annual expenditure is about three million taels, and yet the official dispatches and reports are very slow. . .

Since China has no post office, England, Germany, the United States, Japan, and various other countries have established their own post offices here, and invaded our rights. This is really against international precedent. In 1895 a decree was issued and He-te [Sir Robert Hart], Inspector General of Customs, was ordered to take charge; and since 1896 post offices have been gradually established along the sea-coasts and rivers. These were attached to and concurrently managed by the Inspectorate General of Maritime Customs. . .

(10) *The official collection of opium duties.* [P. 28] Now it is most urgent for us to raise money, and it is difficult to obtain a large amount of funds by the sporadic scraping together of odds and ends. It is difficult to increase again the levy of the *likin* tax, which should be abolished; and it is also hard to make the salt gabelle heavier, since its rates already have been repeatedly raised. Only an additional duty on the "foreign drug" [opium] will not be oppressive to the people but will result in a huge augmentation of financial provisions. We found that in the case of France and Spain, in shipping matches and Luzon tobacco, and in the case of Japan, in collecting and selling foreign and native opium in Formosa, these things were purchased and distributed by government agencies. Now let us imitate this method. According to the Maritime Customs trade reports, in 1899 the import of opium for sale was 5,900,161 piculs [1 picul = 133 lbs.] . . . If we estimate the annual import at six million odd piculs, the total weight is 96,000,000 taels. . . and the total value is 50,000,000 taels including tax and *likin*. We propose that hereafter the government establish offices, and when opium enters the customhouses it be entirely purchased and then resold to private merchants for distribution to all provinces. . . It is estimated that each year we can make a surplus of ten million taels. . .

(11) *More translations of Japanese and Western books.* [P. 31] Today if we wish to adopt political systems from all the nations, we should certainly translate more foreign political and academic works. There are in general three methods of translating books. First, to order each province to conduct research in foreign books, and translate and publish them, and let the ones which produce more translations than others be permitted to ask for a reward from the emperor. Nevertheless the funds are limited and the books thus translated cannot be many. Second, to request that an Imperial decree be publicly circulated among all provincial licentiates of various levels to the effect that those who can translate useful foreign books are to submit them to the emperor for his information through the high officials outside of the capital; they may be rewarded with actual official posts or encouraged with good brevet ranks, and their books may be returned to the various provinces for publication. Thus the cost will be reduced. But there are few important foreign books circulating in China, and the selections cannot be too strict. Third, to request that Chinese ministers abroad

be ordered to investigate the most essential and important books recently published in the nations in which they are respectively stationed, and to invite a thoroughly learned man of that country to be the chief translation official, assisted by the ministers' retinue and students. . .

The above various items are all very important and should be rapidly put into effect. . . As for the unorthodox theories of K'ang Yu-wei, he merely aimed at spreading his own teachings ("K'angism") and treacherously sought to disturb the basic order of things. In reality he has no understanding at all of the essential ideas of Western government and Western knowledge. The various items proposed here are distinctly different from his proposals. And moreover these points have been generally put into operation by Imperial decrees at different times during the last thirty years. Here we only seek to promote and enforce them with the hope of averting imminent calamity. . . We humbly expect that your sacred enlightenment, deep observation, and far-sighted vision will grant an early execution of the proposals, so that all countries may see China's determination to exert every effort to become strong, whereupon their habits of despising and insulting us may gradually die out. This also will let the scholars and the people know that the Court has the intention of renovating our system [lit., to put fresh strings on the bow and pull it anew]. The reactionary people will then modify their blunders, and those who are expecting better government will offer their loyalty. And the heresies that offend the emperor and stimulate uprisings will not arise. Thus the empire will be fortunate indeed. . .

b. *Educational Reform*

The civil service examination system had had a history of more than one thousand years. During the Ch'ing period practical-minded scholars had often raised objections to the formal eight-legged essays required in the examinations, and proposed instead compositions about current affairs.[11] In 1887 mathematics was adopted as an examination subject at the suggestion of a censor,[12] but unfortunately the conservative influence was still so predominant that not many scholars took an interest in this new alternative. Two years after the Sino-Japanese War, in 1897, Yen Hsiu, provincial director of education of Kweichow, memorialized requesting the introduction of a "special examination on political economy" (*ching-chi t'e-k'o*), in order to recruit scholars who were versed in current affairs and had not strictly followed the traditional routine. In the following year Liang Ch'i-ch'ao and more than a hundred other provincial graduates submitted a joint memorial requesting the abolition of the whole civil service examination system. K'ang Yu-wei also presented memorials strongly supporting this change in order to cope with foreign invasion. During the Reform Movement of 1898, a modification in the examination subjects was ordered but not carried out. Finally, early in 1903 Chang Chih-tung, governor-general at Nanking, and Yuan Shih-k'ai, governor-general at Tientsin, submitted a joint memorial, part of which is translated below, to suggest the gradual abolition of the system. Thereafter other memorialists urged a summary abolition, and eventually an imperial decree of September 2, 1905 [13] announced the immediate and permanent cessation of the examinations. They had been held usually once every year or twice every three years since A.D. 622.

To replace the old examinations the Chinese government adopted a new educational program based on Western and Japanese models. This gave the missionary schools a new status, and gradually changed their enrollment. Instead of drawing students exclusively from the children of the poor, they now began to attract those of the elite, that is, the gentry-official class. In the meantime, education abroad, especially in nearby Japan, had become highly esteemed. As many as ten thousand Chinese students were in Japan at one time, whereas only a few hundreds went to Europe and the United States. While some of these students in foreign countries received a relatively substantial education, there were many instances of graduates of short courses in education or law in Japan who at once became teachers or judges on their return.

The change in the educational system also gave sudden recognition to the Chinese students who had been educated in the West since the 1870's. Many of them, including a dentist, were given the *chin-shih* and *chü-jen* degrees. In the educational system, at least, Westernization in form was finally achieved after 1905. This movement, however, did not result in the rapid democratizing of Chinese society, for education was still a luxury of the wealthy; whether the new system developed those "men of ability" so ardently sought after by Chang Chih-tung is also uncertain.

DOC. 51. A MEMORIAL OF CHANG CHIH-TUNG AND YUAN SHIH-K'AI URGING ABOLITION OF THE OLD EXAMINATIONS, 1903. [14]

We consider that it does not matter whether a nation is strong or weak; as long as it has men of ability, it will be prosperous. Nor does it matter whether the time is peaceful or perilous; if there are men of talent, things will be in good order. Indeed, men of ability are the basic stuff of a nation and the foundation of its government. . . The weakness of China today is extreme. Great catastrophes have come in succession and foreign aggressions daily press upon us. It is the moment for us to arise and exert ourselves in action. . .

We reverently admire the arduous life of our Empress Dowager and Emperor who are looking for talented men as if thirsting for water, and who have ordered all the provinces to establish schools, and who again have proclaimed decrees to promote this work. . . Unfortunately, the various provinces which are starting to look into the school situation generally are hesitant or procrastinating, or carry out the order perfunctorily or neglect the order without yet establishing any schools at all. Some schools have been opened but the equipment is very incomplete. When we look into the causes, they say that it is because of insufficient funds and the difficulty of finding teachers. These two difficulties are certainly real [p. 8], but they are not bad enough to cause a great evil. The greatest and most obvious evil, which is the enemy and hindrance to the school system, is the civil service examination. In general, a school is a place to train men of ability, and the civil service examination is to test men of ability. If the civil service examination and school system are coördinated, then the school will be prosperous without our urging. If the school and civil service examinations are uncoördinated, then the school will eventually be a mere name without any substance. Why? Because the multitude compete on the path toward benefits and emoluments, and people are afraid to take up complicated and difficult tasks. The period needed to complete the course in the schools is settled in advance, and it is necessary for one to spend years before he becomes well qualified in his field; on the other hand, one may be successful by sheer chance in taking advantage of the tricks and malpractices in the civil service examinations. Even though the eight-legged essays are abolished and replaced by essays on current policies and classical principles, yet, after all, one's writings are based on the strength of one day and these empty words cannot be compared to actual achievements. . .

China is not without men who are worrying about the times, but we have not yet heard of any of the gentry class who are urging the building of schools. This is also due to the fact that the interest of the multitude is in the civil service examinations, which have been used by fathers and elder brothers to encourage their sons and younger brothers, and by hamlets and villages to urge on their common folk [to become outstanding figures in the future] . . . Thus, as long as the civil service examination is not abolished there is no chance for the schools to be very prosperous, and our students will go on without gaining any actual knowledge, our nation will have no men of ability to meet the crisis of the time, China will be unable to advance to wealth and power, and she will never be able to compete with other nations. Your ministers' hearts ache. . .

[P. 9] We earnestly hope that the civil service examination will be gradually but completely abolished and that schools will be established as numerous as the teeth of a comb and the trees of the forest. Thus we can remove the evils of administration which have been followed for several hundred years in the past, and we can train millions of useful men of ability in the future. By this action the people of all the five continents will be amazed and a myriad generations will be made to show respect. . .

c. Constitutionalism

In order to show the seriousness of her interest in governmental reform, the Empress Dowager sent two official missions to Europe and America in 1905 to investigate foreign constitutional governments. Upon their return in the following year two of the commissioners, Tai Hung-tz'u (1853–1910) and Tuan-fang (1861–1911), jointly presented to the throne a work on "The essentials of European-American government," from which the following passage is taken. Though published in 1907, the original covering memorial was dated in the ninth month of 1906.[15]

This book is significant in many ways. First, it represents the commissioners' understanding of the principles and operation of constitutional monarchy. Tai, an orthodox Confucian scholar-official, and Tuan-fang, a Manchu official with a reputation for vigor and enlightenment, went as far as the dynasty was willing to go in the matter of constitutional government. Their summary of Western constitutionalism is as interesting for what is rejected as for what is accepted. Secondly, this work underlines the utilitarian interest of the reformers of the period: justification for the constitutional form of government is sought in practical rather than in theoretical terms. In the introductory chapter, for instance, the authors explain that the adoption of a constitution would increase the efficiency of the emperor's rule, not detract from it. They stress the expectation that when people are allowed to participate in political affairs, their interest in the nation's needs will be stimulated; whereupon a greater development of resources will follow, and this in turn will facilitate the government's tax collection.[16] Thirdly, such arguments were not intended for the ear of the Empress Dowager only — they were intended also to provide a reasoned basis on which the throne's actions could be publicized to the entire country. It is noteworthy that the book was published within a year of the commissioners' return. A comparison of the arguments contained in this book with the writings of reformers in contemporary journals shows a close affinity in their points of view. It is clear that this work was part of an effort in traditional government circles to win greater support from the scholars and thereby stem the revolutionary tide.

DOC. 52. A Report on Constitutional Governments Abroad, 1906

The thing to be most carefully investigated in the observation of the structure of European constitutional governments is this: what changes are caused by the constitution in the authority of the monarch under a constitutional government as compared with the autocratic rule of the monarch? To know this important point one should study nations which have changed directly from autocratic monarchy to constitutional monarchy. The system of enacting constitutions according to the wish of the people, and then electing the monarch, as in Belgium, Greece, Rumania, etc.; and the system of basing a state on popular consent, as in Italy and Spain; these are actually republican systems although called monarchic, and for the time being we shall not discuss them. Again, we need not discuss the fact that the German Emperor did not depend on his original power in the creation of his empire, but was delegated authority as head of the confederation by the various German states, with the constitution quite resembling that of a republic. [P. 30b] The so-called pure autocratic monarchies that have changed directly into constitutional monarchies are, for instance, the Kingdom of Prussia, the Kingdom of Bavaria, the Kingdom of Saxony and the Austrian Empire. . .

The constitutions of the above countries, such as Prussia, Saxony, and Austria, had all been submitted to the parliaments and amended by them; therefore they are also not constitutions granted by royal order. In the world today only the constitution of Bavaria has the nature of one granted by royal order. It first fixes the powers of the king, and [p. 31] draws up a main article which says that the king is the head of the state and holds the power of the central authority which he exercises according to the provisions of the constitution; that the person of the king cannot be violated, etc. Then the king's various kinds of authority are itemized in the different articles. This is because the influence of the French Revolution spread across all of Europe, so that the people of the various German states also wanted to establish constitutions. Although their kings did not wish suddenly to change their autocratic governments, yet in the circumstances there was nothing they could do but yield to the times, and each granted a constitution. . .

As for the stipulation that the person of the monarch is not to be violated, both the constitution by royal order and that by common discussion include this provision. For the monarch is also human. Perchance he might commit a mistake in policy, which would harm the people and run contrary to the basic purpose of the constitutional government. Or through error he might act contrary to the articles of the constitution. If at such times the hostile criticisms (of the people) are concentrated personally on the monarch, then his powers will be debased and his dignity injured, and henceforth the political system will be destroyed. Therefore the constitutions of the various nations place the monarch beyond the reach of adverse criticism and discussion. . .

But this would make the articles of constitution a mere form without substance, and the situation would be the same as that under an autocratic monarch. Therefore, there must be high ministers to assist the monarch. In case of unsuitable administration or unconstitutional acts, then the monarch's assistants can be blamed for not doing their duty. Consequently, the high ministers of the government must take the responsibility on behalf of the monarch. This is called the system of responsible ministers, which has been clearly provided for in the constitutions of the various nations. . .

[P. 33] Before the enactment of the constitution the monarch holds all the national power, and all political matters of the nation must be decided by him. But no great changes occur after the enactment of the constitution. The monarch remains the highest organ of the state, the constitution only delimiting the respective authorities of the different divisions in the government. Therefore, the monarch's powers consist not only of those written in the constitution. All powers that concern national affairs the monarch exercises, even if they are not written into the constitution. Those powers which the monarch exercises by himself without going through another government agency are called prerogatives [lit., ta-ch'üan, great or high power] by some Western scholars. Because they can be exercised without having to be referred to an article in the constitution, they are thus called "prerogatives"; therefore, there are many that are not specifically stipulated in the constitution. Some other scholars have thought that they could protect the authority of the monarch by specific stipulations in the constitution to show that such and such are the royal prerogatives, so that the other government organs, e.g., parliament, could not encroach upon them; these are called "constitutional prerogatives"; all royal prerogatives are stated in the constitution, and the monarch absolutely cannot exercise those that are not clearly stated. Such a theory is improper and we should take note of this. . .

d. Yuan Shih-k'ai and the Modern Army

Yuan Shih-k'ai (1859–1916), as we have seen, had proved himself an able politician and a leader in the late Ch'ing reform movement under the Manchus. He is best remembered as an army organizer and because as first president of the Chinese Republic at Peking after 1912 he attempted to overthrow the Republic and make himself emperor. After him came the war lords, most of whom had been his army commanders.[17]

Yuan was brought up in an official and military family. With only moderate education, he made his career through his early participation in military programs and as Li Hung-chang's protégé in Korea. He utilized his opportunity to rise to power after the coup d'état of 1898 and the Boxer Uprising had put a premium upon officials who could create and use military force.

The modern Chinese army traces its development from the famous "Hunan Army" (Hsiang-chün) and the Anhwei Army (Huai-chün), developed by Tseng

Kuo-fan and others on a local basis against the Taiping and Nien rebels. A by-product of the Sino-French conflict was the establishment of a Military Preparatory School (*Wu-pei hsueh-t'ang*) at Tientsin, which was suggested by General C. G. ("Chinese") Gordon in 1885. In this school Western methods of military instruction were adopted and German instructors were employed, although the achievement was negligible. After China was defeated by Japan in 1894, Chang Chih-tung, then governor-general at Nanking, organized his "Self-strengthening Army" (*Tzu-ch'iang-chün*), later centered at Wusung near Shanghai and trained by German instructors (see Ch. XVII above). About the same time Hu Yü-fen (d. 1906), director-general of the Peking-Tientsin Railroad, was ordered to organize a modern army, called the *Ting-wu-chün*, which was trained in German style at Hsiao-chan, about twenty miles from Tientsin. Later on this force became the nucleus of the Pei-yang army. At that time Yuan Shih-k'ai was in Peking, where he became a member of the "Society for the study of self-strengthening" (*Ch'iang-hsueh-hui*), the leading society in the Reform Movement, and also established good relations with many high officials, including Jung-lu, then minister of war. Through this connection Yuan was appointed to command the Ting-wu army, which was soon renamed the "Newly Organized Army" (*Hsin-chien lu-chün*). An imperial decree of December 8, 1895, appointed Yuan Shih-k'ai to train the new army at Tientsin, and expressly follow the German army regulations. His Chinese instructors had to learn enough German for the purpose.

From 1896 to 1898 Yuan's energy was spent mainly on this new army. During the Boxer Uprising of 1900, he was fortunately not involved in the international imbroglio. Thereafter Li Hung-chang died, in 1901, and his position as governor-general of Chihli and superintendent of trade for the northern ports was given to Yuan. Jung-lu died in 1903. Meanwhile the Empress Dowager, chagrined at the recent humiliation of China and the dynasty, determined to improve the army as part of her general reform program. In this process Yuan Shih-k'ai had a good opportunity to build up his personal military power through the assistance of his trusted staff members — men like Feng Kuo-chang (1859–1919), Wang Shih-chen (1863–1932), Ts'ao K'un (d. 1938), and Tuan Ch'i-jui (1865–1936), all of whom subsequently became prominent war lords. By the end of 1905, Yuan Shih-k'ai had organized the six divisions of the Pei-yang Army and developed such *esprit de corps* that, even though he was away from his army for a period of years (1907–1911), his officers remained generally loyal to him.

Although he did not carry out as many reforms as his biographers have eulogistically listed, he did, nevertheless, achieve some things which had been suggested or discussed by Li Hung-chang, Chang Chih-tung, and others, notably the abolition of the civil service examinations. His modern detractors of the republican period tend to ignore these pre-republican contributions. When Yuan was governor of Shantung (Dec. 6, 1899–June 16, 1901), he submitted a memorial requesting ten items, viz., more careful issuing of orders and ordinances, training of officials, emphasis on practical studies, increase of useful subjects in the school curriculum, emphasis on travel abroad, a code regulating Chinese ministers abroad, definitions of names, titles, and duties of officials, enrichment of the national revenue, and enlightenment of the people. The reasoning in support of these proposals is along the same line as that of the three memorials of Liu K'un-i and Chang Chih-tung (see Doc. 50). Yuan enforced a few educational reforms, including the opening of a university and elementary and middle schools, in the area under his jurisdiction. He also established a *Chiao-shih-kuan*, an institution to promote advanced study. When Yuan was governor-general of Chihli and grand councillor (1901–1909), apart from building his army, he tried to improve the selection of Chinese diplomatic personnel; to open an agricultural school and an experimental farm in Paoting, and an industrial bureau (*Kung-i chü*) at Tientsin; and to secure financial reform by introducing new taxes and modern banks, in the hope of increasing the government revenues and of paying for the new army, schools, and other enterprises, including a new police force. Yuan was a supporter of the idea of constitutional monarchy — whether he was sincere or hypocritical is another question. Many Chinese students and officers were encouraged by him to study military and political science in Japan; gradually Japanese advisers replaced those from Germany. In short, during this period Yuan chiefly emphasized the training of a modern army, education for the people and good local government. His administrative ability and dominant position undoubtedly influenced the Empress Dowager to endorse some of these reforms. Eventually, after her death, he appeared to many as the only strong man of progressive views who could save China from chaos.

CHAPTER XXI. ECONOMIC DEVELOPMENT

Although this volume is concerned more with ideas than with economics, certain economic concepts have played major roles in China's intellectual history. Let us avoid fruitless argument as to whether or not the "entrepreneurial spirit" is essentially an expression of ideology, and note some of the new ideas of industrial development which appeared in China about the turn of the century, stimulated by the Western example in China and by a new appraisal of Chinese needs and potentialities.

The Western stimulus became more concrete after 1896, when the subsidiary treaty of commerce with Japan gave her people the right "to carry on trade, industries and manufactures" in the treaty ports.[1] By most-favored-nation treatment, other powers received the same privilege. Thereafter foreign factories sprang up like bamboo shoots after rain, seeking to utilize China's cheap labor and raw materials. Japanese, English, and German firms seized the opportunity to open cotton mills in Shanghai, and Chinese industrialists soon followed suit. The rural handicraft industries, which were a sideline for most farm families, could not compete with the cheaper, machine-produced goods. Gradually, the peasantry were compelled to spend some of their hard-earned cash to buy foreign-made cloth, cigarettes, and other commodities.

As a form of government encouragement to Chinese industry, the Tsungli Yamen in 1898 issued regulations whereby a fifty-year monopoly would be granted to inventors of new weapons and a thirty year monopoly to inventors of new utensils for daily use. The numerous concessions for mining and railway development secured by the imperialist powers from 1898 on also moved the Chinese government to take counter measures. Between 1903 and 1911 several projects for industrial development were actively undertaken or encouraged by high officials. Prince Tsai-chen was sent to Europe, America, and Japan to investigate industry. In 1903 a ministry of commerce was set up at Peking; in 1906 it was renamed the Ministry of Agriculture, Industry, and Commerce. A commercial code including a company law was proclaimed.[2] The use of Chinese national products was promoted by leading officials. In 1905, for example, Yuan Shih-k'ai sponsored an industrial exhibit at Tientsin. The Ministry of Commerce built a hall in Peking for the same purpose. The Ministry urged that technical colleges be opened in every province. Doctoral (i.e., *chin-shih*) degrees in industry and commerce were to be conferred on returned students, on the basis of examinations set by the government. In

1910 a huge industrial fair was organized in Nanking by the governor-general, Tuan-fang.

During the years between 1903 and 1908 one hundred and twenty-seven Chinese industrial concerns with a capital of $32,199,800 were registered at the Ministry of Agriculture, Industry, and Commerce.[3] Cotton mills, flour mills, silk filatures, electric plants, tobacco and match factories, and steel foundries were among these enterprises. Also during this decade, through foreign contracts and loans, China completed some 6000 miles of railway construction.[4] To compete against the foreign banks, several modern Chinese banks were opened, including the China Commercial Bank (*Chung-kuo t'ung-shang yin-hang*) in 1897, the Ministry of Revenue (Hu-pu) Bank in 1904, which was reorganized as the Ta-Ch'ing Bank in 1908, and as the Bank of China in 1913. In 1907 the Bank of Communications and the Chekiang Industrial Bank were opened.[5]

This economic growth in China was a pale reflection of the industrialization going on elsewhere in the world and lagged behind the expansion of British, Japanese, and other enterprises in the treaty ports. No Chinese undertakings, governmental or otherwise, could as yet compete with the shipping, docks, textile mills, insurance and banking interests, railway and mining investments of the single pioneer British firm of Jardine, Matheson and Company. Under the steadily increasing pressure of foreign economic development within their country, however, Chinese of the scholar-official class began to embark on new ventures and become themselves entrepreneurs of a new type. The limitations of the "government-supervision and merchant-management" system (see Ch. XIII) had been due in part to the officials' persistence in old patterns of administration — Tseng and Li, Tso Tsung-t'ang and Chang Chih-tung could inaugurate numerous projects but, because of their official duties as territorial administrators responsible for all aspects of government, they had always to delegate the management to others. The result was bureaucracy. Neither the responsible high official nor his delegated manager could live and work from day to day on the job. Neither of them could be moved primarily by the compelling motives of a business man absorbed in costs, prices, and the market.

Among the new generation who achieved prominence in industry after the turn of the century, two men were outstanding — Sheng Hsuan-huai and Chang Chien. Their careers represent two of the various forms of Chinese response to foreign economic encroachment. Both were intensely stirred by nationalist feeling. Although of the official class, neither became a high provincial official. They were not mandarins so much as working executives, specialists in industrial development.

Sheng Hsuan-huai (1844–1916) was born into an official family in Kiangsu. After failing to get a *chü-jen* degree in the provincial examination, he became a secretary to Li Hung-chang, as already noted. In 1873 Li made him manager of the China Merchants Steam Navigation Company, where he worked with two Cantonese compradore-merchants, T'ang T'ing-shu (1832–1892) and Hsü Jun (1838–1911), both of whom later became prominent (Hsü made a fortune in tea and real estate). Since Sheng regarded modern communications as of primary importance for China's national strength, Li made him supervisor of the construction of the Peking-Hankow railway and of the telegraph line between Tientsin and Shanghai. Frequently, when government enterprises got into difficulty, Sheng appears to have been called in as a trouble shooter. When the first cotton mill at Shanghai burned down, Li ordered him to take it over and rebuild it, recruiting the capital from merchants. When the Han-Yeh-P'ing Iron and Steel Works ran short of funds and had to be sold to the stockholders, Sheng Hsuan-huai was chosen to take over the management from Chang Chih-tung. In each case he had a hard time raising funds.

Although Sheng never held a post in the provincial hierarchy higher than that of taotai, he proved his competence in diplomacy as well as industry. He accompanied Li Hung-chang to Chefoo in 1876, and participated in the negotiations with Sir Thomas Wade for the purchase of the Shanghai-Wusung railroad. During the Boxer Uprising he played an important role in keeping South China out of the international imbroglio.[6]

Evidently, Sheng had a natural ability for handling several duties simultaneously — in shipping, telegraphs, railroads, and mining — and his official posts accumulated as time went on. By 1896 he was customs taotai at Tientsin and director-in-chief of most government railway construction, in addition to heading the China Merchants Company and Imperial Telegraphs. These multiple posts moved Gustav Detring to warn Li Hung-chang against him, but the warning went unheeded. Li said Sheng was "a man of an alert mind."

Among his other activities, Sheng Hsuan-huai became the founder of Peiyang College at Tientsin in 1886 and of Nanyang College at Shanghai in 1897, both good technical institutions, where many Chinese engineers as well as political leaders like Wang Ch'ung-hui and Ch'en Li-fu were trained. During the early years of the twentieth century, Sheng wielded great power and his enemies increased in proportion. To avoid sharp criticism in China he traveled to Japan in 1908 on the pretext of seeking treatment for tuberculosis. While in Japan, he met the political and industrial leaders and investigated Japanese industry. In February 1911 he was promoted to be minister of Posts and Communications and vigorously insisted on the policy of nationalization of railways, which served as the fuse to ignite the Republican Revolution of October 10, 1911.

By his foreign competitors in the treaty ports Sheng Hsuan-huai was acknowledged to be energetic and vigorous in the pursuit of his purposes, but he was viewed with deep suspicion. J. O. P. Bland called him an "old fox," [7] and H. B. Morse said that "his honesty was trusted neither by Chinese nor by foreigners." [8] Clean-handed or not, Sheng was certainly very nationalistic in his sentiments. In May 1896 he responded vigorously to Chang Chih-tung's invitation to take the directorship of the Peking-Hankow railway as a means of fighting against foreign aggression. He replied, "I would not think of sparing myself the exertion of a few more years of my energy and strength, if only I could earn some face (lit., a mouthful of breath) for China." [9]

In May 1898, when trying to resist the foreign envoys' threatening demands for railway concessions, Sheng wrote, "I am not afraid of difficulties or danger; I put myself forward and took this job, not caring whether it helps or harms me." [10] There is no doubt that Sheng's aggressiveness accomplished much, and also irritated many people. One of his minor achievements was the founding of the Chinese Red Cross Society (1909). More important was his founding of modern banking in China, as a necessary means of financial defense against the foreign powers, especially Russia. Though Chang Chih-tung was cool to the idea, Sheng went ahead. One of his memorials is translated below.

DOC. 53. SHENG HSUAN-HUAI'S ARGUMENT FOR MODERN BANKING, 1896 [11]

Banking originated in Europe. Its main purpose is to help circulate the wealth and property within a nation so as to meet the needs of the upper and lower classes. Western banking is better than the old Chinese exchange

banks (*p'iao-hao*) or money shops (*ch'ien-chuang*). Since it is protected
by the national government, its rights cannot be usurped and its credit can
be maintained.

After all the nations began to trade with China, the Chinese neglected
banking, and so the banks of England, France, Germany, Russia, and
Japan expanded into China and have taken great profits away from us.
In recent years many Chinese and also some foreign scholar-officials have
clearly seen this situation and have suggested the establishment of banks
to play a major role in our commercial affairs and central administration.
Now we are building railways, which require a heavy initial investment.
Unless we quickly establish a Chinese bank, we shall have no way to circulate the funds which serve as blood in our veins or to stop the control of
our economic life by foreign merchants.

Some critics say that a national bank should supply all its own [govern-
ment] funds as capital; that it should be run by high officials, and should
issue bank notes for the Ministry of Revenue, like the central banks which
manage the financial resources of England, France, and other nations. In
this way a national bank would be an external treasury of the Ministry of
Revenue. But these critics should know that the customs in China and the
West are different; not long ago we learned a lesson from the notes issued
by the Ministry. A government organization which handles business matters will run into numerous obstacles and accumulate evils. Some observers
wish to entrust the raising of foreign funds to Westerners, by whom thousands of taels could be raised in a short time. Such words are sweet to hear,
but the power would be in their hands and the actual advantage or disadvantage would be unpredictable.

Your minister (Sheng Hsuan-huai) thinks that banking is a matter for
merchants; if merchants do not trust the government, the financial power
of the country cannot be concentrated; and if this power is not concentrated, a bank will not be successful. If we wish to begin carefully in order
to get good results, we must accumulate small sums (from merchants) to
make a big fund. I venture to request that a high official be appointed to
select honest and reliable merchants of the gentry class (*shen-shang*) from
all the provinces and recommend them for service as trustees (of the bank).
They should raise five million taels of capital from Chinese merchants and
establish a Chinese bank, first in Peking and Shanghai and then with
branches in other provincial capitals and trading ports. Following Western
business practice, this bank should be managed by the merchants themselves.

Some time ago your minister discussed banking affairs in Shanghai with
Yen Hsin-hou, who has the rank of expectant taotai and is a gentry-merchant
operating the official customs banks (*yin-hao*) which handle the duties at
Canton, Foochow, Ningpo, Shanghai, and Hankow. [P. 15] Yen Hsin-hou
has a broad view of the whole national situation, and is willing to have his
own customs banks incorporated in a national bank so as to make it stronger.
Further, in accordance with the practice of the Hongkong and Shanghai
Banking Corporation (*Hui-feng yin-hang*), we propose, with good paper
and machines, to print banknotes that will circulate along with the silver

currency. The amount of silver on deposit will determine the number of banknotes printed, so that they can be cashed at any time. . . . The employment of personnel and the management of affairs in the bank will follow the regulations of the Hongkong and Shanghai Banking Corporation as a standard. Thus the power of Chinese merchants throughout the nation will be concentrated in the operation of the national banking corporation. If Chinese banks secure only one more cent of profit, they will to that degree recover our rights from the foreign banks.

We should also follow the Western practice whereby banks contribute a certain amount of money to the government when they have a surplus. Regulations should be established in advance and should be strictly observed. Both the merchants and the common people would benefit, and the nation would also benefit indirectly. . .

In November 1896, Sheng Hsuan-huai received verbal instructions from Prince Kung to the effect that the bank should be opened immediately because Russia had secured permission to open Sino-Russian banks at Peking and other places; if China did not establish a bank of her own first, her rights would be entirely lost, like fish caught in one throw of a net. Consequently, the government was most anxious to see the bank succeed without delay,[12] and it was opened for business in June 1897 with a capital of five million taels held by Chinese citizens only.

In spite of his accomplishments, including a huge accumulation of wealth, Sheng Hsuan-huai voiced three regrets about his own life: (1) he had never obtained a higher degree; (2) he had never held a regular governorship; and (3) he had never been to Europe or America.[13] Evidently, he had retained traditional values and ambitions. His younger contemporary, Chang Chien (1853–1926), was a man of different character and ideals.

Chang was born into a farmer's family in Kiangsu, and became a top scholar (chuang-yuan), winning first place among 314 successful candidates in the metropolitan examinations for the chin-shih degree in 1894 — a great honor which helped his future career. Previously he had served as a young official in Korea, in 1882, and his brilliant writing and energetic discharge of duties had caught the attention of Li Hung-chang, Chang Chih-tung, and other high officials. In the critical year of 1895 he could have expected promotion to important positions, but he decided instead to go into the field of industrial development.

Chang Chien thus became known as the top scholar who went into business. He did not like official formalities, and also resented the usual criticism that scholarly bookworms were good for nothing. He was distressed by the Japanese victory and aspired to save China from poverty and weakness. Impressed by Timothy Richard's reform programs for the development of education and industry, and for the improvement of public health and welfare and the popular standard of living,[14] he became interested in his native district, Tungchow, Kiangsu, commonly called Nantung to distinguish it from the northern Tungchow near Peking. This district produced good cotton, which was already being bought up by the Japanese after the war. Chang Chien therefore set to work and founded the famous Ta-sheng Cotton Mill at Nantung in 1898. He served as the managing director and also as liaison officer between the merchant partners and the government officials whose patronage was necessary. Chang's aim in this was explained in the "Mill Agreement" (ch'ang-yueh), drawn up in 1897, part of which is translated below:

DOC. 54. Economic Views of Chang Chien [15]

The establishment of a cotton mill in Tungchow is to aid the livelihood of the people of Tungchow and also to protect China's profitable resources. The cotton produced in Tungchow is soft but tough, with long fibres, the best kind in Asia. Japan needs it badly for her mills. Raw cotton is now taken away and comes back in the form of yarn; this is increasing day by day. We provide resources to others, at the cost of our own substance, and they sell us back the goods which are made out of our resources. . . Our own interest cannot be protected and our people are becoming poorer every day. What can our nation rely upon? . . . For these reasons, in the winter of 1895 Chang Chih-tung memorialized the Throne and recommended that I should manage the cotton mill project. I did not calculate my own meager ability but at once took on the responsibility. Since then I have experienced the greatest inconstancy of human relationships and have been confronted by a thousand misfortunes and frustrations, in addition to frequent changes of the market. For five years I have had to bear insult and ridicule. Fortunately, the enterprise has not ended in collapse, not only because I have used all my limited ability, energy, and wisdom, but mostly because the higher authorities have sympathized with me; the local officials have given me the chance to carry out my plans; and a few gentlemen comrades have assisted and supported me. Now the building of the mill has been completed; the machinery is running; each of my co-workers has already undertaken one particular task as his special duty; each should have his authority defined and should not go beyond it or fail to live up to it. Thus the job will be done.

From this and other statements we can infer that the success of Chang Chien's enterprise was due to several factors: his own patience and endurance; his good connections with the local and higher provincial officials, based in part on the personal repute and high qualifications he had established through the civil service examinations. He was perhaps the first, if not also the last, Confucian industrialist. He worked many years without salary and sometimes resorted to selling his calligraphy in order to raise money for traveling expenses.[16] The hard struggle he had against social convention, which frowned upon any scholar's becoming a "merchant," is indicated in the following retrospective statement made to his shareholders in 1925 at the end of his career: [17]

Since I (Chang Chien) had the misfortune to live in a transitional period of Chinese history, I thrust myself into industrial circles. There I have suffered many hardships, and now in my declining years I cannot endure further distress and humiliation, and must beg the shareholders to recommend an able man to replace me. . . [P. 34] I am also a shareholder; I consider that the mill, the local self-government, and the national industrial development are all directly or indirectly related, and so the mill is of broad significance.

I was of farming stock and an indigent scholar. From youth I did not like to see rich and aristocratic men, nor did I like to interview famous dignitaries. Even if I went to an interview, I would not humble myself. . . . After I was thirty I became enraged at the weakness of China. After forty, when the Sino-Japanese War was concluded, I grew even more angry. I felt pity for our people's lack of ordinary knowledge, the result of our unchanged educational system and the inadequacy of our governmental reforms. I wished to carry out reforms myself, but I had no authority. After careful deliberation from all angles I concluded that we ought to begin with the development of industry. Yet I would have to make connections with rich men in order to develop an industry, and that went against the grain. I pondered it over and over again, and finally decided to give up my personal feelings and "offer my body to feed the tiger." I recognized the virtue of humbling myself for the cause of China, disregarding my private interest so that my purpose could be achieved and my integrity still be maintained. After I had made up my mind I had no regrets.

From 1896 to 1899 my first mill went through a critical period when I had to bear much blame and criticism, and to struggle vigorously for success while still taking a loss. From 1900 to 1901 was a period of gradual upturn; again I was in distress, but the danger was avoided. From 1902 to 1906 was a period of gradual success, and from 1907 to 1915 was a period of peaceful progress. . . For the second mill in 1907 and 1908 I was finding a site and building the factory; there was no gain but a net loss. From 1909 to 1915, however, there was a surplus every year. . . The first mill . . . in a total of twenty-seven years made a combined surplus and regular profit of Tls. 9,964,600. . . [P. 35] The second mill, . . . after it began operation, in sixteen years produced surplus and regular profits of Tls. 3,577,100. The two mills together thus made a profit of more than Tls. 13,481,700. . . The salary and bonuses that I earned, however, over more than twenty years, were mostly used for educational, philanthropic, and public welfare purposes. . .

Chang Chien treated his mill hands paternally and housed them in dormitories, following the Japanese practice. In 1903 he made a trip to that country. The influence of Japanese political institutions and industrial methods can be seen in these excerpts from his diaries:[18]

[P. 3] The Japanese rule their country as though taking care of a garden, or arranging a vase of flowers, for which even a small pebble or a piece of moss has been carefully prepared. Lao-tzu says, "To rule a large country is the same as cooking a small fish." The Japanese understand the essential idea of fixing a small fish. . .

[P. 7] In managing industry, the most important thing the Japanese have is the knowledge that to give is to get. With their material supplies coming from Europe and then flowing to China, they have been able to share in the profits of Europeans and make their country prosperous. Nevertheless, their wages are generally once or twice again as much as those in China. If our government tends to develop commerce, and to benefit the workers, we have five advantages over Japan: (1) abundant natural resources; (2) enough rice and cheap labor; (3) a chance to imitate the strong points of all nations so that the profits will not flow out of China; (4) a chance to meet the needs of our people's daily life so that they will need nothing from outside; and (5) a chance to compete for advancement in civilization with the whole world. . .

In Japan, all industrial manufactures are transported to other nations without paying extra customs duties. As to transportation, their railways are close to their factories and if they are not sufficient, the government subsidizes the products of the factories. The enthusiasm of the nation in encouraging industry is so great! Nevertheless, the country is small, rice expensive, and wages and costs of production are both increasing. The businessmen, however, are still ceaselessly devoting their energies to promoting industrialization. In competition with the civilization of the world, if there is no advancement, there will be retrogression, and this is understood by the Japanese. . .

[P. 13] I went to see a steel works in which steamships and small boats can be built. There are no Europeans among their workers. . . This makes me reflect upon the fact that the size and capital funds of our Shanghai Arsenal are many dozen times larger than those of the Japanese plant, and yet our Arsenal has never built a ship or made an instrument for agricultural or industrial use. Such instruments could be sold to the people at a profit, which could be used to subsidize agriculture and commerce, and then still more people could share the benefit. When we compare the two, what a difference! . . .

When Japanese scholar-officials become government workers or merchants, their selection of a profession is guided by their interests. When they are officials, they are devoted to their government work, and when they are merchants, they are devoted to commercial affairs. Chinese scholar-officials, when they are in official posts, also have some business plans, and when they are merchants, they still have an official air.

By 1910 Chang Chien controlled not only three cotton mills at Nantung and Shanghai, but also steamships and wharf companies to transport his products, a flour mill, an oil refinery, a distillery, and a salt manufacturing company. In a decade Nantung had become an industrial city. At the same time, the new city had gradually acquired a school system, starting with kindergartens and extending to Nantung College. The college included trade, normal, sericultural, agricultural, medical, and engineering schools. An orphanage, an old people's home, a hospital, schools for the blind, dumb, and disabled, and a new jail were also built. Roads, a library, a museum, and parks were constructed.[19] Most of this social development was due to Chang's initiative.

Chang Chien's reputation and moral integrity led to his selection for government posts. He was a leader in the provincial constitutional movement in the 1900's and chairman of the Kiangsu provisional assembly in 1909–1911. Invited by Dr. Sun Yat-sen to enter government service, he became minister of Agriculture and Commerce, and director-general of the National Water Conservancy Bureau from 1913 to 1915. He sponsored China's first company law and bankruptcy law. But Yuan shih-k'ai did not give him much authority to carry out his plans and he soon retired. In 1917 he opened a drama academy at Tungchow to which he invited famous playwrights and actors. In 1920 he invited Liang Ch'i-ch'ao and

John Dewey to give public lectures there. In a preface to the biography written by his son, Dr. Hu Shih says: "He alone opened many new roads: he was for thirty years a pioneer. He created employment for several million people and brought blessings to his locality; his influence was felt all over the country." [20]

The next extract, from Chang's inaugural speech as chief manager of the Han-Yeh-P'ing coal and iron company in 1913, indicates his general faith in industrialization, particularly his conviction that cotton and steel production was essential to China's progress — a view more widely held in China today than fifty years ago.[21]

From an examination of the Maritime Customs trade reports, I have concluded that the cotton and iron industries provide the chief basis of economic power. In the past I have been engaged in the cotton industry, and experienced many difficulties and hardships, with frequent frustrations and recoveries. I am not very familiar with the iron industry. . . Yet it is a ray of hope for China. Today the attention of the various nations is focused on China's only iron mill here. You managers and workers, who have gone through more than ten years of hardship, will not give up your struggle at the half-way point unless your resources are entirely exhausted. . . We should make every effort to go ahead . . . and plan a permanent enterprise for the nation. Employees should be hired only for their ability, and management should aim at actual achievement. . .

In a memorial urging government development of mining, Chang Chien wrote in 1914: [22]

I have learned that in manufacturing there is nothing more important than iron and steel, and in the whole economy nothing of greater importance than a good currency system. Among all the nations in both the eastern and the western hemispheres there is none without a government steel mill and mint and government mines for production of gold, silver, copper, and iron. In peace time these mines supply the needs of society, and in war time they meet the urgent need of the nation. . .

In our newly proclaimed mining law, only salt and petroleum are to be nationally owned; the development of mines is left open to free enterprise so that our government may show that it has no intention of contending for profit with its own people. Nevertheless such ores as iron and lead are not only indispensable [p. 4] for making steamships, rails, and machinery; they also provide the materials for guns and ammunition. The cost of opening such mines is enormous and there will be numerous defects if people are permitted to undertake it by themselves. They should be assisted by the power of the government in order to avoid unsuccessful operation like that of the Han-Yeh-P'ing company.

While Chang Chien's career has not yet been carefully studied and appraised, it is plain that he went far in bridging the gap between Confucianism and modern industry.

CHAPTER XXII. LIANG CH'I-CH'AO AND

NATIONALISM

Liang Ch'i-ch'ao in the early twentieth century became the most influential of all Chinese publicists. When he first rose to fame during the Reform Movement in 1898, his thought had been in line with that of his teacher, K'ang Yu-wei. But after they had both escaped abroad into exile in that year, K'ang made little change in his ideas, while Liang, as a refugee in Japan, a newspaper editor, and a voracious reader of Japanese and other new books, made great progress. Instead of admiring Mencius, he now liked to talk about Rousseau and Montesquieu; instead of urging the protection of Confucianism, he now tried in many respects to go beyond the scope of K'ang's ideas.

In Japan the name of his periodical was changed three times. From 1898 to 1901 it was called *Ch'ing-i pao*, "a paper of public opinions." After 1902 it was changed to *Hsin-min ts'ung-pao*, "a miscellaneous paper for a new people." After 1910 it became the *Kuo-feng pao*, "a paper for the national spirit." The second title has a special significance because, after the repeated failures of the self-strengthening movement and other reform movements, Liang Ch'i-ch'ao realized that not only must China's institutions and political and social systems undergo a change, but the Chinese people themselves must basically be reborn or rejuvenated. Hence the theme of the "new people" or "the renovation of the people" as the major motif of the magazine. It aimed to lead a patriotic, new culture movement.

As the decade after 1900 gave increasing evidence of the impending collapse of the dynasty, the way was opened for the rebel element among the Chinese scholar class to develop their theories of reform and try further to rationalize and understand the disaster which had overtaken China's ancient society. In this period, Liang Ch'i-ch'ao appeared to represent the more significant wing of the rebel reformers. While he was less of a political organizer than Sun Yat-sen, Liang symbolized for the student class the great tradition of Chinese scholarship, face to face with the unprecedented problems posed by the West. His wide-ranging interests and eloquent style gave his writings great force, and there is little doubt that he taught his generation many lessons in the principles of patriotism and citizenship, as well as in political theory generally. The following essay of 1902, "The renovation of the people," from the first issue of his periodical *Hsin-min ts'ung-pao*, had its original classical connotation and has also had its unworthy historical descendant, in the "New people's principles" (*Hsin-min chu-i*), with which the Japanese puppet government of North China after 1937 tried to compete with the "Three people's principles" (*San-min chu-i*) and the Kuomintang. Mao Tse-tung's "New Democracy" (*Hsin min-chu chu-i*) is today a sort of semantic nephew of Liang Ch'i-ch'ao's *Hsin-min*.

After the abolition of the eight-legged essay, young Chinese students were no longer supplied with fixed models to follow in writing essays. Liang Ch'i-ch'ao's articles were widely read for their style in the schools of the Republic as late as the 1930's. He was a powerful and emotional writer, and articles such as this roused a whole generation to formulate and meet new issues. Whatever his eventual place as a philosopher of change in modern China, Liang made an enormous contribution to the promotion of patriotism in the early part of the twentieth century.

DOC. 55. "The Renovation of the People" by Liang Ch'i-ch'ao, 1902 [1]

A state is formed by the assembly of its people. The relationship of a nation to its people resembles that of the body to its four limbs, five viscera, muscles, veins, and corpuscles. There has never been a case where the four limbs have been cut off, the five viscera wasted away, the muscles and veins injured, and the corpuscles dried up, while the body still lived. In the same way, there has never been a nation which could still exist if its people were foolish, timid, disorganized, and confused. Therefore, if we wish [p. 2] the body to live for a long time, the methods of hygiene must be understood. If we wish the nation to be secure, rich, and respectable, the methods for creating a new people must be discussed.

The Renovation of the People as the First
and Most Urgent Matter for China Today

Now I wish to explain thoroughly why a new people is the most urgent and necessary matter. My argument has two bases. One concerns domestic administration and the other concerns diplomatic affairs.

What concerns domestic administration? There are many in the country who are discussing political methods. They would say, A misgoverns the nation or B injures the people; a certain case is a mistake of the government, and a certain system is the fault of officials who have neglected their duty. I do not presume to say that such things are not true. Nevertheless, how is the government formed? Where do the officials come from? Do they not come from among the populace? Is A or B not a member of the citizenry? . . . [p. 3] Why do we have to worry about the lack of a new system, a new government, and a new nation? Even though today we change a law and tomorrow we replace a person, a little painting in the east, a little touch in the west, learning and imitating, I cannot see that there is much help. Why, then, in our country where the new institutions have been discussed for several decades, are the results invisible? It is because we have not yet paid attention to the theory of a new people. . .

[P. 5] What concerns diplomatic affairs? Since the sixteenth century, about four hundred years ago, the reason for European development and world progress has been the stimulation and growth of extensive nationalist feeling everywhere. What does nationalism mean? It is that in all places people of the same race, the same language, the same religion, and the same customs regard each other as brothers and work for independence and self-government, and organize a more perfect government to work for the public welfare and to oppose the infringement of other races. When this idea had developed to an extreme at the end of the nineteenth century, it went further and became national imperialism within the last twenty or thirty years. What does national imperialism mean? It means that the industrial power of the citizens of a nation has been fully developed domestically and must flow to the outside, and thus they industriously seek to enlarge their powers in other (dependent) regions as appendages. The way of doing it is by military power, commerce, industry or religion, but they use a central policy to direct and protect these activities. . . Now, on the Asiatic continent there is located the largest country with the most fertile territory, the most corrupt [p. 6] government, and the most disorganized and weak people. As soon as the European race discovered our internal condition, they mobilized their national imperialism as swarms of ants attach themselves to what is rank and foul and as a myriad of arrows concentrate on a target. They were scattered but they concentrated in this corner, the Russians in Manchuria, the Germans in Shantung, the English in the Yangtze valley, the French in Kwangtung and Kwangsi, and the Japanese in Fukien. All are urged on by the tide of the new "ism" (national imperialism). They cannot help doing this. . .

[P. 7] If we wish to oppose the national imperialism of all the powers today and save China from great calamity and rescue our people, the only thing for us to do is to adopt the policy of promoting our own nationalism. If we wish to promote nationalism in China, there is no other means of doing it except through the renovation of the people.

Today, over the whole country, everybody is worrying about the foreign trouble. Nevertheless, if the foreigners can really cause us trouble, it cannot be ended just by worrying. The stubbornness and aggressiveness of national imperialism is very severe, and yet we are still discussing whether the foreigners can really cause us trouble or not. How foolish we are! I think the existence or non-existence of the trouble will not be decided by the foreigners, but by our domestic condition. In general, all nations are certainly using the same "ism." But why does Russia not apply it to England, and England not apply it to Germany, and Germany not apply it to America, and the various countries of Europe and America not apply it to Japan? It depends on whether there is a chance for doing so or not. . . Thus, in consideration of present-day China, we must not depend upon a temporary wise emperor or minister to allay the disorder, nor expect a sudden rise of one or two heroes from the rural countryside to lead our struggle for success; it is necessary to have our people's virtue, people's wisdom, and people's power of the whole number of four hundred million all become equal to that of the foreigners — then they naturally cannot cause us trouble and we need not worry about them. . .

Explanation of the Meaning of "The New People"

The term "new people" does not mean that our people must give up entirely what is old in order to follow others. There are two meanings of "new." One is to temper and grind what is original in the people and so renew it; the other is to adopt what was originally lacking in the people and so make a new people. Without one of the two, there will be no success. . .

Generally, a nation which can endure in the world must have some peculiar characteristics on the part of its nationals. From morals and laws down to customs, habits, literature, and fine arts, all share a kind of independent spirit which has been handed down from grandfather to father and inherited by their descendants. Thus the group is formed and the nation develops. This is really the fundamental source of nationalism. Our people have been established as a nation on the Asiatic continent for several thousand years, and we must have some characteristics which are grand, eminent, and perfect, and distinctly different from those of other races; we should preserve these and not let them be lost. What is called preserving, however, is not to let (the spirit of the people) naturally appear and grow and carelessly say, "I'm preserving it, I'm preserving it." It is like a tree — unless some new boughs come out every year, its withering may soon be expected; as with a well — unless there is always some new spring bubbling, its exhaustion is not far away. Are the new boughs and the new spring coming from the outside? They are old, and yet we cannot but call them new. Only if we can make something new every day can we find the means to keep the old complete. . .

[P. 9] If we wish to make our nation strong, we must investigate extensively the methods followed by all other nations and races in becoming independent. Selecting their superior points, we can appropriate them to make up our own shortcomings. Now with regard to politics, academic ideas, and techniques, our critics know how to take the superior points of others to fill up our own gaps; but they do not know that the people's virtue, the people's wisdom, and the people's power are really the great source of politics, academic learning, and techniques. If they do not take this but adopt that, neglect the roots but tend the branches, it will be no different from seeing the luxuriant growth of another tree and wishing to graft its branches on to our withered trunk, or seeing the bubbling flow of another well and wishing to take some of the water to fill up our own dry well. Thus, to adopt and make up what we originally lacked in order to renovate our people should be deeply and carefully considered. . .

[P. 10] All the phenomena in the world are governed by no more than two great principles: one is conservative and the other is aggressive. Those who are applying these two principles are inclined either to the one or to the other. Sometimes the two arise simultaneously and conflict with each other; and sometimes the two exist simultaneously and compromise with each other. No one can exist who is inclined only to one. Where there is conflict, there must be compromise, and conflict is the forerunner of compromise. He who is good at making compromises is a great citizen, such as you find among the Anglo-Saxon race. . . Thus what I mean by "new people" are not those who are intoxicated with Western customs, despising the morals, academic learning, and customs of our several-thousand-year-old country in order to keep company with others; nor are they those who stick to old paper and say that merely embracing the several thousand years of our own morals, academic learning, and customs will be sufficient to enable us to stand up on the great earth.

CHAPTER XXIII. SUN YAT-SEN'S EARLY

REVOLUTIONARY PROGRAM

Compared with the imposing prestige of Liang Ch'i-ch'ao, a leader of the scholarly elite who had been for a time near the font of power and might be there again, Sun Yat-sen (1866–1925) in his early days was something of a half-caste. Educated in Hawaii and Hongkong as well as in his native village near Macao, trained in Western medicine and only semi-trained in the Chinese classics, he never became an insider among the upper-class literati. His schemes and promotions, in league with Japanese liberal-expansionists and among Chinese merchants and laundrymen overseas, eventually led to the organization of a following which financed rebellions. Sun and the Kuomintang had their origin on the cultural frontier between China and the West. Like many of his followers, he came from the Canton delta, which had known foreign trade longer than any other area in China and had already led the way in nationalistic anti-foreignism. Sun's thinking was not formed in the Confucian mold nor, in fact, in any particular mold. This fitted him to play a shifting ideological role in a period of rapid change.

The revolutionary movement led by Sun Yat-sen, which he had launched in a minor way soon after the Sino-French war of 1884–85, developed side by side with the imperial reform program. In those first days, however, Sun had not yet reached any conclusive political principles. His program for China's reconstruction developed more slowly than his persistent plotting to overthrow the Manchus.

From the time of the Sino-Japanese war Sun's political ideas became somewhat more definite. Their development can be roughly divided into two main periods. The first is represented by such records as his letter to Li Hung-chang and the Manifesto of the Hsing-Chung-hui (Revive China Society), both dated 1894. The former was a plan for the economic development of China which Sun asserted was necessary for the salvation of the country; reliance on ships and cannon was not enough. As may be seen in the following excerpts,[1] Sun was concerned at this time almost exclusively with developing competent personnel and carrying out technological improvements; his letter does not indicate any interest in the possibility or prospect of social reorganization aside from the adoption of Western technology.

[P. 7] After deep reflection, I realize that the roots of wealth and power in Europe do not lie entirely in solid ships, efficient guns, strong forts, and crack troops, but also in that a man can use his talents to the utmost, a piece of land can produce to the utmost, natural resources can be exploited to the utmost, and commercial goods be circulated almost without restriction. . .

[P. 9] Without good education a man's talents will be wasted; without tactful encouragement, a scholar will live in melancholy in the countryside, and without a rational employment policy, a man in the government may be advanced by sheer good luck. If attention were paid to these three things in their proper order, then a man would be able to use his ability to the utmost. . .

[P. 11] A department in charge of agricultural administration can make the people work hard; special researches on agriculture can improve plant and animal husbandry; and agricultural machines can save human labor. These three procedures should be studied and imitated by our country in order to raise the yield of the land. . .

[P. 12] If machines are widely used, it is easy to open mines, to dredge rivers, and to weave and make cloth, all for the benefit of the people. . . Light, heat, and electricity are examples of common natural resources available to all nations; the degree to which they are put to practical use, however, varies with the degree of technological advance. The five metals and the various kinds of grain, on the other hand, are products of the earth which are not possessed by all nations and which furthermore require skill to produce and use.

[P. 13] A high circulation of commercial goods is contingent upon the removal of [numerous transit] taxes and upon effective laws for the protection of commerce, and possession of many steamships and railways for transport. . . Commerce is of great concern to a nation's wealth and power.

[P. 15] When a man can use his ability to the utmost, all enterprises will be undertaken; when the land can yield to the utmost, people will have enough to eat; when natural resources can be exploited to the utmost, the national economic strength will be great; when commodities can be circulated without restriction, financial resources will be abundant. Thus these four elements are the principal sources of wealth and power, and provide the solid foundations of a nation. . . We need not be concerned about our ability to bring off a large enterprise in this country but we should worry about the lack of people to do it. The weakness of China today is caused not only by the shortage of able people, but also by the large number of ignorant people. The small number of able people can be supplemented by inviting in foreign experts. . . But the large number of ignorant people, even though replaced by others who could do their work, would still try their best to hinder any new enterprise. That is why whenever a new enterprise is undertaken in our nation it is either restricted by precedents or impeded by a flood of criticism. That is the principal cause of the illness of Chinese society. . .

I have admired you, Grand Secretary [Li Hung-chang], . . . [as one] who considers the recruiting of talented men as an urgent matter. . . A person like me may also be drilled and enlisted among your employees. Therefore I disregard the modest dimensions of my own ability in order to seek your recognition. . .

[P. 17] Among the four great items, . . . although the training of personnel in schools to be established throughout the empire should be a matter of high priority, . . . the improvement of agriculture is even more urgent. . . Since our country has attempted to adopt Western knowledge I have never heard anyone speak of the imitation of western agricultural methods. . .

[P. 19] I plan to travel to France this year [1894] to study under famous experts on sericulture. . . I also plan to travel all over the world to investigate agricultural work. . . I sincerely hope that the Grand Secretary will help me to carry out these plans. . .

According to the party historian, Tsou Lu, Li Hung-chang is said to have taken great interest in this letter and to have given Sun a passport in order that he might raise funds abroad for agriculture and sericulture.

Meanwhile, however, Sun observed that Li was old as well as lacking in initiative, revolutionary ardor, and breadth of view; furthermore, China under the Manchu government soon suffered defeat by Japan. He therefore went to Honolulu to organize the Hsing-Chung-hui. Had he been employed by Li Hung-chang as a secretary or in some other capacity he might well have developed into a different person, and had a different career.

The Manifesto of the Hsing-Chung-hui [2] claimed to deal with the political problem of China. Sun was in touch with secret societies, particularly the Triads, who were strongest in South China and overseas, and was now preaching revolution. The Manifesto was mainly a condemnation of the corruption and weakness of the Ch'ing government, while the purpose of the organization was stated to be the revival of China against government repression and foreign aggression. All of this was formulated in rather vague and indirect terms. Republicanism had not yet become a force to attract those who were radically dissatisfied with the existing situation.

According to Sun's own account, it was during his two-year sojourn in Europe (1896–1898) that the general outline of his later *San-min chu-i*, the "Three people's principles," was formed. He discovered that with all their technology and nationalism, the Western nations were still beset by disturbing economic and social problems. Ideas that finally led to the principle of the people's livelihood (*min-sheng*, an ancient phrase) germinated in his mind. Apart from the intellectual influences of the West, Sun had the melodramatic experience of being "kidnapped" or detained in the Chinese Legation at London in 1896 and saved from deportation and death only by the effort of British friends and the Foreign Office itself. This hair-raising episode was a powerful stimulus toward compelling him to bring his revolutionary aims into more concrete form, inasmuch as he seemed thereafter more than ever marked for leadership. Still not completely disillusioned with the old official hierarchy, however, Sun Yat-sen is said to have approached Li Hung-chang again during the Boxer incident and urged him to declare his independence from the Manchu government, so that his independent regime might then become a democratic republic. Nothing came of this proposal.

This incident of 1900 seems to have marked the transition into the second period of Sun's early revolutionary thought. Now the political aim of the revolution had become definitely republicanism, the rallying sentiment of the movement, nationalism. The means was to be revolution by force. Like the French of 1789, Sun believed that all old structures could be torn down and new ones set up in their place; but, in addition, he showed himself also strongly influenced by the nineteenth century cult of science, in that he drew up precise formulae for the revolution, and believed that it could be carried out according to a blue-print.

All this crystallized in the Manifesto issued at the founding of the T'ung-meng-hui at Tokyo in 1905. The program laid down in this document was elsewhere referred to by its author as the "revolutionary program." Political questions were predominant in it. Sun Yat-sen deserves great credit, certainly, for his success in formulating here the central idea of China's modern political revolution: the conception of political tutelage by a provisional government which would train the politically-inert Chinese populace for eventual participation in a constitutional democracy. The three stages set forth in his manifesto of 1905 have remained theoretically valuable ever since, even though political practice has fallen short.

This manifesto of 1905 also strikes a new and truly revolutionary note in espousing the equalization of land ownership — in short, land redistribution — an old device, but a potent one. This idea, among all the desiderata and panaceas which have been quoted above, no doubt appears here because this is one of the first Chinese documents of modern times which was written explicitly for purposes of political revolt. This fact makes it all the more remarkable, however, that no scholar or high official seems to have raised earlier the issue of land redistribution as a possible element in self-strengthening or reform. The fact is that all the long line of individuals we have thus far quoted in this volume had shied away from the idea of fundamental revolution in the Chinese way of life. Before the time of Liang and Sun, they had all failed to consider the possibility of raising the condition of the peasantry to that of literate, property-owning, economically-independent, politically-active citizens. Even Liang was more aware of the "new citizen's" duties than of his rights, while Sun was not able to keep land reform in the forefront of his mind or program. This Western liberal conception, which began to drift into the Chinese scene in the 1900's, had certainly never entered into the calculations of the Empress Dowager or Chang Chih-tung in the declining years of the Ch'ing, for it was antithetic to the privileged status of the landlord-scholar-official class on which the old order was based.

Besides setting forth the aims of the revolutionists, the 1905 manifesto was also to serve as a proclamation by local revolutionary regimes at a future time, wherever an uprising should take place.

DOC. 56. THE MANIFESTO OF THE T'UNG-MENG-HUI, 1905 [3]

By order of the Military Government, on the —— day, —— month, —— year of T'ien-yun,[4] the Commander-in-Chief of the Chinese National Army proclaims the purposes and platform of the Military Government to the people of the nation:

Now the National Army has established the Military Government, which aims to cleanse away two hundred and sixty years of barbarous filth, restore our four-thousand-year-old fatherland, and plan for the welfare of the four hundred million people. Not only is this an unavoidable obligation of the Military Government, but all our fellow-nationals should also take it as their own responsibility. We recall that, since the beginning of our nation the Chinese have always ruled China; although [p. 2] at times alien peoples have usurped the rule, yet our ancestors were able to drive them out and restore Chinese sovereignty so that they could hand down the nation to posterity. Now the men of Han [i.e., the Chinese] have raised a righteous [or patriotic] army to exterminate the northern barbarians. This is a continuation of heroic deeds bequeathed to us by our predecessors, and a great righteous cause lies behind it; there is none among us Chinese who does not understand this. But the revolutions in former generations, such as the Ming Dynasty and the Taiping Heavenly Kingdom, were concerned only with the driving out of barbarians and the restoration of Chinese rule. Aside from these they sought no other change. We today are different from people of former times. Besides the driving out of the barbarian dynasty and the restoration of China, it is necessary also to change the national polity and the people's livelihood. And though there are a myriad ways and means to achieve this goal, the essential spirit that runs through them all is freedom, equality, and fraternity. Therefore in former days there were heroes' revolutions, but today we have a national revolution [Kuo-min ko-ming, lit., revolution of the people of the country]. "National revolution" means that all people in the nation will have the spirit of freedom, equality, and fraternity; that is, they will all bear the responsibility of revolution. The Military Government is but their agent. From now on the people's responsibility will be the responsibility of the Military Government, and the achievements of the Military Government will be those of the people. With a coöperative mind and concerted effort, the Military Government and the people will thus perform their duty. Therefore we proclaim to the world in utmost sincerity the outline of the present revolution and the fundamental plan for the future administration of the nation.

1) *Drive out the Tartars*: The Manchus of today were originally the eastern barbarians beyond the Great Wall. They frequently caused border

troubles during the Ming dynasty; then when China was in a disturbed state they came inside Shanhaikuan, conquered China, and enslaved our Chinese people. Those who opposed them were killed by the hundreds of thousands, and our Chinese have been a people without a nation for two hundred and sixty years. The extreme cruelties and tyrannies of the Manchu government have now reached their limit. With the righteous army poised against them, we will overthrow that government, and restore our sovereign rights. Those Manchu and Chinese military men who have a change of heart and come over to us will be granted amnesty, while those who dare to resist will be slaughtered without mercy. Chinese who act as Chinese traitors in the cause of the Manchus will be treated in the same way.

2) *Restore China*: China is the China of the Chinese. The government of China should be in the hands of the Chinese. After driving out the Tartars we must restore our national state. Those who dare to act like Shih Ching-t'ang or Wu San-kuei [both were traitors] [5] will be attacked by the whole country.

3) *Establish the Republic*: Now our revolution is based on equality, in order to establish a republican government. All our people are equal and all enjoy political rights. The president will be publicly chosen by the people of the country. The parliament will be made up of members publicly chosen by the people of the country. A constitution of the Chinese Republic will be enacted, and every person must abide by it. Whoever dares to make himself a monarch shall be attacked by the whole country.

4) *Equalize land ownership*: [6] The good fortune of civilization is to be shared equally by all the people of the nation. We should improve our social and economic organization, and assess the value of all the land in the country. Its present price shall be received by the owner, but all increases in value resulting from reform and social improvements after the revolution shall belong to the state, to be shared by all the people, in order to create a socialist state, where each family within the empire can be well supported, each person satisfied, and no one fail to secure employment. Those who dare to control the livelihood of the people through monopoly shall be ostracized.

The above four points will be carried out in three steps in due order. The first period is government by military law. When the righteous army has arisen, various places will join the cause. The common people of each locality will escape from the Manchu fetters. Those who come upon the enemy must unite in hatred of him, must join harmoniously with the compatriots within their ranks and suppress the enemy bandits. Both the armies and the people will be under the rule of military law. The armies will do their best in defeating the enemy on behalf of the people, and the people will supply the needs of the armies, and not do harm to their security. The local administration, in areas where the enemy has been either already defeated or not yet defeated, will be controlled in general by the Military Government, so that step by step the accumulated evils can be swept away. Evils like the oppression of the government, the greed and graft of officials, the squeeze of government clerks and runners, the cruelty of tortures and penalties, the tyranny of tax collections, the humiliation of the queue — shall all be exterminated together with the Manchu rule. Evils in social customs, such as the keeping of slaves, the cruelty of foot-binding, the spread of the poison of opium, the obstructions of geomancy (*feng-shui*), should also all be prohibited. The time limit for each district (*hsien*) is three years. In those *hsien* where real results are achieved before the end of three years, the military law shall be lifted and a provisional constitution shall be enacted.

The second period is that of government by a provisional constitution. When military law is lifted in each *hsien*, the Military Government shall return the right of self-government to the local people. The members of local councils and local officials shall all be elected by the people. All rights and duties of the Military Government toward the people and those of the people toward the government shall be regulated by the provisional constitution, which shall be observed by the Military Government, the local councils, and the people. Those who violate the law shall be held responsible. Six years after the securing of peace in the nation the provisional constitution shall be annulled and the constitution shall be promulgated.

The third period will be government under the constitution. Six years after the provisional constitution has been enforced a constitution shall be made. The military and administrative powers of the Military Government shall be annulled; the people shall elect the president, and elect the members of parliament to organize the parliament. The administrative matters of the nation shall proceed according to the provisions of the constitution.

Of these three periods the first is the period in which the Military Government leads the people in eradicating all traditional evils and abuses; the second is the period in which the Military Government gives the power of local self-government to the people while retaining general control over national affairs; the third is the period in which the Military Government is divested of its powers, and the government will by itself manage the national affairs under the constitution. It is hoped that our people will proceed in due order and cultivate their free and equal status; the foundation of the Chinese Republic will be entirely based on this.

[The last paragraph of the manifesto consists of an exhortation to the Chinese people to rise to the occasion, support the ever-faithful Military Government, and shoulder the responsibility of protecting the country and preserving their own ancient and superior race.]

7

IDEOLOGICAL FERMENT AND

THE MAY FOURTH MOVEMENT

1912–1923

CHAPTER XXIV. THE SEARCH FOR NEW PRINCIPLES

a. The Variety of the New Thought

The fall of the Chinese Empire in 1912, after its long decline, came as something of an anti-climax. The rise to power of Yuan Shih-k'ai almost immediately afterward gave the impression that the revolution of 1911 had been one of history's failures. Not only was Sun Yat-sen, the founder of the Republic, disillusioned, but many intellectuals were in a quandary. The old political and ethical code centered on loyalty to the throne had been destroyed, and a new code suitable for parliamentary government had not been established.

Subsequent events have shown, however, that the end of Manchu rule in 1912 and the demise of Yuan in 1916 really served to take the lid off — all sorts of ideological conceptions, movements, fads and experiments bubbled forth, stimulated by the strenuous political events of the period. Within a period of six years the modern generation of Chinese scholars, a considerable number of whom had now had experience abroad, went through the abortive "Second Revolution" of the Kuomintang against Yuan in 1913, Japan's seizure of Kiaochow from Germany in 1914, and her presentation of the Twenty-one Demands in 1915. They also saw Yuan's final failure to become emperor in 1916, China's entrance into the World War, the Russian Revolution and the Allied intervention in Siberia, and finally the struggle over the award of Germany's Shantung holdings to Japan at the peace conference of 1919. It is little wonder that the May Fourth Movement of 1919 ushered in a new era of Chinese history.

The decade from 1912 to 1923, since it is both recent and revolutionary, has been difficult to study. Historians have sadly neglected it. It should appear in time to have been one of the great germinal periods in the realm of Chinese thought. As indicated in our Introduction, this survey makes no attempt to go beyond 1923 because after that date the impact of Marxism-Leninism on Chinese thought and politics obviously becomes one of the central problems awaiting study, and it is treated by others elsewhere.[1] It is also plain that our treatment of the period 1912–1923 is likely to be the least adequate and satisfactory of any section of this survey — which merely accentuates the necessity that it be studied.

This section presents first some selections from Ts'ai Yuan-p'ei, whose thought represented an attempt at synthesis between the Chinese classical tradition and the libertarianism of the Modern European West. Ch'en Tu-hsiu in his early phase similarly reflected the ideas of the French Revolution, with a heavy accent on individual freedom. In his later phase he moved toward Leninism, as did Li Ta-chao. This trend in the direction of the Russian Revolution led to the fundamental split, in which Hu Shih as an apostle of Dewey and pragmatism represents the other line of development. Clearly in these men we have protagonists of the two great camps which have now come to divide the world: it is certainly significant that several Chinese leaders of the period at one time or another had a foot in either camp.

The various strains of thought in the post-1911 period arose out of one great common problem: how to determine and define the values and goals of the new republican era. This effort was necessitated by the deep crisis which had overtaken Chinese civilization, of which all intellectuals were acutely conscious. Conflicts of opinion rapidly developed over fundamental problems such as the relationship between the material and spiritual phases of life, the significance of the scientific method, the merits of materialism and of nationalism, the choice between Westernization or preservation of a "national essence" (kuo-ts'ui), and the doctrines of socialism, anarchism, and communism. All these discussions were attempts at the ideological reconstruction of Chinese life.

Before proceeding to the writings of individuals, let us note some of the protagonists of major attitudes. During and after the first World War, the attitude of revulsion and disgust toward Western materialistic civilization was expressed by Ku Hung-ming, who considered that Western utilitarian culture could not develop the inner mind, and that China's spiritual civilization was so perfect that it could save China and also rescue Western culture from its crisis. Ku regarded Western culture as based on materialism, terrorism, and greed. He strenuously opposed science and machines, warships and railways. He urged his countrymen to cultivate a richer inner life and live in the Chinese mode. As a gesture, he kept his queue against all criticism.

Liang Ch'i-ch'ao in his last phase shared this revulsion toward the West. His account of his travels after the first World War, entitled "A record of impressions during travel in Europe" (Ou-yu hsin-ying lu chieh-lu), argued that Europeans overemphasized science and overdeveloped their material culture. This fostered the habit of serving up the weak as meat for the strong, and created a society where people fought one another. Western civilization was bankrupt; scientific inventions had encouraged warfare and the ruthless destruction of cultural traits. The whole of European society seemed to have sunk into a state of suspicion, melancholy, and fear — in short, into confusion in the spiritual world.

On this issue, Hu Shih parted company with Liang and condemned those who criticized Western culture as materialistic and admired Eastern culture as spiritual. He did not consider the material and spiritual aspects of culture to be alternatives or antitheses, but contended that spiritual culture must be built on a base of material culture. He pointed out that Western culture did not neglect the desires of the human spirit and the mind. He espoused John Dewey's pragmatism.

Wu Chih-hui (Wu Ching-heng, b. 1864–1953), best known as a Kuomintang stalwart, had received the traditional Chinese education, but became a staunch supporter of Western scientific civilization. Except in the writings of political followers, his defense of materialism has not been seriously studied. It appears to represent an influential line of thought among the early Kuomintang leaders.

Philosophical eclecticism was represented in this early republican period by Chang Tung-sun, who has had a long career as philosopher, publicist, and professor. His ideas have changed from one era to the next since the latter years of the Ch'ing monarchy. In the 1940's he became a leader of the Democratic League. During the early part of the first World War he urged that China thoroughly adopt the culture of Western civilization. Later on, from his actual observation of Chinese society, he decided that China could not entirely follow the West. Ever since China had received Western culture, her politics had become more confused, peace had disappeared, society had grown more disturbed, and improvement imperceptible. He concluded that if China adopted Western material culture entirely, Chinese society would develop in an abnormal form. He had the notion that the best way out was to revive China's spiritual culture in order to balance Western material culture.

Another scholar of similar thought was Chang Hsing-yen (Chang Shih-chao, b. 1881–   ), a jurist trained in Japan and England, a specialist on logic and a writer well known for his limpid and terse style. He became the editor of the *Chia-yin tsa-chih*, founded in 1914, and translated the works of Walter Bagehot, John Motley, and others. After advocating a liberal constitutional government, he finally turned against the Western political system, on the ground that China was an agricultural country. To apply the governmental system of industrial countries to an agricultural country was like putting a tiger's skin on a sheep — the latter could never fight against a real tiger. The Chinese spirit was to be content with poverty and to enjoy life, while Westerners stressed money, using it for political activities. Since China's industry was in an infant stage and even her agriculture was not yet highly developed, Chang concluded it was a great mistake for her to try to imitate Western political institutions.

The earliest advocate of anarchism was Liu Shih-fu, a Cantonese who organized the *Hui-ming hsueh-hui* (Society of the cry of dawn) to promote it. In 1907 another Kuomintang leader, Li Shih-tseng (Li Yü-ying), with Wu Chih-hui and others published a "New Era Weekly" in Paris, introducing the theories of Bakunin and Kropotkin to China. After the "Weekly" was suspended in 1910 and Wang Shih-fu died in 1915, this attempt subsided. Following the May Fourth Movement, Wu Chih-hui and Li Shih-tseng returned to China from France, still ostensibly believing in anarchism, but with their ideas greatly modified.

Needless to say, this roster of individual points of view could be indefinitely extended; we have not even mentioned the die-hard classicist Chang Ping-lin (Chang T'ai-yen, 1868–1936), who spent his last years fighting the New Thought and its literary movement tooth and nail, although he had formerly been a revolutionist and an editor of the republican journal *Min-pao* in Japan. There were many other equally distinguished personalities in the early Republic.

In the following sections we have tried to represent the intellectual growth of certain leaders of the day. Events have moved so rapidly in twentieth-century China that by clinging to certain views a radical might find himself soon grown conservative. Serious study should reveal that through all these vicissitudes there was a well-defined trend toward the development of values and cultural ideals among the Chinese intellectual elite, leading up to the revolutionary mass movements of recent decades. It is at least remarkable that Ts'ai Yuan-p'ei, Ch'en Tu-hsiu, Li Ta-chao, Hu Shih, and Liang Ch'i-ch'ao should all have been more or less central figures in the intellectual circles of Peking, members of the same social stratum and community. The examples of Ts'ai's writings chosen from the years 1912 and 1919, like those of Hu Shih in 1919 and 1922 (Ch. XXVI), show a steady growth in the Western liberal tradition; whereas our selections from Ch'en Tu-hsiu in 1915 and 1923 (Ch. XXV) reflect his desertion of individualism and espousal of Marxism as a new path to China's salvation — a step which was less remarked upon in America at the time than it may be in the second half of the twentieth century. Similarly Liang Ch'i-ch'ao, in his facile and masterly survey (Ch. XXVIII) of the turbulent period traversed by the present volume — in so much of which he had himself been a protagonist — shows in 1922 the same faith in rationalism and in progress that had characterized his revolutionary period, much as some of his judgments had changed with the passage of time; whereas Sun Yat-sen, in the passages we quote from 1919 and 1923 (Ch. XXVII), obviously went through a considerable reorientation, almost comparable to that of Ch'en Tu-hsiu.

The comment may be made that those intellectuals who became most active in revolutionary politics were the same ones who deserted the Western liberal tradition, to greater or less degree — almost as though this desertion were a necessary step in the process of organizing revolutionary power in China. Without arguing the extent to which the early Ch'en Tu-hsiu and Sun Yat-sen may be classed as genuine "liberals," or the extent to which they eventually accepted Marxist-Leninist political institutions, it still seems possible to suggest that by the 1920's the problems of revolutionary politics in China had proved impossible of direct solution on a Western-type "liberal" basis. This brings us, by 1923, to the opening of a new era in Chinese history, and a stopping-place for this survey.

b. Ts'ai Yuan-p'ei and Freedom in Education

Ts'ai Yuan-p'ei (1867–1940) was the leading liberal educator of early Republican China. He served as the first minister of education of the Republic (1912–1913), chancellor of National Peking University (1917–1927), and co-founder and director (1928–1940) of the *Chung-yang yen-chiu-yuan*, or Academia Sinica, the highest research institute of Nationalist China.[2] Through his early campaign for freedom in education, the May Fourth Movement of 1919 was fostered and the "new tide" of thought was largely made possible. Many eminent political and academic leaders of the past generation in China were trained at Peita (i.e., Peking University, *Pei-ching ta-hsueh*) under Dr. Ts'ai's influence.

Ts'ai Yuan-p'ei was remarkable because he had received a traditional Chinese education and had risen to the top as a member of the Hanlin Academy, and yet was not confined by Confucian patterns of thought. On the contrary, he revolted against the formality of Confucianism, proposing the abolition of the worship of Confucius in the schools, and promoting the scientific study of the Confucian classics under the new academic departments of Chinese literature, history, and philosophy — but not as a required subject for every student.

Dr. Ts'ai became well versed in Western philosophy, taking particular interest in Kropotkin, Darwin, Nietzsche, Wundt, Le Bon, and other similar writers. In 1912, after resigning from the first Republican cabinet, he went to Europe and made a study of world civilizations at the University of Leipzig. He wrote a book dealing with the principles of philosophy while he was in France during the first World War and another volume on the history of European esthetics. His history of Chinese ethics (*Chung-kuo lun-li-hsueh shih*, 1931) was also succinctly and ably written. He is generally considered a "synthesizer of Western and Chinese thought," [3] but his main contribution was undoubtedly in promoting freedom of education and freedom of thought. He believed academic institutions should be free from government control or interference. Kuomintang writers have hailed the intellectual movement guided by Ts'ai Yuan-p'ei as "aimed at a rebirth of the old Chinese civilization by discovering the foundation of Western strength and absorbing its essence into their own philosophy so as to effect a new synthesis on an intellectual and spiritual basis." [4] He was unquestionably outstanding as a man of principle and integrity. Although a senior member of the Kuomintang, he resigned his positions and retired to Hongkong for the rest of his life when he became dissatisfied with the trend of events at Nanking.

The following document shows the strong Kantian trend of Ts'ai's thought and his consistent effort to find correspondences between Confucian and Western ethics and philosophy, in the period when he was China's first modern minister of education.

DOC. 57. Ts'ai Yuan-p'ei's Views on the Aims of Education, 1912 [5]

In recent days I have been drafting new school regulations with my associates in the Ministry of Education to prepare for the calling of a higher education conference. I have had the honor to be given some grand ideas by my comrades, but there are few that concern educational policy. Hence I express my own humble ideas first as a prelude. I shall be fortunate if educators in the nation will correct me.

There are two great kinds of education: one is subordinate to politics, the other is above politics. During the monarchical period (I refer also to constitutional government of a monarchical nature) educators followed the policy of the government and considered the model education to be purely subordinate to government. In the republican period, educators can set up a standard based upon the situation of the people and thus we may have education beyond political control.

Near the end of the Ch'ing dynasty the education which was subordinate to the government, and which was widely talked about by educators, was called "military education for the citizen" (*chün kuo-min chiao-yü*). Generally speaking "military education for the citizen" is contradictory to socialism, and there have already been signs of its decline in other countries. Nevertheless, in our country, where strong neighbors are all oppressing us, we have to plan hastily for self-protection, and our national rights which have been lost during successive years are, in the circumstances, difficult to recover without relying on military power. Moreover, after a revolution by the militarists, it is hard to guarantee [p. 190] that there will not be a period when the militarists will wield political power. Unless we adopt a universal military system, we shall have no way to balance the military power, and the militarist group will become a permanent special caste in the whole country. Hence today we really must adopt the so-called "military education for the citizen . . ."

There is a second kind of education which is subordinate to government and which is called "utilitarian education" (*shih-li chu-i chih chiao-yü*), in which the people's livelihood forms the nucleus of common education. Those who advocate this most rigorously go to an extreme in saying that all general learning is entirely included in forestry, cooking, sewing, metallurgy, carpentry, and masonry. This theory was created in America but has recently been popular also in European countries. In our country the treasures under the earth have not been developed, the organization of industrial circles is still in its infancy, the unemployed are numerous, and the nation is extremely poor. Thus utilitarian education is certainly a matter of priority.

These two policies constitute the principles for strengthening our troops and enriching the nation. Although troops may be strengthened, however, this trend may be overdeveloped into private fighting or into national aggression [p. 191]. Then what can we do? The nation may be enriched and yet it may be unavoidable for the educated to cheat the ignorant, for the strong to cheat the weak, and so produce a great gap between the rich and the poor and the tragedy of a bloody war between capitalists and workers. Then what can we do? The answer is to teach the morality [*tao-te*, ethics] of citizenship. What is the morality of citizenship? It was put forth during the French Revolution in the phrase, "liberty, equality, and fraternity." The essential ideas of morality are wholly included in these. . . [With quotations from the Confucian classics, Ts'ai then suggests that *i* (righteousness), *shu* (reciprocity), and *jen* (benevolence) roughly correspond to the principles of the French Revolution, p. 192.] These three principles [*i, shu*, and *jen*] are really the foundation of all morality and should be included in the moral education of citizens.

An education that includes moral discipline for citizens should be considered as the final goal. I would say "not yet," however, because moral education for citizens is still not above politics. What is called the best government in the world has for its goal no less than the greatest happiness of the greatest number. The "greatest number" is made up of many individuals. The individual's welfare consists of sufficient clothing, adequate food, and avoidance of catastrophe or harm. This is no more than our present society's ideal of welfare. One person's welfare is added to [p. 193] that of others to become that of the majority of people. The goal is still the same. The discussions in the legislative branch, the executive action of the administrative branch, and the protection exercised by the judicial branch of the government are all aimed at the welfare of the people. Even if we progress to the point spoken of in the "Li-yun" where "the great doctrine applies to all" [*ta-tao wei kung*],[6] and reach what the socialists call the golden age of the future, when every person will do the utmost that he can and every person will receive what he needs — these goals, after all, are the same as the ideals of present society. Probably the goals of politics and law are also working for happiness, and all education which is subordinate to politics and law is, at its best, also like this. . .

[P. 197] The two principles of military citizenship and utilitarianism are used to make up for our inadequacy in self-protection and self-preservation. Moral education is to make people work for mutual protection and mutual preservation, and all this is instrumental in breaking the habit of scheming for one's own interest and in eradicating the (sense of) difference between you and me. From this, people can progress to the promotion of education in the light of reality.

What is the method for promoting the conception of reality? The answer is that, on the negative side, with regard to the phenomenal world, we have nothing to dislike and nothing to be obstinate about; while on the positive side, we are very anxious to, and we gradually do, advance toward understanding the world of reality. We must follow the general rule of freedom of thought and freedom of expression, and not allow any one branch of philosophy or any one tenet of religion to confine our minds, but always aim at a lofty universal point of view which is valid without regard to space or time. For such an education I can think of no other name than "education for a world view" [shih-chieh-kuan chiao-yü]. Education for a world view, however, is not something to chatter about every day. Moreover, its relation to the phenomenal world cannot be described in dry and simple words. Then, in what way can we reach it?

The answer is, through esthetic education [or, education for artistic appreciation, mei-kan chih chiao-yü]. Mei-kan is a conception combining beauty and solemnity and is a bridge between the phenomenal world and the world of reality. This concept was originated by Kant [p. 198] . . . In the phenomenal world every person feels the passions of love, hatred, fear, surprise, happiness, anger, sadness and pleasure, and these feelings vary according to the phenomena of departure, reunion, life, death, disaster, good fortune, and catastrophe. As for the fine arts, such phenomena are used as sources of inspiration, and make those who look at representations of them have no other feeling than that of artistic appreciation. For instance, the gathering of lotus seeds and the cooking of beans are work for food, and yet when they are written in a poem they arouse other interests. The blazing red volcano or a strong wind wrecking a boat are terrible and dreadful scenes, but when they appear in a painting they turn out to be worth exhibiting and appreciating. That is, with regard to the phenomenal world we have nothing to dislike and nothing to be obstinate about. When you feel related to actual phenomena neither by craving nor by loathing but are purely absorbed in artistic appreciation, then you will become a friend of the Creator and will be close to the conception of the world of reality. Therefore, if an educator wishes to lead the people from the phenomenal world to the conception of the world of reality, he must adopt esthetic education.

On these five points there should be no special emphasis or negligence in today's education. The principle of military citizenship, the utilitarian principle, and the moral principle are the three which belong to political education. (The moral education of ancient China occasionally had reference to a world view and that should be discussed separately.) The two principles of the world view and esthetic education are above politics. . .

[P. 200] When we base ourselves on these five principles and distribute them among all the school subjects, the percentage of each principle will vary according to the nature of each subject. . . The proportion shall be ten per cent for military citizenship, forty for utilitarianism, twenty for moral education, twenty-five for esthetic education, but only five per cent for the world view.

[P. 202] During the Manchu dynasty there were the so-called imperial educational purposes, namely, to inculcate loyalty to the emperor, respect for Confucius, promotion of public spirit, promotion of military spirit [p. 203], and promotion of usefulness. Loyalty to the emperor is not suited to the republican form of government; respect for Confucius is contradictory to the freedom of belief. . . These two need not be discussed. The promotion of military spirit is the principle for military citizenship; the promotion of usefulness is the principle of utilitarianism; the promotion of public spirit is what I have called moral education for citizenship. Their scope may be necessarily different in breadth or narrowness, but essentially they are the same ideas. The world view and esthetic education are things the Ch'ing dynasty did not mention, but I pay close attention to them. Therefore, I have particularly explained these points and illustrated them, asking advice from modern educators in the hope that they will give them their candid discussion.

The letter translated below was published in reply to criticisms advanced by the famous translator Lin Shu (Lin Ch'in-nan), who was one of the conservative members of the Peita faculty at the time. Written a bare six weeks before the outbreak of the May Fourth Movement, Ts'ai's eloquent advocacy of freedom of academic thought epitomizes the spirit of a period of creative effort, untrammeled by orthodoxy; in 1919 that of the Confucian empire had finally been dissolved, while the orthodoxy of the modern party-governments had not yet taken its place.

DOC. 58. Ts'ai Yuan-p'ei's Policy for Peking University, 1919 [7]

[P. 323] In connection with the university I have two policies, as follows:

(1) With regard to academic ideas, I act according to the general rule of the various universities of the world, following the principle of "freedom of thought" and adopting the policy of tolerating everything and including everything. . . Regardless of what schools of academic thought there may be, if their words are reasonable and there is a cause for maintaining them, and they have not yet reached the fate of being eliminated by nature, then even though they disagree with each other, I would let them develop in complete freedom [p. 324]. This idea has been explained in the foreword of the *Peking University Monthly*. [Note: This foreword was written in November 1918. Part of it reads, "What is called a university is not merely a place for a majority of the students to attend classes on time and to be furnished with the qualifications for becoming graduates. It is actually an organization for academic research by professors and students working together. By research we mean not merely the learning about European culture, but also the necessity of making further discoveries on the basis of European culture; it is not merely for preservation of the essentials of our national culture (*kuo-ts'ui*), it is also necessary to use scientific methods to expound the real nature of our national essentials."] [8]

(2) With regard to professors, their knowledge is the main thing. When they give lectures in the university, the only limitation on them is that they do not contradict the first policy. Their words and actions outside the university are entirely their own affair. This university never makes inquiries nor takes responsibility for such words and actions. For instance, the idea of restoration of the ,Manchu emperor is rejected by the Republic, but among the professors of this university there is one who wears a long queue and still maintains the theory of restoration [i.e., Ku Hung-ming]; but

because he teaches English literature, which has nothing to do with Chinese politics, I let him do as he wishes. The sponsors of the *Ch'ou-an-hui* [lit., "Society for the preparation of peace," but actually for making Yuan Shih-k'ai emperor] are criminals in the eyes of public opinion. Among the professors of this university there is such a man [Liu Shih-p'ei]; but because he teaches ancient Chinese literature, which has no relation to politics, I let him continue. The visiting of prostitutes, gambling, and the taking of concubines and such matters are forbidden by the "Society for the Promotion of Morality" of this university (*Chin-te-hui*); but among our faculty members there are occasionally those [e.g., Ch'en Tu-hsiu] who like to write love poems in praise of prostitutes, and who consider the taking of a concubine and associating with prostitutes as romantic actions and gambling as a pastime. If they do not neglect their school work and do not mislead the students into falling as they have, then I also, for the time being, let them continue with their teaching. Generally, it is very difficult to procure men of ability. If we sought for perfection and asked for completeness, it would probably be difficult to establish a university. Moreover, there is certainly a natural boundary between public and private life. . .

CHAPTER XXV. EARLY CONVERTS TO MARXISM

If republicanism was to be the answer to China's political problems, what was to be the nature of her intellectual life in this new era? The post-1911 period down to 1923 saw all sorts of experimental attitudes on the part of leaders in the realm of thought — for example, Nietzsche was a source of reference for Ch'en Tu-hsiu, Hu Shih, and Ts'ai Yuan-p'ei, among others. The experiments and gropings of these years included the attempt to transplant the terms of Western ideology into the thought of republican China; the effort to create a new vernacular literature; and spirited debates over such questions as centralism versus federalism in politics or the relation between science and philosophy of life. The same decade also witnessed the disillusionment of some of the intellectuals with Western liberalism and their subsequent acceptance of dialectical materialism.

Ch'en Tu-hsiu (1880?–1942) participated in all these developments. Beginning as a scholar with a good literary training in the traditional style, he became deeply influenced by the West, the culture of which he thought was represented in its essence by the French. He was a revolutionary before the overthrow of the Manchu dynasty, and continued to be an enemy of traditional conventions thereafter. He gave active support to the new literary movement; he praised the combativeness, individualism, and utilitarianism of the Westerners in opposition to the decadence of Chinese society. In 1916 he became dean of the School of Letters of Peking University, and took a leading part in the intellectual developments which led up to the May Fourth Movement of 1919. As chief editor and a constant contributor to the monthly magazine *La Jeunesse*, "New Youth" (*Hsin-ch'ing-nien*), his influence over the rising generation of Chinese students was tremendous. The main themes of his credo at this time were science and democracy: "We are convinced at present that only these two gentlemen ["Mr. Science and Mr. Democracy"] can cure the dark maladies in Chinese politics, morality, learning, and thought," he wrote in January 1919.

The Versailles Peace Conference, however, the Shantung question, the Chinese Republic's relapse into warlord politics, and the successes of the Russian Revolution all combined to turn him against his early faith in Western liberalism and toward the new socialist Russia and its ideology. It is difficult to determine the exact date of his change of mind, but it appears that his iconoclasm had reached a climax sometime in 1918, when a short article of his entitled "On the destruction of idols" was published in *Hsin-ch'ing-nien*. In this he included in his objects of attack not only Chinese conventions but also a part of the modern Western ideology, the theory of the national state — which he declared produced war and was a device for the protection of the rights of the privileged classes. It was evidently time for a re-evaluation of his aims, time to build an ideology that could meet the situation more adequately. With the help of Western liberalism, he had torn down the traditional Chinese system; but now, in the process of rebuilding, he used other new materials. By 1921 he had become a convinced Marxist and took part in the founding of the Chinese Communist Party, of which he was the leader and general secretary until 1927. Ch'en made undeniable contributions to the new cultural movement. The first and third of the following items represent the two major periods of his thought.

DOC. 59. CH'EN TU-HSIU'S "CALL TO YOUTH," 1915 [1]

The Chinese compliment others by saying, "He acts like an old man although still young." Englishmen and Americans encourage one another by saying, "Keep young while growing old." Such is one respect in which the different ways of thought of the East and West are manifested. Youth is like early spring, like the rising sun, like trees and grass in bud, like a newly sharpened blade. It is the most valuable period of life. The function of youth in society is the same as that of a fresh and vital cell in a human body. In the processes of metabolism, the old and the rotten are incessantly eliminated to be replaced by the fresh and living. . . If metabolism functions properly in a human body, the person will be healthy; if the old and rotten cells accumulate and fill the body, the person will die. If metabolism functions properly in a society, it will flourish; if old and rotten elements fill the society, then it will cease to exist.

According to this standard, then, is the society of our nation flourishing, or is it about to perish? I cannot bear to answer. As for those old and rotten elements, I shall leave them to the process of natural selection. I do not wish to waste my fleeting time in arguing with them on this and that and hoping for them to be reborn and thoroughly remodeled. I only, with tears, place my plea before the young and vital youth, in the hope that they will achieve self-awareness, and begin to struggle. What is this self-awareness? It is to be conscious of the value and responsibility of one's young life and vitality, to maintain one's self-respect, which should not be lowered. What is the struggle? It is to exert one's intellect, discard resolutely the old and the rotten, regard them as enemies and as the flood or savage beasts, keep away from their neighborhood and refuse to be contaminated by their poisonous germs. Alas! Do these words really fit the youth of our country? I have seen that, out of every ten youths who are young in age, five are old in physique; and out of every ten who are young in both age and physique, nine are old in mentality. Those with shining hair, smooth countenance, a straight back and a wide chest are indeed magnificent youths! Yet if you ask what thoughts and aims are entertained in their heads, then they all turn out to be the same as the old and rotten, like moles from the same hill. In the beginning the youth are not without freshness and vitality. Gradually some are assimilated by the old and rotten elements; then there are others who fear the tremendous influence of those elements, who hesitate, stammer and stall, and dare not openly rebel against them. It is the old and rotten air that fills society everywhere. One cannot even find a bit of fresh and vital air to comfort those of us who are suffocating in despair.

Such a phenomenon [p. 2], if found in a human body, would kill a man; if found in a society, would destroy it. A heavy sigh or two cannot cure this malady. What is needed is for one or two youths, who are quick in self-consciousness and brave in a struggle, to use to the full the natural intellect of man, and judge and choose all the thoughts of mankind, distinguishing which are fresh and vital and suitable for the present struggle for survival, and which are old and rotten and unworthy to be retained in the mind. Treat this problem as a sharp tool cleaves iron, or a sharp knife cuts hemp. Resolutely make no compromises and entertain no hesitations. Consider yourself and consider others; then perhaps society can hope to become clean and peaceful. O youth, is there anyone who takes upon himself such responsibilities? As for understanding what is right and wrong, in order that you may make your choice, I carefully propose the following six principles, and hope you will give them your calm consideration.

1) *Be independent, not servile.*

All men are equal. Each has his right to be independent, but absolutely no right to enslave others nor any obligation to make himself servile. By slavery we mean that in ancient times the ignorant and the weak lost their right of freedom, which was savagely usurped by tyrants. Since the rise of the theories of the rights of man and of equality, no red-blooded person can endure [the name of slave]. The history of modern Europe is commonly referred to as a "history of emancipation": the destruction of monarchical power aimed at political emancipation; the denial of Church authority aimed at religious emancipation; the rise of the theory of equal property aimed at economic emancipation; and the suffragist movement aimed at emancipation from male authority.

Emancipation means freeing oneself from the bondage of slavery and achieving a completely independent and free personality. I have hands and feet, and I can earn my own living. I have a mouth and a tongue, and I can voice my own likes and dislikes. I have a mind, and I can determine my own beliefs. I will absolutely not let others do these things in my behalf, nor should I assume an overlordship and enslave others. For once the independent personality is recognized, all matters of conduct, all rights and privileges, and all belief should be left to the natural ability of each person; there is definitely no reason why one should blindly follow others. On the other hand, loyalty, filial piety, chastity and righteousness are a slavish morality. (Note: The great German philosopher Nietzsche divided morality into two categories — that which is independent and courageous is called "morality of the noble," and that which is humble and submissive is called "morality of the slave.") Light penalties and light taxation constitute the happiness of slaves; panegyrics and eulogies are slavish literature; . . . noble ranks or magnificent mansions are glory only to slaves; resplendent tablets and grand tombs are their memorials. That is because such persons, by submitting to the judgment of others regarding right and wrong, glory and shame, instead of depending on their own standard of judgment, have completely annihilated their independent and equal personalities as individuals. In their conduct, whether good or bad, they cannot appeal to their own will-power, but are confined to receiving merits or demerits (from others). Who can say that it is improper to call such persons slaves? Therefore, before we speak of contributing to mankind in moral example or in deed, we must first make this distinction between the independent and the servile.

2) *Be progressive, not conservative.*

"Without progress there will be retrogression" is an old Chinese saying. Considering the fundamental laws of the universe, all things or phenomena are daily progressing in evolution, and the maintenance of the *status quo* is definitely out of the question; only the limitation of man's ordinary view has rendered possible the differentiation between the two states of things. This is why the theory of creative evolution, "L'Evolution créatrice," of the contemporary French philosopher Henri Bergson, has become immensely popular throughout a whole generation. Considered in the light of the evolution of human affairs, it is plain that those races that cling to antiquated ways are declining, or disappearing, day by day, and the peoples who seek progress and advancement are just beginning to ascend in power and strength. It is possible to predict which of these will survive and which will not. Now our country still has not awakened from its long dream, and isolates itself by going down the old rut. . . All our traditional ethics, law, scholarship, rites and customs are survivals of feudalism. When compared with the achievement of the white race, there is a difference of a thousand years in thought, although we live in the same period. Revering only the history of the twenty-four dynasties and making no plans for progress and improvement, our people will be turned out of this twentieth-century world, and be lodged in the dark ditches fit only for slaves, cattle, and horses. What more need be said? I really do not know what sort of institutions and culture are adequate for our survival in the present world if in such circumstances conservatism is still advocated. I would much rather see the past culture of our nation disappear than see our race die out now because of its unfitness for living in the modern world. Alas, the days of the Babylonians are past. Of what use is their civilization now? "When the skin has vanished, what can the hair adhere to?" The progress of the world is like that of a fleet horse, galloping and galloping onward. Whatever cannot skillfully change itself and progress along with the world will find itself eliminated by natural selection because of failure to adapt to the environment. Then what can be said to defend conservatism!

3) *Be aggressive, not retiring.*

While the tide of evil is now rushing onward, would it not be rare virtue for one or two self-respecting scholars to retire from the world, to keep themselves clean? But if your aim is to influence the people and establish a new tradition, I suggest that you make further progress from your present high position. It is impossible to avoid the struggle for survival, and so long as one draws breath there can be no place where one can retire for a tranquil hermit's life. It is our natural obligation in life to advance in spite of numerous difficulties. Stated in kindly terms, retirement is an action of the superior man in order to get away from the vulgar world. Stated in hostile terms, it is a phenomenon of the weak who are unable to struggle for survival. . . Alas! The war steeds of Europe are intruding into your house. Where can you quietly repose under a white cloud? I wish that our youth would become Confucius and Mo-tzu and not [the hermits] Ts'ao-fu and Hsü Yu,[2] and I do not wish so much that our youth be Tolstoi and Tagore (Note: R. Tagore, an escapist poet of India) as that they become Columbus and An Ch'ung-ken [the Korean patriot who assassinated Prince Ito on October 26, 1909].

4) *Be cosmopolitan, not isolationist.*

Any change in the economic or political life of one nation will usually have repercussions over the whole world, just as the whole body is affected when one hair is pulled. The prosperity or decline, rise or fall of a nation of today depends half on domestic administration, and half on influences from outside the country. Take the recent events of our country as evidence: Japan suddenly rose in power, and stimulated our revolutionary and reform movements; the European War broke out, and then Japan presented her demands to us; is this not clear proof? When a nation is thrown into the currents of the world, traditionalists will certainly hasten the day of its fall, but those capable of change will take this opportunity to compete and progress. According to the pessimists, since the opening of the treaty ports our country has been losing territory and paying indemnities to the point of exhaustion. But according to the optimists, we would still be in the age of the eight-legged essay and the queue were it not for the blessings of the Sino-Japanese War of 1895 and the Boxer Uprising of 1900. Not only are we unable to support an isolationist and closed-door policy, but circumstances also are unfavorable to it. . . If at this point one still raises a particularist theory of history and of national circumstances and hopes thereby to resist the current, then this still indicates the spirit of an isolationist country and a lack of knowledge of the world. When its citizens lack knowledge of the world, how can a nation expect to survive in it? A proverb says, "He who builds his cart behind closed gates will find it not suited to the tracks outside the gates." The cart-builders of today not only close their gates, but even want to use the methods contained [p. 5] in the chapter on technology in the *Rites of Chou* for use on the highways of Europe and America. The trouble will be more than not fitting the tracks.

5) *Be utilitarian, not formalistic.*

The social system and the thought of Europe have undergone a change since J. S. Mill's advocacy of utilitarianism in England and Comte's advocacy of positivism in France. More recently their system and thought have undergone another change, with the great advancement of science in Germany, where material civilization has reached its pinnacle of achievement. In all that concerns the administration of government, the aims of education, and the fashions in literature and the crafts, there is nothing that is not focusing on the road of better livelihood and greater usefulness, like ten thousand horses galloping toward the same point. Meanwhile all things that are formalistic, utopian, and useless to practical life are almost completely rejected. The great contemporary philosophers, such as R. Eucken of Germany and Bergson of France, although they do not consider the present materialistic civilization perfect, all discuss the problems of life (Note: The English word is "life," the German "leben," and the French "la vie") as the goal of their teachings. Life is sacred. Because the blood of the present war has stained life's bright banner, the Europeans will waken entirely from utopian, empty dreams.

Generally speaking, concern for usefulness and better livelihood, respect for actuality and disdain for illusion were characteristic of the ancient people of our country, whereas our present social system and thought are inherited from the Chou and Han dynasties. Empty formalism was emphasized in the *Rites of Chou*, and under the Han dynasty Confucianism and the Taoism of Lao-tzu were elevated to high positions, while all other schools of thought were interdicted. The age-long precepts of ethical convention, the hopes and purposes of the people — there is nothing which does not run counter to the practical life of society today. If we do not restring our bow and renew our effort, there will be no way to revive the strength of our nation, and our society will never see a peaceful day. As for praying to gods to relieve flood and famine, or reciting the *Book of Filial Piety* to ward off the Yellow Turbans [i.e., bandits] — people are not infants or morons, and they see through these absurdities. Though a thing is of gold or of jade, if it is of no practical use, then it is of less value than coarse cloth, grain, manure or dirt. That which brings no benefit to the practical life of an individual or of society is all empty formalism and the stuff of cheats. And even though it were bequeathed to us by our ancestors, taught by the sages, advocated by the government and worshiped by society, the stuff of cheats is still not worth one cent.

6) *Be scientific, not imaginative.*

What is science? It is our general conception of matter which, being the sum of objective phenomena as analyzed by subjective reason, contains no contradiction within itself. What is imagination? It first oversteps the realm of objective phenomena, and then discards reason itself; it is something constructed out of thin air, consisting of hypotheses without proof, and all the existing wisdom of mankind cannot be made to find reason in it [p. 6] or explain its laws and principles. There was only imagination and no science in the unenlightened days of old, as well as among the uncivilized peoples of today. Religion, art, and literature were the products of the period of imagination. The contribution of the growth of science to the supremacy of modern Europe over other races is not less than that of the theory of the rights of man. . . Our scholars do not know science, therefore they borrow the *yin-yang* school's notions of auspicious signs and of the five elements to confuse the world and cheat the people, and the ideas of topography and geomancy to beg for miracles from dry skeletons (spirits). Our farmers do not know science; therefore they have no technique for seed selection and insecticide. Our industrialists do not know science; therefore goods lie wasted on the ground, while we depend on foreign countries for everything that we need in warfare and in production. Our merchants know no science; therefore they are only concerned with obtaining short-term profits, and give not a thought to calculating for the future. Our physicians know no science; not only are they not acquainted with human anatomy, but also they do not analyze the properties of medicines; as for bacteria and contagious diseases, they have never heard of them. They can only parrot the talk about the five elements, their mutual promotions and preventions, cold and heat, *yin* and *yang*, and prescribe medicine according to ancient formulae. Their technique is practically the same as that of an archer! The height of their marvelous imaginations is the theory of *ch'i* (primal force), which even extends to the techniques of professional strong men and Taoist priests. But though you seek high and low in the universe, you will never know what this "primal force" exactly is. All these nonsensical ideas and unreasonable beliefs can be cured at the root only by science. For to explain truth by science means proving everything with fact. Although the process is slower than that of imagination and arbitrary decision, yet every step taken is on firm ground; it is different from those imaginative flights which eventually cannot advance even one inch. The amount of truth in the universe is boundless, and the fertile areas in the realm of science awaiting the pioneer are immense! Youth, take up the task!

The author of the next item, Li Ta-chao (1888–1927), is now honored by Chinese Communists as the principal party-founder, a distortion of history evidently necessitated by the fact that the first head of the party, Ch'en Tu-hsiu, was later condemned and expelled. Li Ta-chao was a professor of political science and economics, and a returned student from Japan. Like Ch'en Tu-hsiu, he was an active leader of Chinese youth through his writings and lectures at Peking University. It is said that while teaching at that institution in the years 1919–1925, he offered courses on historical materialism and socialism; from his own writings in *Hsin-ch'ing-nien* it is clear that his interest in Marxist ideology had begun only after the Russian Revolution. Unlike others of his time, however, he was quick to assert the merits of the Marxist-Leninist revolution without going through a prolonged period of skeptical observation, as the following article testifies. Though he was one of the leaders in the founding of the Chinese Communist Party in 1921, he suffered an early death in April 1927, at the hands of the warlord of Manchuria, Chang Tso-lin; he was spared the subsequent intra-party conflict between the Stalinists and Trotskyites, and the fate of ostracism which overtook Ch'en Tu-hsiu.

Certain parts of the following article still show a non-Marxist approach to history, but there were signs that Li was engaged in hard study of Marxist theory during 1918 and 1919. In the latter year he stated his opinion that "this is a period of transition between the era of individualism and that of socialism and humanism." [3]

DOC. 60. LI TA-CHAO, "THE VICTORY OF BOLSHEVISM," NOVEMBER 15, 1918 [4]

"Victory! Victory! The Allies have been victorious! Surrender! Surrender! Germany has surrendered!" These words are on the national flag bedecking every doorway, they can be seen in color and can be indistinctly heard in the intonation of every voice. Men and women of the Allied powers run up and down the street in celebration of the victory, and in the city of Peking the soldiers of these nations loudly blast forth their triumphal songs. Now and then, echoed amid the noises of celebration and rejoicing, you hear the tinkling sound of some German merchant's shop window being shattered, or that of the bricks and tiles taken off the von Ketteler Memorial Arch [a memorial to the German Minister killed by the Boxers]. It is indeed needless to describe the happiness of the people of the Allied powers who are living in our country. . .

But let us think carefully as small citizens of the world; to whom exactly does the present victory belong? Who has really surrendered? Whose is the achievement this time? And for whom do we celebrate? If we ponder over these questions, then not only will our non-fighting generals' show of strength and our shameless politicians' grasping of credit become senseless, but also the talk of the Allied nations, that the end of the war was brought about by their military forces defeating the military force of Germany, and their mad celebrations will be entirely without significance. And not only are their celebrations and boasts meaningless, but even the fate of their political system will probably [p. 443] be the same as that of German militarism, and vanish with the latter in the near future.

For the real cause of the ending of the war was not the vanquishing of the German military power by the Allied military power, but the vanquishing of German militarism by German socialism. It was not the German people who surrendered to the armed forces of the Allied powers, but the German Kaiser, militarists and militarism who surrendered to the new tides of the world. It was not the Allied nations but the awakened minds of the German people that defeated German militarism; and the failure of German militarism was the failure of the Hohenzollern [Chinese text here inserts "Bolshevism" in English, by error] German imperial family and not that of the German nation. The victory over German militarism does not belong to the Allied nations; even less does it belong to our factious military men who used participation in the war only as an excuse [for engaging in civil war], or to our opportunistic, cunningly manipulative politicians. It is the victory of humanitarianism, of pacifism; it is the victory of justice and liberty; it is the victory of democracy; it is the victory of socialism; it is the victory of Bolshevism [Chinese text inserts "Hohenzollern" by error]; it is the victory of the red flag; it is the victory of the labor class of the world; and it is the

victory of the twentieth century's new tide. Rather than give Wilson and
others the credit for this achievement, we should give the credit to Lenin
[These names are inserted in English], Trotzky, Collontay [Alexandra
Kollontai], to Liebknecht, Scheidemann, and to Marx. . .

Bolshevism is the ideology of the Russian Bolsheviki. What kind of
ideology is it? It is very difficult to explain it clearly in one sentence. If we
look for the origin of the word, we see that it means "majority." An English
reporter once asked Collontay, a heroine in that [Bolshevik] party [p. 444],
what the meaning of "Bolsheviki" was. The heroine answered. . . "Its
meaning will be clear only if one looks at what they are doing." According
to the explanation given by this heroine, then, "Bolsheviki means only what
they are doing." But from the fact that this heroine had called herself a
Revolutionary Socialist in western Europe, and a Bolshevika in eastern Europe, and from the things they have done, it is clear that their ideology is
revolutionary socialism; their party is a revolutionary socialist party; and
they follow the German socialist economist Marx as the founder of their
doctrine. Their aim is to destroy the national boundaries which are obstacles
to socialism at present, and to destroy the system of production in which
profit is monopolized by the capitalist. Indeed, the real cause of this war
was also the destruction of national boundaries. Since the present national
boundaries cannot contain the expansion of the system of production brought
about by capitalism, and since the resources within each nation are inadequate for the expansion of its productive power, the capitalist nations all
began depending on war to break down these boundaries, hoping to make
of all parts of the globe one single, coördinated economic organ.

So far as the breaking down of national boundaries is concerned, the
socialists are of the same opinion with them. But the purpose of the capitalist
governments in this matter is to enable the middle class in their countries
to gain benefits; they rely on world economic development by one class in
the victor nations, and not on mutual coöperation among humanitarian,
reasonable organizations of the producers of the world. This war will cause
such a victor nation to advance from the position of a great power to that
of a world empire. The Bolsheviki saw through this point; therefore they
vigorously protested and proclaimed that the present war is a war of the
Tsar, of the Kaiser, of kings and emperors, that it is a war of capitalist governments, but it is not their war. Theirs is the war of classes, a war of all
the world's proletariat and common people against the capitalists of the
world. While they are opposed to war itself, they are at the same time not
afraid of it. They hold that all men and women should work. All those who
work should join a union, and there should be a central administrative
soviet in each union. [P. 445] Such soviets then should organize all the
governments of the world. There will be no congress, no parliament, no
president, no prime minister, no cabinet, no legislature, and no ruler. There
will be only the joint soviets of labor, which will decide all matters. All
enterprises will belong to those who work therein, and aside from this no
other possessions will be allowed. They will unite the proletariat of the
world, and create global freedom with their greatest, strongest power of

resistance: first they will create a federation of European democracies, to serve as the foundation of a world federation. This is the ideology of the Bolsheviki. This is the new doctrine of the twentieth-century revolution.

In a report by Harold Williams in the London *Times*,[5] Bolshevism is considered a mass movement. He compares it with early Christianity, and finds two points of similarity: one is enthusiastic partisanship, the other is a tendency to revelation. He says, "Bolshevism is really a kind of mass movement, with characteristics of religion. . ." Not only the Russia of today, but the whole world of the twentieth century probably cannot avoid being controlled by such religious power and swayed by such a mass movement.

[P. 446] In the *Fortnightly Review* Frederic Harrison says: "Savage, impossible, and anti-social as Bolshevism is, we must realize that it is also an emotional disturbance that is very solid, very wide, and very deep. . .

In his book *Bolshevism and World Peace*, Trotzky writes: "In this new revolutionary era a new organization shall be created by unlimited proletarian socialist methods. The new organization will be as great as the new task. Amid the mad roar of the cannon, the crash of temples and shrines, and the wild blast of patriotic songs from wolf-like capitalists, we ought to be the first to undertake this new task. With the death-music of hell about us, we should maintain our clarity of mind, and clearly perceive and realize that ours will be the one and only creative force in the future. . ."

From this passage it is plain that Trotzky holds that the Russian revolution is to serve as a fuse to world revolution. The Russian revolution is but one [p. 447] of the world revolutions; numerous revolutions of other peoples will successively arise. . .

The above are all statements made before the end of the war, and before the outbreak of the socialist revolutions in Germany and Austria. Today Trotzky's criticisms have been justified. The comments made by Messrs. Williams and Harrison have also been upheld. There are the Austrian revolution — the German revolution — the Hungarian revolution — and recently there have been reports also of the rise of vigorous revolutionary socialist parties in Holland, Sweden, and Spain. The pattern of the revolutions generally develops along the same line as that in Russia. The red flag flies everywhere, the soviets are established one after another. Call it revolution entirely *à la Russe*, or call it twentieth-century revolution. Such mighty rolling tides are indeed beyond the power of the present capitalist governments to prevent or to stop, for the mass movement of the twentieth century combines the whole of mankind into one great mass. The efforts of each individual within this great mass, following the example of some of them, will then be concentrated and become a great, irresistible social force. Whenever a disturbance in this worldwide social force occurs among the people, it will produce repercussions all over the earth, like storm clouds gathering before the wind and valleys echoing the mountains. In the course of such a world mass movement, all those dregs of history which can impede the progress of the new movement — such as emperors, nobles, warlords, bureaucrats, militarism, capitalism — will certainly be destroyed as though struck by a thunderbolt. Encountering this irresistible tide, these things will be swept away one by one. . . [P. 448] Henceforth, all that one sees around him will be the triumphant banner of Bolshevism, and all that one hears around him will be Bolshevism's song of victory. The bell is rung for humanitarianism! The dawn of freedom has arrived! See the world of tomorrow; it assuredly will belong to the red flag! . . . The revolution in Russia is but the first fallen leaf warning the world of the approach of autumn. Although the word "Bolshevism" was created by the Russians, the spirit it embodies can be regarded as that of a common awakening in the heart of each individual among mankind of the twentieth century. The victory of Bolshevism, therefore, is the victory of the spirit of common awakening in the heart of each individual among mankind in the twentieth century.

DOC. 61. CH'EN TU-HSIU'S ARGUMENT FOR HISTORICAL MATERIALISM, 1923 [6]

[The first few pages explain the controversy then being waged among Chinese intellectuals over the question whether or not science could determine one's philosophy of life. This was the problem of the influence of modern scientific thought upon values.] Chang Chün-mai [Carson Chang, a Chinese minor-party political leader, who later founded the National Socialist or Social Democratic Party] lists nine philosophies of life, and maintains that they are all subjective, intuitive, synthetic and voluntaristic, and arise out of the monomial nature of personality; that they are not objective, rational, analytical or determined by the scientific law of cause and effect. Now after viewing his nine philosophies of life we can see that, first, whether there is a large family system or a small family system is purely a natural phenomenon during the transition from a patriarchal society based on an agricultural economy to a military-nationalist society based on an industrial economy.

Secondly, the high or low position of women in relation to men and the marriage system (which governs this relationship) are both due to the fact that in an agricultural-patriarchal society the wife and children are regarded by the husband and parents as tools of production, as a kind of property; while in an industrial society the family handicrafts go out of date and are replaced by the system of hired labor, so that one need not treat the family as a tool of production. Therefore the feminist movement naturally begins to flourish.

Thirdly, the systems of common or private property: in the primitive communal society there was neither the possibility nor the necessity for private property, since men were weaker than the beasts and needed to form groups and coöperate for survival. . . When we reached the agricultural stage of permanent habitats and granaries [p. 6] (to facilitate grain preservation), as independent producers the small farmers needed only to possess land, and not to coöperate in group effort. This gave rise to the idea of private property. In the stage of industrial society, the system of independent production by family handicraft can no longer exist, since thousands and tens of thousands of people are organized within one coördinated coöperative unit; any man who has no work cannot eat, and without tools he cannot work. But no one has the tools of production, because these are already privately possessed by a few capitalists. Therefore unless the tools of production are taken over by the public, every man will have to sell his labor to the capitalists. Thus arises the idea of public ownership of property.

Fourthly, the controversy between the conservatives and the reformers: this is due to the fact that although economic changes have occurred in the present society, the organization of the old society, which is not suited to this changed condition, still persists and restricts the development of change; therefore classes with different economic interests naturally are engaged in conflict, according to the speed or slowness of change.

Fifthly, as to the different opinions regarding matter and spirit, they are the special concerns of a few persons: generally speaking, not to mention the manual laborers in factories, even the twenty- or thirty-dollar-a-month compilers at the Commercial Press worry daily about the insufficiency of food and clothing; so who has the time — like Chang Chün-mai and Liang Ch'i-ch'ao — to discourse on the so-called spiritual civilization and Eastern culture? . . . [Four further points are here dealt with.]

[P. 7] The above nine different kinds of philosophies of life are all determined by different objective causes and effects. Social science can analyze them one by one and offer rational explanations. It is hard to find one which is without an objective cause, or rather which has arisen without grounds out of a person's subjective, intuitive free will.

Liang Ch'i-ch'ao is indeed more intelligent than Chang Chün-mai. He says, "Chün-mai lists nine items of 'I vs. not-I,' which he holds cannot be explained by scientific method; I think, however, that eighty or ninety per cent of them have to be explained by the scientific method." Liang Ch'i-ch'ao adopts the attitude of a fence-sitter [p. 8]. He disagrees on the one hand with Chang Chün-mai, and on the other with V. K. Ting [China's leading modern geologist, d. 1935]. It is Liang's opinion that: "Of life's problems, the majority can, and must be, solved by scientific method. But there is a minority — perhaps the most important part — that is above science."

His so-called "majority" means those matters in human life that concern the reasoning power; his "minority" means those that concern emotion. He said: "Since the problems touch on actual matter, then of course they are determined by the various laws in the environment — both as regards time and space." True, things that involve the reasoning power cannot be separated from actual matter; but is it also true that things of emotion do not touch upon actual matter? How the senses are stimulated and how they react, how emotion arises, these are common knowledge in psychology. . .

[P. 9] All these statements about hereditary patterns, conscience, intuition, and free will are determined by the differing conditions of existence of different peoples at different times: a person born into a Hindu Brahmin family will naturally be averse to killing people; if he were born into the home of an African chieftain he would naturally consider that, the more people he killed, the greater would be his glory. . .

[P. 11] We believe that only objective material causes can change society, can explain history, and can determine one's philosophy of life. This is the "materialistic interpretation of history." We want to ask Mr. V. K.

Ting and Mr. Hu Shih: do they believe the "materialistic interpretation of history" to be the whole truth, or do they believe that, apart from materialism and above science, such things as the idealism advocated by people like Chang Chün-mai can also exist?

(November 13, 1923)

CHAPTER XXVI. HU SHIH AND PRAGMATISM

IN CHINA

Hu Shih (1891–) was an early contributor and one of the editors of *Hsin-ch'ing-nien* (*La Jeunesse*) in its pre-communist phase and a close associate of Ch'en Tu-hsiu. While a student in the United States (1910–1917) he had become a disciple of John Dewey; and he has openly acknowledged his intellectual indebtedness to John Stuart Mill, Thomas Huxley, and John Morley. The fundamental views which he developed in this early period have persisted with remarkable consistency throughout his thinking in subsequent years.

In 1917 Dr. Hu became professor of philosophy and chairman of the department of English literature at Peking University, posts that he held until 1926. By the time of the May Fourth Movement in 1919, Hu Shih was already well known for his rebellion against the traditional style of writing and his vigorous espousal of the written vernacular (*pai-hua*) as a literary medium. After leaving Peita for a four-and-a-half-year absence in England, America, and Shanghai (1926–1930), he returned in 1931 to become dean of the College of Arts and Letters. From 1932 to 1937 he was the chief editor of "The Independent Critic" (*Tu-li p'ing-lun*), a weekly journal of opinion which continued in the main stream of China's pre-Marxist liberal thought.

Hu Shih's advocacy of vernacular literature was an outgrowth of his training in pragmatic philosophy, a relationship that becomes clear when the two following items are read together. He got an immediate response from young Chinese intellectuals and students as soon as his proposals for literary reform were made public in 1916–17. One of his friends, Ch'ien Hsüan-t'ung, even went so far as to suggest the eventual abolition of the ideographic script.

In his own scholarly career Hu Shih applied the attitude of doubt and criticism which he believed was an essential element of the New Thought. On the one hand this was expressed in his re-examination of the classical heritage of the past; his many critical commentaries on classical and literary works, as well as his unfinished history of Chinese philosophy, are important contributions to Chinese learning. On the other hand, he engaged himself in comparing Chinese systems of thought with Western ones; even in the period before 1923 his field of interest included the advocacy of individualism and the emancipation of women.

After the founding of the Chinese Communist Party by Ch'en Tu-hsiu and others in 1921, Hu Shih found himself in basic disagreement with them in their views of life and its problems. Three trends in Chinese thought were discernible after the First World War: first, that represented by the old-style scholar and translator of Western works, Yen Fu, who was disillusioned with the application of Western institutions to China and turned back to the traditional fold (see Ch. XVI), thus losing influence in the new culture movement; second, that represented by Ch'en Tu-hsiu and Li Ta-chao, who began the effort to introduce new elements into Chinese thought through Marxism; third, that represented by Hu

Shih, who continued in his belief of the values of Western liberalism. During the thirty years from 1919 to 1949, this last belief remained largely dominant in Chinese academic circles.

DOC. 62. Hu Shih, "The Significance of the New Thought," 1919[1]

Study the problems. Introduce academic theories. Reorganize our national heritage. Recreate civilization.

Part I. Several articles explaining the "New Thought" have recently appeared in the newspapers. After reading these articles, I feel that their characterization of the New Thought is either too fragmentary or too general, neither an accurate explanation of it nor an indication of its future tendencies. . . From my own observation, its basic significance lies merely in a new attitude. We may call this [p. 153] "a critical attitude." The critical attitude is, in short, to distinguish anew the merits and demerits of all things. In more detail, the critical attitude involves several special prerequisites:

(1) Of the traditional systems and conventions, we must ask, "Do these systems still possess the value to survive today?"

(2) Of the teachings of sages and philosophers handed down from ancient times, we must ask, "Are these words still valid today?"

(3) Of all behavior and beliefs receiving the blind approval of society, we must ask, "Is everything that has been approved by the public necessarily correct? Should I do this, just because others are doing it? Is there no other way that is better, more reasonable and more beneficial?"

Nietzsche said that the modern era is "an era of re-evaluation of all values." These words, "re-evaluation of all values," are the best explanation of the critical attitude. In former days people said that the smaller a woman's feet, the more beautiful they were; now we not only deny the "beauty" of bound feet, but say that foot-binding is "inhumanly cruel." Ten years [p. 154] ago opium was offered to guests in homes and stores; now opium has become a prohibited article. Twenty years ago K'ang Yu-wei was a feared and radical reformer, like a big flood or a fierce beast; now he has become an old curio. It is not K'ang Yu-wei who has changed, but his evaluators, and accordingly his value has also changed. That is a "re-evaluation of all values. . ."

Part II. [P. 155] When expressed in practice, this critical attitude tends to adopt two methods. One is the discussion of various problems, social, political, religious, and literary. The other is the introduction of new thought, new learning, new literature, and new beliefs from the West. The former is "study of the problems"; the latter is "introduction of academic theories." These two things comprise the methods of the New Thought.

These two tendencies can be observed by a casual glance at the contents of new magazines and newspapers of the past two or three years. On the side of studying the problems, we can point to (1) the problem of Confucianism; (2) the problem of the literary revolution; (3) the problem of a unified national language; (4) the problem of the emancipation of women; (5) the problem of chastity; (6) the problem of ethical conventions; (7) the problem of educational reform; (8) the problem of marriage; (9) the problem of the father-son relationship; (10) the problem of the reform of the drama . . . and so on. On the side of the introduction of academic theories, we can point to the special issues "On Ibsen" and "On Marx" of the *Hsin-ch'ing-nien*, the issue "On contemporary thought" of the *Min-to* [The people's tocsin], the issue "On Dewey" of *Hsin-chiao-yü* [The new education], the theory of *ch'üan-min cheng-chih* [total democracy] in *Chien-she* [Reconstruction], and the various new Western theories that have been introduced in such newspapers and magazines as the *Peking Morning Post*. . . [and other papers in Peking, Shanghai, and Canton].

[P. 156] Why must problems be studied? Because our society is now undergoing a period in which its foundations are shaken. Many customs and systems which were not questioned have become difficult issues owing to their failure to meet the needs of circumstance and satisfy the people; therefore we cannot but thoroughly study them, cannot but ask whether or not the old solutions were wrong; if they were wrong, wherein the mistake lies; and when the mistake is discovered, whether there is a better solution, or whether there is any way that will better meet the demands of the present time. For example, the question of Confucianism never arose before. Later, when the civilization of the East came into contact with that of the West, the influence of Confucianism gradually weakened; whereupon a group of Confucianists attempted to restore its dignity by resorting to governmental laws and decrees, not knowing that such high-handed methods would only rouse in people a sort of skeptical reaction. Therefore when the Confucianist Society was the most active, around 1915 and 1916, the anti-Confucianists were also the most numerous. It was at this time that Confucianism became a problem. At present most enlightened people have already broken through these illusions regarding it, and this problem is gradually subsiding, so that when the parliamentary members of the *An-fu* clique passed the resolution defining Confucianism as the basis of moral cultivation, no one in the country even paid it any attention.

Again, take the instance of the literary revolution. Heretofore education has been the special privilege of a small group of "scholars," and has not concerned the majority of the people; therefore the difficulties of the language have not constituted a problem. In recent years education has become a common privilege of all the people, and every man knows that universal education [p. 157] is indispensable; so gradually some people began to realize that the classical style is really not suited to education for all, so then classical versus vernacular style became an issue. Later others felt that writing only textbooks in the vernacular style was not effective because no one in the world would be willing to learn a language that was of no use except in textbooks. . . If we wish to advocate a vernacular education, then we must first advocate a vernacular literature. The problem of the literary revolution was thus engendered. Now that the National Education Association has unanimously passed a resolution to change the primary school textbooks into the vernacular, moreover, more and more people are writing in the vernacular, and this problem is gradually subsiding.

Why do we have to introduce academic theories? This probably can be explained in several ways. First, some persons are convinced that China lacks not only cannon, warships, telegraphs and railways, but also new ideas and new learning; therefore they introduce as many modern Western theories as possible. Secondly, some persons deeply believe in certain theories themselves, and wish to spread and develop them; therefore they exert themselves to advocate them. Thirdly, some persons are unable to do actual research work themselves, and feel that it is easier to translate ready-made theories; therefore they are glad to engage in this kind of middleman's business. Fourthly, while studying concrete social or political problems one has to do destructive work on the one hand, and on the other hand to make out a prescription to fit the malady. This is not only difficult in itself, but also can easily offend others and cause trouble; therefore one may prefer to embark upon the introduction of academic theories and, under the beautiful phrase "study of academic theories," one [p. 158] can avoid being accused as an "extremist" or radical, as well as succeed in sowing a few seeds of revolution. Fifthly, those who study a problem cannot limit their discussion to the problem itself; they have to approach it by considering its meaning in the context; and when one extends the study of a problem to the realm of this sort of significance, it is necessary to rely on various theories as material for reference and comparison. Therefore the introduction of academic theories usually aids in the study of problems.

Although the above five motives differ from one another, they all embody the "critical attitude" to a greater or lesser degree; they all express a dissatisfaction with old learning and thought, and a new awakening to the spiritual aspect of Western civilization. . .

Part III. [P. 161] In the above we have mentioned the two practical expressions of the "critical spirit" of the New Thought. Now we must ask, "What is to be the attitude of the New Thought movement toward the old learning and thought of China?" My answer is, "It should also be a critical attitude."

Under analysis, our attitude toward the old learning and thought should be threefold: first, opposition to blind obedience; second, opposition to compromise; third, advocacy of a reorganization of our national heritage.

Blind obedience is the opposite of critical-mindedness. Since we advocate a "re-evaluation of all values," we naturally must oppose blind obedience. This need not be elaborated.

Why must we oppose compromise? Because the critical attitude recognizes only one right and one wrong, one good and one evil, one suitability and one unsuitability — it does not recognize any compromise of the ancient and modern, or of the foreign and the Chinese. . . [P. 162] Compromise is the natural tendency of human indolence; it does not require our advocacy. The majority of people can probably, with effort, walk only thirty or forty *li* while we go a hundred *li*. Now if we start talking of compromise and only go fifty *li*, then they will not move even one step. Therefore the duty of the reformer is to set his goal in the right direction and go forward, not to turn back and talk of compromise. There will inevitably be numerous laggards and cowards in society to come out for compromise.

In its positive aspect we make only one proposition regarding our attitude toward the old learning and thought, that is: "to reorganize the national heritage." To reorganize the national heritage means finding order out of chaos, finding the relations of cause and effect out of confusion, finding a real significance out of absurdities and fantasies, and finding true value out of dogmatism and superstition. . .

Part IV. . . [P. 164] From my personal observation, the future tendency of the New Thought should be to lay emphasis on the study of problems important to life and society, and to carry out the task of introducing academic theories through studies of these problems. . . What is the sole aim of the New Thought? It is to re-create civilization. Civilization was not created *in toto*, but by inches and drops. Evolution was not accomplished overnight, but in inches and drops. People nowadays indulge in talk about "liberation and reform," but they should know that there is no liberation *in toto*, or reform *in toto*. Liberation means the liberation of this or that system, of this or that idea, of this or that individual; it is liberation by inches and drops. Reform means the reform of this or that system, of this or that idea, of this or that individual; it is reform by inches and drops. The first step in the re-creation of civilization is the study of this or that problem. Progress in the re-creation of civilization lies in the solution of this or that problem. (November 1, 1919, 3 A.M.)

We have chosen Dr. Hu's following summary of the new literary movement, because it depicts so well the various phases of its early development as well as the main tenets of its major advocates. The terms *pai-hua* and *kuo-yü* are often interchangeably translated; the latter literally means "national dialect," but from the time of the literary revolution, especially in the context of the present piece, it has also assumed a second meaning of "vernacular," which is *pai-hua*.

DOC. 63. Hu Shih, "On the Literary Revolution," 1922 [2]

The Chinese classical style was already a dead language two thousand years ago. That was why in the time of the Emperor Wu-ti of Han [140–87 B.C.] Prime Minister Kung-sun Hung [200–121 B.C.] memorialized: "The decrees and laws that have been issued . . . are written in an elegant style, with profound literary expressions, and are an exquisite bestowal of your grace. But the petty officials are smatterers who cannot thoroughly ascertain their meaning and have no means of announcing them clearly so as to instruct the people below." Even at that time the petty officials were unable to understand the decrees and laws written in elegant style. But the government was obliged to advocate this kind of dead classical style for its political needs, and it devised a way to encourage the common people to study the classical style: all who could "master more than one classic" were given official posts, and "the more widely read were to be employed first." Beginning in the Han dynasty, this method underwent gradual revisions until it became the system of "literary examinations." This system of literary examinations prolonged the life of the dead classical style for fully two thousand years.

[P. 189] But the vernacular literature of the populace could not be suppressed. Though aristocratic literature had the upper hand in these two thousand years, yet popular literature also continued quietly and unobtrusively to develop. . . [The following two pages trace the evolution of vernacular literature since the Han, which the author divides into five major periods represented by the following: (1) the "musical poem" of Han; (2) the vernacular poetry and Buddhist lectures of T'ang; (3) the poetry of uneven verse of Sung; (4) the ballads and drama of Chin and Yuan; (5) the novel of Ming and Ch'ing. The last is held to have been the most influential literary force in China during the last five hundred years.]

[P. 191] China's vernacular had long been put in a definite written form, had spread far and wide, and had produced many first-class works in the living language; but the vernacular had not yet received the recognition of the general public. Why was this? There are two major reasons: one was the continuation of the civil service examinations; the other was the lack of a conscious advocacy of the use of the vernacular. . .

[P. 193] The conscious advocacy of vernacular literature began only with the literary revolution movement since 1916. In two respects this movement is different from the movements for vernacular newspapers and alphabetization. First, there is no distinction between "us" and "them" in this movement. The vernacular style not only is an instrument for "enlightening the people's minds," but also is the only instrument for the creation of Chinese literature. The vernacular style is not a bone fit only to feed the underdog, but a treasure which the people of the entire country should appreciate. Secondly, this movement honestly attacks the authority of the classical style, and regards it as "dead literature." Although the previous movements for vernacular newspapers and alphabetization admitted that the classical style is difficult to understand, they nevertheless kept on feeling that "we of the upper classes are not afraid of the difficulties — 'you can only be a man above men if you can take the hardest of hardships.'"

[P. 194] At its inception the idea of a literary revolution consisted only of a few persons' private discussions, and was not formally published in the journals until January 1917. The first article, "A preliminary discussion of literary reform" by Hu Shih, was still in a vein of very peaceful discussion. . . [p. 195]

Ch'en Tu-hsiu's special character lies in his determination to go straight forward. At that time Hu Shih was still in America, where he wrote Tu-hsiu:

'The rights and wrongs of this matter cannot be determined in a day, nor by one or two persons. I hope very much that people in China will cooperate with us to study this problem calmly. When discussions reach a mature stage, the rights and wrongs naturally will become clear. It is true that we have already raised the banner of revolution and cannot retreat, yet we should not maintain that what we advocate is absolutely right and not tolerate correction by others.'

(April 9, 1917)

This shows that Hu Shih recognized the literary revolution as being still in a stage for discussion. He was then engaged in writing poetry in the vernacular style in order to prove that it was suitable as a medium for verse; therefore he entitled his volume of poetry "A collection of experimental poems," or "Trials" (Ch'ang-shih chi). This attitude of his was too pacific.

The literary revolution would have had to go through at least ten years more of discussions and trials, if his method had been adopted. But Ch'en Tu-hsiu's courage exactly counterbalanced this defect of overcautiousness. Tu-hsiu replied:

'My opinion is that, while tolerance of different opinions and free discussion are the basic principles of the development of learning, nevertheless the rights and wrongs of the theory — that in the reform of Chinese literature the vernacular should be regarded as the main object — are already very clear, and we definitely will not allow discussion by opponents [p. 198]; we must consider our theory as the absolute right and not allow others to correct us.'

At the time such an attitude rather aroused the objection of the general public. But had it not been for Ch'en Tu-hsiu's spirit of 'not allowing discussion by opponents,' the movement for a literary revolution would not have received so much attention. For opposition signifies interest.

During 1917 much correspondence on literature appeared in *Hsin-ch'ing-nien*, in which much of the discussion by Ch'ien Hsüan-t'ung could supplement the ideas of Hu Shih. In January 1918, *Hsin-ch'ing-nien* renewed its publication under the rotating editorship of Professors Ch'en Tu-hsiu, Ch'ien Hsüan-t'ung, Shen Yin-mo, Li Ta-chao, Liu Fu [d. 1934], and Hu Shih. Throughout the year its articles were all written in the vernacular style. The main theme of Hu Shih's essay, "On a constructive literary revolution" (April 1918) was stated to be:

'The purpose of my article "On the establishment of a new literature" can be covered in four simple words: "vernacular literature, literary vernacular." The literary revolution we advocate aims only at the creation of a vernacular literature for China. Only after there is a vernacular literature can there be a literary vernacular. Only after there is a literary vernacular can our vernacular become the real national spoken language. . .'

[On pp. 199–206 the author deals with the growth of several vernacular magazines in Peking in 1918, and the intensification of the conservative opposition, especially the debate in 1919 between Lin Shu (the old-style scholar and translator of Western novels, who died in 1924) and Ts'ai Yuan-p'ei. Then the students' May Fourth Movement gave a further impetus to the development of the vernacular press.]

[P. 207] Although the student movement of 1919 and the new literary movement are two distinct matters, yet a close relation exists between them in that the effect of the student movement was to facilitate the spread of the vernacular over the entire country. Moreover, after the May Fourth Movement the enlightened elements in the country gradually came to realize the importance of the "revolution of thought." Therefore toward the new trends they adopted either an attitude of welcome, or of study, or of tolerance, and gradually reduced the old attitude of hostility, so that the movement for literary revolution was able to develop freely; this was another close relationship. Consequently, after 1919 the spread of the vernacular progressed at "a thousand *li* a day." More and more poetry also was written in the vernacular. In 1920, a ministerial decree was issued by the Ministry of Education, requiring the use of the vernacular style in all primary school textbooks for the first and second grades, beginning that autumn. . .

According to this order, the change from classical to vernacular textbooks in the entire primary school would not be completed before the present year [1922]. But the lower and upper levels of the educational system are related; when one hair is pulled the whole body can be affected. When the first and second grades changed to vernacular, the junior normal schools perforce [p. 208] also had to change, and most of the upper primary schools also followed suit. When junior normal schools changed, the senior normal schools were also obliged to change. Many middle schools also voluntarily adopted vernacular textbooks. Although this action of the Ministry of Education was based on the resolution of the National Education Association, much was contributed by the members of the Society for the Study of Vernacular Language, an association formed in 1916, whose active members were connected with the Ministry. When the vernacular literature movement had matured, there was little opposition to the idea of vernacular textbooks; therefore the Society for the Study of the Vernacular Language was able to induce the Ministry of Education to accomplish this important measure of reform when Deputy Minister for Education Fu Yueh-fen was the acting minister . . . [pp. 208–211 deal with more recent opposition from the classicists. The last paragraph, pp. 211–213, evaluates the achievements of the new literature during the last five years.]   (March 3, 1922)

CHAPTER XXVII. SUN YAT-SEN'S

REORIENTATION OF THE REVOLUTION

Among modern political leaders, Dr. Sun seems to have been remarkably adaptable, having not only different ideas at different times, but even conflicting ideas at the same time. Possibly this lack of consistency is to be expected in a man who was primarily a political leader, not a political theorist. Sun picked up many ideas somewhat indiscriminately and wound up as a syncretic thinker rather than a systematic one. His writings over the years included a bit of everything.

The adoption of Western political thought as the theoretical justification for the Chinese Revolution reached a climax at the time of Sun's inauguration as the president of the provisional government at Nanking early in 1912. The provincial delegates then declared: "We, the descendants of Han, have groaned under the searing oppression of the Manchus; and, admiring the systems of equality of the American and the French peoples, we have met and planned together . . . for the overthrow of tyranny and restoration of the rights of man. . ." At the same time, the emphasis on nationalism (which did not oppose but included the Manchus) was made clear in Sun Yat-sen's speech after he was given the seal of office: the task of the provisional government, he said, was to seek unity of race, unity of territory, unity of military administration and unity of national finance. In all this early and rather casual expression of revolutionary aims, there was no indication of how this Chinese republican revolution on the Western model was to be combined with changes in social structure such as were implied in the "revolutionary program" and others of Sun's pronouncements.

After the establishment of the Republic, Dr. Sun persisted in his belief that Western constitutional democracy was the answer to China's troubles. Having renounced the presidency in favor of Yuan Shih-k'ai, Sun asserted in 1912 that, since nationalism and the people's rights had been achieved, he would now devote himself to improving the people's livelihood as director-general of railway development. The Kuomintang as a political body openly seeking legislative power was mainly put together by Sun's lieutenant, Sung Chiao-jen. Yuan therefore had him assassinated in 1913.

After this first effort at parliamentary government in China had been thwarted, Sun Yat-sen in 1914 swung to another extreme. In Japan he organized the Chinese Revolutionary Party (*Chung-hua ko-ming-tang*) — a secret group to be controlled autocratically by Sun as Leader (*Tsung-li*), to whom all members swore personal loyalty. The stated aim of this new centralized party — three years before the Russian revolution — was one-party government.[1] How much this effort accomplished is uncertain; Sun was soon working again with the Kuomintang. At the same time he retained his faith in the ultimate possibility of constitutional democracy, after the party had performed its task of political tutelage. He still maintained that the carrying out of his original "revolutionary program" (see Ch. XXIII) could solve China's problem of political reorganization. His military campaigns against northern warlords were at first "campaigns for the protection of the constitution," by which he meant that the legitimate government at Peking, established by the consent of the opposing parties in 1912, and its draft constitution must be the object of support, in deference to the idea of the rule of law. In 1917, he wrote "A primer of democracy" (*Min-ch'üan ch'u-pu*) which dealt exclusively with parliamentary procedure. The Russian Revolution of that year roused his interest, but produced no immediate effect on his political thinking. What socialist influence there was in his teachings had already been worked into the principle of the people's livelihood.

The establishment of the Canton Military Government in 1921 marked another turning point in Sun's outlook. He now acknowledged that the mere "protection of the constitution" was not enough to further the cause of the revolution: henceforth the revolutionaries would have to conduct their campaign under a separate government. At the same time the power of the Russian Revolution had begun to impress him, and in the straits to which he was reduced in 1922–23 he did not hesitate to begin the reorganization of the Kuomintang on soviet structural lines. In speeches made at this time he stressed the role of the Party as the foundation of the state, the importance of strict organization and discipline within the Party, the subjection of the individual member to the Party, and the need of ideological propaganda. With his Russian advisor, Michael Borodin, at his elbow, these things appeared to Sun in 1924 to be the immediate and urgent desiderata of the revolutionary cause.

In the economic sphere, Sun had felt before 1923 that China's problems were to be solved by a two-fold plan on a national scale: China must carry out, first, the policy of the equalization of land ownership and the nationalization of capital; and secondly, the industrialization of the country supported by foreign loans. On the latter point a detailed plan entitled the *Shih-yeh chi-hua* (lit., industrial plan; English version: *The International Development of China*) was drawn up by Sun in 1917–18. This work was based on an interesting blend of two assumptions, that the expanded war-time economy of capitalist nations demanded large foreign outlets for investment, and that China could look to these Western capitalist nations for help through a financial transaction pure and simple. Sun's reasoning appears to have been that, since China was striving to become a nation just like the Western democracies, they could therefore help one another out of difficulties. By absorbing the surplus capital of the Western nations after the World War, China would help the latter to prevent an economic collapse; meanwhile China could benefit from this financial aid in her industrialization. This conception, like so many of Sun's other dreams, was shattered after 1919 and soon smothered by the spread of Leninist thought in Kuomintang circles.

His post-war disappointment with Western support made Sun look to Russia. The reorganization of the Kuomintang in 1923–24 shifted the emphasis of his thinking to the realm of political strategy and control. In order to broaden the basis of support for the revolution, members of the recently founded Chinese Communist Party were admitted into the Kuomintang as individuals in 1923. The first detailed exposition of the *Three People's Principles* did not appear until late 1924, and the exposition of the principle of the people's livelihood was cut short by Sun's departure from Canton and subsequent death (March 1925). These famous lectures embody the outline of his political doctrine, which had been proclaimed nearly two decades earlier after the founding of the *T'ung-meng-hui* (see Doc. 56); but at the same time it is apparent that Marxism-Leninism was beginning to have its effect on Sun's thinking, as evidenced in his much-touted "three policies" of 1924, which included support of the Soviet Union.

The following item indicates the rather unfocussed and groping character of Sun's thinking before his alliance with communism.

DOC. 64. SUN YAT-SEN'S THEORY OF KNOWLEDGE AND ACTION, 1919 [2]

In these days of scientific advancement all who create things must first acquire the knowledge for the task before they dare begin the work. . . So in all enterprises one must be able from one's knowledge to construct ideas and images, from the ideas and images to produce a set of agenda [i.e., things to be done], and on this set of agenda as a base, to work out a careful plan, and by following the plan to apply one's effort. In this way, no matter how advanced or intricate the enterprise nor how stupendous the construction, the aims can all be easily achieved by an assigned date. Nowadays the radio and the airplane are the most advanced and intricate of things; the most stupendous of engineering projects are the more than 1,200,000 *li* of railroads in the United States (when the United States took all the American railways under government management on December 13, 1916, the total mileage was 397,014 miles, with a capital of U.S. $19,600,000,000, which is equal to $39,200,000,000, in Chinese silver dollars) and the Suez and Panama Canals. Yet when their scientific principles were known and their sites had been studied, the plans were drawn up by engineers, and these plans were put into practical application; then they became matters of no difficulty at all. These are all real facts that can be verified. People of our country can know the truth about them with a little investigation.

As for my work in revolutionary reconstruction, I have based my ideas on the current of world progress, and followed the precedents in other countries. I have studied their respective merits and demerits, their gains and losses, considered the matter thoroughly [p. 51], and given it mature thought. Then I drew up the "Program of Revolution," and fixed the progress of the Chinese revolution into three periods. The first is the period of military government; the second, the period of political tutelage; the third is the period of constitutional government. [The rest of this paragraph gives a summary of the "Program of Revolution," explaining the plan for a five-power constitution.]

[P. 52] When the Republic was first established in 1912, I strongly urged putting the "Program of Revolution" into effect, in order to achieve the goal of revolutionary reconstruction and the application of the Three People's Principles. But most of our Party members were hesitant, and thought it could not be done. Although I repeatedly explained and argued, it was all to no avail. They all held that my revolutionary ideals were too high; that "it is easy to know a thing but difficult to carry it out." Alas! Were my ideals too high? Was it not rather that the knowledge of our party members was too low? Therefore I could not help becoming discouraged and disappointed. For the destructiveness of revolution precedes the constructiveness of revolution in due order, and they complement each other. Now, since no revolutionary construction had been begun since the destruction of revolution, that meant there would be no revolutionary reconstruction. Since there was no revolutionary reconstruction, what use would there be for a revolutionary president? That was why I, desiring to retire after the establishment of the Nanking Government, continued the armistice [with Yuan Shih-k'ai] and renewed peace negotiations. Now that the situation has changed, many persons have criticized me, saying that I should not have consented to peace negotiations and abdicated the presidency after the establishment of the government at Nanking. But suppose I had continued to be the president, while, after the successes of the destruction [of the revolution, i.e., by Yuan], most Party members no longer abided by their revolutionary pledges, nor submitted to the views of the Leader; in that case, even if the Revolutionary Party could have united China, it would still have been no more than substitution of new bureaucrats for old ones. As to the fundamentals of the governance and cultivation of the nation, or the basic plan for the people's livelihood, we would have been totally unprepared. That would have amounted to exchanging one tyrant for another. Hence there was no need for me to be president. [The next paragraph re-emphasizes the statement that his retirement from the presidency was caused by the revolutionaries' not putting revolutionary reconstruction into practice.]

[P. 53] What is revolutionary reconstruction? It is extraordinary reconstruction, and also rapid reconstruction. There is ordinary reconstruction, which follows the natural course of society and is done according to the trends of circumstance. This is the reconstruction that differs from the revolutionary. In a revolution extraordinary destruction is wrought — such as the decapitation of the monarchical system and the overthrow of absolutism. . . [P. 54] In these extraordinary times only extraordinary reconstruction can inspire the people with a new mind and make a new beginning of the nation. For this reason the "Program of Revolution" is a necessity.

Now let us observe the great revolutions that took place before our Republic, of which the most world-shaking were the American and French. The political system of America was determined after the revolution, and for more than one hundred years there has been no change in it. Except for one civil war arising out of the question of Negro slavery, there has been no major disturbance in that country. We can indeed say that once the revolution was accomplished America's political system became fixed and unchanging; there was prolonged good administration and internal peace; civilization advanced and economic development became the best in the world. On the other hand, France after the revolution was beset by major disturbances; the political system was changed five times — twice into the monarchical system and thrice into the republican — until, eighty years after the revolution, a militarist emperor was defeated and captured by a foreign enemy. Then republicanism became secure. Compared with the United States, their respective peace and disturbance, gains and losses, are as different as heaven and earth. Why? People who comment on the problem mostly say that Washington was generous and humble in behavior, and therefore at the beginning of their nationhood refused the crown; but that Napoleon, bursting with ambition and aiming at world conquest, began with a republic and ended with an empire. Yet these people do not realize that the course taken by a nation is determined by the psychology of the multitude; if the direction is set, then it certainly cannot be altered by the intelligence of one or two persons who have risen to leadership through force of circumstance. For neither Washington nor Napoleon was an initiator of the American or the French Revolution. After the thirteen American colonies had begun their campaign against England, Washington was asked to command their troops; and Napoleon rose from an obscure position after the outbreak of the revolution in France. If the positions of these two individuals had been exchanged, the results would probably have been the same. Therefore the different aims of Washington and Napoleon arose not out of their personal virtues, but rather out of the traditions of their countries.

The continent of America had always been a wilderness. The English had colonized it just a little over two hundred years. The English people loved adventure and were endowed with self-governing abilities. After reaching America they forthwith established institutions for self-government, and gradually became thirteen colonies. . . [p. 55] It was not so with France. Although France was an advanced and cultured country in Europe, with an intelligent, energetic population, and although for a hundred years before the revolution she had been under the influence of revolutionary theories and, further, had the American precedent to rely on; still she was unable to attain the republican form of government with one leap out of revolution. Why was that? It was because her political system had always been an absolute monarchy, and her government had always been centralized; she possessed no new world as the area for development and no self-government as foundation.

[P. 56] China's defects are the same as those of France; moreover, the knowledge and political ability of the Chinese people are far behind those of the French. And yet I wished to attain a republican constitutional government in one step after the revolution. How should this have been brought about? That is why I devised a transitional period in order to repair our defects. During this period we are to carry out a constitutional government, so as to train and guide the people, and to effect local self-government. . . [The rest of this paragraph and the three following repeat the need for the period of tutelage, and maintain that failure to put it into effect has cost the revolutionaries a certain amount of sympathy among the Europeans and Americans.]

[P. 57] Others again have queried whether the six years of political tutelage would not be the same as the "enlightened despotism" advocated by narrow-minded scholars? The answer is that the aim of enlightened despotism is despotism itself, whereas that of political tutelage is republicanism. Therefore there is the difference between heaven and earth betwixt the two. Take, for instance, the present World War. All nations participating in it, be they republics or monarchies, have ceased their constitutional government and resorted to military government. The people's traditional freedoms of movement, of speech, and of organization, are all abolished; even food and drink and business are controlled by the government [p. 58]. Yet no criticisms are raised in these countries. Instead the people sacrifice their lives for the nation, because they aim at victory and survival. When other nations which have already had constitutional government can stop its operation, how can we immediately put constitutional government into effect at the beginning of the revolutionary war, when the constitutional regime has not yet come into being and we are just embarked on seeking it through the revolutionary war? That is really a puerile and illogical idea! [In the next two paragraphs, the American policy in the Philippines and the regencies of the duke of Chou and others are cited as examples to support the theory of political tutelage.]

[P. 59] Well then, why is it that the destructive phase of the revolution has succeeded but the constructive phase has failed? The difference lies between knowledge and ignorance. In the destructive revolution I had attempted ten uprisings and ten times had failed. That was because at that time the majority of the Chinese people still did not realize that they were conquered by the Manchus, so they lived in a stupor and died dreaming, and regarded the revolution as unprincipled rebellion. Later the revolutionary trend became gradually more prevalent, and most people came to realize that the Manchu Dynasty ought to be abolished, and that the Chinese race ought to be restored to power. Consequently, it was possible to overthrow the Ch'ing Dynasty with one single stroke, as easily as turning one's palm. As to the constructive revolution, however, not only was the general populace ignorant of it, but also the Revolutionary Party did not know what it meant. In a revolutionary mission, the most difficult thing is to destroy and the easiest is to reconstruct. Now why is it that we have succeeded in the difficult but failed in the easy? It is because it is easy to do; therefore people do not realize how essential it is, and so neglect it; such is the cause of failure. . .

[P. 60] There is a common saying that the four hundred million Chinese are like a sheet of loose sand. What is the means by which these four hundred million grains of sand can be united into a coördinated, organized country ruled by law? It is necessary to start with oath-taking, so that one's mind can be set upright on the proper course and one's sincerity be assured; then we can hope to attain [the various stages listed in the famous classical quotation from the *Great Learning*] self-cultivation, ruling the family, administering the nation, and bringing peace to the whole world. Nowadays there is no civilized nation under the rule of law that does not take the pledging of an oath as the basic procedure of the rule of law. . . [The rest of this paragraph presents further arguments in support of oath-taking, citing oaths of citizenship and public office in foreign countries as examples; then Yuan Shih-k'ai's oath on assuming the presidency is explained.]

[P. 62] A race is an aggregation of human beings; a human being is ruled by the mind; and the nation and the government are the manifestations of the psychology of a group. Therefore the foundation of a nation is first based on the working of the mind. Hence when the people and officials of the Manchu Dynasty give their allegiance to the Republic, they must first show their honesty and sincerity; that is why the ceremony of oath-taking is necessary. Yet the members of the Revolutionary Party did it when the party was being organized, but do not do it while national reconstruction is being carried out. Thus the ambitious, progressive and fearless spirit of Party members was sufficient to bring about destruction, but such powers were lost during the time of national reconstruction, and so there has been no actual achievement in construction. These were the consequences of action and non-action. But the reason for their non-action was not that they were unable to act, but that they did not know the urgent necessity of doing so. Therefore I say, "Whatever can be known can certainly be carried out." Is there anyone who still thinks it is idealistic? [In the last paragraph of this chapter Sun proceeds to draft the form of an oath which he holds ought to be taken by every loyal citizen of the Republic, and lays down the procedure by which it is to be administered.]

The following speech, a sort of Party harangue, is from the period when Sun was taking Michael Borodin's advice in reorganizing the Kuomintang. It has some relevance to events three decades later.

DOC. 65. Sun Yat-sen's Adoption of the Russian Party system, 1923 [3]

Comrades: the present reorganization of our Party aims at the largest possible expansion of the influence of our Party in the various provinces of China's interior. Hitherto the influence of our Party has been mostly overseas. Therefore our Party has bases and members overseas, but its influence in the interior of China has been very weak. Consequently throughout the years the struggle of our Party in our country has depended exclusively on military force. When our military forces have won the day, our Party accordingly has won with them; when military force has failed, our Party also accordingly has failed. Therefore the sole purpose of the present reorganization of the Party is to enable us to avoid relying exclusively on armed force, and to rely on the power of the Party itself. By "the power of the Party itself" I mean the mind and strength [i.e., the support] of the people. Henceforth our Party should regard the mind and strength of the people as that of our Party and it should use the mind and strength of the people in its struggles. Popular support and military force can be employed simultaneously without contradiction. But between the two, which should be the foundation, and which is the more dependable? To rely on military force alone is not dependable, because the victories and defeats of military forces are inconstant. Our Party must first have a basic strength as its foundation before we can hope to rely on military force. Without such a basic strength as our foundation, military force is undependable even if we possess it.

There have been three times of success when our Party struggled with the use of military force in the interior of China. The outbreak of revolution at Wu-ch'ang [1911], the overthrow of the Manchu Dynasty, and the establishment of the Republic: that was the first success of our Party's military force. Yuan Shih-k'ai wanted to become emperor; the anti-Yuan campaign was started and his regime was overthrown [1916]: that was the second success of our Party's military force. When Chang Hsün [1854–1923] tried to restore the Manchu emperor [1917], we launched the campaign to protect the Constitution [of 1912]. Subsequently Hsü Shih-ch'ang [1856–1939] resigned from the presidency and Ch'en Ch'iung-ming revolted against us [1922], and the warlords of the north also joined the campaign for the Constitution: that was the third success [p. 315] of our Party's military force. But all three successes did not enable us to attain the aim of the revolution. That is, although military force had succeeded, the revolution still had not been accomplished, because our Party still lacked power. What was the power that we lacked? It was the support of the people. . .

[P. 319] The above account shows that the struggles of our Party have depended mostly on military force; therefore the victories and defeats came intermittently. If this situation continues for a prolonged period, there will never be any hope of success for our Party, and there never will be a day when our Three People's Principles can be realized. Therefore the present reorganization has been initiated. What is expected of this reorganization? It is expected that out of this our Party will be able to build up a central force. From this day forward all comrades must apply themselves earnestly to the revolutionary task. All comrades must make the revolutionary task their own life-long task, must bring about the complete realization of the Three People's Principles and the Five Power Constitution. Only then can our Party be considered as having succeeded. But we cannot rely [p. 320] exclusively on warfare for this success, because in warfare we must depend on military men, and the majority of the general run of the present military men do not understand ideology. . .

[P. 321] Why has not our Party engaged in organized, systematic, and disciplined struggle before? It was because we lacked the model and the precedent. Now we have a good friend, Mr. Borodin, who has come from Russia. The Russian Revolution took place six years later than that in our country, and yet after one revolution the Russians have been able to apply their principles thoroughly; moreover, since the revolution the revolutionary government has daily become more stabilized. Both are revolutions: why have they succeeded in Russia, and why have we not in China? It is because the Russian Revolution owed its success to the struggle of the Party members: on the one hand the Party members struggled, on the other hand they were aided by military forces, and so they were able to succeed. Therefore, if we wish our revolution to succeed, we must learn the methods, organization, and training of the Russians; then there can be hope of success.

But many people hold that the regime in Russia is controlled by the Bolshevik Party and, if we learn from Russia, would we not be learning from Bolshevism? These persons do not realize that, while it was true that before the outbreak of the revolution in Russia there was much Bolshevik thought — for the leaders of the Russian Revolution were mostly men of deep learning and lofty and profound ideals, consequently it was inevitable that some of their theories were radical and extreme — yet the Russians do not act only according to ideals but base most of their actions on fact, just as in traveling one must choose and take the road that one can go through. [P. 322] Therefore at the time of the Russian revolution there were many political parties, such as the Social Democratic Party, the Democratic Revolutionary Party, etc., but they could not all succeed, and the one that has succeeded today is the Communist Party. The reason behind the Communist Party's success is that it suits the desires of the majority of the Russian people, so all the Russian people support it.

When he first came, Mr. Borodin told me that the Russian Revolution has undergone six years of struggle through various ways, but in retrospect today it is seen that nationalism has been the thing that appeals most to the Russian people. The Russian people suffered extremely under the bondage of the Great Powers. The suffering they underwent during the great European War was forced on them by the Great Powers. The shaking of the Tsar's regime was due to his participation in the Great War together with the Great Powers, thereby inciting the opposition of all the Russian people, and they rose in revolution against the Tsar. . . After the success of the Communist Party's revolution, its renunciation of foreign debts evoked the vigorous opposition of the Great Powers. England, the U.S.A., France, Japan and others all rose and attacked her. At that time Russia was surrounded by enemies in eight directions, and the troops of the Great Powers had already reached St. Petersburg. The dangers of the situation really exceeded that at Canton a few days ago. The reason for Russia's being able to resist such strong enemies lay entirely in the struggles of the Russian people and of the Party members; therefore they have been able to eject the foreign forces, establish an independent nation, and are no longer the slaves of the Great Powers. Furthermore, they are also able to eliminate foreign economic aggression. . . [The next few lines explain how the ideology of the Russian Communist Party coincides with the Three People's Principles.]

[P. 323] Both our Party and theirs advocate the Three People's Principles. Although the ideology is the same, yet our Party does not possess good methods; therefore it is slow in achieving its goal. Their vision is great and their learning deep, and they can devise good methods. If we want our revolution to succeed we must follow their example. Heretofore in the accomplishment of the revolution each of us has fought on his own; henceforth we must fight as an organized group and engage in a disciplined struggle. Since we wish to learn their methods, I have asked Mr. Borodin to be the director of training [4] of our Party; he is to train our comrades. Mr. Borodin is extremely experienced in party management. It is hoped that all comrades will sacrifice their personal prejudices and earnestly learn his methods. Although it has only been a very short time since the establishment of the local branch offices of our Party, yet according to the reports of various comrades the results are already highly visible. If this continues, the day of final victory for our Party will certainly arrive. . .

CHAPTER XXVIII. LIANG CH'I-CH'AO'S REVIEW OF CHINA'S PROGRESS, 1873-1922

In 1922 the leading Shanghai newspaper, "Shun Pao" (*Shen-pao*), was fifty years old and its editors asked Liang Ch'i-ch'ao, who was also fifty, to survey the developments of the past half century. Liang's effort to appraise China's progress, condensed below, is in optimistic terms, but one can hardly avoid the feeling that the writer had resolutely made up his mind not to be downhearted. In the few remaining years of his life, Liang devoted himself to philosophical and classical studies. His faith in what the West could offer China seems to have been deeply shaken by the First World War. In 1920 he had written: [1]

Since Darwin's discovery of the principle of the evolution of species, a great revolution has occurred in intellectual circles over the whole world. His service to learning must be acknowledged. But afterwards his theory of the struggle for existence and survival of the fittest was applied to the study of human society and became the core of thought, with many evil consequences. This great European war has nearly wiped out human civilization; although its causes were very many, it must be said that the Darwinian theory had a very great influence. Even in China in recent years, where throughout a whole country men struggle for power, grasp for gain, and seem to have gone crazy, although they understand nothing of scholarship, yet the things they say to shield themselves from condemnation are regularly drawn from Yen Fu's translation of T. H. Huxley's *Principles of Evolution*. One can see that the influence of theory on men's minds is enormous. No wonder that Mencius said, "These evils, growing in the mind, do injury to government, and displayed in the government, are harmful to the conduct of affairs." Perhaps the Europeans' current fondness for the study of Laotzu is in reaction to this theory. . .

Again in 1923, Liang Ch'i-ch'ao wrote of a West that was withered, dry, and sick from "spiritual famine" because of its pursuit of material things: [2] "Of the methods of relieving spiritual famine I recognize the Eastern — Chinese and Indian — as, in comparison, the better. Eastern learning has spirit as its point of departure; Western learning has matter as its point of departure. . ."

In the following essay of 1922, Liang stresses first the physical growth of the people of China and then their spiritual awakening to political consciousness as a nation.[3] We quote from it here as a conclusion to this volume.

Part II. There has been a great task on which, during the last five thousand years, our ancestors have continually expended much effort and which has never been interrupted. During the last fifty years, it still has been vigorously carried on, and furthermore it has been fruitful. What is this task? To give it a name, I call it "the expansion of the Chinese race." Originally our Chinese race consisted merely of a few small clans with a few bases in Shantung, Honan [p. 41], and other places. During the several thousand years that followed it has been slowly growing . . . growing . . . until it has become a high and peerless race, and has established this vast and majestic nation.

The Chinese race has grown in two ways: through assimilation of the numerous alien tribes in and outside of our territory, and through colonization by our own people on the frontiers year by year, thus enlarging our territory. . . In the last fifty years there have been great successes. . .

1. After the Taiping Rebellion, the Miao Rebellion in the Southwest followed and spread very widely. It required more than ten years before it was suppressed; however, the suppression this time had some characteristics of a fundamental solution. Hereafter I dare say that China will have no such term as the "Miao bandits." The fact is that "our race versus the Miao race" has been a great public problem ever since the time of the Yellow Emperor and of the Emperors Yao and Shun. The uproar had been going on for several thousand years and still it was not entirely solved. It was only within the last fifty years that the very last paragraph of the essay on the Yellow Emperor's campaign against Ch'ih-yu [a legendary rebel] was completed. This is indeed a matter of history which is worth putting down in a special description writ large.

2. The revolution of 1911 and the abdication of the Manchu Emperor have great political significance. . . Formerly the race of the eastern barbarians had caused us trouble for seventeen or eighteen hundred years. . . At last came the group of Manchus who occupied China the longest and were also the most thoroughly assimilated. The Manchus may be considered as the great conglomeration of the eastern barbarian tribes, and they can also be considered as the great conclusion of the eastern barbarian tribes. During the last fifty years the sinification of the Manchus has advanced full speed, until the [1911] revolution, after which every Manchu was capped with a Chinese name. Hereafter there will be really no Manchus in the world. This amounts to our absorbing all the eastern barbarian tribes who have been active during the last two thousand years, and transforming them into a part of the Chinese race. This concludes a great stage in the expansion of the Chinese race.

3. The movement of the people in the interior in the two directions of northeast and northwest has also been a great task of the last fifty years. Formerly the Manchus had planned to use the land in the Three Eastern Provinces [Manchuria] as an old base area to which they could always retire. . . Since the wars between China and Japan, and between Japan and Russia, this area has become a potentially belligerent zone, communication facilities have been opened wide, and economic conditions have abruptly changed. Although on the one hand, many privileges have fallen into the hands of others, on the other hand the degree of close relationship between the people inside and outside Shanhaikuan has increased several times. The people of the Three Eastern Provinces and those of Shantung and Chihli gradually have been merged into one group. Moreover let us take a look in the direction of the northwest. Ever since Tso Tsung-t'ang established [the

governor-general's] office in Kansu and Shensi, the influence of the interior has daily extended in that direction. During the Kuang-hsü period [1875–1908] Sinkiang was established as a province, and hence the thirty-six states in the Hsi-yü [the western region], whose relations with us since the two Han dynasties [B.C. 206–200 A.D.] had been sometimes rather close and sometimes attenuated, may be considered completely incorporated into Chinese territory and made the same as the interior. . .

4. The work of overseas emigration has also greatly developed during the last fifty years. Since the Ming dynasty, the people of Fukien and Kwangtung have been emigrating on a large scale to the various places of the southern ocean [lit., Nan-yang, including in general, Southeast Asia, Singapore, Batavia, Java, etc.]. More recently, following the development of commerce by the Europeans, our emigrants have also established some real foundations of economic power. Furthermore, in America, Australia, and other places that had no contact with us before, the question of Chinese immigration has become a world problem. . .

Racial expansion is a matter worth celebrating; and because of this, it can be proved that our race is just in its age of youth; it has not yet reached adulthood and is still growing every day. . .

The most regrettable thing is that in several other directions we have entirely failed: first, Taiwan; second, Korea; and third, Annam. . . We must realize that, while our people are able to go forward, other races can also do so. Hereafter, if we make no new efforts, I fear that the only way will be to go backward, and we shall have no more opportunity to continue our expansion.

Part III. [P. 43] In the realm of learning and thought, we cannot but recognize that there has been considerable progress, and that actually a way of great progress has been opened for the future. In this the most vital turning point is the abolition of the civil service examination system. This system has had more than one thousand years' history, and can really be regarded as deeply rooted and firmly based. Its greatest shortcoming was to make the minds of the scholars of the whole country hypocritical, traditional, and vague, and thus block all sources for the development of learning and thought. The movement for abolition of the civil service examination had already begun nearly fifty years ago. Kuo Sung-tao, Feng Kuei-fen and others had all briefly expressed some ideas to this end. By the time of the 1898 Reform Movement, the so-called new party of that time, including K'ang Yu-wei, Liang Ch'i-ch'ao and their group, may be said to have used their whole energy in launching a general attack against the civil service examination system. After about ten years from first to last, and after undergoing a great number of vicissitudes, this obstacle to civilization was finally broken down. Now these past events seem to be ordinary, but from the point of view of an historian of the last fifty years they must be counted as of great importance.

After these fifty years, what knowledge can we present to other people? It is embarrassing to say that there is practically nothing. But the minds of the scholars have been changed to a very large degree. I remember that in 1876 there was a minister to England, Kuo Sung-tao, who wrote a travel account in which there was a paragraph which said in effect, "The present barbarians are different from former barbarians; they also have two thousand years of civilization." Good Heavens, this was terrible! When this book reached Peking the public anger of all the officials and scholars in the government was aroused. Everybody denounced him; every day he was accused; the matter was not concluded until the printing blocks of the book were burned by imperial decree. So little time has passed since then, yet the phrase "new cultural movement" has now become a habitual slogan of all learned societies. Ma-k'o-ssu [Marx] is almost competing for the seat of honor with Confucius, and I-pu-sheng [Ibsen] is nearly overthrowing Ch'ü Yuan [343–290 B.C.]. Whether this kind of psychology is correct or not is another question, but in general the radical change of thought of the last forty-odd years was indeed never dreamed of during the preceding four-thousand-odd years. . .

An old proverb well says that "when one keeps on learning, then one realizes that one's knowledge is insufficient"; and during the last fifty years the Chinese gradually have realized their own insufficiency. This little consciousness, on the one hand, is the cause of the progress of learning; and, on the other, it may be counted as the result of the progress of learning.

In the first period our mechanical articles were first realized to be insufficient. This realization gradually started after the Opium War until in the period of T'ung-chih [1861–1874] foreign troops were borrowed to suppress the civil war. Hence people like Tseng Kuo-fan and Li Hung-chang acutely felt that the solidity of foreign ships and the effectiveness of foreign cannon were really superior to ours. . . Therefore the shipyard and academy in Fukien and the arsenal at Shanghai and other institutions were gradually established. But during this period the world of thought was little influenced. During this time the most memorable things were the several science books translated by people in the arsenal. To us now these books may seem archaic and superficial, but among the groups of translators there were several who were quite loyal and devoted to knowledge. It was really a painstaking enterprise for them to produce such works then, because at that time no scholars could speak a foreign language, while those who could speak a foreign language did not read books. Therefore these translations really blazed a trail for "the experts in Western knowledge who did not understand foreign languages" in the second period.

In the second period there was a feeling of insufficiency concerning our [political and social] institutions. After the defeat by Japan, people with good minds in the nation really seemed to have met a thunderbolt in a dream. Accordingly, they wondered why the great and grand China should have declined to such a degree, and discovered that all was due to her bad political system. Therefore they took *"pien-fa wei-hsin"* [i.e., to change the statutes and to reform] as a big banner and launched a movement in society. The ardent leaders were the people like K'ang Yu-wei and Liang Ch'i-ch'ao. The people in this group were well trained in Chinese learning, but as for foreign languages they actually could not understand a single word. They could not tell others "what foreign knowledge consisted of and how to learn it." They could merely shout in loud voices every day, saying, "The old stuff of China is insufficient; many good points of the foreigners should be learned." Though these words sound general and undefined [lit., like swallowing a date whole], yet at that time they produced a tremendous effect. The political movement was a failure, with the exception of the above-mentioned abolition of the civil service examination system. . . This really opened a new phase for the future. During this period many schools were opened at home and many students went to study in foreign countries. . . The most valuable productions in the academic field were the several works translated by Yen Fu, who introduced some of the main currents of nineteenth-century thought into China. It is regrettable, however, that too few people in the nation could understand them.

In the third period there was a feeling that the foundations of our culture were insufficient. The duration of the second period, comparatively speaking, had been very long — from the war of 1894 to 1917 or 1918 — twenty years. Though great changes were wrought in the political arena, the realm of thought remained much the same. In brief, during this score of years we always felt that our government and laws, etc., were far inferior to those of others, and we were vexed at not being able to bring others' political organizations and forms one by one into our country. We took for granted that if this could only be done, myriads of other problems would be solved. [P. 45] It is almost ten years since the success of the [1911] revolution but all that we hoped for has proved vain, item by item. As we have gradually thought back, in our disappointment, we have realized that a social culture is a whole unit, and as such it definitely cannot make use of new institutions with an old psychology. By degrees there has grown up a demand for a reawakening of the whole psychology. At the conclusion of the great European war a great deal of active spirit was added to the tide of thinking of the whole world. Among the recently returned students there appeared quite a few able persons, who exerted their courage to promote a complete emancipation movement. Therefore during the last two or three years a new epoch has been demarcated.

The progress of thought in the three periods, if we try to measure between the people of the first and last periods, will be immediately very clear. In the first period [the pioneers] like Kuo Sung-tao, Chang P'ei-lun, Chang Chih-tung, and others, were regarded as very new monsters. When it came down to the second period, Sung-tao and P'ei-lun were dead, but Chih-tung was still living, and in the first half of this period Chih-tung was still regarded as a promoter of new things; but by the latter half he was considered simply an exponent of conservative, absurd ideas. In the second period K'ang Yu-wei, Liang Ch'i-ch'ao, Chang Ping-lin, Yen Fu, and others were all brave scholars of the world of thought, standing in the first line of battle. During the third period, when many new young men ran to the front lines, these people [of the second period] were pushed behind, one by one, and some have entirely withdrawn or retired from the ranks. This kind of phenomenon, the new replacing the old, may prove that the circulation of fresh blood in the world of thought during the last fifty years has been very rapid. It may prove that the body and spirit of the world of thought are gradually becoming healthy and strong.

If we take a number of fifty-year periods in our history to compare with the fifty years just past, great progress has indeed been made in this last half-century. If, however, we take our last fifty years and compare them with the last fifty years in other countries, we shall be utterly ashamed. Let us take a look: what has the United States done in fifty years? What has Japan done in these fifty years? What has Germany done in these fifty years, and what has Russia done in these fifty years? Although politically their successes and failures are not the same, and their suffering and happiness are not equal, yet as to their academic and thinking elements, all may be considered to have advanced a thousand *li* a day. Even England, France, and other old nations — which one is not running forward as if flying? We have been talking noisily of new education for several decades. Let us ask our scientists, do we have one or two things which may be considered inventions of world importance? Ask our artists, do we have one or two productions which can be offered for world appreciation? And in our publication circles, do we have one or two books which are important works of the world? Alas, we had better wait until after the third period and see what it may bring.

Part IV. [P. 46] "We may grudgingly grant that all other things have progressed in the last fifty years; only government, I am afraid, has entirely retrogressed." This remark is being made by almost a myriad mouths with one voice, and it is difficult even for me to object to it. Nevertheless in the last analysis [lit., looking from the inside of the bones] it may also be said that in the last fifty years what has advanced most in China is precisely the government.

Fundamentally, government is formed by the opinions of the people. Not only is democratic government built on the opinions of a large number of people, but even dictatorship and oligarchy are also built on the opinions of a large number of people. Any kind of government always needs the active support or at least the tacit consent of a large number of people before it can exist. Thus the awakening of our citizens toward government is the general source of political progress. The actual politics of China in the last fifty years may indeed be said to have retrogressed and not progressed; but from the point of view of the citizen's self-consciousness, the concept has actually become clearer day by day, and furthermore has enlarged day by day. Self-consciousness: what are we conscious about?

First we are conscious that all who are not Chinese lack the right to control Chinese affairs.

Secondly, we are conscious that all Chinese have the right to control Chinese affairs.

The first is the spirit needed for the establishment of a national state [lit., *min-tsu chien-kuo*]. The second is the democratic spirit [lit., *min-chu*]. It is not that these two kinds of spirit had not existed before, but the ideas had frequently been dormant, vague, and confused. In the last fifty years — actually, the last thirty years — the ideas have been expressed very clearly.

I dare say that, after the Manchu abdication, if there should again be another race who wished to imitate the attempt of the Five Barbarians, the Toba Wei, Liao, Chin, Yüan and Ch'ing, "to enter to be the masters of China again," that is something that would never happen till the seas dry up and stones rot. I dare say that once the signboard of the Republic has been hung up, hereafter in thousands and myriads of years it will never be taken down again. Regardless of whether you are as wise and sagacious as Yao and Shun, or as strong and tyrannical as the First Emperor of the Ch'in or the founder of the Ming, or as cunning as Ts'ao Ts'ao and Ssu-ma I, if you wish again to be the emperor of China, no one will ever allow you to do so. This fact should not be lightly regarded. . .

In sum, during the most recent thirty years, of the tasks which have been accomplished by our nationals, the most important is the fundamental extermination of a government dominated by foreign people [p. 47] for more than one thousand years. . . The second is the permanent destruction of the absolutist monarchical government of more than two thousand years. . . And moreover, these two achievements are by no means unexpected coincidences; they have really been achieved by the fundamental awakening of the people, who have exerted the greatest effort before they could accomplish them. Seen from this point of view, the period can really fit the meaning of the word progress.

During the last ten-odd years since the establishment of the Republic, the political phenomena have indeed been disgusting; but I think we should not be too disappointed, because these phenomena have been caused by two special factors, and these factors are going to disappear soon. The first one is that, during the time of the revolution, because the power of the people themselves had not yet become sufficient, they could not help relying on traditional influences.

The second factor is that it is normal for all matters in society to have their ups and downs. From 1894 and 1898 to 1911 benevolent people and scholars dedicated to a worthy cause have really been worked to the point of physical and mental exhaustion. The most regrettable thing is that many people who struggled for ideals died martyrs of the times. Their successors could not immediately take up the task. Therefore the interregnum has become a dark and colorless period; but I think this period will soon be over. The former leaders seem to have reawakened, caught their breath, and renewed their struggle. The fighting power in the rear has, furthermore, become stronger day by day. In these circumstances a new spirit and a new phase will naturally appear.

In summary, I am completely optimistic in regard to the political future of China. My optimism, however, has grown from the pessimism of ordinary people. I feel that China during the last fifty years has been like a silkworm becoming a moth, or a snake removing its skin. These are naturally very difficult and painful processes. How can they be accomplished easily? — only if biologically it is possible to function during the necessary change or removal, and if psychologically there is consciousness of the necessity for change and removal. Then, after we have undergone the unavoidably difficult and painful process, the future will be another world. Therefore, while everyone may consider that our political life is retrogressing, I feel that the possibility of its progress is very great.

Liang Ch'i-ch'ao had been among the most eloquent of China's intellectual leaders during three decades. This retrospect of 1922, in addition to the intrinsic interest of its analysis, shows the continuity between China's traditional ethnocentrism and her modern nationalism. In so doing it points toward more recent decades, and forms a suitable stopping point in our survey.

POSTFACE. A FURTHER APPROACH
TO THE PROBLEM

Although this chapter can hardly sum up the significance of the materials quoted above, it can suggest certain lines of further analysis. This study describes a part of the heroic and ominous process of modern history. It is almost (but not quite) superfluous to remind ourselves that this process is a totality of many interrelated parts and that words are at best poor slippery tools with which to build a mental image of it. Sun Yat-sen in history, for example, represents a compound of peasant social background and Chinese and Western education, a quest for the betterment of his countrymen and for political leadership, for national regeneration and personal fulfillment — in what single formula can we neatly understand him?

While all the major paths of modern learning must no doubt be followed, in so far as they seem to lead onward, our chief effort should be to pursue those lines which seem likely to penetrate most deeply and broadly the terra incognita before us. Two such main approaches to the study of Modern China in the century from 1839 to 1923 are here suggested — one socio-economic and one psycho-ideological. They are not mutually exclusive; to some extent, each includes the other. Let us try to describe them in the simplest way, without special terminology.

The socio-economic approach is the more obvious of the two. From one point of view, for example, the failure of China to modernize was a failure of her ruling class and its institutions — of the landlord-scholar-officials whose way of life was incompatible with effective westernization. Li Hung-chang and his colleagues could try to satisfy both their desire for private gain and their official duty as bureaucrats by organizing industrial enterprises, as in fact they did. But if this officially-fostered industrialization was to be a continuing success, the bureaucrats in charge had to venture their entire careers and fortunes in it, become investors and genuine entrepreneurs in industrial development, and thereby cease to be mandarins. This they did not do. China in the late nineteenth century developed neither true *Zaibatsu* nor "robber barons." As Cheng Kuan-ying so eloquently complained (Ch. XIIIa), the officials did not become businessmen. Instead they seem to have retained the ancient ideals of the landlord-gentry class; the profits of their industries went into landowning, not into increased factory production, because land had always been regarded as the safest form of investment. While this analysis is oversimple, it indicates how the traditional "oriental" supremacy of officialdom over the merchant class may have impeded the rise of a system of negotiable property rights, protected by corporation law instead of official favoritism, and capable of supplying the investment capital needed for industrialization.

In short, the Chinese ruling class would not or could not mobilize its resources to take the plunge into modern industrial life; it evidently feared that it might lose its old agrarian-based prerogatives and yet fail to gain equivalent power as a new capitalist class.

Plainly this type of analysis, if systematically pursued, can penetrate the structure of the old Chinese society and its social and economic institutions. Old-style family relationships, connections between the landlord-gentry in the villages and officials in the imperial administration, the wide powers of the latter over large-scale economic activity — a great multitude of such problems await further analysis through the written record.

The psycho-ideological approach has a different emphasis. It is concerned first of all with the traditional Chinese ideologies — the systems of values and beliefs which supported and sustained the old order. Secondly, it is concerned with the slow and many-faceted breakdown of those ideologies under the corrosive influence of Western power and Western ideas. Thirdly, it seeks to analyze the absorption and adaptation of those Western ideas which interacted with persisting elements of the old order. In short, this approach studies the ways in which modern Chinese have sought to create new systems of value and belief to replace the no longer adequate ideology of the disintegrating traditional order.

As we watch Neo-Confucianism losing its grip upon the mind of modern China, we enter a phase of intellectual history in which this second approach is particularly fruitful. When ancient institutions are no longer perpetuated by contemporary thought and conduct — when Liang Ch'i-ch'ao attacks the Confucian monarchy in order to save the Chinese nation, when Chang Chih-tung and Yuan Shih-k'ai propose to abolish the civil service examinations in order to improve the bureaucracy, or Hu Shih and Ch'en Tu-hsiu discard the classical style in order to make Chinese writing more useful — then ideas are likely, purely as ideas, to play a particularly important role in history. At such times, we suggest, the individual mind is more free to innovate, less trammeled by conventions and considerations of orthodoxy or of personal prestige, more aware of the great variety of possibilities with which mankind is confronted. In the crises of revolutionary change, leaders project their own personalities, and even minor traits. Dr. Sun's Japanese name, Nakayama, becomes in its Chinese equivalent, *Chung-shan*, the new name for universities, boulevards, and a style of clothing. The revolutionary innovators borrow ideas from everywhere — Britain, Japan or the French Revolution, the Protestant Bible or the *chin-wen* school of textual criticism, even from the New York dentist Maurice William whose book is mentioned in the *Three People's Principles*. To some degree there occurs a process of natural selection among ideas, which gain currency through their applicability — real or illusory — to the needs of China's leaders.

At the same time feelings become more intense and motives more complicated. As the inherited institutions and habits of thought lose validity, intellectuals experience tension and anxiety, greater hopes and fears. The experience of modern China must be studied through psychology as well as economics and social organization. Eventually, patriotic and revolutionary causes sweep individuals into great organized movements, and social psychology becomes a major, though neglected, key to our understanding. Such insight seems particularly necessary now, when so many Chinese have succumbed to a totalitarian communist faith, based upon the pre-Freudian, rationalistic economics and sociology of Marx and Lenin, as well as upon the vigorous nationalism of the Chinese people.

This second approach to China's cultural metamorphosis, by way of the ideas and motives of leading individuals, is more obviously suggested by the materials in this volume. Our selections generally represent the Chinese élite, not the common people. These personal statements and responses of Chinese leaders no doubt exemplify the working of basic institutions and provide data for socio-economic analysis. Yet each of these writers must be studied as a human personality, moved by his pride of culture or devotion to the throne, by his hatred of official corruption or of the foreign invader, as the case may be.

When such case histories are grouped together and compared, many trends and uniformities appear — such as the sequence of major influences from Britain in the nineteenth century, Japan in the decade to 1911, America during and after the First World War, and subsequently Soviet Russia. It is evident that Western influence has been conveyed, more than we generally realize, through the medium of Japan and thus blended with forms of Japanese influence. The most significant political trend has been the gradually increasing concern of China's intellectual élite for the political awakening of the mass of the people, their education and mobilization in the task of national regeneration. After the turn of the century, members of the Chinese upper class evince more interest in the peasantry as potential citizens of a modern state. The new thought of the May Fourth Movement at length acknowledges the Gargantuan problem, how to bridge over the ancient bifurcation between the illiterate farming population and the intellectual élite. Since this bifurcation facilitated, perhaps necessitated, political tutelage by a party dictatorship and since it now contributes to totalitarianism, it still remains a great impediment to real democracy in China.

No matter how we approach it, and there are many ways, the strenuous effort of China's leaders to meet her modern problems is a main thread of world history — tangible and accessible to study, and of crucial import for the future of Western democracy. Throughout the century surveyed above, the greatest need was to imbue the effective leadership of the day with a deeper understanding of modern world history. Further research may show that the Confucian élite of the late Ch'ing period failed to avoid revolution in large part because their educational reforms did not recruit China's native talent broadly enough nor train a younger leadership adequately and in time. Similarly, it may be concluded that the doom of the Kuomintang was sealed from the time when Dr. Sun failed to convince the scholars of Peita that his *Three People's Principles* could give them intellectual leadership. As for the learning received by China's leaders from Western Europe and America, we can hardly say, at the end of the first century, that it has been an entirely constructive influence. Perhaps the moral is that we cannot really help another society unless we first understand it ourselves.

INDEX OF DOCUMENTS

GENERAL INDEX

ERRATA

On page 26, *for* Ssu-ko-lan *read* Su-ko-lan

On page 101, *for* Mr. [George] Stephenson *read* Mr. [Sir MacDonald] Stephenson

On page 116, *for* the inventor of the locomotive, George Stephenson *read* an English engineer, Sir MacDonald Stephenson

INDEX OF DOCUMENTS TRANSLATED IN THE TEXT

(in many cases condensed or excerpted)

INDEX

Abacus, 16

Abeel, Rev. David (1804–1846), 41, 134

Academia Sinica, 234

Academic freedom, championed by Ts'ai Yuan-p'ei, 234, 238–239

Agricultural administration, improvement of, urged, 202, 224

Agricultural schools, Chihli, 210; advocated by K'ang Yu-wei, 148

Ai-lun (Ireland), 26

Aiguebelle, Paul d' (1831–1875), 80

Allen, Rev. Young J., edits Wan-kuo kung-pao, 134; urges political and social reform, 147

Alphabetization of Chinese, 256

American Presbyterian Press, 51

American Revolution, 261–262

Amherst mission (1816), 20

An Ch'ung-ken, 243

An-fu clique, 253

Anarchism, 232; advocated by Wang Shih-fu, Li Shih-tseng, and others, 233

Anglo-Chinese war, Second (1857–1858), 46

Anglo-Japanese alliance (1902), 127

Anhwei Army. See Huai-chün

Annam, French conquest of, 122, 127, 152, 269

Anti-Boxer martyrs, 190–193

Anti-Christian feeling, 14–15, 187

Anti-foreign feeling, of Empress Dowager, 89

Anti-foreign movement, in Canton (1841), 35–36

Anti-Manchu movement by early Ch'ing "nationalist" thinkers, 7–11; by secret societies, 11–12, 56; T'an Ssu-t'ung, 157; statements by Sun Yat-sen, 228–229

Anti-missionary movement, 135; condemned by Chang Chih-tung, 173–174; by T'an Ssu-t'ung, 158

Army: modern, developed by Yuan Shih-k'ai, 209–211; of the Green Standard, see Lü-ying; regulations, German, followed by Hsin-chien lu-chün, 210; Japanese, to be copied, 201. See also Hsiang-chün, Hsin-chien lu-chün, Huai-chün, Pei-yang Army, Ting-wu-chün, Tzu-ch'iang-chün

Arsenals, Lanchow, 81; Kansu, 171; Shanghai, 64, 111; Shantung, 171, 270, 218; Szechwan, 171; construction of, urged, 35, 53, 202; inefficiency of, criticized, at Tientsin, Shanghai and Nanking, 159

Attitude of the British, French, and Americans toward Chinese in 1840's, 33

Bakunin, 233

Bagehot, Walter, 233

Bank of China, 212

Bank of Communications, 212

Banks, 212; proposed by Hung Jen-kan, 58; introduced by Yuan Shih-k'ai, 211; foreign, in China, 214. See also Bank of China; Bank of Communications; China Commercial Bank; Hongkong and Shanghai Banking Corporation; National bank; Russo-Chinese Bank

Barbarian, explained, 18

Barbarians, use of to control barbarians, 29; advocated by Wei Yuan, 30–35; criticized by Feng Kuei-fen, 53; by T'an Ssu-t'ung, 157

Benoist, Michel, 18

Bergson, Henri, 242, 244

Black Flags, Chinese irregulars in Annam, 122

Bland, J. O. P., 213

The Bogue or Hu-men, 28

Bolshevism, 246–249, 266

Bolshevism and World Peace, 248

Book of Changes, 171

Book of Filial Piety, 244

Book of History, 15, 171

Book of Rites, 7, 147; quoted on beginning reform in the school, 170

Borodin, Michael, advises Sun Yat-sen, 259, 264–265; director of training in Kuomintang Party, 266

Boxer circulars, quoted, 188–189

Boxer movement, origin of, 187–188

Boxer notices, quoted, 189–190

Boxer Protocol (1901), 187

Boxer Uprising, 135, 187–193

Brenier, M., 62

Bribery, obstacle to modernization, 87; taken by Empress Dowager, 89–90

Bridgman, Rev. E. C. (1810–1861), 134

British East India Company, 152

Brown, J. M., 62

Buddhism, 13–14

Bureaucracy, dominates traditional China, 4; in industry, 212

Burlingame, Anson, 62, 97, 98

Burlingame Mission, 97

Business schools, advocated by K'ang Yu-wei, 148

Cabinet government, urged by Wang K'ang-nien, 164

Calculating rods, 16